Contents

WITHDRAWN

Childhood

We work with leading authors to develop the strongest
educational materials in child care, bringing cutting-edge
thinking and best learning practice to a global market.

Under a range of well-known imprints, including
Longman, we craft high quality print and electronic
publications which help readers to understand and apply
their content, whether studying or at work.

To find out more about the complete range of our
publishing, please visit us on the World Wide Web at:
www.pearsoned.co.uk

Childhood
Services and Provision for Children

Phil Jones, *Leeds Metropolitan University*
Dorothy Moss, *Leeds Metropolitan University*
Pat Tomlinson, *Leeds Metropolitan University*
Sue Welch, *Leeds Metropolitan University*

PEARSON
Prentice
Hall

Harlow, England • London • New York • Boston • San Francisco • Toronto • Sydney • Singapore • Hong Kong
Tokyo • Seoul • Taipei • New Delhi • Cape Town • Madrid • Mexico City • Amsterdam • Munich • Paris • Milan

Pearson Education Limited
Edinburgh Gate
Harlow
Essex CM20 2JE
England

and Associated Companies throughout the world

Visit us on the World Wide Web at:
www.pearsoned.co.uk

First published 2008

ISBN: 978-1-4058-3257-1

British Library Cataloguing-in-Publication Data
A catalogue record for this book is available from the British Library

10 9 8 7 6 5 4 3 2 1
11 10 09 08 07

Typeset in 9.75/13 Minion by 73
Printed and bound in Great Britain by Ashford Colour Press, Gosport

The publisher's policy is to use paper manufactured from sustainable forests.

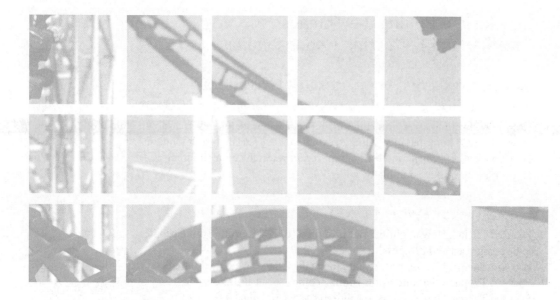

Author Acknowledgements

The editors would like to thank the Childhood and Early Years Teaching and Research Group, and students of children and young people across Leeds Metropolitan University.

Publisher Acknowledgements

We are grateful to the following for permission to reproduce copyright material:

p. 32 from 'Parents and children give their views on smacking' in *The Guardian* (07/07/04) © Kathleen North; NF3.1 from Office for National Statistics www.statistics.gov.uk/census, pp. 67–70 from Office of National Statistics and pp. 84–87 from *National Curriculum on line* http://www. nc.uk.net/nc_resources/html/ks1and2.shtml. Reproduced under the terms of the Click-Use License; Table p. 34 from *Big Business, Small Hands*, Save the Children (01/01/2000 ISBN 1-84187-030-7), NF4.1 from *House of Commons (2004) Select Committee on Work and Pensions Second Report Session 2003–4* (31st March) www.publications.parliament.uk/pa/cm200304/cmselect/cmworpen/ 85/8506.htm. Parliamentary material is reproduced with the permission of the Controller of HMSO on behalf of Parliament; p. 107 two unnumbered figures from *Global Education Digest*, UNESCO Institute for Statistics (2004, p. 25); pp. 86–7 from *The National Curriculum, London*, DfEE/QCA (2000, pp. 10–13) Crown Copyright material is reproduced with the permission of the controller of HMSO and the Queen's Printer for Scotland, pp. 249–250. Reproduced by permission of SAGE Publications, London, Los Angeles, New Delhi and Singapore from Moss, P. and Penn, H., 1996; *Transforming Nursery Education, London,* © Moss, P. and Penn, H., 1996; Equal Access? Appropriate and Affordable Childcare for every Child, Institute for Public Policy Research (IPPR), London (Stanley, K., Bellamy, K. and Cooke, G., 2006, p. 36).

In some instances we have been unable to trace the owners of copyright material, and we would appreciate any information that would enable us to do so.

List of Contributors

Fraser Brown is a teaching fellow and Reader in playwork at Leeds Metropolitan University. Previously he has worked as an adventure playworker; a project coordinator and regional leisure officer; director of Children First Training Agency; and as a lecturer at Sheffield College. He has a number of publications in the field of play and playwork. He is a trustee and co-founder of Aid for Romanian Children, a charitable trust that focuses on two causes: improving the plight of Roma children in Cold Valley village, Transylvania, and improving conditions at the Sighisoara paediatric hospital.

Marian Charlton is head of community and youth studies at Leeds Metropolitan University. Her teaching is in social policy, family and community studies. She is qualified as a community social worker. She is actively involved in several community-based projects and is currently chair of governors in a community primary school. She has three grown-up children and five grandsons. Before going to university as a mature student she worked as a play group coordinator, a welfare assistant with special needs children and a youth worker.

Ros Chiosso is a senior lecturer in community and youth studies at Leeds Metropolitan University. A welfare rights adviser, community educationalist and community activist, her experience and knowledge base is drawn from 20 years of both paid and voluntary work in many diverse communities. Her publications to date are practitioner-focused and include contributions to the *Community Work Skills Manual* (2001).

Ruth Cross is a lecturer in health education and health promotion at Leeds Metropolitan University. Having Registered Nurse status, a BSc (Hons) in health psychology and an MSc in health education and health promotion she has wide experience in health, health-care services and health provision both in the UK and in Sub-Saharan Africa. She teaches aspects relating to child health and child health promotion on the BA Childhood Studies course at Leeds Metropolitan University.

Anna Gray is a student at St Aidan's High School, Harrogate. She is 17 years old and enjoys an active social life. She has chosen to stay in the sixth form at her school to stay with her friends. Anna would like to add that she is a young person with Down's Syndrome.

Christine Hines is a senior lecturer in childhood studies and course leader of early childhood education at Leeds Metropolitan University. She was formerly responsible for Foundation degrees in early childhood and worked as a head teacher in a primary school for several years.

Phil Jones is a Reader in childhood studies, Leeds Metropolitan University. He has worked with children in a variety of settings, and coordinated international arts and therapy projects involving children in the UK, Greece, Portugal, Ireland and the Netherlands. He has lectured on areas such as play and the arts therapies in a number of countries including the US, Canada, France, Greece, Italy, Portugal and the Netherlands. His sole authored work includes *The Arts Therapies: A Revolution in Healthcare* (Routledge) and *Drama as Therapy* (Routledge) which has also been published in Greek, Korean and Chinese.

Jane Kettle is associate dean and head of the School of the Built Environment at Leeds Metropolitan University. With a background as a housing practitioner, she has been involved in the delivery of vocational planning, housing and regeneration education for ten years. Her publications are in the area of housing and social policy, and she has co-authored a book examining the opportunities for professionals to engage children in decision-making processes in planning and the built environment.

Dorothy Moss is a principal lecturer in childhood studies at Leeds Metropolitan University. A welfare rights advocate and community activist for 10 years, Dorothy moved into lecturing in welfare rights and community practice in 1988. She worked primarily on courses related to youth and community development and social welfare with law. She currently teaches social theory and social policy related to childhood. Her research and publications are in the areas of social theory, social justice and gender.

Yinka Olusoga is a senior lecturer in early childhood education at Leeds Metropolitan University. She has experience as a class teacher in early years and primary settings and has worked with children and parents in socially and culturally diverse communities. Her research is in the field of philosophy of education, and she particularly focuses on personal and social education and on children's friendships.

Georgina Spencer is Liaison Librarian for the School of Humanities and Education at Keele University. She was, until recently, Learning Adviser for Education at Leeds Metropolitan University where she supported students and staff in finding and using information effectively. Her interests lie particularly in the area of using ICT in the delivery of Information Skills training for students and staff at all levels. She is currently developing a library WebCT module at Keele University for dissemination in September 2007.

Pat Tomlinson is faculty registrar and a principal lecturer at Leeds Metropolitan University. Pat is a trained teacher who became involved in project development with children's community organisations for 10 years and was subsequently a training consultant for play and child care. Her scholarly activity has focused on curriculum development in child and play studies and participatory research including feasibility studies, project management and objective-setting exercises with child-care providers.

Gary Walker is a senior lecturer in childhood studies at Leeds Metropolitan University. Previously he was education coordinator for children in public care in a local education authority. He has worked in a variety of social and educational care settings since 1980. He is a qualified social worker with experience of child protection and child care. He has worked as child protection training coordinator for a local education authority, offering training, guidance and support to schools.

Sue Welch is currently principal lecturer in childhood studies at Leeds Metropolitan University. Although she is a qualified teacher and an educational psychologist she is very interested in children's lives outside education. This is reflected in her first degree in social administration and her experience in working with looked after children and with families of children under 5 as well as experience in teaching and as an advisory teacher.

Chapter 1

Introduction

PAT TOMLINSON

When people consider the notion of childhood, they bring to it a range of ideas, themes and perspectives. These are drawn from their own experience and interpretation of the world and the views they have encountered. Scholars and students of the subject are no different. We embark on our respective courses of study and learning in the full knowledge that we have all experienced childhood yet not readily appreciating how different and diverse that experience might have been for those of a different social position to our own and in relation to different services.

The concept of childhood in the 21st century may appear to be a high profile affair. Politicians, researchers, academics, professional practitioners and commercial entrepreneurs consider, investigate and at times exploit notions of childhood. Within the UK, children, usually within the context of family, may appear to dominate social, fiscal and economic policy. Budget speeches by the Chancellor of the Exchequer from the turn of the century to the time of writing reflect this with reference to child tax credits, children's trust funds, investment in education and opportunities for budding sports Olympians. Diverse professional areas such as health, youth justice, education and social

work are involved differently in aspects of child development, care and welfare. Commerce and industry exploit childhood in a variety of ways, for example Marketlooks (2001), a website providing market analysis, identified the growing concept of the 'tween' market, children between 8 and 12, that provides revenue to the tune of US$170 billion per annum. From manufacturing to service industries childhood is big business. The 'Toys and Games Market Report 2005' shows that since the year 2000 the UK market for traditional toys and games has grown by 21 per cent to a value of £2.13 billion in 2004.

Within this broad and complex framework the study of children and society has emerged as an area of multidisciplinary scholarship incorporating education, sociology, social psychology and social policy. Historically children have tended to be studied as an adjunct or subordinate to other categories. Sociology has traditionally studied children within the context of family. Social policy has tended to study children within the context of adult needs, for example, early years from the perspective of parenting, young people from the perspective of social control, while education has focused on the child as a developing adult and an investment in the

1

future. Although such approaches are still evident there has been a move to explore childhood in its own right. This move considers the cultural, social, educational and political context of children's lives and explores experiences of childhood from a child's perspective. The contributors to this book are from many professional, academic and service user backgrounds, yet share a common objective: to consider children and the experience of childhood as a distinct and important aspect of their scholarship and practice.

The focus of the book is predominantly services and provision for children in the UK. It explores broad underpinning perspectives on children's services, information about particular provision and critical issues related to meeting the needs and wants of children. Although concerned to centre on UK provision and services authors are mindful of international and global debates and actions related to childhood. Within this context chapters variously identify the influence of global agencies such as the United Nations and relationships to services with an international perspective. The book addresses key questions within the context of the changing face of service provision, critical debates about childhood and the voice of the child. These questions include:

- What relationships between the state and the child does service provision reflect?
- How is service provision seen from a children's rights' perspective?
- How are children's views taken into account in relation to services?

The book is informed by two contemporary perspectives on childhood: firstly, the idea that childhood is socially constructed and that the rights of the child should be centre stage; secondly, the long-standing recognition of the social divisions of childhood where emphasis is placed on excluded, oppressed and marginalised groups of children including those in poverty, looked-after children, refugee children, child offenders and young people. We explore the influences shaping policy (economic, social, political and cultural) both top down, through the impact of national and international law and policy, and bottom up, through

social movements for change, community development and the child's perspective and influence, alongside snapshots of policy and case studies. We discuss the status of the child, the extent to which the child's voice may be heard in the development of policy and the rhetoric and realities of children's rights. There has been a growth in multi-professional approaches and a recognition that both the status and understanding of those involved with the children's workforce need to develop. In this complex and changing environment, not only is it essential to know about prevailing policies and provision but to appreciate the critical context within which these exist.

The broad range of ideas, critical debates and examples of policy and practice raised provide insight into important ideas about the social construction of concepts of childhood discussed within the book. We examine how dominant ideas in themselves create opportunities and constraints for children. In the sense that childhood could be considered to be to some extent a 'fiction', the argument is that we need to unpick that fiction if we are to serve children's interests best. However, it is also important that we recognise the material realities of children's lives, for example finance, shelter, environment and the quality and quantity of services available to support children. As well as 'childhood' being an 'idea', individual children's lives are real and children are socially and historically positioned in relation to ever-changing material forces. The existence of war and the unequal distribution of wealth are two examples. Alcoff points out that we need to study peoples' lives in the context of the relationship between ideas and material 'realities' (1997, p. 343). It is the way that ideas *about* children and their *lived realities* interact that should be the focus of attention. Goldson et al. (2002) argue that we must not lose sight of the major material inequalities children experience because our attention is too drawn to the ways in which children are conceptualised. Both aspects of the study of childhood are important and we hope that we have drawn on such debates evenly and holistically.

The book brings together, within a critical framework understanding and discussion of a significant range of services and their impact on children's lives.

How the book is structured

The book is divided into four parts, each providing different perspectives on childhood provision and services. Part I provides the critical framework which establishes the debates, discussions and dilemmas across children's provision and services. This is developed in the four chapters where theoretical debates and essential concepts and themes are introduced. These areas are children's rights, the politics and economics of childhood, inequalities between children and the impact of adult perceptions and images of children on policy. The intention of Part I is not to arrive at definitive answers to questions but to introduce a range of critical perspectives on children's services which can be drawn on to reflect on and evaluate other chapters.

Part II covers specific areas of provision and service for children providing some contextual background, outlines of provision and critical questions in relation to particular areas. The debates developed in Part I inform the chapters of Part II in different ways. Each chapter is distinct and autonomous, but together they form a broad and contemporary picture of policy, provision and service for children in the UK. Some chapters provide a historical context, some focus on snapshots of contemporary policy and others discuss directly critical questions about the shape and direction of contemporary provision. It has not been possible to cover every single service for children or all scenarios across children's lives but the range of services covered has been carefully selected to be representative of the diversity of children's services and ensure the inclusion of specialist services such as play and youth alongside the monolithic provision of education and health.

Part III draws on a range of case studies to exemplify the critical framework of the book in practice and to see the real life impact of provision and services discussed in Part II. These case studies include perspectives from those involved in developing services, those working in them and children using the services. The selection of case studies reflects the key questions highlighted earlier. So, for example, the relationship between the state and perspectives on children's services is explored in two examples of community development. Issues of children's rights are examined through the experiences of a teacher of refugee children and a child's personal account and insight as a recipient of children's services.

Part IV provides a practical resource for getting the most out of the book and out of study in general. It focuses on the way that the book might be used as a learning resource and the way that knowledge and understanding of the shifting terrain of children's services and provision may be updated. It offers an accessible guide to those studying childhood services and is structured around questions related to accessing information and academic research, using book-based learning, journals and the Internet. It shows how libraries support this and how analytical skills can be developed and used to aid interpretation of text. It is concerned with building the confidence of those engaged with learning about children and childhood. Reflective activities are integrated throughout the book and this part focuses directly on ways in which particular themes and issues are developed across the book and important strands of research and thinking might be highlighted.

Features of the text

Each part has an opener that identifies the aims of the part and details each chapter included in it. It also indicates the relationship with the other parts of the book and suggests guided reading and links.

Each chapter lists the key questions it is discussing at the start and offers a number of reflective activities that individual readers or groups can get involved with to strengthen their understanding of the text. These can be undertaken without recourse to other sources of information. Each chapter has an annotated bibliography to support selected reading.

Readers can approach the text from any point and will find signposts and guidance to enable broadening of the theme or topic across the book.

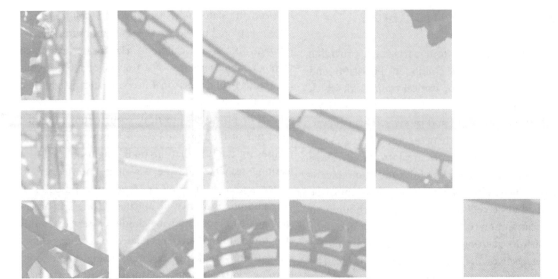

Debates, Discussions, Dilemmas: The Critical Framework

What is the aim of Part I?

The first four chapters act as a grounding for the rest of the book. These include an introduction to relevant theories and concepts; the meanings and implications of children's rights; key debates about contemporary political issues relating to children and childhood; the ways in which processes such as social exclusion affect children and their families along with an analysis of the pictures of children contained within policy.

Guide to reading Part I

Part I gives a broad analysis, and can be read to familiarise the reader with key concerns across children's services as a whole. The chapters can be read independently or together. They can be used to help understand critical issues that are raised in other parts of this book.

Links To Part II		Links To Part III
	Chapter 2 Childhood: Rights and Realities	
Chapter 6 Education: Service or System?	This chapter examines debates about children's rights and the ways childhood is constructed within societies.	Chapter 14 The Swings and Roundabouts of Community Development
Chapter 10 Safeguarding Children		Chapter 18 The Venture
	Chapter 3 The Politics of Childhood	
Chapter 9 Children Who Offend	This chapter considers the ways particular areas of service provision are tied to the wider context of economic related issues and political debates.	Chapter 17 Educating Refugee Children
Chapter 11 Day Care Services for Children		Chapter 18 The Venture
Chapter 13 Children's Experience of Community Regeneration		
	Chapter 4 The Social Divisions of Childhood	
Chapter 6 Education: Service or System?	This chapter analyses how the social divisions of class, race and community are related to the exclusion faced by children.	Chapter 15 Mind the Gap
Chapter 8 Provision for Child Health		Chapter 17 Educating Refugee Children
Chapter 10 Safeguarding Children		
	Chapter 5 Pictures of Children	
Chapter 7 Youth Services and Provision	This chapter looks at ways in which pictures of children as investment or threat can be seen behind government policy.	Chapter 16 The Anna Rebecca Gray Interviews
Chapter 12 Services to Children's Play		

Chapter 2

Childhood: Rights and Realities

SUE WELCH

The quality of a child's life depends on decisions made every day in households, communities and in the halls of government. We must make those choices wisely, and with children's best interests in mind. If we fail to secure childhood, we will fail to reach our larger, global goals for human rights and economic development. As children go, so go nations. It's that simple.

(UNICEF, 2005a)

Introduction

This chapter addresses the relationship between children's rights and services and provision for children. It is concerned with the questions

- What do we mean by children's rights?
- Who is responsible for ensuring children's rights are upheld?
- What status do children have within our communities?
- How effective are services in responding to children's rights?

It isn't the intention of this chapter to arrive at definitive answers to these questions but to raise further questions and issues that challenge assumptions and allow for discussion and reflection on a range of views.

The focus is on provision in the UK, primarily England and Wales as policy and provision in Scotland is sometimes different. Some comparisons are made with other countries where different approaches illustrate different ways of thinking. Children's rights are the focus of much debate, both within the UK and internationally, as individuals and governments struggle to identify what rights children should have and how these can be upheld in practice. These debates are important in considering services and provision made for children and underlying them are ideas about how we construct our ideas of childhood and children.

The chapter starts by looking at the 1989 United Nations Convention on the Rights of the Child (UNCRC). It identifies what the convention says about children's rights and the rights of others and points to some issues arising from this. It goes on to consider some of the difficulties around who is responsible for upholding children's rights.

The chapter looks at issues in relation to the status of children in our society and communities and identifies some of the tensions and contradictions in the way we think about childhood and children. The particular tensions are:

- Childhood as important in itself versus childhood as preparation for adulthood
- Children as vulnerable people versus children as capable
- Children as victims versus children as villains

This leads to examination of how these tensions affect the way we provide services and provision for children.

Finally, issues identified during the chapter are drawn together with further questions raised for consideration.

What is meant by 'children's rights'?

Debates about children's rights are sometimes affected by the way the term 'rights' is interpreted so it is worth considering what is mean by a 'right'. Simplistic media representations sometimes use the term as though it means having complete freedom to do as you please because nobody can stop you from implementing your rights. However, this is a misconception. Rights are also linked with responsibilities. One of the chief responsibilities is to respect the rights of others so when there is conflict between the rights of two individuals or groups there has to be negotiation between the individuals or groups about how to make this work. For example, while I have a right to make decisions about what car to drive I also have a responsibility to consider the effects on others of driving that car, for example the amount of pollution it generates, the speed at which I drive, the safety of passengers that I carry. Some of these responsibilities might be enshrined in laws, for example those that identify speed limits and safety standards, but others are personal responsibilities that need me to make decisions that are not purely selfish, such as the engine size and how I drive the car.

Some societies (e.g. in the US, Australia, the UK) have a strong individualistic approach to how society works with the rights of individuals being stressed. Other societies (e.g. in Latin America, Asia) stress the importance of the group and consider that the individual should relinquish some individual rights because of the rights of the wider society. This relationship between the rights of the individual and the rights of the rest of society is at the heart of many debates. For example, graffiti can be seen as an individual's right to free expression but may also be seen as an encroachment on the rest of society's rights to an unspoilt environment. If you consider these different points of view you will see how difficult it is to achieve a solution without further discussion of the boundaries of 'free expression' and what an 'unspoilt environment' might be.

Do all rights have the same status?

If an individual has a right to something it places an obligation on others to ensure that that right is met. Sometimes this is a moral obligation: something that we feel we ought to do. Sometimes it is a legal obligation: something that we have to do by law. So, although we may say that someone has a right to food and shelter, unless there are legal imperatives that someone, usually the state, has to provide these, the safeguarding of that right will depend on the voluntary actions of others.

Consequently we need to talk about different kinds of rights. Franklin (2002) identifies the contrast between moral rights and legal rights: moral rights where we think something ought to happen but we can't guarantee that it will and legal rights where there is a clear obligation on an individual or state to ensure that a right is upheld. He points out that claims to moral rights are often a precursor of these becoming legal rights, for example the campaigns to ban smoking in public areas preceded legislation to enforce this. Franklin makes a further distinction between welfare rights and civil or liberty rights. Welfare rights are those rights that are concerned with ensuring individuals are given protection and are provided with the basics for survival. Civil or liberty rights focus on self-determination: the right to participate in decisions that affect an individual and society.

Reflective Activity 2.1

Children's rights and children's needs

Which of the following 'needs' that are often the heart-felt cry of adults would you apply to children:

'I need a cigarette.'

'I need a drink.'

'I need peace and quiet.'

'I need to be left alone.'

Conversely which of the following needs that are often identified with children would you apply to adults?

'Children need firm discipline.'

'Children need to have difficult decisions made for them.'

'Children need strict routines.'

1 What does this tell you about the concept of 'need'?

2 What difference does it make when you change the word 'need' to 'have a right' in these statements. Why might this make adults feel more comfortable with the concept of children's needs rather than rights?

3 Think about where these ideas about children's needs have come from.

We will look at this later in the chapter when thinking about childhood as valued for itself versus childhood as preparation for adulthood.

'Rights' and 'needs'

An important distinction to make in relation to rights is the difference between 'rights' and 'needs'. While the two are related there is a significant difference in the implications of using the term 'rights' rather than 'needs'. As Hill and Tisdall (1997) point out: when we talk about rights there is the expectation of entitlement to something; when we talk about needs there is a sense of deficiency. Adults tend to be much more comfortable talking about children's needs rather than their rights but are likely to see children's needs as different to adults' needs.

Within the context of rights and needs children are constrained by the social divisions across the societies in which they reside. Children may be construed as needy or entitled because of their social context, such as class, economic circumstances, gender or ethnic background. Within such a framework children can be differentiated and discriminated as being worthy of rights due to high familial status or unworthy due to perceived or actual deficiency.

These aspects are considered in more detail in Chapter 4, The Social Divisions of Childhood.

The United Nations Convention on the Rights of the Child

The very term 'children's rights' suggests that there is something different that means children have different rights to the rest of the population. The most important document in relation to children's rights is the 1989 United Nations Convention on the Rights of the Child (UNCRC). In 1991, through ratification of the treaty, the UK committed itself to ensuring that the principles of the UNCRC would be incorporated into UK law.

The 1989 Convention consists of 54 articles. Of these articles 41 identify the human rights to be respected and protected for every child under the age of 18 years and require these rights to be implemented in the light of the Convention's guiding principles.

The United Nations Children's Fund (UNICEF, 2005) identifies the Convention's four guiding principles as

- Non-discrimination (Article 2) which

   1. States Parties shall respect and ensure the rights set forth . . . without discrimination of any kind, irrespective of the child's or his or her

parents' or legal guardian's race, colour, sex, language, religion, political or other opinion, national, ethnic or social origin, property, disability, birth or other status.

2. States Parties shall take all appropriate measures to ensure that the child is protected against all forms of discrimination or punishment on the basis of the status, activities, expressed opinions, or beliefs of the child's parents, legal guardians, or family members.

- Best interests of the child (Article 3) which states

  In all actions concerning children, whether undertaken by public or private social welfare institutions, courts of law, administrative authorities or legislative bodies, the best interests of the child shall be a primary consideration.

- Survival and development (Article 6) which

  1. States Parties recognize that every child has the inherent right to life.

  2. States Parties shall ensure to the maximum extent possible the survival and development of each child.

- Participation (Article 12) which

  1. States Parties shall assure to the child who is capable of forming his or her own views the right to express those views freely in all matters affecting the child, the views of the child being given due weight in accordance with the age and maturity of the child.

  2. For this purpose, the child shall in particular be provided the opportunity to be heard in any judicial and administrative proceedings affecting the child, either directly, or through a representative or an appropriate body, in a manner consistent with the procedural rules of national law.

The 41 articles that identify children's rights are often referred to in three main groups: the 3 Ps. These are:

- provision to ensure children's survival and development (welfare rights);

- protection from abuse and exploitation (welfare rights);

- participation in decision making (liberty rights).

It is clear from the Convention that rights should not be thought of individually but as a whole. However, there are potential difficulties that arise which include conflict between types of rights and interpretations of significant phrases such as 'best interest' and 'due weight'. The definition of child is not without its critics and the status of the relationship between child and parent can be hotly disputed. There is a potential conflict between welfare rights and liberty rights. Farson (1974) and Holt (1975) both cited in Archard (1993) point to the difference in nature of these rights. Welfare rights don't require children to do anything – others have to act to ensure these rights. Liberty rights allow children to exercise these rights if they choose. A number of authors (e.g. Monk, 2004) have questioned the interpretation of 'in the best interests of the child' and what this means in practice because of the potentially adult-centred notion of what is in the best interests of a child. It is a commonly held view that the adult knows best yet we see the results daily of adult actions which jeopardise children within their homes and communities. The interpretation of 'the views of the child being given due weight in accordance with the age and maturity of the child' again relies on a judgement being made about the capabilities of an individual and this may be based on a 'deficit model' of children's capabilities (i.e. that children do not warrant the same status and importance as adults), thus implying that an adult's view is weightier than a child's. The definition of a child also raises argument. For example, the Convention's definition,

Every human being below the age of eighteen years unless under the law applicable to the child majority is attained earlier.

(UNCRC, 1989)

clusters together newborn babies and children of 17 as though they were a homogeneous group. Another important tension is the relationship between the rights of the child and the rights of parents or primary carers. As parents are more powerful than children, when there is conflict between children's rights and parents' rights, parents' rights may be given more consideration both in formal and informal settings, for example choice of school or visiting rights across split families.

Reflective Activity 2.2

Children's rights in practice – thinking through difficulties

In a divorce case the parents want joint custody of their children, a 5-year-old boy and a 12-year-old girl, although they will be living 300 miles apart. The children have friendships at school and in the neighbourhood where they currently live and where the father will remain. The children want to stay with their father and would like the mother to visit them some weekends.

1 What do you think should happen?

2 What do you think would be in the child's best interests?

3 What assumptions are you making when you make this decision?

4 Have the children respected the rights of the parents?

5 How have you taken into consideration the evolving capacities of the children to make decisions?

The above activity is meant to help you to think about why these situations might be problematic.

Who is responsible for ensuring children's rights are upheld?

Human rights are considered to be highly important in today's world.

All human rights – civil, political, economic, social and cultural – are inherent to the human dignity of every person. They do not constitute an option and are not open to free and arbitrary interpretation, nor are they neutral. They stand for clear values and require a commitment to make them work; to act and promote actions that ensure their realization; to express concern, voice criticism and foster change in cases where rights are denied or neglected.

Human rights are meant to inform and guide development policies. Human development is only meaningful and sustainable when designed to ensure the realization of human rights.

(UNICEF, 2005b)

If rights are taken seriously then it is important to consider how rights are upheld and who is responsible for ensuring this. The UNCRC makes it clear in Article 42 that the state has responsibility 'to make the principles and provisions of the Convention widely known … to adults and children alike' and in Article 18 to

> render appropriate assistance to parents and legal guardians in the performance of their child-rearing responsibilities and shall ensure the development of institutions, facilities and services for the care of children.

Articles 19 and 20 identify the state's responsibility to protect the child from 'all forms of abuse, violence, exploitation and neglect'.

In doing this states need to bring their national legislation into line with the provisions of the convention except where the national standards are already higher. Article 44 describes how states are then accountable for their actions through providing reports every five years to the committee on the rights of the child. However, it is also clear in Articles 3, 5, 9, 10, 18 and 27 that the Convention sees the primary responsibility for children's care and guidance to be with the family and parents. The state is expected to support parents in this task by providing 'material assistance and support programmes'.

While this may sound straightforward the extent of state 'interference' or 'intervention' is the source of much political debate. The debates around this focus on two different points of view. The first point of view is that parents and carers know what is best for their children and have a right to bring up their children as they think fit; the second that the state has a role in supporting parents and protecting children. According to the first point of view, the state should not interfere unless the child is in danger. This is known as the 'liberal standard' and is explained by Archard (1993) who identifies three elements:

- commitment to the importance of 'the best interests of the child';
- parent and carers have the right to autonomy (freedom to bring up their children as they see fit) and privacy (no-one can intrude in the family without consent);
- there are clear conditions that identify when it is appropriate for the state to intervene.

Within British culture the last of these elements is usually in relation to children suffering abuse or neglect. When there is sufficient evidence that a child is 'at risk of significant harm' and the 'best interests' of the child are in danger, the state can interfere with the parents' and carers' rights to privacy and autonomy. However, the assumption explicit in The Children Act 1989 is that the best place for a child to be is with their family.

Different types of rights (provision, protection and participation) within the Convention can be seen to have different implications for the role of parents and carers and the role of the state. As we saw earlier in the case of the divorce proceedings there may be times where the rights of the child and the rights of the parent or carer are in potential conflict. The role of the state in such an instance is to identify a proper balance between the two. The 'liberal standard' (1993) suggests that the state would only interfere if the child is at risk of significant harm. It is expected that the parent or carer would be a source of *protection* but where the child needed protection from abuse or exploitation by the parent or carer themselves the state would need to intervene.

See Chapter 3, The Politics of Childhood.

In contrast there is an expectation in the Convention that the state has a more positive role in supporting parents and carers in making adequate *provision* for their children. Fiscal policy, education services, welfare benefits and health and social services are all forms of state intervention but are generally seen as being there to support parents and carers in upholding children's provision rights. The manner in which provision is made and its availability is dependent on political decisions and fiscal policy, which are in turn influenced by ideology and power and economic conditions. Thus services may be provided directly by the state from taxes, privately purchased according to income, charitably provided in terms of need or publicly supported through tax relief or benefits. So political decisions and economic circumstances concern how much provision and what type of services are provided and which parents and carers can access what provision. The UNCRC notes throughout that provision should be to 'the fullest

This is explored in more detail in Chapter 3, The Politics of Childhood.

possible extent' but also that this will be 'in accordance with national conditions and within their means'. Political responses to this problem vary according to the emphasis that is put on individual responsibility.

Since ratification of the UNCRC, children's *participation* rights have gradually been given more consideration through The 1989 Children Act and more recently The 2004 Children Act. In the UK there have been

| This is explained in more detail in Chapter 19, Searching and Researching Childhood. |

some moves towards the state ensuring that children take a more active role in decision-making in services that are provided for them although the role of the recently appointed Children's Commissioner in England has been criticised for being 'weak', 'lacking a rights focus' and being 'under political control' (Community Care, 2004). However, the state does not intervene in children's

Reflective Activity 2.3

A 'new vision' of the child?

UNICEF argues that the UNCRC provides a 'new vision' of the child.

> Children are neither the property of their parents nor are they helpless objects for charity. They are human beings and are the subject of their own rights. The Convention offers a vision of the child as an individual and as a member of a family and community, with rights and responsibilities appropriate to his or her age and stage of development.

The convention was ratified by the UK in 1991 so the vision is now over 10 years old. By now we should be able to see aspects of this vision in practice.

Think about children that you know.

1 Do you think they are viewed by their families as individuals with rights and responsibilities? Explain why by giving examples of how families show this.

2 Do you think they are viewed by their communities as individuals with rights and responsibilities? Explain why by giving examples of how communities show this.

participation rights within the family unless there is a dispute between parents, as in the divorce case. The tension between children's participation rights and parents' responsibilities to protect children is a constant dilemma and occasionally these burst into the headlines. You can find out about these cases through journal searching.

What status do children have within our communities?

While the UNCRC identifies what rights children should have, the European Convention on Human Rights, which was incorporated into British law through the 1998 Human Rights Act, identifies what rights all humans should have. The 1998 Human Rights Act covers everyone in the UK, including children, and Fortin (2002) explains that if a child considers that their rights are being infringed by the government or a public agency, he or she can bring that grievance to a civil court under the Human Rights Act. The rights contained in these two documents have many areas of overlap but also some significant differences. The differences are mainly in two areas:

- Liberty rights (e.g. the freedom to vote, to own property, to marry) are features of the Human Rights Act but not the UNCRC.
- Protection rights, against abuse, exploitation and neglect, are part of the UNCRC but not the Human Rights Act.

This difference could suggest a difference in status where adults, through their right to engage in political decisions and be economically independent, can wield power over children who rely on them for their protection and provision. Alternatively, children could be seen as young citizens who are involved in those decisions that are appropriate to their age and stage of development, helped by sensitive adults who have the 'best interests' of the child in mind and who listen to and take seriously their point of view to make sure they are protected but not 'over protected'.

In relation to services that are provided for children, government policy and practice is influenced by voters and tax payers. Children are neither voters nor tax payers. Children's views are mediated through their parents and carers as full citizens, who will act 'in the child's best interests' until the child reaches the age of 18 when he or she becomes a citizen in his or her own right. So, even services that are concerned entirely with children, such as preschool, primary and secondary education, have no requirement for children to be part of decision-making: parents and carers are those who have to be consulted.

> This is discussed in more detail in Chapter 6, Education: Service or System?

Archard (1993) identifies two different points of view: the caretaker thesis and the liberationist thesis. The 'caretaker thesis' considers that children should only be accorded rights of protection and provision, not participation, because they may make mistakes that could seriously influence their later life. Supporters of this thesis consider children are not experienced enough or rational enough to make important decisions for themselves so adults, acting in their 'best interests', need to make these decisions for them. The caretaker thesis has been criticised by many advocates for children's rights. Liberationists such as Holt (1975) and Farson (1974), cited in Franklin (2002), argue that children should have the same liberty rights as adults because they should be given equal status with adults. They acknowledge the developmental argument put forward in the Convention, but don't consider that an argument based on children's lack of rational thought and lack of experience is a strong enough argument to deny children liberty rights. Franklin summarises the 'liberationist' critique in Table 2.1.

Table 2.1 The 'Liberationist' Critique

Argument	Example
Children of all ages are able to make rational and informed decisions	Cases of children as young as 6 being able to consider the implications of invasive medical treatment and determine their wishes
While children may lack experience in decision making they cannot get experience if they are never allowed opportunities to do so	A child who is never asked to participate in decisions made by the family (e.g. where to go on holiday, what food to buy, what TV programmes to watch) will not learn how to weigh up different points of view in order to reach a decision
Making mistakes is part of the learning process and children as well as adults need to be allowed to do this	A child who is always protected from taking risks will not know what the consequences of 'risky' decisions are so will not learn from making mistakes
Adults are not denied the right to make decisions on the grounds that they might make mistakes	Adults make many 'bad' decisions (e.g. marrying the wrong person, leading an unhealthy lifestyle) but are still given the right to make important decisions
Age requirements for rights are arbitrary and inconsistent	Children are legally allowed to marry with consent at 16 but cannot vote until 18
If liberty rights were conferred on the basis of competence many adults would be denied these rights	Many adults who have the vote know nothing about the candidates or parties in an election. If their competence to vote was tested they might lose their right to vote
Children can do nothing to change their status as they have no access to decision making	If children's status is linked to their age and economic dependence they can do nothing to change either of these things
Treating all those under 18 as a single group obscures legitimate reasons to argue for greater liberty rights	Arguments about increasing children's rights can be ridiculed by using a newborn infant as the example

Source: Franklin (2002), pp. 23–5.

In 2003 the 'Think Tank', Demos, produced the suggestion that children should have a vote from birth. Demos suggested that most of the debate is around a reduction of the franchise from 18 to 16. Whereas this tinkers with notions of adulthood it does not address participation of children. Some consideration was given to exercising the vote on behalf of a very young child or holding the vote in safe-keeping until the child is ready to use it.

> Parents could be encouraged to cast the extra vote in consultation with their child, and to think explicitly about the child's interests. But in any case, children's votes would reinforce the importance of families with children as an electoral constituency.
>
> (Thomas, 2003)

Katz promotes a different perspective suggesting that,

> It is at local level that young people's lives are most likely to be affected by their input. That means hearing the angry under-fives complaining about the filthy paperless toilet in their local playground. Or the young woman who has been passed from one service to another and is now in a young offender's institution with heroin addiction. It means letting kids contribute to decisions about school playgrounds and dinner menus. (Katz, 2003)

He views consultation at a local level about situations that directly affect them is a more constructive and realistic way of enabling the participation of children in decision-making. He believes that allowing someone else to exercise the child's vote would undermine progress to date, particularly given the conservative attitudes of many parents towards children's rights. Professor Priscilla Alderson of the Institute of Education reminds us that,

> Chapter 18, The Venture: Case Study of an Adventure Playground, gives examples of how this has been done.

> The whole idea of someone voting for someone else destroys so many powerful good legal traditions – the United Nations Convention on the Rights of the Child states that children have a right to express a view as soon as they can form it.
>
> (Alderson, 2003)

As Katz reminds us, 'It is their views we want – not their parents'.'

While these two writers differ in their approach to thinking about giving children a voice they both agree that children's voices should be heard and that they should be treated as 'citizens'. The concept of children as citizens has gained momentum in the last 10 years and since 2002 citizenship has become a statutory part of the English National Curriculum for Key Stages 3 and 4 (secondary school). This identifies targets for all children to achieve from the age of 5 onwards and is based on children learning about citizenship and their responsibilities (although not their rights). This move has been criticised as tokenism by Scott (2002) who points out the difficulty of learning about citizenship and participation without the opportunity to engage in meaningful opportunities to make decisions either in school or in the community.

> This is important in Chapter 4, The Social Divisions of Childhood, where citizenship is considered in this formal sense rather than as here, as a participant in society.

This idea of citizenship being concerned with rights and responsibilities needs to be considered alongside the idea of 'formal citizenship' or 'belonging' to a particular country.

Reflective Activity 2.4

Giving children a voice – how?

The above ideas are about attempts to think about ways of giving children a voice.

1 What do you think of Thomas's idea that parents should be able to cast a vote for children until they can do this themselves?

2 Do you think this would influence the status of children within society?

3 How do the ideas of liberationists and caretakers fit with these points of view?

The previous discussion has indicated that the way we think about children and young people will influence the way we think about their status, the rights they should have and the services that we provide for them. Here we look at three ways of thinking about childhood and children that influence how children's rights are reflected in service provision.

> Chapter 5, Pictures of Children, considers some of the language, concepts and attitudes that build up pictures of children that influence policy and practice initiatives.

Childhood as important in itself versus childhood as preparation for adulthood

The investment in children and mothers today will be the guarantor of the well-being and productivity of future generations. Indeed, children are our most accurate measure of development.

(Carol Bellamy, UNICEF Executive Director, Dublin, October 1997, cited in UNICEF)

The quotation highlights the first tension in how we think about children and childhood. Bellamy suggests that a reason for providing services for children (and their mothers) is because the investment will pay off in the future by ensuring that the adults of tomorrow are productive and happy. She may be using this as an argument because the view that children should be provided with services because they are children doesn't have such a strong political appeal. The earlier discussion concerning the status of children suggests that in the UK the higher status of adults through being voters and tax payers leads to the likelihood of services reflecting the interests of adults rather than children. During the terms of office since 1997 of the New Labour government children have been high on the political agenda but we need to look at the sort of services that have been developed to see whether they are concerned with children experiencing childhood or with children as prospective adults. Chapters in Part II, particularly those focusing on education, play and day care, consider this further.

Developmental psychology has added weight to the 'investment' argument for service provision by proposing that the environment, including the actions of adults, has an impact on the way a child develops. If we can decide what sort of adult we want to produce we can attempt to provide the 'best' environment possible to mould the child into the 'best' adult. This sort of thinking identifies the child as always 'becoming' rather than 'being' (James and Prout 1997) with provision being focused on what the child needs in order to move on to the next stage rather than what they need as the human being they are in the present. In contrast, most of the services provided for adults are concerned with their current context not as a preparation for what is to come next. For instance we don't usually suggest that adults in their 60s need to have their freedoms restricted because they might incur this in residential care in their next stage of life. Thinking of children as a future adult rather than the child they are at the moment is also behind some of the interpretations of 'in the best interests of the child' and 'children's needs'. Going beyond the basic needs of food, water and shelter developmental psychology suggests what psychological conditions are necessary for development. For example, Kellmer Pringle (1974), whose writing underpins much of the development psychology and child work practice of today, suggested there are four basic needs:

- love and security;
- new experiences;
- praise and recognition;
- responsibility.

The implication is that if these needs are not fulfilled the child will not become the adult we want them to be. As we saw in Reflective Activity 2.1, establishing what an individual 'needs' is subject to interpretation and Woodhead (1997) shows how ideas about needs are linked with our social construction of childhood and influenced by our culture. While the UNCRC is concerned with children's rights, articles concerned with provision and protection are underpinned by thinking about children's needs so the same concerns can be expressed about the assumptions behind these articles: do they reflect what children have a right to

Reflective Activity 2.5

Assumptions behind provision

Think about the following in the light of these ideas about children's needs and rights and children as 'beings' as opposed to 'becomings'.

Testing of children in school

Children are tested at the ages of 7, 11 and 14 in the core subjects and many find this a stressful event. Why do children need to be tested? How does the stress that children suffer meet children's rights to the 'highest attainable standards of health'? (Article 24)

The type of play facilities provided for children

What range of play facilities exist in your area? Are they available to all children or are there restrictions to access imposed by payments or access for children who are disabled? Who has decided that these are appropriate play facilities? On what basis? Are there other things that children might value?

Children starting formal education at five

In many European countries (Denmark, Sweden, Norway, Finland, Iceland and Switzerland) children don't start formal education until they are 7. Before this age provision is focused on providing care, play and leisure opportunities for children.

Why do children in the UK start formal education at 5? Who benefits from this?

because they are human beings or what we think they need in order to become the adults of tomorrow? Promoters of participation rights are more concerned with the child as a 'being' who can contribute to decisions about their current needs and rights. Consequently we should be looking critically at some of the assumptions behind provision we make for children in terms of the assumptions about what children need, what they have a right to and whether the 'best interests' of the child in the present are being served or the 'best interests' of the future adult.

You might also look at the chapters in Part II to identify what assumptions are being made in the services described there, for example Chapters 6, 11 and 12.

Children as vulnerable versus children as capable

This section is concerned with the assumptions behind provision for children in relation to their perceived vulnerability. Jones (2004) identifies the change in use of the word 'vulnerable' from one that needs further definition (e.g. 'vulnerable to disease' or 'vulnerable to abuse') to a much more general adjective (e.g. 'vulnerable children'). When used in this way it suggests that children are vulnerable in many, unspecified ways and gives the impression that, as vulnerable beings, they need protection. However, unless we specify how children are vulnerable we are in danger of over-protecting them. The previous section on childhood for its own sake versus preparation for adulthood identified developmental psychology as an influence on the way we think about children and what they need and suggested that if the identified needs weren't fulfilled a child's development would be at risk. This reinforces the idea of general vulnerability.

Bee (2002) shows how Piaget's theory of cognitive development puts forward the idea that children think differently at different stages of development so until children reach adult ways of thinking they aren't capable of rational thought or taking responsibility. This leaves them vulnerable to exploitation if they aren't protected. However, more recent research (Donaldson, 1978) has cast doubt on this difference in quality of thinking and suggests that in meaningful contexts children's thinking is very similar to that of adults. This kind of evidence suggests that we should be supporting children's thinking in everyday decision making rather than assuming their overall vulnerability.

Oakley (1994), writing from a feminist perspective, parallels the status of children with that of women in the UK at the beginning of the 20th century. She suggests that when the group (women or children) is identified as vulnerable it legitimises the use of power over them as a form of protection. From this perspective it becomes very important to identify specific vulnerability to ensure that this power isn't abused.

Some of the ways we might class children as vulnerable are

- physically vulnerable to exploitation or abuse;
- sexually vulnerable to exploitation or abuse;
- emotionally vulnerable to exploitation or abuse;
- socially vulnerable to exploitation or abuse;
- vulnerable to illness and disease;
- economically vulnerable to the effects of poverty.

If we then involve children in the discussions around their vulnerability we may be able to reduce the possibility of wielding power without taking away the protection that some children may well need.

As Piagetian ideas about children's restricted intellectual capabilities have been challenged, subsequent work with children has attempted to acknowledge their capabilities and has found that 'children become competent by first being treated as if they are competent' (Alderson, 1993). In the same way that it is important to identify in what ways children might be vulnerable it is also important to identify in what ways individuals can be seen as capable so we don't overestimate their capabilities and consequently increase their vulnerability. The UNCRC identifies children as being potentially vulnerable in articles that are concerned with protection from abuse and exploitation and in provision of services that support their survival and development. It also acknowledges children's developing capabilities in the articles concerned with participation.

As we saw in the section on the status of children there is a danger in grouping all children together as a homogeneous group. While there are few that would argue that a newborn child is vulnerable to physical abuse it is more difficult to argue that all 17-year-olds are physically vulnerable. Similarly differences in genetic factors and experiences may lead some children to be more socially, emotionally, sexually or intellectually developed than others. In this case Jason could be seen as a capable 10-year-old who has many social, emotional and physical abilities. In the UK these abilities are considered unusual at this age and Jason could be seen to be vulnerable to exploitation because it isn't seen to be the norm for children to behave in this way. However, in other societies it is quite acceptable for children of his age to take such responsibility. By talking

Reflective Activity 2.6

Who is vulnerable?

Jason is 10 years old and lives with his mother and younger brother. His mother suffers from depression and often relies on Jason to get himself and his brother up and ready for school. He also shops, prepares meals for them all in the evenings, goes to the launderette and keeps the house clean and tidy. Jason takes these responsibilities very seriously and both boys appear well cared for. His mother is able to keep going because of the support Jason gives her in these ways and because he is sensitive to her difficulties. He is concerned that if he tells anyone what is happening his mother may be blamed.

1 How do you respond to this?

2 In what ways do you think Jason might be vulnerable?

3 What evidence would you look for to help you to identify whether Jason was vulnerable or not?

4 What capabilities does Jason show?

5 What sort of service is needed to support and protect Jason without wielding power?

to Jason about how he feels and what he would like to happen it might be possible to appreciate his capability and identify any areas of vulnerability. Under current legislation he is economically dependent on others and therefore is potentially vulnerable to poverty and, as we saw in the section on the status of children, this may influence how he is perceived and listened to.

Children as victims versus children as villains

The final area of tension that we are going to consider is closely linked with the previous section. Concepts of children's vulnerability stemming from developmental psychology can also identify children as victims of the environments that they live in. The progress towards the ideal adult can be marred by the circumstances surrounding the child's development. Archard (1993) identifies two opposing beliefs about the 'nature' of children: the idea that children are innately good and born innocent and the contrasting idea that children are innately sinful. In the first case it becomes important to attempt to protect the child's innocence from the potentially corrupting environment; in the second, it becomes important to reform or educate the child into accepted ways of behaving. The first instance suggests children may be victims of the environment that they live in and need to be protected from anything that might sully their innocence. The second instance suggests that children are villains who should be controlled. Both instances identify children as problematic and see the solution in forms of control. Neither sees children as active participants in identification of what is problematic or in finding solutions.

When children are seen as victims the identified problem is that of finding ways of protecting them from sources of contamination. Solutions may take the form of censorship (e.g. barring viewing of specified films) or physical constraints (e.g. not being allowed out without supervision). Media representations of what happens when these solutions fail and children are abused, murdered or exploited have portrayed children as innocent victims and made calls for more legislation and policies to protect children from the various sources of threat (e.g. increasing security in schools, calls to ban advertising aimed at children, increased surveillance, restrictions on the risks that children are allowed to take). Viewed from a child's point of view some of these restrictions might appear to be actions that shut down desirable activities and decrease their privacy and freedoms.

Franklin (2002) shows how media representations of children have changed over the last twenty years to increasingly emphasise a view of children as a group who are at least troublesome if not evil. Perhaps in response to the restrictions designed to protect children as victims, the behaviour of some children is now seen as much more challenging. Here the identified problem is not one of finding ways to protect children but of finding ways to make children conform to what adults perceive as appropriate standards of behaviour. Solutions to the problem tend to be in terms of increasing control over children and young people. While the UNCRC is pointing to the need for children to participate in decisions according to their developing capabilities

government policies have been focusing on the control of children and young people. In earlier sections of this chapter we considered the status of children and the relationship between the rights of children and the rights of adults. This is particularly relevant here as Franklin (2002) suggests that one of the possible causes for this 'demonisation' of children might be the fear of losing control that adults have. He identifies the priority that is usually given to adult rights when there is a conflict between children's rights and adults' rights. This was reinforced in the previous discussion around citizenship of children being economically dependent on

Reflective Activity 2.7

Concerns about media portrayals of children

> The government's chief adviser on youth crime has called on politicians and the media to stop calling children 'yobs' and warned that Britain risks demonising a generation of young people.
>
> In an interview with the *Observer*, Professor Rod Morgan, chairman of the Youth Justice Board, said this country was throwing out contradictory messages about its attitude to children. He said that while, on the one hand, children represented the country's aspirations for the future, on the other, they were being condemned as thugs in hooded tops. (Bright, 2005)
>
> . . . children have fewer rights in our society than we do, and policies which affect them profoundly are rarely framed in terms of their needs. Nowhere is a lack of joined-up political thinking more obvious than in the failure to connect the problems of children with the 'problem' of children.
>
> (Williams, 2002)

These two quotes identify concerns about the way we are portraying children and the policies that are being implemented.

1 What concerns are being expressed?

2 What do you think the authors would suggest as ways forward?

adults and having no right to vote so remaining comparatively powerless.

Chapter 9 looks more closely at the provision for children who commit crimes. The chapter outlines the changes in legislation and helps us identify the influences of perceiving children as victims and children as villains. In considering the previous tensions the opposing viewpoints led to different actions whereas in this section we have seen that constructing children as either victims or villains leads to similar types of action that restrict and or punish children. Using either of these constructions may result in an abuse of power by adults who use either construction to justify their actions.

How effective are services in responding to children's rights?

Services within the UK are predicated on the welfare/caretaker focus of children's rights with the dominant view being of the state operating in the 'best interests' of the child within the context of the family.

Chapter 3, The Politics of Childhood, provides further discussion of this.

Primary social and welfare services afford parents the power to determine the child's schooling, make decisions on health care and tend to intervene on a child's behalf only in cases of extreme neglect or abuse.

Chapter 13, Children's Experience of Community Regeneration, highlights the absence of the child's voice in consultation and decision-making on housing and community development. Chapter 14, The Swings and Roundabouts of Community Development, shows how often children's recreational provision becomes the catalyst for community development. At both policy and delivery levels children are ostracised from involvement in decisions which directly affect their lives while being used as a means of gaining interest and action for adult demands.

By considering examples of current policy we can identify how the tension between vulnerability in some areas and capability in others might be taken into consideration. In the recent Department of Education and Skills paper *Birth to Three Matters* (Sure Start, 2002) children are identified as being vulnerable and needing to be dependent on adults while in the same paper the child was described as a 'strong child, a healthy child, a skilful communicator and a competent learner', demonstrating some tension between perception and reality.

Chapters in Part II consider policies and provision across a range of services for children and you will find the tension between vulnerability and capability occurring in these chapters, particularly Chapter 10, Safeguarding Children.

Contradictory perspectives can also be taken such as limited decision-making in secondary schools through school councils but no control over the curriculum, yet in the context of offending being deemed to be criminally responsible from the age of 10.

Conclusion

The questions identified at the beginning of this chapter were

- What do we mean by children's rights?
- Who is responsible for ensuring children's rights are upheld?
- What status do children have within our communities?
- How effective are services in responding to children's rights?

The answers to these questions are not straightforward as the discussion throughout the chapter has shown. This discussion provides some insight into the complexity of the subject. Children's rights are primarily laid down in the UNCRC but it can be seen that this is not without criticism because of debates about the sort of rights children should have, the emphasis on

▶

an individualistic construction of society and the potential conflict between liberty rights and welfare rights. While the family is seen as the primary upholder of children's rights the state is seen to have a role in supporting families but the way this is done raises issues about parental autonomy and privacy and the economics of funding the support needed.

Issues concerning the status of children revolve round participation rights and how far children are treated as citizens within society. Treating children as a homogeneous group is particularly problematic here in drawing a distinction between adults and children. The way we support children as citizens and help them to learn about their rights and responsibilities is important across all service provision.

The way services respond to children's rights is influenced by the way childhood is constructed within societies and the way children are perceived. The tensions identified in the chapter can be seen to polarise views. When looking at the chapters in Parts II and III you might go on to consider whether it is possible to acknowledge that

- childhood is important in itself *and* as a preparation for adulthood
- children are vulnerable *and* capable

By acknowledging these tensions we may provide services that support children's liberty rights as well as their welfare rights and involve them as full citizens of our society. However, pursuing media constructions of children either as victims or as villains is likely to cloud discussion and lead us away from the important issues discussed in this chapter.

Annotated reading

Archard, D. (1993) *Children: Rights and Childhood*, London: Routledge

A very thorough and detailed discussion of problems associated with the idea of children's rights.

Children's Rights Alliance for England <www.crae.org.uk>

This reports on news and initiatives across England in relation to children's rights. It includes access to reports made on children's rights in the UK which give areas for action.

Franklin, B. (2002) *The New Handbook of Children's Rights*, London: Routledge

This contains chapters written by different people who are specialists in different areas of children's rights. It is essential reading for anyone who is interested in this area and gives illustrations of policy and practice.

James, A. and Prout, A. (eds) (1997) *Constructing and Reconstructing Childhood: Contemporary Issues in the Sociological Study of Childhood*, London: Falmer

This is a challenging read that discusses ways we construct childhood and the implications of these. Particularly relevant to the points made in this chapter is Martin Woodhead's chapter on Psychology and the cultural construction of children's needs.

UNICEF Convention on the Rights of the Child <http://www.unicef.org.uk/crc/convention.htm>

The full text of the 1989 Convention on the Rights of the Child can be found here with further information about the Convention and the work that UNICEF undertakes in an attempt to ensure these rights are met.

The Politics of Childhood

PAT TOMLINSON

Imagine a country where children are consulted, listened to and taken seriously; where opportunities prevail for children to be involved in decision-making and the democratic process; where children, as a matter of course, are able to make positive contributions to the well-being of their communities and neighbourhoods; where children's participation stemming from political and social imperatives is regarded as just and normal; and where children need no convincing that democracy works for them.

(Matthews, 2001)

Introduction

This chapter explores two dominant spheres of influence on children's lives – politics and economics. It examines three substantial questions as to how these influences affect children and the experience of childhood. The discussion considers the effects of politics and economics on children within their families, communities and nations.

- How are concepts of childhood shaped by political and economic influences?

- What is the relationship between politics, childhood and the status of the child?

- Political and economic policies: why do we need to consider the child's perspective?

The areas covered in this chapter are complex and overlapping. The purpose is to explore some key debates, not resolve them. This chapter does not focus on explaining different political perspectives, rather it explores the impact on children, the quality of services provided, the economic contexts in which they live and the way children's voices may be excluded from political debates. It explores their experience in relation to the families, communities and nations they live in, giving consideration to the international context.

Within a nation, the status, rights, responsibilities and obligations attributed to children affect their experience and life chances. Children as members of a nation state and part of the international community are susceptible to political and economic influences. Arguably they are more susceptible than other sectors of the population as they have greater vulnerability due to age, developmental stage and relative powerlessness. There are no democracies in the world that give children the franchise and few that provide suffrage below the age of 18.

> Throughout the world, 18 years of age is by far the most common minimum age for voting. Some 142 countries set their voting age at 18 for at least one of their chambers of parliament: 171 chambers altogether have a franchise at 18. Only three, Korea, Indonesia, and the Sudan, set the voting age at 17, with a further three, Brazil, Cuba, and Nicaragua, permitting voting at 16, and just one, Iran, setting the age at 15. (Bassam, 2003)

These variations stem from a range of political and economic factors influencing the status of children. The relationship between childhood, politics and economics is complex. To unravel this, we need to explore the effects of political beliefs and economic actions on the experience children have of their childhood in the confines of the family but also beyond in their communities and countries of residence. We also need to examine international and global influences. We live in a global society, operate in a global economy and engage politically on an international stage (Deacon, 2003). This is experienced at an everyday level, for example developments in global communication are available in most children's homes via the Internet and a simple perusal of the weekly UK shopping basket shows the extent of world trade. Children experience events taking place in international politics on a daily basis directly or through their television screens. Thus at both a micro and a macro level children see and feel the impact of global economics and politics. Indeed the United Nations suggests that the impact of world events on children is intense and at times disproportionate to other sectors of the population.

> Children are always among the first affected by armed conflict. Even if they are not killed or injured, they can be orphaned, abducted or left with psychological and psychosocial distress from direct exposure to violence, dislocation, poverty or the loss of loved ones.

HIV/AIDS is tearing at the very fabric of childhood. Around 15 million children under the age of 18 had been orphaned by the pandemic by the end of 2003. (UNICEF, 2004)

Both in global terms, that is, when discussing elements 'covering or relating to the whole world' and international terms, when examining issues 'concerning or involving two or more nations' (Collins, 1987) children are centre stage.

How are concepts of childhood shaped by political and economic influences?

This section explores the political and economic factors shaping childhood in different parts of the world. There are tensions between discourses about children

and their experience in childhood. Thinking of the spheres of influence in our lives can be difficult and complex. As children, we frequently do not know the extent or range of external influence on our childhood experiences and rarely do we have opportunity to change things beyond the boundaries of home.

Legislation and policy concerning children and their families is extensive. Yet many children who are directly affected by such legislation are barely aware of its existence let alone involved in its consideration. For example, policies such as highway and housing developments have significant effects on the safety and quality of living space for children but are consistently seen as adult issues only. On the rare occasions children become involved it is within family and community neighbourhoods over such concerns as school crossing patrols and parking at the school gates. Yet when consulted children highlight their desire to be free to discover and access their own play space beyond 'designated' spaces and indicate traffic problems as the main constraint in doing so. The ability of children to affect decision-making is also limited in areas directly focused on policy for children, for example provision of schooling for children is determined by adults within the political arena. Policy tends to focus on larger political agendas, sometimes parental rights but rarely children's rights (Hill and Tisdall, 1997). The pervasive adult perspective is that children lack the maturity to make decisions for themselves.

> Chapter 13, Children's Experience of Community Regeneration, explores these issues in more depth.

Even as adults we can remain naive about the range of influences that affected our childhood experiences and the impact these had on our future prospects. As Daniel and Ivatts argue,

> [children] are principal recipients of welfare services, and their experience . . . will do much to determine not only their present well-being but also their future life chances. Yet they make shadowy appearances at best in most of the social policy literature. (1998, p. 1)

Given this seeming contradictory situation, of children often divorced from the politics which determine the services they receive, it is necessary to examine the reasons for this and the way that wider political and economic interests influence the status accorded to children within their homes, their neighbourhoods and their nations. Analysis of the status accorded to children on a personal and collective level raises questions about their relative powerlessness, their rights and their exploitation.

The discussion focuses on the impact of poverty and social exclusion. This area starkly reveals the impact of political ideology and economic context on the experience of childhood: how different political perspectives address issues of poverty and social exclusion, and how different perspectives conceptualise the relationship between the two. Wealth and poverty are clearly major determinants of social inclusion or exclusion but, beyond that, what is at their root? Pierson (2000) examines a number of approaches to social exclusion. These reflect different political perspectives. Some socialist and social democratic perspectives emphasise the redistribution of wealth as the only effective way to alleviate poverty. Others, more associated with the right of the political spectrum, argue that poverty is reinforced through over generosity to the poor and that the welfare state, although intended to alleviate poverty, has created an 'underclass' overly dependent on the state who have lost the motivation to create wealth themselves. These differing perspectives provide very different explanations for the same phenomena. Each discourse works from a particular set of assumptions and explanations of how the world works and incorporates its own set of values (Rogers, 2001). When these differing perspectives are acted upon at the level of policy, then services to children and the impact on their lives will be very different. Clearly the concept of social exclusion is broader than that of poverty and is concerned with wider issues such as discrimination, inequality and lack of opportunity (DWP, 2003).

> See Chapter 4, The Social Divisions of Childhood, for further discussion.

Moss and Petrie (2002) make it clear that the politics and economics of childhood are not static but shift in relation to economic and ideological trends. For example, as the demands for an increasingly educated workforce grow, the period of childhood extends to enable the fulfilment of these economic demands. This is evidenced by the massive expansion in young people continuing in full-time education beyond the minimum school leaving age. In the mid-1970s two-thirds of young people left school on reaching the age of 16. This changed significantly by the 1990s with 80 per cent of young people staying on in full-time education post-16 (Coles, 1998). Census 2001 data shows this trend continuing into the 21st century. The Labour Government target in the UK is that 50 per cent of all children should enter higher education. The notion of the child as an economic asset affects the larger discussion of the relationship between the family and the state's responsibility for children. The state, community and family may view children as primarily economic assets reared for their future productivity. This has been a commonly held view historically in the UK from the feudal system to the Industrial Revolution. Within this perspective the child is considered an economic resource essential to the well-being of the family and society. Prior to the recognition of the value of an extended education, children were expected to contribute to their communities as early as possible rather than remain a cost through a prolonged period of childhood and not place undue burden on the resources of the state through personal or collective expectations of social welfare and care.

As well as being viewed as economic assets, some communities have recognised that children require their social needs to be addressed, including their health, welfare and education. Children may be

Reflective Activity 3.1

The child as an economic asset?

The South Asian Coalition on Child Servitude claims that India has the largest number of working children in the world. Many of these children are in 'bonded child labour'. This is the phenomenon of children working in conditions of servitude in order to pay off a debt. The debt that binds them to their employer is incurred not by the children themselves, but by their relatives or guardians – usually by a parent. In India, these debts tend to be relatively modest, ranging on average from 500 rupees to 7,500 rupees, depending on the industry and the age and skill of the child. The creditors-cum-employers offers these 'loans' to destitute parents in an effort to secure the labour of a child, which is always cheap, but even cheaper under a situation of bondage. The parents, for their part, accept the loans. Bondage is pay for the costs of an illness, perhaps to provide a dowry to a marrying child, or perhaps – as is often the case – to help put food on the table.　　　(Bachpan Bachao Andolan, 2007)

Reflect on the ethical concerns raised by this situation and ways in which it might be changed. Consider the absence of state welfare and levels of poverty in countries where such practices persist. Also consider how children are being seen by adults in the wider community.

Reflective Activity 3.2

The child as a social asset?

The Child Welfare Scheme in Nepal.

Through the efficient use of funds, Child Welfare Scheme empowers and enables its local partners to work with communities to reduce poverty and improve the health, education and opportunities of disadvantaged children and youths in order to give them a second chance in life. At least 85 per cent of funds donated to CWS are used directly for project activities. To date CWS has helped 11 mountain village communities build and manage their own Day-Care Health Centres. CWS has also set up drinking water projects and established programmes to build smokeless stoves in many villages' houses. In addition, CWS undertakes activities for street youth in Pokhara, including a health clinic and a vocational training and reintegration centre.　　　(CWS, 2007)

1　What view of the child is evident in such practices in Nepal?

2　Compare and contrast this situation with that of 'bonded children' in India supported financially and emotionally within their families. Communities may adapt environments to facilitate child development. The state and other establishment entities such as religious organisations may support the welfare and care of children. In general children may be viewed as social assets. The extent of prevailing views across and within countries can be varied depending on the social and political context at a micro and macro level. This will affect the size of resources available for children's welfare and care services and the social status afforded to children.

Clearly in both the above examples the economic value of the child is considered. In the latter case, however, the emphasis is on supporting their health, education and welfare in the longer term. The child is socially valued beyond their economic worth, being conceptualised as having the right to health care and welfare. Policies that address the social value of the child, such as the right to state education, protective child labour legislation and gender equality, are considered in more detail later in the chapter.

The commonly held view across the main political parties in the UK is that the value of family life lies in its privacy from state intervention. Indeed most UK government policy and legislation has been based on this premise. There is little encouragement to view children as independent individuals, separate from parents and other family members (Fortin, 2002). Indeed, until recently the most significant piece of legislation in England and Wales for child-care and family services, the 'Children Act 1989' rests on the belief that children are generally best looked after within the family with both parents playing a full part and without resort to legal proceedings. This rhetoric remains in spite of extensive changes to children's lives resulting from more diverse family circumstances and differential family experiences. In the UK and elsewhere throughout the world children experience changing patterns of family life. Split families, step-parents and siblings, lone-parent households and family displacement mean that a child can be faced with changing and challenging situations throughout childhood (Harper, 2003).

A fuller discussion of this legislation can be found in Chapter 10, Safeguarding Children.

Across the globe children are experiencing family displacement as refugees and asylum seekers as a result of war, pestilence and economic upheaval. In January 2004 over 7.5 million children were classed as refugees, making up 45 per cent of the refugee population. Such children may be left homeless, parentless and stateless through these extreme circumstances. In 2003, some 12,800 unaccompanied and separated children applied for asylum in 28 industrialised countries (UNHCR, 2005).

The experience of educating refugee children is explored in Chapter 17.

Even within the embrace of their own homes, for many children the idealised notion of a two-parent heterosexual family in a stable child-rearing setting is a myth. The UK Census 2001 reveals that dependent children still make up a substantial number of people, some 11.7 million. Overall, almost a third of households contain dependent children and one in nine has children under 5. The majority of dependent children live with both natural parents (65 per cent). However, many children have different experiences of family. 22.9 per cent or 2,672,000 dependent children live in lone-parent families, 91.2 per cent of which are headed by the mother. More than one in ten dependent children live in a stepfamily (1,284,000). In addition to the total of dependent children, over 45,000 children under 16 live in communal establishments. Many children live in 'workless' households with over two million (17.6 per cent) in households where there are no adults in work. Approximately 149,000 children under 18 provide unpaid care within their family. Figure 3.1 on p. 27 shows the continuing decline in marriage and the increase in divorce in the UK through the second half of the 20th century.

Such diversity means that there is a tension in the politics of UK family life. There is a pragmatic approach which recognises the diversity of family life, for example the introduction of civil partnership rights for same sex couples in 2005. However, stereotypes of the heterosexual nuclear family as a 'safe haven' persist. This was highlighted in 2007 when attempts to legislate against the discrimination of gay people in relation to the provision of goods and services led to a heated debate around whether Catholic adoption agencies

Figure 3.1 Marriage and divorce patterns since 1950.

<http://www.statistics.gov.uk/census/>

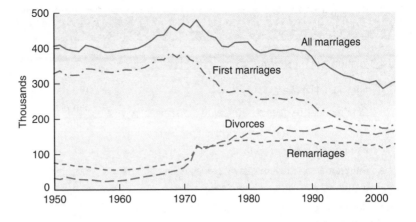

should be granted exemption on the grounds of religious belief and conscience from considering lesbians and gay men as prospective adopters.

Reference to children in political debate is framed mostly within the notion of 'diminished capacity'. This phrase encapsulates the commonly held view that the child is not always able to represent him- or herself or has less decision-making capability than adults. It is widely acknowledged that parents are in charge of their children and responsible for them. Much of the political and economic debate concerning children centres on where parental responsibility ends and state responsibility begins. The literature examining children in society generally encompasses the premise that children have little formal control particularly beyond the family and are relatively powerless to influence the vagaries of their political and economic environments (Hill and Tisdall, 1997; Foley et al., 2001 and Qvortrup et al., 1994).

> Chapter 2, Childhood: Rights and Realities, and Chapter 5, Pictures of Children, explore these concepts in different ways.

Within the realms of social policy it is commonly accepted that three perspectives of children dominate: the child as victim, investment or threat (Daniel and Ivatts, 1998; Foley et al., 2001; Prout, 2003). The emphasis will vary according to wider political aims, economic context and the age of the child. Whatever the case, these three idealizations or stereotypes deny children their status as full human beings.

Whether perceived as threat, victim or investment the child is considered beholden to rather than equal to the adult population. These stereotypes can be compounded by other inequities such as gender, class, differing ability or ethnicity. A child in poverty, for example, may be more frequently identified as a threat than a wealthy child. The impact of multiple inequalities on children's experience and future prospects is discussed later in this chapter when reviewing the circumstances of children's lives.

> These constructs of childhood are discussed in depth in Chapter 2, Childhood: Rights and Realities.

Generally, the concept of 'family' is dominant over that of childhood throughout the world. Childhood is viewed from within the family context, not as a distinct construct in itself. It is based on the view that children are invisible in and indivisible from the family unit. Common parlance supports this theme and professional training and practice is frequently family focused rather than child-centred. Within UK policy for children the emphasis is more on the welfare and safeguarding of children rather than their rights.

> Inequalities are also discussed in Chapter 4, The Social Divisions of Childhood.

This section has considered a range of complex and overlapping political and economic influences on childhood in different parts of the world. Key questions

Reflective Activity 3.3

Dominant concepts of the child

Child as threat

- Children may be seen as a threat to the social order.

- The emphasis is on 'problem families' with unruly and uncontrolled children.

- Children are portrayed as 'evil' beings needing to be instructed and retrained into 'good' adults.

- Society is characterised as needing protection from children rather than to be protective of them.

- Notions of 'depraved' and 'deprived' begin to come together.

- The gap between childhood and adult worlds appears to widen.

- The use of this concept reflects disillusionment with a support and prevention ethos in social policy to a more authoritarian and policing emphasis.

Child as victim

- Child as victim is associated with ideas about the abuse of children which in turn may be stereotypes, for example emphasis on 'stranger-danger' rather than the more real risks of danger in the home.

- Theories that emphasize child as 'victim' may explain things such as delinquency by referring to child neglect and abuse (by the family, community or state).

- The use of this concept may lead to more support and prevention in social policy, but the emphasis on children as passive and vulnerable may not always be in their best interests.

Child as investment

- Children may be viewed as investments to satisfy future society needs.

- Population policies may be introduced to influence both quality and quantity.

- Children may be viewed in terms of their potential to produce economic wealth for themselves and society.

- 'Success' in the future may be the focus.

- The child as 'investment' influences approaches to various aspects of social policy, such as education and health.

1 Consider each of these concepts in turn. In what circumstances might they be emphasised by politicians?

2 Consider them in relation to portrayals of children in art, literature, film and advertisement. How are they reinforced?

---

are raised. It has explored the way wider political agendas, unconcerned with children per se, may influence policy towards children. For example, in relation to social exclusion differences in political perspective lead to widely differing policies, some supporting welfare state provision, others conceptualising it as damaging. Moving to consideration of how children are conceptualised in political discourse, it has discussed the idea of children as

See discussion of welfare and liberty rights in Chapter 2, Childhood: Rights and Realities.

economic assets. How far does the idea of the child as an investment or an economic resource drive political agendas? At one extreme the example of bonded labour is given, at another the idea of extended education for the child is linked to economic demands. Questions have been raised about other conceptualisations of children, where the emphasis may be their care and welfare and where the child may be more socially valued in their own right. It has addressed the changing patterns of family life, the tensions in family policy that arise and the way that the concept of 'family' is frequently emphasised over that of childhood. Stereotypes of childhood abound in political discourse about children and the voice of the child often goes unheard by politicians.

What is the relationship between politics, childhood and the status of the child?

This section explores how differing perspectives on childhood influence the status afforded to children and how these are in turn shaped by political and economic priorities. The complexity of ideas about childhood and the way these are drawn on by politicians and policymakers is often overlooked. Where children are considered they may be viewed solely as economic investments. Their care and welfare might be considered but their status in society as full human beings far less so. In addition, where the child is the centre of consideration, the emphasis has tended to be on their welfare and the role of the family rather than their status in society. The themes of inclusion and exclusion are now drawn on to explore the power of children and their participation in political and economic decision-making.

At the beginning of the 21st century the elected UK government began a consultation on the health, care, protection and welfare of children. As a result of the high profile inquiry into the death of Victoria Climbié, responding to public and professional concerns about weaknesses in child protection strategy, children were once again on the government agenda. Victoria Climbié was a young child abused and finally murdered by her carers in spite of being brought to the attention of a range of welfare agencies. The Victoria Climbié Inquiry (Laming, 2003) led by Lord Laming resulted in a wide range of recommendations for change to child protection work. The result was the Green Paper, 'Every Child Matters' which summarised its proposals as being:

> designed both to protect children and maximise their potential. It sets out a framework for services that cover children and young people from birth to 19 living in England. It aims to reduce the numbers

of children who experience educational failure, engage in offending or anti-social behaviour, suffer from ill health, or become teenage parents.

(DfES, 2003b, p. 6)

A range of initiatives were proposed, involving significant restructuring of services to support parents: provision of early intervention and effective protection strategies for vulnerable children; improvement of accountability and integration of child protection work; and the instigation of workforce reforms. In contrast to 'Every Child Matters' concurrent Home Office activity saw the advent of the Anti-Social Behaviour Order (ASBO) from 1 April 1999 which is being used as a means of restraining children and naming and shaming them within communities.

> Chapter 10, Safeguarding Children, and Chapter 11, Day Care Services for Children, explore different aspects of these changes in greater detail.

For further discussion of ASBOs see Chapter 9, Children Who Offend.

The dichotomy of the two approaches demonstrates the ambivalent relationship between the political administration and children. It reflects the polarisation of two prevailing concepts of the child mentioned earlier and articulated by Prout (2003) that public debate swings between children as victims, in need of protection from harm, and children as a threat to social order coming from problem families producing unruly and uncontrolled children. The concept of children as 'evil' beings needing to be instructed and retrained into 'good' adults is part of our social and cultural heritage (Daniel and Ivatts, 1998). The emphasis is on society needing protection from children rather than the protection of children. Such perspectives ensnare children in the political headlights of parliamentary debate and policy but rarely engage children in the consultative processes that influence such policy.

There is, of course, a 'third way'. Prout (2003) suggests we find a 'more adequate way of representing childhood' (p. 4). As a society we can view children as citizens, seeing children as holders of human rights too. There is evidence of political moves to consider this approach, for example the preamble to the Convention on the Rights of the Child (UN, 1989) seeks to accord children the human rights status of adults while proclaiming children as 'entitled to special care and assistance'. All but two countries of the world have ratified the Convention. While the extent of ratification is laudable it is not a guarantee of implementation.

> Concepts of citizenship and the Convention are discussed in more detail in Chapter 2, Children's Rights and Realities.

Ratification of the Convention implies a legal requirement to meet its intentions and ratifying countries are required to report on progress towards this. However, independent nations must create internal statutes, policy and resources to ensure enactment and devise penalties for defaulters. Despite the Convention being seen by the United Nations Children's Fund (UNICEF) as the most 'universally accepted human rights instrument in history', the organisation provides evidence on a daily basis of contraventions of some of the most fundamental protocols of the Convention. The

Reflective Activity 3.4

Undermining the status of the child: case examples

Child slavery

Although slavery is illegal everywhere, it continues to exist in some parts of the world. Its existence is rarely acknowledged by citizens of advanced industrialised countries, despite the fact that it is a part of the global economy. The term 'slavery' is rarely used anymore. Instead, slavery is usually referred to as 'bonded labour' or 'human trafficking'. Children are particularly vulnerable to the new slavery. According to the International Labour Organisation (2002) report, 'A future without child labour', 73 per cent of these children – approximately 180 million – are working in the worst forms of child labour – including prostitution, bonded labour, trafficking and hazardous work. Moreover, the figures also show that slavery is not dead, with some 5.7 million children trapped in forced and bonded labour.

Slavery is prohibited in Article 15 of the Universal Declaration of Human Rights and numerous other international human rights' treaties. The trafficking of children is specifically prohibited under several international conventions, including the 1989 United Nations Convention on the Rights of the Child, yet many consumer products such as chocolate and carpets are produced using child slave labour.

Forced early marriage

Across the globe, children, primarily girls, are forced into early marriage. It is difficult to estimate the number of early marriages because many early marriages are unregistered and unofficial, but the highest rates appear to occur in Mali, Niger, Uganda, Burkina Faso and Cameroon. Girls as young as 8 or 10 years old are forced to be married, often with much older men. Recently, UNICEF has publicly demanded an end to child marriages. A study on the practice declared that it often inflicts physical and emotional anguish on young girls and deprives them of the right to give free and full consent to marriage and the right to education.

Despite its pervasiveness, forced early marriage has rarely been viewed as a human rights violation in itself. Nonetheless, it violates Article 16 of the Universal Declaration of Human Rights, as well as several other human rights' treaties, notably the Convention on the Rights of the Child, the world's most widely ratified human rights treaty.

1 Consider the two examples above where the status of children is undermined. What political and economic priorities may have allowed these abuses to continue despite the UN Convention on the Rights of the Child?

2 Remember that abuse of children occurs in both the developed and developing worlds. Abuse may relate to both lack of resources and to the low status of children in a community. Think of examples where the status of children may have been undermined in the UK.

contraventions raise issues not only for nations directly involved but for international communities around the world. The two activity boxes (3.4 on p. 30 and 3.5 on p. 32) explore the undermining of the rights of the child in different countries of the world including the UK. They draw attention to examples of oppressive social practice and how the low status of children allows political and economic exploitation to take place.

Within its first term of office (1997–2001) the UK New Labour government began to show interest in the rights of children and young people, through establishing the Children and Young Person's Unit (CYPU) in England and the Children's Parliament in Scotland. These were both concerned with developing an overarching strategy covering children's services and a vision for children and young people. The Children's Parliament aims to provide opportunities for children up to the age of 14 to engage in local, national and international democratic processes. The intention is to enable direct contact with adults who matter at the highest of levels, specifically with appropriate ministers and the Commissioner for Children and Young People. The CYPU no longer exists, having been incorporated into the Department for Education and Science (DfES). Some of the principles surrounding consultation with children and young people have continued, not least the electoral commission's enquiry into the minimum voting age (Electoral Commission, 2004) which may yet offer young people entry into the decision-making processes of the country. Contrary to this optimism rests the demise of the unit itself. The unit embarked on a set of service principles centred on Prout's notion of children as 'social persons' including such criteria as 'centered on the needs of the young person, empowering, inclusive, equitable and non-discriminatory' (CYPU, 2001a, p. 12). These principles have been promoted by the government, with departments being encouraged to consult with children and young people and develop a plan for participation of children in policy development and implementation. There are several examples of this in both Parts II and III.

However, the differential status of children and adults continues and is demonstrated by the heated debate in Parliament in 2004, resulting in a three-line whip of Labour Members of Parliament, over the challenge to the retention of a clause in the Children's Bill allowing parents to smack their children. In 1998 the government had commissioned a survey of adult views on smacking children. The results of the survey supported the right of parents to use physical punishment as part of child-rearing practice (ONS, 1998). This resulted in a government White Paper in 2000 on 'chastisement' which gave the legal right to parents to physically punish their children. The clause has now been retained in the Children Act 2004. Children's views on 'chastisement' were not surveyed: a clear demonstration of the differential political influence between the franchiseless child and the vote-holding parent. On the one hand, participation is encouraged while, on the other, political action continues to support the physical punishment of children by their parents. The above example shows how entrenched social and cultural perspectives of child rearing within society and family outweigh international perspectives of children's rights in political policy. Ultimately, the political concern to maintain the electoral support of parents led the government to cast aside a children's rights agenda. Britain is not alone in showing anomalies between its political action and international agreements on children's rights. There are many examples that UNICEF identifies. Wider political and economic agendas frequently undermine children's rights and lead to their exclusion from the political process.

In the above section we have explored ways in which the status of children may be undermined despite political attempts to legislate in their favour. We have explored examples from different parts of the world where despite the ratification of an international convention protecting children's rights and giving them a place in the political process, their status has been seriously undermined. We have given a more detailed example from the UK where the tension between children's rights as an articulated agenda is undermined by other political interests, such as maintaining electoral support for example.

Political and economic policies: why do we need to consider the child's perspective?

The third question examines what impact political and economic policies have on children's everyday lives and the importance of considering their needs, experiences

Reflective Activity 3.5

Undermining the status of the child: the political process

Parents and children give their views on smacking

Michael, 54, architect, father of two aged 10 and 12
Parents should be able to do what they damn well want! I don't want the government telling me what to do. Frankly, if people want to smack their kids, they will.

Martin, 28, quantity surveyor, two children
I last hit my son two days ago. He was pushing his baby sister and creating mayhem. Before he was born, I vowed never to hit my children, and every time I do – which isn't often – I hate myself for it. Hitting is a sign of parental weakness. Parents should be able to provide parameters without resorting to smacking. It's a cowardly act and I wish I could stop for good. What happens when the smacking stops working? Do you smack them harder? It's a slippery slope and I intend to get off it for good.

Margaret, 41, three sons
All my children have been smacked at one time or other. I am neither ashamed nor proud of that fact, I just felt it necessary at the time. The threat of smacking has been an effective method of discipline. I discovered early on that harsh words simply weren't enough. I smacked my eldest son as a toddler when I was at my wits' end. I realised that last-resort smacking doesn't work – for them or me. My children know I love them which I believe is the main issue in this debate. Smacking is tolerable in a parent–child relationship if the kids know that they are loved and cared for.

Jonathan, 38, retail manager, two children
The first time I hit my eldest daughter was the last. She was five years old and was throwing a wobbly in the supermarket. Perhaps it was my embarrassment more than anything but I didn't see any option. I smacked her on the bottom a couple of times. It was

her look of total shock and confusion that made me want to cry. At that instant I felt a terrible father; I knew I was out of control. I wondered, would I hit her every time I was tired or anxious? There have been times when I've come close to smacking her again, but I always think of her face that day. I've never hit my younger daughter and hope to God I never do.

Joanna, 26, part-time bank worker, one child
When I witnessed my brother smacking his daughter, I was amazed at my reaction. I had smacked my son on and off since he was two, the last time being earlier that same day. Seeing my niece hit changed my whole perception of smacking. She started screaming and I felt like I was looking at child abuse. Here was this terrified little girl looking up at the person she trusted most – it seemed so wrong. Since I stopped smacking him, my son's behaviour has not deteriorated – if anything, it has improved. We are both calmer for not fearing, and not giving smacks. (*The Guardian*, 7 July 2004)

The facts
- Since Sweden banned smacking over a decade ago, child deaths at the hands of parents have fallen to zero. In Britain they run at one a week. Smacking has been banned in 12 European countries in the past 30 years.

- The British government has refused to move from its position that parents should be allowed to use 'reasonable chastisement'.

- Children's charities point out that hitting someone over the age of 18 could put the assailant in court. Hitting a child is perfectly legal.

1 Consider the views of the parents. How do their attitudes reinforce or undermine children's rights?

2 Why do you feel the political response in the UK took the form it did?

and perspectives. Vlyder (2001) in his contribution to a report for UNICEF makes a vigorous case for economic policy to orient its thinking with a child-centred perspective. He considers much of the policy development in these areas to be ignorant of children's needs and wants, at best giving consideration to children through family strategy while at worst ignorant of the significant and differential impact of macro policy on the economic circumstances of children. For many interested in understanding childhood and working with children, it can seem a tenuous and tortuous connection from child care to macroeconomics. Micklewhite (2000) simplifies and clarifies the discussion by reminding us that economics is about improving the lives of people, and children are people, who we have seen earlier are subject to some of the worst excesses of economic exploitation (e.g. trafficking and abuse). These examples and others discussed in this section have an international economic context that requires a macroeconomic perspective. The intention here is not to examine or discuss economic theory but to consider economic policy as it affects children at the everyday level. Again we see a potentially disproportionate impact of global economic policy on children. For example, dominant macroeconomic trends at the end of the 20th century show evidence of increasing differentiation between children who benefit most from the growing affluence of the Western world and those who benefit least. A recent study based on Organisation for Economic Cooperation and Development (OECD) data showed growing income inequality between children arising from a range of conditions including population demographics, political policy and economic strategies (Oxley et al., 2001). The inequitable political status discussed earlier tends to subordinate children as a significant group yet quantitative data suggests otherwise. Overall, 37 per cent of the world's population are children. In Africa, children actually form the majority of the population. Even in Europe, with its much older age structure, nearly a quarter of the population are children (UNICEF, 1998). Children therefore form a large fraction of the world's population. This in itself raises significant economic and political issues when it is set alongside data showing the significant impact of children on households, an essential unit of political and economic strategy. It cries out for attention within the global economic strategy.

United Nations data show that half the world's population is living in poverty and the gap between rich and poor is widening. On a global scale the experience is desperate with 2.8 billion families living on less than 2 dollars a day. Kofi Annan, then UN Secretary-General, conveyed the essence of this experience in his speech in October 2000 for the International Day for the Eradication of Poverty when he said,

> Almost half the world's population lives on less than two dollars a day, yet even this statistic fails to capture the humiliation, powerlessness and brutal hardship that is the daily lot of the world's poor.

The demographics of childhood imply that children are in the majority of those facing this awful situation. Christian Aid (2001) argues that there will be little chance of eradicating child poverty amongst the poorer nations of the world until the economic agencies of the rich northern countries are politically coerced to write off Third World debt. In a recent spending review, the Chancellor announced a large increase in the UK's aid budget. He announced that by 2007–8, total UK aid will rise to nearly £6.5 billion a year. Part of the increase in the Department for International Development's (DFID) budget was specifically earmarked for the provision of multilateral debt relief. Brown, in a DFID press release (2004) said:

> Too many countries are still being forced to choose between servicing their debts and making the investments in health, education and infrastructure that would allow them to achieve the millennium development goals and so we must do more.

However, this in itself while desirable will not improve children's lives unless the political will to do so prevails in respective nations of the world. Those who use and abuse children for political and economic gain will not necessarily cease to do so because the straitjacket of poverty through debt has been lifted. Within this context, any consideration of political and economic influences on childhood requires us to take an international and global perspective. Indeed Micklewhite (2000) concludes that 'key economic variables on which economic policy operates can all be given a child dimension'.

The extent of a country's natural resources and ability to generate wealth runs alongside the means of wealth production and distribution. The use of child labour within a nation state demonstrates the intricacies of the political and economic axis. One obvious tension is the ever-increasing demand of the rich Western consumer for cheap goods and the expectations of shareholders for increased profit that contrasts with the political rhetoric of politicians and public alike against exploitation of children and young people. Direct action is full of good intent but does not always produce the desired outcomes. For example, boycotts in the Western world of goods produced by the unethical use of child labour can be counterproductive if the only source of a family's income is the earnings of its children. To close this down through lack of demand only results in greater poverty and consequently hardship for the children concerned. The inter-relationship between country economies historically, which has led to the unequal distribution of resources globally, provides a context within which we must try and understand the continuance of child labour. It is only by addressing the

Reflective Activity 3.6

Change for children: addressing political and economic issues

Analysis of action			
Political	**Economic**	**Social**	**Cultural**
National and local child welfare policy and provision	Strategic and operational business partnerships	Welfare reform through legislation and policy	Validating and valuing the status of childhood
Ideological stance on education provision	Corporate responsibility	Educational reform through legislation and policy	Adopting an equality perspective
Family support programmes in times of need	Local focus on improvement in conditions	Effective policing of legislation and policy	Raising and reforming familial expectations
Regeneration policies in areas of need	Adult employment strategies	Anti-poverty strategies	Community perspectives on childhood

Save the Children believes all children have the right to be protected from dangerous and exploitative work. We don't believe in banning all children's work because for some it is a valuable part of growing up, and banning it can drive them into more dangerous work. We work with governments, companies and others to find alternative sources of family income. We consult children and communities to find ways of improving the working conditions of those who have no alternative, and providing schooling. We stress the need to tackle the root cause of child labour, poverty.

Save the Children (2000) Big Business, Small Hands

1 Summarise the areas of action being outlined in your own words and try and think of examples in each case.

2 Reflect on the strengths this strategy has for protecting children from dangerous and exploitative work. You may wish to visit the Save the Children website to examine a current example of its work in this area: <http://www.savethechildren.org.uk/>

wider political and economic context of such practices, together with the conditions in which children across the world live, that they may be overcome. A primary need is to consult closely with the children themselves (and their families and communities).

To help understand the intricacies of the issue the Save the Children organisation has identified a comprehensive matrix of involvement and action by states if exploitation of child labour is to be eradicated. The table in Reflective Activity 3.6 on p. 34 summarises Save the Children's analysis of the complexity of the problem. To tackle one sector does not provide the solution. Only a comprehensive approach will do. This approach must also permeate the different strata of society: family, community and state.

Child labour is sometimes exploited in the much wealthier UK, but on a far lesser scale (UNICEF/United Nations Children's Fund, 2007). However, global relationships and interests also influence children's lives in wealthier countries and shape policy towards children. A key example is the idea that individuals should be enabled to create their own wealth and that this leads to economic growth and healthy competition. This neo-liberal economic theory is dominant within international political and economic organisations. Within this set of beliefs, inequality may be seen as an inevitable outcome for some children. These beliefs shape children's lives in both richer and poorer countries.

In the UK the New Labour government has stated that it seeks the eradication of child poverty by 2020 and current fiscal and social policy is intended to facilitate this. As the 'UK National Action Plan on Social Inclusion 2003–2005' states

> The fight against poverty is central to the UK Government's entire social and economic programme.
>
> (Department for Work and Pensions, 2003, p. 3)

However, it does not show any intention to dramatically redistribute wealth. The main aim is to lift some of the very poorest, particularly children, out of poverty. Statistics published by the Child Poverty Action Group show the disproportionate impact of poverty on children within poor families. Poor families make up 25 per cent of the population, which includes

3.3 million children (Children's Rights Alliance for England, 2005) based on a commonly accepted indicator of poverty of half of average income after housing costs adopted by the Households Below Average Income Unit (HBAI) of the Department of Work and Pensions. Variable indicators are increasingly used based on 50, 60 and 70 per cent of contemporary median income both before and after housing costs, ensuring that the statistics of poverty are complex and variable. However, the impact indicators are similarly reflected whatever the measure used. Poverty impacts on children's lives in many ways including going without essentials, inadequate housing, lack of participation in leisure, higher death rates and ill health and poor attendance and outcomes at school. Some progress has been made towards the long-term goal of the alleviation of child poverty with the numbers of children living in poverty reduced. However, the proportion of children in the UK living in poverty is still one of the highest in the original 15 states of the European Union.

For further discussion on poverty and health see Chapter 8, Provision for Child Health.

The approach to tackling poverty and social exclusion by New Labour is a departure from the previous Conservative administrations. However, the approach contains a mix of political aims, only some of which are concerned with the well-being of poorer children. These aims include integrating the unemployed back into the workforce and reducing the welfare benefit bill in certain areas. There is little focus on wealth redistribution as such, the main focus being the introduction of a protective minimum wage (at a relatively low rate), the topping up of low wages and the provision of financial and service support for child care. This is considered to both benefit children and enable more women (in particular lone parents) to return to the workforce after having children. Harsher sanctions have been brought in for unemployed families (in terms of cooperation with job search activities and compulsory work for welfare schemes) and lone-parent benefit has been abolished. Clearly part of this programme of change is improving services to poor children and lifting children out of poverty, but there is also a wider economic and employment agenda.

The impact of such intervention depends on the perspective taken. For the individual family with children whose income rose by 17 per cent between 1997 and 2003 and the additional 20 per cent of parents who now have enough money to see to the necessities of life each month, the change is significant. As the system of tax credit support is means tested, not all those entitled claim. In terms of a comparative picture children in the UK are at a noticeable disadvantage across the EU (the 15 states) with 23 per cent of children living in poverty as opposed to 18 per cent across the rest of the European Union and only 5 per cent in Denmark. The redistribution of income in 2005 shows the poorest tenth of families 6 per cent better off and the richest tenth with a 3 per cent reduction in net income (Toynbee and Walker, 2005).

While the statistical shift is small the question is how great the political shift is from previous administrations. The political perspective prevailing throughout the 1980s and early 1990s was that wealth acquisition and employment circumstances were viewed as a personal responsibility and children's care and learning experiences were insufficiently addressed. In the 1970s gradual disillusion with the welfare state (seen as holding back the poor), increasing unemployment and social problems led to an upsurge in the belief in individual endeavour to meet need and the benefits of private provision over public services (neo-liberalism). This led to the election of a Conservative government in 1979. Over the next 10 years a free market political philosophy was developed which included the withdrawal of state subsidies to many areas of production and manufacturing in the UK and the opening of markets to global imports. This led to considerable job losses and to an increase in welfare dependency, income differentials and poverty within the population (Bradshaw, 1990). By 1997 some aspects of this approach were challenged and a Labour government was elected on a promise of greater social cohesion and alleviation of social ills. However, its support of the wider free market employment and trade strategies remained.

Since 1997, in targeted areas of deprivation, there has been growth in state provision of under 5s services through the Government-funded Sure Start project. Sure Start is the Government's programme to deliver the 'best start in life' for every child by bringing together early education, child care, health and family support (at the time of writing this strategy is being reviewed). There has also been a shift in the focus of fiscal policy towards poor families and an increase in front-line staff in education and health (DoH, 2003). The UK has seen significant change in the focus of political and economic policy affecting children between the end of the 20th century and the beginning of the 21st. Before 1997, the notion of poverty within government had virtually disappeared with euphemistic phrases such as 'low-income families' taking over. In the government of the day's report to the United Nations' Committee on the rights of the child there was no mention of poverty, in spite of 4.1 million children living below the poverty line (based on half average income after housing costs). Since 2000 the Chancellor of the Exchequer's speeches have been peppered with concerns about children in poverty and alleviating the burden, although the emphasis on 'social exclusion' has sometimes diverted attention from growing inequalities in wealth. Children became more visible in some aspects of policy. The introduction of the 'baby bond' (Children's Trust Fund) rolled out in 2005 is a clear example. Although a new small financial investment in children, the emphasis is on motivating parents to 'save' money for their children rather than simply delivering state benefits to them.

Clearly there is a wide diversity of family life within and between countries. Child-rearing practices vary, household sizes vary and adult views of children's status and prospects vary. Attitudes within the family may be influenced by wider political debates outside the family. The income and employment status of adults within the family, spending patterns and family size and structure give rise to the economic conditions within which the child thrives, survives, stumbles or falls. Whether children themselves must contribute to the household income through their labour will depend on the extent of economic need coupled with how childhood is conceptualised in the wider culture.

Any political intervention, whether it be the introduction of new services for children or the introduction of protective legislation for children, will be felt in the families and communities where children live.

The effect of such changes can only be measured by long-term research. For example, the introduction of Sure Start in the UK came in conjunction with a cut in lone-parent benefit and compulsory interviews for work for lone parents. The impact for the child in the lone-parent family will relate to all those factors. Outside the UK, intervention to protect children from exploitative work, unless carried out in consultation with children and families, and in parallel with other means of them increasing their incomes, could backfire, as Save the Children point out. There is a need to place children's interests at the heart of political and economic strategy, and consultation with both children and their families is paramount.

Conclusion

In this chapter we have considered the complex area of the politics of childhood. We have considered the differences in children's lives related to the economic context, political ideologies and the status they are granted by adults. Are they viewed solely as economic assets? If so, are they viewed in the short term as providers of labour for the household to help fill immediate needs or in the longer term as assets to the nation? Are they socially valued? As social assets is childhood inevitably extended and supported by social policy? A major theme in the chapter has been that of 'diminished capacity' where parents or at times the state determine the best interests of the child. The focus of policy historically has more commonly been the family than the child. Although new child-centred initiatives have come about, there are questions as to how effective they are and where they have been undermined.

Children have been commonly viewed as victim, investment or threat. Such perspectives bring children to the forefront of political debate but do not involve them in the discussion. Alternatively, we can view children as citizens with independent and informed voices. Unfortunately, attempts to do this are often undermined by non-compliance, for example in relation to the United Nations Convention of the Rights of a Child. There is differential political status between the child and parent in democracies. Even when political authority encourages participation, political action often undermines the rhetoric. It reinforces the exclusion rather than inclusion of children in the political process.

Macroeconomic policy approaches largely ignore children's needs and wants. United Nations data shows that half the world's population is living in poverty and the gap between rich and poor is widening. Global economics and political action have a serious impact on the experience of childhood. The crux of the question is how we transform political and economic agendas to put at their centre concepts of children as citizens, to consider and respond to their interests and needs and to further their well-being. In some countries, such as Canada and South Africa, all policy decisions have to be measured against potential outcomes for children. This is not the case in the UK. Students of childhood and child work professionals and practitioners must learn to identify the ways in which political actors use and abuse concepts of childhood and the way that wider political aims and economic contexts influence the shape of services and provision for children.

Annotated reading

Brannen, J. and Moss, P. (eds) (2003) *Rethinking children's care*, Buckingham: Open University Press

Looks at care from the perspectives of children, parents and care workers; provides discussion on economic, social and political change from modernity to late modernity. It looks at four key issues: the conceptualisation of care; how care translates its public policy into practice; the nature of the care relationship; and how care might be transformed in the future.

Pierson, J. (2002) *Tackling Social Exclusion*, London: Routledge

A comprehensive text considering what is meant by social exclusion and ways in which government policy is attempting to tackle the problem. It covers a wide range of approaches that professionals working in this arena might take to combat social exclusion.

Toynbee, P. and Walker, D. (2005) *Better or Worse?: Has Labour Delivered?*, London: Bloomsbury

A thorough audit of hospitals, schools, trains, climate change, the constitution and the countryside. Figures show that Britain is safer, better educated, better off all round. But people don't believe it and the polls reveal this growing public mistrust. The book gets away from the personalities and the spin to reveal the true political picture of Blair's Britain.

de Vylder, S. (2001) Chapter 10 'A macroeconomic policy for children in the era of globalization', in Cornia, G. A. (ed.) *Harnessing Globalization for Children: A Report to UNICEF*, Florence: UNICEF

This report represents a comprehensive effort to assess the impact of the latest wave of globalisation on children. It examines the kinds of policy and programme that can best harness globalisation's benefits on their behalf. It considers how the impact of globalisation on child well-being varies depending on a number of factors, including geography, differences in family conditions and domestic policies, the evolution of global markets and international rules of the game that control global exchange. It goes on to examine what measures are likely to promote child-friendly globalisation at the beginning of the 21st century.

Chapter 4

The Social Divisions of Childhood

DOROTHY MOSS

A young mother and her four year old child have become the first family to be evicted from their home under a pilot scheme which takes away all benefits from failed asylum seekers who do not leave Britain voluntarily.

(*The Guardian*, 29 August 2005)

The client's son who has learning difficulties and developmental delay attends a mainstream school and has been excluded from numerous school activities including the Christmas play, assemblies, school trips as the school believe he would not benefit from these activities and would disrupt other children.

(Disability Rights Commission, 2005b)

Introduction

This chapter is set within the context of childhood as a social construct acknowledging that children experience many different childhoods. The experience is influenced by the relationship between the child, the family and the state. It focuses on access to services and provision for groups of children who face barriers or may be deliberately excluded from mainstream services and provision as the quotations at the start of the chapter exemplify. The concept of 'social divisions' is first explored. The chapter is then structured around six areas of questioning:

- How do inherited wealth and material inequality shape access to services and provision in childhood?

- How do country of birth and formal citizenship shape access to services and provision in childhood?

- How do heritage and home shape access to services and provision in childhood?

- How do 'ability' and impairment shape access to services and provision in childhood?

- How do gender and sexual identity shape access to services and provision in childhood?

- What is meant by the concept of 'minority' children?

Finally the chapter explores the way that these factors interrelate in shaping children's access to services and provision. A central theme is inequalities between children and their different experiences related to the social divisions of class, 'race', gender, sexuality and ability. Some groups of children emerge as especially vulnerable: children refused refugee status; travellers' children; disabled children; children in local authority care; children who are sexually exploited; children who experience homophobia. In some of these cases specialist services and provision have been developed and examples are discussed in this chapter and in the final section of this book. As the focus of the chapter is on children who are excluded, a critical stance towards current policy is taken.

What does the concept 'social divisions' mean and how does it relate to children's access to services and provision?

Children are not a unified group. They come from widely differing backgrounds and their access to services and provision is unequal. Although they share common characteristics in terms of age, relative dependency on caregivers and their shared status as children, in this chapter we consider the social divisions of childhood, how these arise and how they affect access to services and provision of different groups of children.

Many factors make a difference to children's access to services and provision. Familial wealth clearly makes a difference as some services can be purchased, for example private education, private health care and leisure (Novak, 2002). Discriminatory attitudes and institutional processes make a difference to how children are treated by service providers. For example, disabled children often have less access and fewer rights in relation to mainstream services such as schooling (Disability Rights Commission, 2005a); black boys of African Caribbean heritage are more likely to be excluded from school (London Development Agency, 2004); and refugee children may have very few rights to mainstream services while waiting for their refugee status to be decided or if their families' applications have been rejected (Cunningham and Tomlinson, 2005).

Reflective Activity 4.1

The social divisions of childhood

'It is impossible even to think about people without immediately encountering 'social divisions'. We automatically perceive other human beings as being male or female, black or white, older or younger, richer or poorer, sick or well, or friend or foe. In forming a perception of them, we place them in pigeon holes, adapting our behaviour and attitude to them in terms of the slots we have placed them in. . . .

'When we talk about social divisions, we mean those substantial differences between people that run throughout our society. A social division has at least two categories, each of which has distinctive material and cultural features. In other words, one category is better positioned than the other, and has a better share of resources . . .

'However, social divisions are not 'natural': they are the outcome of previous social interactions, events, decisions and struggles. They are 'socially constructed', so that while there are always social divisions, their precise form varies from society to society.' (Payne, 2000)

1 Identify some of the social divisions that affect children's lives.

2 Which of these groups might have a better share of resources, for example money, housing?

3 How might these divisions affect children's access to major services and provision such as health care, education, justice, income, housing and social work support? (Part III might help you with this)

How do inherited wealth and material inequality shape access to services and provision in childhood?

Novak argues,

> It is an obvious – although significantly neglected – fact that the living standards, opportunities and life chances of children differ enormously. In a society such as Britain's that is grossly unequal and deeply divided by social class it would be strange were it otherwise. (2002, p. 59)

Here Novak is linking material inequality with social class, which is a complex concept. In every day usage the term 'class' often refers to the official classification of occupations (e.g. class one may be the professional class and class five, unskilled workers). However, Best (2005) discusses other meanings of the term 'class', considering several dimensions including wealth, income, social status and political power. Here the main focus of class divisions is on differences

> Chapter 19, Searching and Researching Childhood, demonstrates the ways those studying poverty might explore research to examine the question 'Why are children poor?'

in wealth and income and how these may lead to different access to services for children. Novak (2002) points out that in 1979 one in ten children lived at or below the poverty line in the UK whereas in 1999 the figure was one in three (see Figure 4.1). The numbers had reduced to one in four by 2003/4 (CPAGa, 2005). The official measure of poverty in the UK is Households below Average Income (HBAI), defined as 60 per cent of median income after housing costs.

Although the Government has made steps towards reducing the numbers experiencing childhood poverty, 3.5 million children are still affected in the UK and in addition financial inequality has grown. Carvel and Elliot point out that,

> After adjusting for inflation, the poorest 10 per cent of households earned £100 a week in 1971, while the richest 10 per cent earned about £320. By 2002–3 the household incomes of the poor were still under £170 a week, while those of the rich had swelled to nearly £670. The inequality gap between the two groups more than doubled to about £500 a week. (2005, citing Brewer et al., 2005)

Although measures of inequality are not measures of poverty as such, they point to the conditions in which poverty arises and to the experience of relative deprivation (CPAG, 2001).

Figure 4.1 Children in low-income households in Britain. (House of Commons, 2004.)

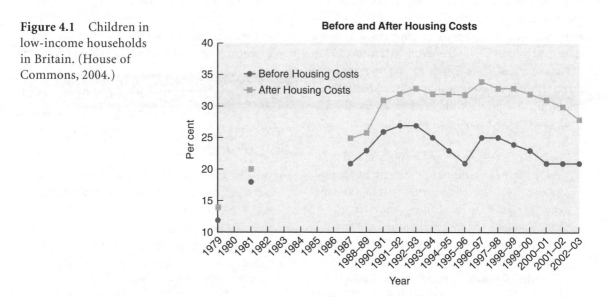

The inheritance of family wealth reinforces class inequalities over generations. The implications of huge differences in material wealth are evident:

> Put a child from an unskilled or semi-skilled family background next to one from a professional or managerial background, and one will live 10 years longer than the other, be less likely to die at birth, in infancy and childhood, will suffer fewer diseases and live a healthier mental and physical life. It is no accident.
>
> (Novak, 2002, p. 63)

Although adults decide how their wealth is spent and this spending does not always benefit their children, there is no doubt that familial wealth creates great opportunities for children in relation to education, leisure, health, well-being and career opportunities:

> The cementing of class inequalities begins at an early age, and among the myriad of ways in which the privileges, or deprivations, of social class are passed down from one generation to the next, formal education systems figure centrally.
>
> (Novak, 2002, p. 65)

Wealthier families can afford private education for their children, where staff:student ratios are lower; their children can get more individualised attention and are more likely to succeed academically. However, there is evidence to show that children from state schools are more successful in higher education because they are more used to working independently (Harrison, 2003).

Opportunities for children to improve their life chances, through gaining qualifications and better-paid employment, depend on their equal access to high-quality services such as education and health care.

> The level of intergenerational mobility in society is seen by many as a measure of the extent of equality of economic and social opportunity. It captures the degree of equality in life chances – the extent to which a person's circumstances during childhood are reflected in their success in later life, or on the flip side, the extent to which individuals can make it by virtue of their own talents, motivation and luck.
>
> (Blanden et al., 2005, p. 2)

They go on to show the importance of the relationship between educational attainment and income and point out that there was less social mobility for children born in 1970 compared with children born in 1958. They argue that this partly relates to the link between income and educational achievement. The better off had more opportunities to stay on at school and go to further and higher education. They conclude that the

> expansion of higher education in the UK has benefited those from richer backgrounds far more than poorer young people. This occurred over a period when means-tested student support declined sharply in the UK.
>
> (p. 12)

Chapter 6, Education: Service or System?, gives further context to the influences on educational provision.

It is yet to be seen whether the Government's target to widen participation in higher education to 50 per cent will redress this situation in the longer term.

Although children from the lowest-income households are the focus of a wider range of state services and provision, in many areas of service provision children from wealthier households benefit more, in particular when private services are considered. In relation to education, better-off children tend to stay on at school longer, they go to the 'better' state schools (in terms of examination results), they enter higher education and many also have access to private education

Reflective Activity 4.2

Wealth and social mobility in childhood

1 Why do you think children from poorer families get less opportunity to stay on at school and enter higher education?

2 Consider the situation of poorer children and richer children in relation to access to other services and provision, such as health and leisure, as well as education.

(which is sometimes subsidised by the state) (Bynner & Joshi, 2002). In relation to health, better-off families tend to use health services on a more regular basis, they may experience better health due to living in less polluted environments and have better nutrition. Better-off children may also use libraries and leisure services more often than poorer children. They are also more likely to benefit from subsidised transport systems because of their greater mobility. Poorer children may benefit more from particular specialist services targeted at them such as Sure Start, Connexions, community regeneration projects (which tend to be located in poorer neighbourhoods) and some state benefits, but many areas of spending on children's services and provision do not reach the poorest children when they are not targeted.

How do country of birth and formal citizenship shape access to services and provision in childhood?

Entitlement to services and provision in childhood is limited in relation to the country of a child's birth and/or the country of their parents' birth. There are many rules that affect entitlement to benefits and services related to nationality and citizenship. Entering the UK is very difficult if you are not a formal citizen. If you succeed in gaining entry, in order to prove entitlement to certain services of the welfare state, you must also prove you 'belong' or are 'settled'. If this is not the case, families claiming benefits and services will encounter a number of barriers.

'Nationality' is the status defining a person as belonging to a community.

'Citizenship' is concerned with the relationship between an individual and the state so individuals can enjoy civic rights but are also bound by civic duties. (Fransman, 1994)

Those without formal citizenship must apply under the appropriate legal rules. These legal rules vary from country to country. Does the country need foreign labour for economic reasons? Does the government actually welcome diversity? Is the government and population hostile to particular groups of potential immigrants? All these factors shape a country's citizenship and nationality legislation. Some of these legal rules have been considerably tightened in the UK. Lack of formal citizenship limits entitlement to services. Those children living within the UK without full British citizenship may be denied services or treated differently. Nationality and formal citizenship can only be gained automatically in the UK if one of the parents has citizenship. Otherwise, a person has to show they have been legally settled for some years and even then the status is discretionary. A critic of a dictatorial and cruel ruling regime in Nigeria fled to the US in 1994, having heard that he was about to be arrested by that regime. He was subsequently charged with treason and his adult daughter was put on a hit list. She also fled Nigeria and on her way to the US she fell ill in London and gave birth prematurely. The baby was born on British soil. What nationality was the baby? Was the baby Nigerian? The Nigerian consulate in the UK was hostile and refused to enter the baby on his mother's passport. Was the baby British? No, the British Nationality Act 1981 withdrew automatic nationality by birth in Britain in an attempt to reduce the rights of those whose parents were born overseas. The majority of children affected by this change came from black and minority ethnic communities (Fransman, 1994, p. 288). Neither of the baby's parents was British. Although both parents had US visas 'the US barred the newborn' because that government had friendly relations with the Nigerian regime. The baby was caught up in 'The white man's red tape', as the Grandfather (Wole Soyinka) pointed out despite every child's right to an identity in Article 8 of the United Nations Convention on the Rights of the Child (UN, 1989). The baby was stateless. Finally, after much pressure, the British supplied a travel document, valid for a single exit, or, as Wole Soyinka described it, a 'sneak deportation order'. Wole Soyinka's family's plight was reported in a *Guardian*

Chapter 2, Childhood: Rights and Realities, discusses citizenship further.

article by Maya Jaggi on 7 July 1999 entitled 'Swaddled in red tape'.

The situation of those applying for refugee status (asylum seekers) is particularly difficult. The rights of families facing upheaval or persecution in their country of origin have been dramatically reduced in many countries, reflected also in negative media coverage of their plight. Asylum-seeker children are extremely vulnerable and the 1989 United Nations Convention on the Rights of the Child says that states should be aware of the special rights that these children should have because of their vulnerability. However, several states, for example, Australia, have chosen to provide services for them in segregated settings, thereby reducing their rights rather than protecting their rights. Similar proposals exist in the UK (enacted in the Immigration and Asylum Act, 2002) but at the time of writing have not come to full fruition. Children whose families have been refused refugee status are particularly at risk of harsh treatment in the UK, being subject to deportation orders and sometimes kept in detention prior to deportation. Abdullah Shakil, aged 7, is a case in point. His mother had fled an abusive husband in Kuwait. He speaks of his experience in detention in Scotland after his mother had been served with a deportation order.

> Chapter 17, Educating Refugee Children, discusses the effects of this in more detail.

> In Dungavel I helped my mum. I helped her with the baby and I was quiet because my mum wanted to sleep. And my mum said we had to be quiet because she said she didn't want to get into trouble. I don't like it if my mum cries and she would cry if she got into trouble I think. We tried to be good, but sometimes it was hard. Sometimes we were sad and cried.   (*The Guardian*, 9 October 2003)

> Chapter 10, Safeguarding Children, identifies in more detail how *Every Child Matters* (DfES, 2003) in reality means that some children matter more than others.

More recent legislation (the Asylum and Immigration Act 2004) 'threatens children with destitution and possible removal from their families' if asylum applications have failed (Cunningham and Tomlinson, 2005, p. 253). The stateless child and the asylum-seeker child are sometimes denied the protection afforded to other children in UK law.

How do heritage and home shape access to services and provision in childhood?

Patterns of migration for work, both to and within the UK, together with class and income inequalities have led to significant differences between the communities where children live and their experience of community. This in turn affects children's access to services and provision. For example, families encouraged to enter the UK for work in the 1950s and 1960s, from South Asia and the Caribbean, settled in areas where work was available (e.g. in the wool and steel industries). People who hold extreme views about repatriation ignore the fact that the UK needed them to do jobs that white people would not do.

However, much of this work disappeared in the economic recession of the 1970s and 1980s and such communities now suffer relatively high unemployment. Better-off families have been migrating to the suburbs; some of the wealthiest are beginning to move into gated communities (see Reflective Activity 4.3) characterised by fences and gates which cut them off from the rest of the area. Such communities have developed in many countries of the world, particularly the UK, the US and South Africa, and are evidence of the growth of inequality in such countries. The children who live in gated communities tend to be from wealthier families, who may run businesses, work in professional jobs in other parts of the city or commute quite long distances to work. The gated community has appeared in most wealthy areas of Britain.

> Chapter 3, The Politics of Childhood, explains how the economic climate influences children's lives.

Chapter 13 looks in detail at community regeneration and identifies the government's intention that 'nobody should be seriously disadvantaged by where

Reflective Activity 4.3

Access to services and provision: two communities

The two case studies below are fictional although based on reality.

communities. However, health, environment and housing are poor.

The inner-city neighbourhood

Many people living in the inner city are first, second and third generation migrants from different parts of the world. They include refugees from the Second World War (Ukrainian, Polish, German, Estonian); people settled in the UK in the 1950s and 1960s having been actively recruited by the British government to fill labour shortages (South Asian and Caribbean); and more recent asylum seekers (from areas of war and upheaval). A lot of children live in the inner-city community. There are relatively high unemployment levels and insecure employment because the local industry closed down in the 1970s and 1980s. There is a lot of movement in and out of the community. A mixture of housing includes some owner-occupied or rented, but in a poor state of repair. Families who own them are not well off enough off to keep them in good condition. Landlords scrimp on repairs. There are few green spaces. One park has been recently improved. Busy dangerous roads run though the community but side streets have traffic calming measures. This is a vibrant community, and many religions and nationalities are represented; there are lots of areas of growth and development and many strong local organisations trying to work together across all

The gated community

This community is characterised by security. There are main gates, one of which is closed after 7pm. Residents have their own means of access. In addition individual houses and apartment blocks are gated off and some houses have high walls around them. Houses have very big gardens. There are CCTV cameras trained on most parts of the community. Unless invited by residents, outsiders are not allowed beyond the gates. The area contains some services including a pub-restaurant, supermarket, golf course, cricket pitch, hairdressers and nursery. The area has lots of green safe spaces where no cars can drive. There are traffic calming measures throughout. There is a good playground. The housing is very well maintained and expensive. Children tend to go to the local private schools although some are boarders. The children come from a number of different backgrounds but their households are all relatively wealthy.

(Adapted from Wainwright,
The Guardian, 28 November 2002)

1 What quality of life issues might there be for children in the communities described above?

2 How would access to services and provision differ for children in the respective communities?

they live' (Neighbourhood Renewal Unit, 2005). Despite this, the two very different fictional communities described in Reflective Activity 4.3 would provide different pathways to services for children. A number of factors, including their family's class position, level of income, geographical heritage, patterns of mobility and migration, wider social attitudes and personal choices related to safety and belonging, would influence the types of communities in which children live. Access to services and provision and prospects would be dramatically different. Children say that they want stability, safety, social acceptance and space for play and leisure

(Chawla and Malone, 2003), but their experience varies dramatically in relation to where they live.

How do 'ability' and impairment shape access to services and provision in childhood?

Ability is a gateway to services and provision in the UK. The selection of the 'more able' within the educational system is still prevalent and determines access to better

schooling. The move to identify the 'gifted and talented' in schools (DfES, 2005a) is evidence of this. Children so identified may be offered additional summer schools and top-up teaching, for example. There are major questions as to how 'ability' is defined. It is no coincidence that the majority of those whom society deems more academically able also come from financially better-off backgrounds. Ability may have nothing to do with innate gifts and talents (see Reflective Activity 4.2). Those children who do not reach the benchmark of 'ability', however that may be socially defined, might find themselves receiving different and sometimes lower levels of service and provision. Clearly the idea that one child is 'more able' than another is a relative concept which depends on the benchmark being used. Abilities are not fixed and all children have different strengths.

As we have seen so far in this chapter, inheritance, place of birth and residence create unequal opportunities for children. In this section we consider the way that ability shapes access to services and provision, drawing on the understanding of disability activists and researchers. Is 'disability' the opposite of 'ability'? Is 'disability' innate to the individual or is it socially constructed in the same way that our ideas about 'ability' are? Medical definitions of disability have historically focused on what is 'wrong' with the individual, who is considered 'abnormal' or different from 'the norm'. Who defines 'the norm' is

Chapter 6, Education: Service or System?, explains how different ideas about what education is for are important in influencing which abilities are valued.

Chapter 8, Provision for Child Health, explains and challenges this 'medical model'.

therefore a critical issue. This approach has been challenged in more recent times. Mike Oliver, a disability activist and researcher has challenged medical definitions of disability, arguing that they have failed to consider the disabling barriers within society that disabled people face. He points out that

Not only do these definitions medicalise and individualise the problems of disability but they do the same to the solutions (policies) that are applied. Thus services too are based upon an individualised and medicalised view of disability and are designed by able-bodied people through a process which disabled people have had little or no control.

(Oliver, 1990, p. 6)

In contrast he identifies that

disabled people . . . have dispensed with the intricacies and complexities of the (medical) definitions and instead propose the following two fold classification.

Impairment lacking part or all of a limb. Or having a defective limb, organism or mechanism of the body.

Disability the disadvantage or restriction of activity caused by contemporary social organisation which takes little or no account of people who have physical impairments and thus excludes them from the mainstream of social activities.   (p. 11)

The Disability Rights Commission (2004) argues that 'Samuel' (see Reflective Activity below) was treated less favourably than other children, he was made more visible and humiliated, and he was treated as a problem rather than a person. No reasonable adjustments were made to cater for his needs. As a result of the school's actions he missed a year of education.

Oliver (1990) has pointed out that the patronising or hostile treatment of disabled people in society comes from deeply embedded ideologies (ways of thinking) that disability is a personal tragedy and that individuals are afflicted by disabilities. In this way society denies responsibility for the conditions in which disabled people live. Disabled children have been historically segregated and isolated in separate schools and institutions. Despite policies of inclusion espoused by government, practices of segregation and isolation still arise in mainstream settings which result in less-favourable treatment of disabled children. Many mainstream schools lack the facilities needed to meet the inclusion of all pupils.

Laura Middleton discusses the way that, historically, disabled children have been 'screened out' of mainstream services. Screening is a process whereby able-bodied people removed disabled children from mainstream settings because it was considered better for society as a whole (Middleton, 1992). She considers this screening process in relation to birth, family acceptance, medical treatment; education; the market place; growing up and sexuality; acquiring skills; getting somewhere to live; and gaining employment. Although there has been progress in relation to the inclusion of disabled children in some mainstream services, children still face huge barriers, as the case of Samuel demonstrates below.

Reflective Activity 4.4

The access of disabled children to services and provision

'Samuel' (not his real name), a pupil with hearing impairment and autism was isolated from his peers through exclusion from school. He attended a hearing impairment unit in a mainstream school. On his first day at school his mother was told to send him to school in a red jumper rather than the school uniform jumper which was blue. This arrangement was later changed so that he was allowed to wear a blue jumper but with a fluorescent disc sewn on the back. The school's justification for this less-favourable treatment, which caused the pupil a great deal of upset, was that it would enable them to keep an eye on him as they weren't used to dealing with autistic children. Despite full-time support through his statement of special educational needs the school was unable to develop an effective means of communication or to ensure his safety. He was excluded from school in November 2003 after he climbed up the wall bars. 'Samuel's' family appealed against his treatment, using Disability Discrimination legislation.

(Disability Rights Commission, 2004)

Consider Mike Oliver's discussion of disability in relation to 'Samuel's' case study.

1 Is 'Samuel' 'disabled' because of his learning difficulties or because of the society he lives in and the school setting he experiences?

2 How might society gain from having children like 'Samuel'?

3 Think of other examples of discrimination against disabled children and how these might affect their lives.

How do gender and sexual identity shape access to services and provision in childhood?

Although the rights of girls and lesbian and gay young people are now more firmly established in the UK than in past years (e.g. there are legal sanctions in the UK against discrimination) there are still many ways that access to services and provision are limited because of gender and sexual identity. For example, although girls are now achieving relatively well at school in the UK, patterns of inequality persist in relation to the types of career and education opportunities available for both girls and boys. Thomas (1990) explores the experiences of male and female students and the meanings they attach to particular aspects of the curriculum. Her research focuses on the way that science and arts subjects are associated with masculinity and femininity respectively. This shapes the choices of students.

Many children face active hostility if their behaviour is seen to deviate from that which is considered 'normal' for their sex. Although girls may be more actively encouraged to participate in sports and boys to develop domestic skills, for example, than was historically the case, they still may face hostility and exclusion by their

---

Reflective Activity 4.5

Children's sexual identity: reinforcing conformity

Sue Lees discusses her 1980s' research

> Girls walk a narrow line: they must not be seen as too tight, nor as too loose. Girls are preoccupied in their talk with sexuality, and in particular with the injustice of the way in which they are treated by boys. Defining girls in terms of their sexuality rather than their attributes and potentialities is a crucial mechanism of ensuring their subordination to boys. 'Nice girls don't' is a phrase all girls understand, even if standards of sexual morality are more liberal. The terms of abuse are so taken for granted that girls do not question them and are drawn into judging other girls in terms of their reputation . . . The only security girls have against bad reputations is to confine themselves to the 'protection' of one partner.
> (Lees, 1993, p. 29)

Lees quotes the words of two teenage girls (Jacky and Leiser) to reinforce these points:

> [Jacky] A boy can be called a stud and people like and respect him – they have no responsibilities, they can just be doing what they want and if they're called a stud they think it's good. (p. 30)

> [Leiser] I think it's made a sin for women to enjoy sex. From the time we begin enjoying sex we're called slags, or we can't have too many friends that

are men. The ones who have good rapport with men are called slags, and the ones who don't are simply called tight bitches. (p. 30)

Boys too are put down if they fail to conform to gender stereotypes,

> Some boys were different, talked about their feelings and were non-competitive and sensitive. But to avoid teasing and being accused of being 'wimps', they have to keep their heads down. Boys have to protect a 'masculine' facade of toughness, hardness and superiority. To call a boy a 'poof', a 'buttyman' . . . is derogatory . . . this term in denoting lack of guts suggests femininity, weakness, softness and inferiority. Boys are under pressure to disassociate themselves from anything female in order to 'prove their masculinity'. (p. 91)

1 Having read these extracts of research from the 1980s, do you feel similar pressures exist for children and young people today? In what way have things changed?

2 Think about the verbal banter and abuse between children you have heard or have experienced yourself? What impact might this have on children's choices for the future about education, employment and relationships?

peers. Dominant ideas about gender and sexuality are actively reinforced by processes of labelling. This may take the form of verbal banter, verbal abuse and sometimes physical abuse from peers. Such ideas are reinforced in the media and by the way goods are marketed to children, even to the extent that Lego is now available in pink for girls. Such ideas are also often reinforced in the family. Sometimes children are actively excluded from participation in the mainstream because they are seen to have broken unspoken rules of behaviour. Sometimes children choose to keep their 'heads down' and not step out of line so as not to be labelled as 'different'.

There is still strong evidence that to break away from normative expectations about gender and sexuality can be very hard. There is evidence of extensive bullying of young gay and lesbian people, and high risks of suicide and homelessness amongst this group (Stonewall, 2005). Violence against and harassment of girls is also a major issue, as is violence amongst boys in general (often seen as a card of masculinity) (Muncie, 2004). Activists from the women's and lesbian and gay rights' movements have worked hard over the years to develop organisations that counter some of this hostility and negativity and develop confidence and self-esteem amongst young people. For example, Getaway Girls (2005) is a voluntary organisation in Leeds, working with young women and aiming, 'To support young women to improve their confidence, self-esteem and ambitions, offering a variety of opportunities and new challenges to expand experiences'. In Manchester, the Albert Kennedy Trust was set up because of the tragic death in 1989 of a 16-year-old boy who fell to his death from the top of a car park in Manchester while trying to get away from a group of violent homophobic attackers. The aims of the Albert Kennedy Trust (2005) are,

> To improve attitudes within society towards lesbian and gay young people. To promote greater understanding of lesbian and gay young people wherever they live. To provide accepting, supportive and caring homes for lesbian and gay young people who would otherwise be homeless or in a hostile environment.

Teachers in schools need far more training and support to deal with awareness raising and bullying associated with sexual identity.

What is meant by the concept of 'minority' children?

In what way is the concept 'minority' problematic in relation to services for children? Does it simply draw attention to children's group membership? Does it draw attention to 'minority needs' (for example, minority religious beliefs)? Does the concept 'minority' trigger different treatment by service providers? Should it? In recent years the concept 'minoritised' has been used to draw attention to the process whereby some groups are treated less well by service providers on the grounds of 'race' or 'culture' (Forbat, 2004; Burman et al., 2004). In the UK a black child of Afro-Caribbean heritage is clearly in the minority compared with a child of white European heritage. In the Caribbean, of course, black children are in the majority.

This section will use 'race' as an example of being in a minority group. In relation to the concept of race, there is in fact no pure race and the term is often used as a euphemism for other identifying factors such as colour, country of origin or religion. The concept has historically been used to conceal racism.

> Because racial prejudice is so deeply embedded in our society, it comes as no surprise to many people to learn that the concept of race is a social construct, and a recent one in human history. It did not emerge until the early days of capitalism . . . The myth of a Black race that is inferior was developed to rationalise the institution of enslavement of Black [people] from Africa.
>
> (Jennes, 2001, p. 306).

The tailoring of children's services to meet the different needs of individual children is important, for example the recognition of an individual's language or dietary needs is imperative. Sometimes, however, difference in treatment is generalised to a 'minority' group on the basis of ill-informed stereotypes. Individual circumstances may be lost sight of when children are treated as part of a group. Stereotypes about 'race' and 'culture' may determine service provision with negative consequences. Sensitivity to cultural difference may override respect for children's rights. This section goes on to consider why this might happen.

The assumption that children as a group share a common experience and have equal access to services and provision in the UK is challenged in this chapter. There has been more recognition by the state that service providers need to recognise and cater for children from different backgrounds in order to ensure equality. The promotion of racial equality is now a duty under the Race Relations Amendment Act 2000 and discrimination against children in many areas of services provision is outlawed. Yet, however strong equality legislation may be, there is no doubt that some children continue to be treated less fairly than others. These children, who often come from minority groups, are also 'minoritised' in relation to service provision.

At the extreme, some children's entitlement to equal treatment in relation to service provision has been deliberately removed by government. Children of asylum seekers who have been refused refugee status face deportation, detention and the threat of removal from loving parents (Cunningham and Tomlinson, 2005). The rhetoric of *Every Child Matters* is undermined by this abuse of their human rights. Children of travellers come from communities with a strong sense of history and identity, but insecurity of residence, exclusion from many mainstream areas of life and active hostility from the wider community. They and their families have faced major persecution, including forced evictions, and there are many instances where the state had failed to protect them. But even where service providers try to create equal access for children

Reflective Activity 4.6

Young carers in South Asian communities

Speaking about her experiences as a child living with a disabled mother, Karita expressed deep frustration with social services.

> They seem very judgemental. They keep giving us an Asian social worker even though we've asked for non-Asian. They say mum's Asian. We say she can understand English.   (Shah and Hatton, 1999, p. 61)

Karita was not concerned that she had an Asian social worker as such, but that the attitude of the worker who visited her was that it was her duty to support her mother. Social workers of all backgrounds are capable of such judgemental attitudes, but Karita felt she would have been less likely to get such a response from a 'white' worker. The reality was that the quality of support and choice available to Karita had been predetermined by the family's minority ethnic status and assumed language to such an extent that Karita's rights to services and support had been seriously undermined.

> The 'colour blind' approach had sometimes been replaced by an approach which was regarded as 'culturally sensitive' but in fact relied on blanket

stereotypes about different ethnic groups. Those service professionals who had strong expectations about the proper role of South Asian young carers, based on such blanket stereotypes concerning family obligation, gender and culturally specific roles, were perceived by the young carers in this study to be judgemental and unwilling to provide service support.   (p. 61)

Consider Karita's and her mother's needs for services and support.

1 What do you think the disadvantages of a 'colour blind' approach to Karita's circumstances would have been (i.e. an approach that ignores the fact that Karita is from a black and minority ethnic group)?

2 What has been the effect of 'cultural sensitivity but blanket stereotyping' (i.e. an assumption that children from one particular black and minority ethnic group will need a particular approach tailored to their generalised needs)?

3 What approach do you feel would be more helpful than either of these approaches?

of all backgrounds, subtle forms of discrimination may continue, albeit less intentionally and sometimes with the aim of 'cultural sensitivity'.

There is no doubt that service providers must adapt to the circumstances and needs of different social groups. The approach of ignoring all differences has rightly been abandoned. However, the approach of overgeneralising the needs of particular groups, or categorising groups along crude 'racial' lines is equally discriminatory. What is essential is that all children are given equal rights in relation to services. These include equal rights to services (no child should be excluded by law); the right to be involved in decision-making; the right to evaluate services; and the right to recognition of diverse needs. Simplistic 'racial matching' is a dangerous practice and any practice that overrides children's rights, even with the aim of 'cultural sensitivity', will have the opposite effect. A child's 'culture' is their daily experience of life, not some fixed and static set of beliefs and practices owned by other people in their community. Similar examples of overgeneralisation can be identified in relation to other minority groups, for example considering 'disabled' children as a group without considering their individual experiences. True sensitivity involves engaging directly with, listening to and hearing about the child's experience.

Conclusion

Year one students on a childhood studies degree programme in 2004 were exploring divisions in childhood. They came up with the following terms which they remembered as terms of abuse that they had heard in their own school playgrounds. Many of these terms are highly offensive and denigrate children in relation to their assumed race, ability, gender, sexuality, class and appearance:

Geek; you shop at Netto; tommy two stripe; snobs; NHS glasses; scruff; scrubbers; tramp; mirror minger; freakoid; specky 4-eyes; Billy no-mates; zylem seekers; estate bird; batty boy; short arse; gay boy; slapper; slag; tart; belly bouncer; goofy; dumb ass; you live in a skip; your mum shops at Aldi; nurd; ponse; council kids; window licker; retard.

Clearly the terms above reflect the main social divisions that children experience, some of which have been discussed in this chapter. The language differentiates the children involved from each other and it reinforces existing social divisions on a daily basis. Often unwittingly, children are involved in reproducing the divisions and demarcations of class, race, gender, sexual identity, age and ability that run through the social system and that they learn from their families, the media and their peers. Even where they don't understand the terms being used interestingly they reflect the divisions in access to services we have discussed so far in this chapter.

There is a hierarchy of social values associated with certain social positions (i.e. society values some groups over others) and children reflect the complexity of this in their playground language. They choose to differentiate themselves from groups who are considered socially inferior: lesser in some way or 'different' from the norm. In this way they protect themselves from abuse. The consequences for children are that many seek to be 'normal' to avoid the stigma of being labelled and others remain bullied and excluded.

Divisions in access to childhood services and provision are reinforced at a number of levels. Direct discrimination is evident in the experience of Samuel who was humiliated by the teachers at his school (Reflective Activity 4.4). Those children who experience a lesser quality of service, for instance because of where they live or how much money they have, face indirect but still severe discrimination (Reflective Activity 4.2 and Reflective Activity 4.3). Karita faces discrimination as the result of institutionalised processes that have arisen over time, intended initially to benefit her and her mother, but in fact overgeneralising and neglecting her needs (Reflective Activity 4.6). Wole Soyinka's grandchild and Abdullah Shakil face state discrimination. Their human rights are undermined and their rights to the services received by other children removed by law. Their cases demonstrate that there are children who are considered not to matter; that is, the political interests of the state have overridden their needs and rights as children. Their existence puts paid to the notion that 'every child matters' in the UK or if we accept the rhetoric as based in reality, then these children are no longer considered to be children in UK law.

▶

Critical questions arise from this chapter relating to the barriers facing different groups of children in relation to access to services and provision. To what extent should cost determine access to important services for children? Better-off children usually have more access to higher-quality provision because their families can afford to pay. To what extent should the lack of formal citizenship and nationality limit children's entitlement? Is it right that any children living in the UK should be subject to detention and deportation when they have committed no offence? Why should where you live make a difference? For example, what is the effect of parental choice of school in terms of perpetuating unequal schooling outcomes? We know that better-off parents move to the catchment areas of schools that achieve higher results. What is the impact for children of poorer backgrounds? What does inclusion mean? Does it just mean no longer segregating provision for disabled and other groups of children or does it go much wider than this, for example does exclusion still operate even when children's provision is integrated? How can the stereotyping related to gender, sexuality and minority status and other social divisions be seriously challenged? How can blanket generalisations be avoided while at the same time the different needs of children be recognised and catered for?

Consider for example the very positive experiences of Anna in Chapter 16, The Anna Rebecca Gray Interviews.

In this chapter we have identified the ways that material inequality, citizenship, heritage, community, ability, minority status, gender and sexuality create barriers to services and provision for children. In some areas specialist provision has developed to cater for the needs of particular groups but there is clearly inequality in access for many children. The social divisions of childhood are complex. Just because a child is black or has impairments does not in itself mean their access to support will be more problematic. Each child is a member of many different groupings and the issue of access to services is different for each individual.

Membership of a particular group does not always lead to inequality of access to services, but powerlessness, abuse, lack of freedom of choice and active exclusion by the state (as is the case with children of asylum seekers) is a reality for many children.

Annotated reading

Cunningham, S. and Tomlinson, J. (2005) '"Starve them out": does every child really matter?: A commentary on section 9 of the Asylum and Immigration (Treatment of Claimants, etc.) Act 2004', in *Critical Social Policy*, Vol. 25(2) May, London: Sage, pp. 253–75

An example of the undermining of children's rights to services and protection in the UK. Quite difficult to read because of the references to law, but extremely important for understanding the way in which children's rights can be overridden for political reasons.

Lees, S. (1993) *Sugar and Spice: Sexuality and Adolescent Girls*, Harmondsworth: Penguin

Although written some years ago, a fascinating account of the ways in which girls are pressured to conform to gendered stereotypes and the ways they deal with this.

Novak, T. (2002) 'Rich children, poor children', in Goldson, B., Lavalette, M. and McKechnie, J. *Children Welfare and the State*, London: Sage

A clear analysis of the different service outcomes for children from rich and poor backgrounds.

Oliver, M. and Barnes, C. (1998) *Disabled People and Social Policy: From Exclusion to Inclusion*, London: Longman

An overview of a range of policies and political debates related to disability and society.

Payne, G. (ed.) (2000) *Social Divisions*, Basingstoke, Palgrave

An overview of social theory in relation to the full range of social divisions discussed in this chapter and more.

Shah, R. and Hatton, C. (1999) *Caring Alone: Young Carers in South Asian Communities*, Barnardo's

A case study of the experiences of children being looked after by disabled parents to whom they give assistance.

Chapter 5

Pictures of Children: What Are the Attitudes Behind Services and Provision?

PHIL JONES

Images represent social interactions and social relationships.

(Kress and van Leeuwen, 1996, p. 121)

Introduction

This chapter will examine the kinds of images or pictures of children created within the services established for them.

The emphasis in considering services for children is usually on the social, political or economic impact of a particular initiative or provision on the lives of children. Analysis is often based on the ways in which the content of the service will affect aspects of a child's life. This is usually framed within debates about the social or political framework or beliefs concerning the efficacy of the intentions and actions of aspects of policy or legislation.

This chapter will look at service provision and connected policy and legislation from a different

perspective. It will ask:

- What pictures of children are being created and how do these develop within service provision?
- How do we see contemporary 'pictures' of children?
- What implicit or hidden pictures are present in contemporary service provision?

The quote at the start of this chapter suggests that images can't be taken at face value. Images or pictures reflect different views, attitudes and relationships within society. Here the term 'pictures' does not mean photographs or paintings: it refers to the images of children that words can create. This chapter takes this idea and tries to look at the pictures which can emerge if we look carefully at the words within various documents concerning children's services. In essence the chapter tries to help 'read' and analyse documents about children. It avoids accepting the scene for what it appears to be but looks more closely, taking what we are given in documents as clues, rather than concurring with the pictures of children within the material at their apparent face value. It encourages us to be 'active readers' (Haw, 1998, p. 24), questioning the meanings behind documents and proposals. In this way it also encourages a questioning attitude, to be active and alert to the images of children within initiatives and developments for children.

While the chapter will focus on contemporary examples, the first case example is historical as it can be easier to identify the pictures behind policies and descriptions of services when they seem to be very different from the ones that we are used to and that we find around us. At times we can be so immersed in the cultural attitudes and ideas of our own time and country that it can be hard to stand apart to try to see what is happening. So, to help illustrate this process of identifying the pictures of children behind children's services the first case example comes from another era – a hundred years ago. The pictures seem to have some clear differences from those in 21st-century UK, and therefore can be easier for us to see.

The second and third examples explore 'pictures of children' within a more contemporary UK situation. They look at two recent policy frameworks to help see what pictures are within and behind the descriptions of services for children. Each one is chosen to represent a different strand or perspective on contemporary services for children.

What pictures of children are being created and how do these develop within service provision?

Working for Children 2004–5 (2004) reported that £40 billion was spent on children's services in England alone, with more than 4 million people in England reportedly working with children (2.4 million in paid

work, 1.8 million unpaid). This figure included 43,100 social services staff, 437,200 teachers, 274,500 paid child-care staff, 37,000 foster families and 51,000 youth workers. Documents guiding the work undertaken by departments overseeing children and workers such as these have an enormous impact on children's lives. These consist of policy documents, frameworks to guide the development of new initiatives and guidelines for practice or ways of working with children. Policies and policy documents may consider areas such as initiatives, structures, descriptions of provisions, spending targets or the reallocation of resources relating to different aspects of children's services.

The contents of these proposals and initiatives are not neutral, though they are often presented as if they are only practical descriptions of services for children, or the redistribution of resources. However, the development or design of services and the effect they have on children is not merely a matter of, for example, creating play centres for disadvantaged children or support structures for children who are homeless. There are hundreds of different ways that services can be provided for children. National or local government makes choices about what it says it is going to do, what it actually does and what it is not going to do. The choices that are made by a government reflect, for example, ideas about children and their upbringing, as well as reflecting the ways that a government wants children to grow into adults. The choices also reflect ideas about the following:

- the nature of the relationship between children, their family and community;

- the role that national and local government should play in children's lives;

- how to respond to demands or changes within society that concern children.

Connected to these ideas are factors such as how governments see children's relationship to areas such as economics, work, gender, reproduction, sexuality, race and disability. Importantly, then, behind or contained within every document are ideas about what children are, how they should relate to their families and the community around them, what they should do. These are often less explicit than the overt focus – but they

Reflective Activity 5.1

Making pictures

'Pictures' in this context involves looking at the following areas about the ways children are seen:

- the kinds of ideas about who children are and what they should be like;

- what they should and shouldn't do;

- the ways children and young people connect to others, especially those who have a role in their lives, or provide services that are concerned with them;

- the ways children relate to the world around them.

1 Create a simple drawing of a child. By the drawing make some speech bubbles. Inside the bubbles put some words that you think children might say about what they want in life. Now around them write some names of people such as 'mother', 'father', 'friend', 'teacher', 'social worker', 'play worker' or agencies such as 'school', 'health service', 'mosque', 'church' or 'law enforcement'. By each agency put a speech bubble. Again, inside each bubble put words that you think the person or agency might say and that shows something about how they see children.

2 Discuss the different pictures that emerge from this, the different ways you think people 'see' children.

3 Reflect on what the words you have chosen tell you about the pictures you have of children.

fuel and drive the ideas and approach – so it is important to learn to see them. That is what this chapter will help the reader to do: to begin to identify the pictures of children within such proposals and initiatives.

Picturing children: what are the differences between words, action and image?

What a government says it aims to do and what it actually does may be very different. The things that are said may differ from what actions or services emerge. What a government seems to be saying it wants to do, and why it wants to do it may, once we look at the picture of children behind what is being said, be more complicated than at first glance. This book will include a considerable amount of commentary on the relationship between what is said by government compared with what is actually done.

In this way, we can say that the services a government provides reflect attitudes towards children. At times the attitude may be very explicit. For example, a government may directly say that it wants to support 'children's rights', or it may say that it believes that only married mothers and fathers should bring up children. At others, though, the attitude may be less explicit, but, by examining the way a government talks about what it is going to do we can see attitudes or pictures that are behind its actions, the image of children it has.

These different pictures reflect different ideas about children. Any policy or service is created within debates, arguments and different opinions about children.

The following considers a particular example in order to identify the pictures behind the description of what is to be provided for children. Historically services for children have often been provided by religious organisations or voluntary societies. Amongst the first agencies concerned with the welfare and protection of children were philanthropic and charitable institutions such as Barnardo's. The following example concerning welfare and care for homeless and destitute children in the early 20th century contains an interesting and important picture of children.

Case Example 5.1

Waifs and strays

The following excerpt concerns children's services. It is from the *Handbook for Workers* involved in 'Homes for Waifs and Strays' and was published by the Church of England (1904).

Read the text and then reread it looking at some of the areas listed after the extract.

The Homes

These are, as a rule (chiefly on the score of healthiness), established in country districts, not in large towns . . . There can of course be no wholly efficient substitute for a mother's love, a father's Christian example and rule, but, so far as it is possible to supply the lack of these, the training and shelter afforded by the Society do give to the children what otherwise, in all probability, they would never know – the priceless blessings of a Christian home . . .

The homes can be classified in three divisions . . . There are homes for destitute children . . . Homes certified by the Local Government Board for the reception of pauper children under the provisions of the Pauper Education Act of 1862 . . . [and] Homes certified by the Home Office as Industrial Homes . . . The children committed under the provisions of the Industrial Schools Acts of 1866 and 1881 are paid for by the Treasury, and also in some cases by the committing authority. The payment made, however, rarely covers the cost, and here the State and private benevolence must work hand in hand. As the name implies, some industry is taught in these Homes – farming, gardening, tailoring, etc.

Placing Children in Service

The following rules have been specially approved by the Executive: (1) As each situation offers or if found for a child, one member should be appointed by the Local Committee to take the responsibility of advising them as to whether the situation is a suitable one for the child, and on what terms it should be accepted. The Committee shall require a satisfactory reference from each person who may wish to engage a child. (2) Each Local Committee shall report twice in the year to the Executive on the welfare of the child placed out in their responsibility. (3) Each employer who engages a child should promise that, in the event of the child leaving its situation, the Hon. Secretary of the Home would at once be communicated with. The Hon. Secretary shall upon the receipt of such communication, arrange for the child's return to the Home, or provide for it in some other way. (4) Children should be placed with members of the Church of England . . .

Ladies especially will understand how important it is that girls should not be sent in service under such conditions as will lead them to become mere 'drudges', and two years careful training for domestic servants by the matron will in great measure prevent this. Many ladies, interested in the welfare of our children, have very kindly received girls into their houses as 'pupil-servants', with the results that they have been able eventually to command good wages as house, parlour, nurse and laundry maids. (Handbook, 1904, pp. 5–9)

Reflective Activity 5.2

Picturing children: waifs and strays

Make a list of all the words you can find in this text that are used to describe or refer to children. Now discuss them using the following general questions:

1   What is emphasised in these words?

▶

2 What kind of picture of children do the words you have listed create?

3 What aspects of childhood seem left out to you as a 21st-century reader?

Now look at these more specific questions:

Look to see how the relationship between child, family, community and the services provided for them, or the state is described in the *Handbook for Workers* extract.

4 What kind of picture of the child in relationship to their family or to the 'home' does this create?

5 Does this contrast with your views or images of what a 'home' should be for a child, or how a child connects to their family, or to the services that relate to them?

Now compare your pictures with some of the ones identified below.

Words in the text used to describe or refer to children:

Pauper   Waif   Destitute   Domestic servant
Drudge   Pupil-Servant

The words used to describe children *all* relate to money or work. This is really the only framework used to identify them. Virtually every time a child is referred to they are 'pauper', 'waif' or 'destitute', all of which refer to their lack of money and support. They are called 'domestic servants' and 'drudges', which both see them only in terms of work roles. Even the name used to refer to them in relation to education concerns work, 'pupil-servants', or their financial status, 'pauper education'. The *Handbook* creates an image of children as only mattering in terms of their poor financial status and their actual or potential capacity to work.

Words in the text used to describe the relationship between child, family, community, services

and state:

Industrial Homes   Priceless value
Ladies kindly receive girls   sent in service

The picture painted of the relationship between any child, their family, community and state primarily reflects this. The homes provided by the Church of England are also primarily seen in terms of money and work. Examples of this include them being called 'Industrial Homes', the primacy placed on the children being prepared for service. Where other areas are mentioned they are usually couched in terms which are linked to money transactions, buying, selling and value. Examples of this include the love and religious guidance from a mother and father being described in words taken from the market place – 'priceless value', or the idea that children are given and taken like bought objects 'ladies . . . kindly receive girls'. Although framed in the moral gloss of religion, the child is seen as a debt and as an investment – the picture created is one where the child has a price label attached, their 'cost' by being a 'pauper', and that state and religion link to put money into the training of a child so that they can be made to work.

All the actions which children are involved in depict them as objects that things are done to. They are 'committed' to the homes, they are 'paid for' and 'placed in service', 'received' or 'sent in service'. This creates an image of the child as passive and without any voice. The use of the word 'it' to our eyes in 21st-century UK, creates an image of an object, a thing, not a living gendered person. There is no real focus upon their needs and there is no notion of the child having any rights, for example. The picture of the child is one of them being silent – no reference is made at all to what they might

Compare this with the discussion of children's rights in Chapter 2, Childhood: Rights and Realities.

▶

want, or to their voice on any aspect of their present or future. The image is one where adults make decisions for the children and the assumption is that the children would not expect to do anything other than what they are told to do.

The idea that a child might be placed in a situation where they might be at risk is only briefly visible. The assumption is that it is enough for adults to be 'responsible' for the child and that one member of the executive decides that the 'situation' is 'suitable'.

For further discussion see Chapter 10, Safeguarding Children.

The only criteria are that the people who the child will serve are Christians, and that two visits a year are sufficient to monitor the child and their situation.

Then and now: parallels and differences?

Contemporary concepts of such social divisions related to economic and social status are defined and discussed in Chapter 4, The Social Divisions of Childhood.

We can draw both parallels and differences between the pictures of children this 'Homes for Waifs and Strays' document creates and those within contemporary UK documents relating to children's services. We might draw parallels in that poverty still creates enormous differences in the way children live, and the way that children who are wealthy have one set of experiences and have expectations that are enormously different from those who are poor.

We might see differences between the pictures of children who are seen as objects within services with all decisions made about them, where the child is silent and is 'done to', and those reflected in approaches which try to emphasise consulting and listening to children.

Such pictures can be seen within the debates in Chapter 12, Services to Children's Play.

Such child-centred approaches try to involve them in decisions about service design and delivery and their own lives, and sees children as having rights that must be acted on. The contemporary situation is informed by a developing emphasis on pictures of actively engaged children where they are involved in decision-making, design, development and evaluation of services, rather than as objects referred to as 'it', where adults are active and the children are still, silent and to be used.

How do we see contemporary 'pictures' of children?

Harker (2005) discusses the 10-year child-care strategy of the New Labour government in the context of images of children reflected within government policies of other European Union member states. She asserts that the UK has lagged behind other industrialised countries, for example 'some 30 years' behind Scandinavia. Her point is that the UK needs to look at the discoveries and findings of other states regarding areas such as the way children are seen within the services.

Harker says that UK services for child care usually depend on quantifiable indicators such as staff:child ratios or testing through looking at specific outcomes that can be counted, such as the ability to perform certain singled out skills or aptitudes such as reading, rather than, 'the totality of a child's experience . . . the best early years services are based on a child-centred understanding of education and care' (p. 12). She goes on to describe the different pictures of childhood behind such an approach to service provision. Look at Harker's comments on the educational approach taken by pre-school initiatives developed in Italy by Reggio Emilia in Chapter 6, Education: Service or System?.

Their approach is informed by an image of a child, not as an empty vessel into which the right ingredients must be poured, but as a being with extraordinary potential. Great emphasis is placed on encouraging curiosity and innovation, with

both children and teachers engaged in a constant process of discovery. The child is not seen as a passive recipient of education or care, but as an active participant.   (Harker, 2005, p. 12)

Here she's saying that the kinds of ways that children are pictured affects the ways services are provided. She's contrasting the Reggio Emilia approach which has behind it a picture of children as individuals with 'amazing potential' with one often found in the UK that pictures them as empty passive vessels into which adults pour things. She says that this results in very different services and experiences for children. Reggio Emilia, she says, offers children 'the strongest foundation for life' (p. 12) as they develop their own sense of identity, self-worth and ability to develop independency and their own strengths. The picture is of a child and adult in a relationship that involves discovering and developing together. The second offers an altogether more passive picture of children where they are 'empty', where they are defined by, and have to grow into, shapes entirely provided by adults.

Here you can see that pictures of children reflect tensions about the ways in which children are seen, and that the pictures governments have can vary. The pictures inform the way services are provided. Such a picture, therefore, has a real effect on the way children

receive services and the ways in which they develop. Identifying these pictures is not just an intellectual exercise, as this example shows: the pictures have great influence on the ways in which children's lives are lived. Examining documents concerning children in this way can help to look critically at the way children are being seen. This in turn helps us to see whether children are being best served by these pictures, or whether they impede or hinder the way children receive services.

In trying to see the pictures of children within the texts, as we've seen, it can be useful to look at the themes and issues reflected in the way bodies such as the government describes what it intends. By looking closely at *what* is being said, *how* it is being said, and then *standing back and analysing* what is behind the documents talking about services, we can begin to identify what kinds of views of children are *fuelling* the initiative or provision.

In looking at childhood a number of authors have described themes or tensions in the way society sees children. These ideas are not static, and there is not only one set of ideas in operation at one time. However, certain themes are often involved in the way children are looked at. We will now consider some of these themes to assist in forming a framework to help us look at the pictures that emerge from policy and service documents.

The themes are:

- Child, family, community and state
- Empty vessel versus active potential
- Need, rights and risk
- Investment
- Difference

Key theme: child, family, community and state

One of the areas of debate and tension in the pictures created of children concerns the relationship between child, family, community and state.

Tensions exist around the roles of family, community and state in the bringing up and socialisation of children. Service providers' images of children often reflect concerns that families, educators and providers of support services are not enabling children to turn into 'worthy citizens' (Hill and Tisdall, 1997, p. 247): thus perpetuating a view of children as wayward beings needing to be reformed. Coleman and Rowe (2005) in their research with children and young people saw many of these themes reflected in the comments made by young people about the lack of real consultation, and engagement between government themselves. Children's voices echoed this theme,

> 'People say we need to know this stuff, but its not happening to us. The thing is we can't vote yet, so why should we get involved?' (Boy, 15)

> 'You don't want to listen to people who talk about politics.' (Boy, 14)

> 'If a politician comes on the telly you switch off the TV.' (Boy, 14)

> 'I'm more interested in the news than politicians.' (Boy, 14)

Others took the view that governments could learn from young people, but

> 'they shouldn't stereotype us – stereotyping is the worst thing.' (Boy, 16)

'They reject the notion of citizenship as a set of rules to be disseminated by government and absorbed by future citizens.' (Coleman and Rowe, 2005, p. 7)

What we see are contradictions between the emerging pictures of children in terms of their relationship to their families, to the resources in their local community and to the government that makes decisions about services. To better understand and interpret the pictures of children conveyed in service policy and proposals we must raise questions such as:

- Are children seen as the property of families or as independent individuals?
- Do pictures emerge of children who are supported in their growth by government provision?
- Is the picture one where children are being controlled by the government through the services it provides to fit proscribed notions of what a 'good adult' will be?

Key theme: needs, rights and risk

Another tension has been identified concerning whether children are seen as objects of concern and dependent on adults, or agents in their own right capable of opinion, decisions and actions on their own behalf. Are they, for example, active participants in society rather than individuals for whom others 'know best' and make decisions?

Hill and Tisdall (1997) talk about the way needs are often seen as,

> mainly the responsibility of parents and families within the private sphere of the home, although wider society has a role in supporting families to do so. The collective needs of populations or communities are part of the realm of social policy which examines the nature and extent of societal responses through provision of services, financial benefits and legal regulation. (Hill and Tisdall, 1997, p. 39)

Wyse has pointed out that the UK has been strongly criticised by the United Nations Committee on the

Rights of the Child (UN, 2000) for its lack of progress on prioritising children's rights. He links this to an embedded, historical attitude towards children,

> The UK is criticized for doing little to adopt a rights-based approach because of a dependency on the philosophies of service, welfare and interest. The word 'rights' hardly appears in UK legislation.
>
> (Wyse, 2004, p. 100)

In our further discussion of case examples we will see how much the state is seen to be 'serving' children within specific and stringently defined contexts compared with promoting children's rights and views per se. We will also look at how much large and powerful organisations say they know what children need and will look after their welfare, compared with acknowledging children's rights.

Again, we can use these debates to create questions to help us see what pictures emerge of children in terms of needs, rights and risks.

- Are they seen as individuals who have rights or as individuals who need to be looked after by others who make decisions for them; should they be 'seen and not heard'?

- Is the picture of children's relationships to services such as education or protection one where they are connected by a risk relationship?

- Are children seen as individuals or pictured only as a series of needs which may be met?

Key theme: difference

Our final theme is one of difference and whether one way of providing a service is sufficient for all children, or whether and how differences between children in terms of economic status, gender, race, culture, disability or sexuality can be addressed. Daniels and Macdonald (2005) describe diversity in a way which can be useful when thinking about the importance of all children fully participating in services with their

> Chapter 6, Education: Service or System?, raises this debate within the context of a national curriculum.

differences acknowledged. They say that the range of areas where difference can occur is very broad and that diversity is

> about recognising this range of differences in people and valuing people as individuals, respecting their differences and their differing needs. It is also about accommodating differences so that an individual can play a full part.
>
> (Daniels and Macdonald, 2005, p. 1)

So what pictures emerge of children in terms of difference?

- Are they pictured as a single identity where all children are pictured as more or less the same?

- Is difference ignored within a 'one size fits all' attitude?

- If difference is acknowledged, is it seen in terms of a deficit from the 'norm' where difference is seen as being less than the majority?

- Is a child's individuality pictured as an advantage in creating and developing diversity, where difference is valued and celebrated? Or is it seen as something that needs to be modified or changed to become less different?

- Is the view one where any service needs to be devised, resourced or made available so that the service can reflect difference in the children who use it? Or is difference ignored and any child who does not fit the way the service is provided made to feel that they are a problem?

What implicit or hidden pictures are present in contemporary service provision?

As stated earlier, we will examine two specific areas of contemporary service provision for how they address the questions raised in the key themes. Each area is looked at through analysis of the explicit focus of the service or provision; examination of how the language and concepts embedded within the service's policy and practice reveals contemporary attitudes and debates about children; and analysis of these pictures examining how the key themes are considered:

- **Case Example 2**: an introduction from one of the main initiatives concerning the National

- Framework for Children, written by John Reid (DoH, 2005).

- **Case Example 3**: material from 'Youth Matters' (DfES, 2005g).

Case Example 5.2

The National Services Framework: Hansel, Gretel and poverty?

Every Child Matters: Change for Children (DfES, 2005c) was described by the government as a programme of local action designed to implement 'whole system transformation of children's services' (p. 2). It includes what it calls the 'development of the children's workforce, and the integration of front line delivery and the processes that support it' (p. 4). A number of sets of documents were published to provide guidance on areas such as children's trust governance and strategic planning. These were aimed at all managers of services that 'impact on children and young people', including corporate planners and head teachers. These documents are designed to support the effective delivery of services. 'The Common Assessment Framework' was designed to provide 'a common approach to needs assessment that can be used by the whole children's workforce' (p. 4).

> Further discussion of this area of children's services can be found in Chapter 10, Safeguarding Children.

'National Services Framework: Young People and Maternity Services (Standard 1)'

FROM John Reid's Introduction

Inequalities still impact on children and young people. Some find it difficult to access the services they need, simply because of where they live or because of their circumstances. Child poverty, though greatly reduced, still means that children and young people from disadvantaged backgrounds risk not realising their full potential as they grow and develop into adolescence and adult life . . . At the heart of the National Services Framework is a fundamental change in our way of thinking about children's health. It advocates a shift with services being designed and delivered around the needs of the child. Services are child-centred and look at the whole child – not just the illness or the problem, but rather the best way to pick up any problems early, take preventative action and ensure children have the best possible chance to realise their full potential. And if and when these children grow up to be parents themselves they will be better equipped to bring up their own children. (DoH, 2005)

Standard 1 sets its focus as the promotion and delivery of health and well-being of all children and young people through a coordinated 'programme of action, including prevention and early intervention wherever possible, to ensure long term gain, led by the NHS in partnership with local authorities. (Part 1 Standard 1)

▶

Reflective Activity 5.3

Picturing Children: National Services Framework

1 This introduction talks frequently of activities, actions and changes involving the state, child and health services. Examples of this are the 'programme of action' or 'a fundamental change'. Make a list of the phrases describing actions relating to children in this description of services.

2 Look to see how the relationship between child, family community and the services features in these actions. What kind of picture of the child in relationship to their family, the community around them and to the state emerges?

3 Try to collect your words and short phrases around the key themes that this chapter is exploring:

   • Child, family, community and state
   • Empty vessel versus active potential
   • Need, rights and risk
   • Investment
   • Difference

4 Now compare your pictures with some of the ones I've identified below.

Child, family, community and state

'difficult to *access* the services they need', '*not realising* their full potential as they *grow and develop*', 'children *grow up to be* parents themselves'

The active words that create a picture of certain kinds of relationship are words such as 'access', 'not realising' and 'grow up to be' which are all linked to the child growing and developing, or being hindered in their growth by different things getting in the way.

The talk of a fundamental 'change' in thinking relates to the relationship between state and child – the services are not seen as something which exist as static monolithic slabs, but ones which are to be designed around helping the child in actions like 'growing', 'developing' and using services. The picture here is one where the child is supposed to be at the centre and the state supports their use of services and their growth.

Empty vessel versus active potential

'*not realising* their full potential' 'the best possible chance *to realise* their full potential'

The picture of the child here also focuses upon the future. In the very short excerpt 'full potential' is mentioned twice in relation to the child's future. The image is one whereby services can be used in a *fight* or *struggle*. The words create a picture where there is a combat with two sides: on the one hand 'inequality' and being stuck outside, and on the other 'services'. Poverty especially is pictured as a key negative adversary who stops and stunts children. This enemy is used in an image in relation to growth and development. Here the picture is of poverty sealing off a child who will then not grow or develop. Children who are outside this sealed-off area are seen to grow through being 'equipped', having 'chances'. Services are pictured as a champion, centred round the child, picking things up, taking preventative action, ensuring chances, or as a good gardener ensuring maximum 'growth' and 'development'.

The picture is of the child as a separate person, almost set apart from the situation they have grown up within or which they live in now. Though brief mention of 'circumstances' is made, the emphasis is repeatedly placed on the child as an individual apart from others, on them being individually equipped and services seeing them as an individual. They are 'whole' on their own, the attention is on *this* rather than them being pictured within the contexts they live in, and that the contexts need to change in order to help them. On the one hand, this creates an image of services trying hard to see each and every child as an individual; on the other, it does not create

▶

any sense of the child's relationship to the people around them, to 'groups', or communities in change together. The image is more one where access to services will result in an individual child being seen and given services to help them alone to better themselves. We could say that this picture cuts out the larger picture and doesn't look at the wider causes that have created the child's 'disadvantaged background' in the first place.

Need, rights and risk: around the child

> 'designed and delivered *around* the needs of *the child*'

Within the excerpt above we could argue that, although there is much emphasis on 'potential', and the child is seen at the centre, they are not themselves very active – they are tended to and worked upon or around. The focus is on the child and their needs – but the picture is one where the services are active in creating a shape to fit 'around' the child. There is no mention of the child's own voice or of rights and demands. These also stay outside the picture. Others do things around or for them such as designing or delivering. You could say that the picture is one where the child is passive, whereas the service agencies and workers are active.

Investment: Hansel and Gretel and breadcrumbs

> 'difficult to *access . . . where they live*'

As analysed above, the picture of children is one where deprivation is linked to poverty – but the attention to rectifying this is seen to be to create access to services, not to consider why the poverty is in the child's life and environment in the first place. It's as if there is no history around the child, or no system in which they live and that has produced the poverty in their community or family. In this way the *background* of the child's poverty isn't in the

picture at all – it moves out of the frame. The picture focuses on the aspect of the child's poverty that concerns the way other children can gain better 'access' to services. If you like, poverty becomes only a way of stopping children arriving at the services. The words paint a very physical, almost geographic image:

> Some find it difficult to access the services they need, simply because of where they live or because of their circumstances.

To my mind the picture is one where poverty snatches away the child's map of where to find services, rather like the birds and creatures eating up Hansel and Gretel's breadcrumb trail. The image is one whereby services change the way they meet children in order to make sure the services know how to find the children who are poor. In this way no real picture is given of what is in the children's lives that causes the poverty: it's as if all that needs to happen is that a route to services is made for them.

Summary

Here we see that, by examining the words carefully, pictures of children that are not explicit when we first read the National Services Framework become apparent. These are important and show ideas that lie behind the seemingly purely practical proposals and ways of working. The picture created here tries to show the child as full of potential and growth. It tries to create services that respond to the child, but the picture reveals the child as rather passive in the face of workers and agencies who work 'around'

> See Chapter 4, The Social Divisions of Childhood, about the difference between rhetoric and action relating to the multiple causes of inequality.

them by identifying what they need and how they should grow into 'equipped parents' themselves. The child is also seen as an individual outside of the context that resulted in their disadvantage. The picture doesn't show the background and reasons for the child's poverty.

Case Example 5.3

Youth Matters: Living as Shopping? Opportunity cards and ASBOs

This Case Example focuses on a UK government Green Paper, 'Youth Matters' (DfES, 2005g) which, in part, aimed to consult on provision for young people, especially targeting 13- to 19-year-olds (p. 6). The government response to this, 'Youth Matters: Next Steps' (DfES, 2006d), aimed to 'set out the vision for empowering young people, giving them somewhere to go, something to do and someone to talk to', focusing on services and facilities for young people. Fourteen 'pathfinder' local authority areas were initially used to 'pilot' initiatives which were described as giving more 'flexible and accessible information, advice and guidance', and 'better targeted support' for young people experiencing difficulties (p. 6).

'Youth Matters: Next Steps' places its work in the context of 'empowering' young people and says that it wants to place children at the 'centre of our policies and services'. The government said that there were 'three principal ways' it intended to implement 'Youth Matters':

- through a personalised, differentiated approach which responds to the needs of every young person, while recognising that group or neighbourhood approaches are also needed
- putting purchasing power in the hands of young people and supporting them to make choices and influence provision
- involving young people in local decisions about what is needed in their communities

(DfES, 2006d, p. 6)

By looking at the consultative document, 'Youth Matters', we can begin to reveal what pictures of young people are behind the way the government began to approach such an initiative and formulated such 'principal ways' guiding their work and ideas. It says that there are 'more opportunities' for young people than in 'previous generations', and situates these opportunities as being there for teenagers to 'take advantage of' in order to make a successful 'transition to independent adulthood' (p. 11). It emphasises education and training in relation to this, talking about 'rising standards' and a higher proportion of teenagers taking part. It then goes on to identify areas where there is 'little improvement' or what it calls 'poorer outcomes'. Schools, colleges, youth services, Connexions, mainstream services such as health and targeted support services are all mentioned as 'having a role to play' (p. 11).

It is interesting to examine the way these services, and their relationship to children and young people, are depicted to look at the way pictures of children and young people emerge in this area. Three sections of the 'Youth Matters' dealing with services will be looked at as samples to develop these pictures in terms of themes identified earlier in this chapter.

Youth Matters

The government's 'Youth Matters' was presented to Parliament in July 2005. The overt picture communicated to teenagers within the consultative document starts with,

Somewhere to go? Something to do?

How would you make life better for teenagers?

The choices you make now – and that includes what you choose to do in your spare time – will affect what happens later in your life. Are there things you want to do where you live but can't? And do you know where to go for information and advice about making decisions in your life? We want to improve local opportunities to help you make the most of your teenage years. We have lots of ideas about how to improve things, but we need to know what you think. (2005, p. 2)

▶

Boxes in the questionnaire contain 'quotations' which are not linked to an actual, real individual, but are supposed to be the 'voices' of teenagers. One, for example, runs as follows:

Encouragement

'What I need is a card that gives me discounts on things to do and in the shops, and lets me prove my age. If it could also be topped up with money to spend on activities, then I'd have more choice in what I do. I'd also help more in the community if my contribution was recognised in some way'

Here are further quotations from 'Youth Matters'. These will be used to look at the pictures of 'youth' that emerge from within and behind the language.

Youth Matters

This first chapter sets the scene for our proposals by exploring how today's teenagers are doing and analysing the services currently available to them.

Young People Today – Most young people are doing well

43. Most young people today enjoy their teenage years and make the transition to adulthood successfully.

45. Today's young people are:

- learning more – 53.7 per cent of pupils in England now achieve 5 or more GCSEs at grades A*-C1, and the percentage of 16–18 year olds in learning had increased to 75.1 per cent by 2003;

- enterprising – 15 per cent of 16–18 year olds in England are thinking about starting their own business and another 5 per cent are already engaged in some form of entrepreneurial activity;

- contributing – 45 per cent of 16–24 year olds participate at least once a month in informal volunteering – the highest level for any age group.

46. In recent years some key outcomes for teenagers have shown marked improvement:

- smoking among young people aged 11–15 years has fallen from 13 per cent in 1996 to 9 per cent in 2004;

- between 1998 and 2003, the under-18 conception rate, while high by international standards, fell by 9.8 per cent;

and

- levels of drug use among 11–15 year olds have fallen slightly since 2001 while use of serious drugs has remained stable.

Young people face challenges in growing up

47. However, the teenage years are also a time of transition and challenges – these can relate to a wide range of issues including study, money, employment, self-esteem, health, housing, parents and relationships.

These challenges may be greater for young people who have disabilities, for those with special educational needs (SEN), for those who are homeless or who are in care and for teenagers from some black and minority ethnic groups . . . A survey found that 68 per cent of homeless households believe their children were experiencing problems at school as a direct result. (p. 12)

Services for Young People Today

55. Government funded services are not the only – or even necessarily the most important – source of opportunity, challenge and support for young people. Parents are the strongest influences on their children's lives. The voluntary and community sector also plays an important role independent of Government, often providing innovative ways of reaching some of the most vulnerable young people who are at risk of being missed by other services. Faith, sports and other youth groups, scouting, guiding and other national youth movements and schemes such as the Duke of Edinburgh's Award Scheme and Community Service Volunteers between them provide millions of opportunities for young people each year.

56. But public services do have a key role to play. It is important that they strike the right mix of support and challenge, particularly when teenagers are involved in anti-social behaviour and crime. (p. 14)

▶

Reflective Activity 5.4

Picturing Children: Youth Matters

In these excerpts from 'Youth Matters' certain words and themes recur.

1 Make a list of terms used to describe what teenagers do, or should do, which are seen as 'positive' or 'negative'.

2 Now make a list of words and phrases that describe what the government is 'doing' or 'offering' to young people.

3 What do they emphasise? What pictures of young people do they promote? What picture of the relationship between young people, services and the government do they seem to reflect?

4 Again, try to collect your words and short phrases around the key themes that this chapter is exploring:
 • Child, family, community and state
 • Need, rights and risk
 • Investment
 • Difference

5 Now compare your pictures with some of the ones I've identified below.

Child, family, community and state: choosers and improvers

'*choices* you make now ... what you *choose* to do'

'*We want to improve* local opportunities to help you ... We have lots of ideas about how to improve*'

'expanding *opportunities* ... *learning* more ... *enterprising* ... *entrepreneurial* activity ... *contributing*'

Here the emphasis is on 'choice': the word is repeatedly used. It creates a picture of the teenager typified by being in a position to make choices. The picture is of a government that wants to help the teenager make 'choices' about how to use their spare time, to make things better locally and to provide information so that the teenager knows where to go for help to make decisions. The picture of a teenager in the 'Encouragement' box is one who wants to own a card and be able to prove their age, who wants to have top-ups with money to spend on activities and their contribution to the community recognised. As the National Children's Bureau highlights, this view of teenagers may be simplistic. It published the views of Hamish McCallum, a 15-year-old, to illustrate this point:

> Youth Centres are not for everyone. In fact only a small percentage of young people say that they would like to use one' stressing that young people tend to like to be 'different' rather than organised into activities. He says that the 'opportunity card' could be 'a waste of time and money' as the rewards might be seen to be 'shoddy' and might not make 'the slightest bit of difference.
>
> (NCB, *Opinion,* 4 August 2005)

To summarise, the young person is pictured as an enthusiastic 'chooser' and buyer whose choices are defined by government 'activities' in order to fill their 'spare' time and who wants accreditation for these, in order to be a force for good in their local community.

The young people are not the initiators of activities, they are purchasers. The picture is one whereby their participation is largely seen in terms of an economic model of purchasing and developing as a consumer. The image is almost one of teenager as a developing shopper in relation to their community and to their government, who provides them with the things they want to offer.

Further discussion of the individual as purchaser of services can be found in Chapter 8, Provision for Child Health.

Needs, rights and risk: the absent background

'the most vulnerable young people who are *at risk of being missed* by other services'

'Government funded services are not the only – or even necessarily the most important – source of *opportunity, challenge and support* for young people. Parents are the strongest *influences* on their children's lives'

'*things you want to do* where you live but can't . . . where to go for information and advice about *making decisions* in your life . . . a card that *gives me discounts* on things to do and in the shops . . . *more choice* in what I do. I'd also help more in the community if *my contribution* was recognised in some way'

Part of the picture is apparently focused on support for teenagers who have 'needs' or are 'at risk'. The role of the government in the image created by the text is to listen and to offer support in a market of choice and buying. However, the picture of the 'successful' teenager is one painted of a particular type and is created in a particular way: one who takes 'opportunities'. Here the picture of a teenager is seen largely as an economic asset to be trained, honed and encouraged in specific areas. The government provides services in a way that links directly to these areas. It's pretty black and white. Absent from the picture is anything outside of economic success, or of education outside of government-defined priorities of percentages in attendance or exam successes.

The Learning and Skills Council in its published response to this Green Paper echoes some of these concerns. The use of ASBOs and this aspect of 'Youth Matters' is challenged by them in the following way:

Overall we feel the Green Paper is inconsistent and unhelpful in its references to young offenders. Of course, young people must not be allowed to disrupt the activities of other young people, but it is important to bear in mind that those young people have already been 'punished' by the courts through a range of community or custodial sentences. They should not be further punished by having benefits or opportunities withdrawn from them. . . . it would have been helpful if the Green Paper had acknowledged that youth offending is very often an indication of disadvantage, deprivation and a lack of facilities and opportunities to become involved in positive activities!
(Learning and Skills Council, 2005, p. 6)

This echoes concerns that the image of young people as consumers leaves out of the frame issues such as deprivation and poverty in the Youth Matters' picture of children as card-carrying free shoppers and choosers.

Here the notion of teenagers' rights or self determination is reduced to choosing which activities they would prefer over others which are all provided for them, and which are continually referred to as 'bettering'. Here the teenager is seen as an individual who, both at school and in time outside school, is in need of improvement within organisations defined as 'improving' by the government, and which are, once examined, carefully seen as picturing the young person as a particular type of opportunity taker, whose choices are all linked to being a successful force in the market economy.

The following is another excerpt:

Youth Matters Options

a. Youth matters contains a range of proposals designed to improve outcomes for young people. This section of the RIA focuses on the proposals which have a significant impact on the public, private and voluntary sectors. It looks specifically, therefore, at options considered when developing proposals for increasing participation in constructive activities including proposals for influencing both the demand and supply of constructive activities for young people . . .

The paper goes on to suggest options for action. These include RIA points 36 and 37:

▶

- developing a paper voucher scheme where a young person is given vouchers to 'spend on activities';
- a national card scheme with centralised 'delivery and management' where young people have an activities budget and that 'young people to spend on their choice of constructive activities' to aim to create 'the development of a market to meet the needs of young people'.

These would be marketed along with a rewards and discount system.

A further option is for RIA 40:

- a voluntary national scheme supporting local cards. Here local authorities develop their own 'opportunity cards' which could be 'topped up' with funds for young people to use on a 'range of constructive activities'.

However, the children's version says that 'young people who abuse opportunities or commit crimes should not be given these top-ups' (p. 2) and in the questionnaire this is extended to include 'young people who misbehave' (Question 10, p. 2). The option is described as involving 'national branding, marketing and negotiation of discounts to promote activities' (RIA 40, 2005, p. 2).

The government invites organisations which supply goods and services to young people to 'put themselves forward' to offer discounts on the card for young people to 'benefit' from them (RIA 46, 2005, p. 2). Parents, grandparents and local authorities can 'supplement' the government's contribution safe in the knowledge that the cards can only be used for 'beneficial' activities.

On one level this material seems to contain a proposal to increase activities which teenagers can take part in within their 'free time'. However, once you begin to look at the proposal from different perspectives other pictures emerge. Let's return to our examination of the pictures within these words of children and young people at risk.

The card system begins to create an image of the relationship between child and government which,

on the one hand, is one where the government shows children how to become consumers. This act of consuming is seen, on the other hand, as a way to address inequalities or disenfranchisement. Any problems the teenagers are experiencing are not seen in terms of underlying causes such as poverty or inequality, housing or disenfranchisement – there is, as we remarked earlier, no background to the young person's life in this picture. Instead the young person who is 'disadvantaged' or who commits crime is pictured in relation to more access to the act of consuming activities.

The picture of a young person's relations with government is also one where the card becomes a means of the government regulating behaviour through a reward and punishment system of controlling the supply of market treats. The system is also one where their purchasing power to become these things can be added to if the teenager is disadvantaged, but their access to the market selling these properties is reduced if they misbehave.

Difference: minority or majority?

'the great majority', 'a small minority'

The document uses a good deal of division, separating out young people into one sort or another. It isn't apparent on first looking, but through the section of 'Youth Matters' this division of difference occurs.

Youth Matters says that most (so we can say 'majority' here) young people 'today . . . are doing well' and that, 'most young people today enjoy their teenage years' and 'successfully' make the transition to adulthood. It goes on to talk about the 'great majority' and if you look at this section you'd imagine that the detail of the picture it will go on to give is of this 'majority' and the characteristics that make them successful and enable them to do well. Yet when we look carefully this divided picture is not what it seems.

The successful 'majority' picture is actually *not* a picture of the majority of young people from the

▶

Reflective Activity 5.5

Majority and Minority

One way the Youth Matters material creates a picture of young people is by choosing to divide up, separate and draw out differences between young people through the way it uses 'majority' and 'minority'.

Create a list of 'majority' and 'minority' things the excerpt says about young people. Under each of these two terms place words and descriptions you think can be placed under these headings based on what is said in the excerpt from 'Youth Matters'.

evidence the government selects to colour its picture. It uses statistics, but, with one exception, the statistics it cites actually uses minorities of young people to define this so-called 'majority' who are supposed to be doing well! The three areas it uses to create a picture of difference around 'doing well' and 'not doing well' are learning more, enterprising and contributing. As we saw above the other side of the picture is typified immediately after by a contrast with young people who are smokers, pregnant under 18 and who use drugs. Yet for 'enterprising' it uses statistics of only 15 and 5 per cent engaged in 'entrepreneurial activity' – this means that 80 per cent are not. In terms of contributing it says that 45 per cent are informal volunteers in some kind of activity – again this means that 55 per cent are not. The one majority statistic it uses is that 53.7 per cent of pupils achieve 5 or more GCSEs at grades A*–C1, which means that 46.3 per cent do not – only a slight majority.

It seems here that the picture of the 'majority' being successful is not built up of actual majority statistics or groups of young people who really are in the majority, but by characteristics that the government want us to think are successful, doing well but are actually minority groups of young people. Here the picture the government wants to put forward is different than the actual majority, which is

of a picture where the majority are not involved in entrepreneurial activities or making voluntary contributions to their community. So the difference between majority success and minority 'challenge' is not as clear cut as the words seem initially to suggest.

We can see that, by examining the words and the pictures they create, it is possible to see that the government wants to advocate a certain kind of 'majority', the successful young person, but is using slight of hand to create pictures of what they want rather than what is there, without seeming to do so. By looking at the pictures created by the words we see behind the apparent image a different picture or at least a less clear one. The picture of two kinds of youth, with a division into one being from a positive majority and the other from a minority which is characterised by not being enthusiastic volunteers and entrepreneurs is more complex.

Summary

In 'Youth Matters', we see once more, by examining the words carefully, pictures of children that reflect certain attitudes and beliefs that are not obvious when first looking at the proposals. As this chapter has shown, these are important and show ideas that lie behind the seemingly purely practical proposals and ways of working. The young people are not the initiators of activities, they are purchasers. The picture is one whereby their participation is largely seen in terms of an economic model of purchasing and developing as a consumer. The image is one of teenager as developing shopper in relation to their community and to their government, which provides them with the things they want to offer. Here the picture of a teenager is seen largely as an economic asset to be trained, honed and encouraged in specific areas. This image of young people as consumers leaves out of the frame issues such as deprivation and poverty in the Youth Matters picture of children as card-carrying free shoppers and choosers. The picture of a young person's relations with government is also one where the card becomes a means of the government regulating behaviour through a reward and punishment system of controlling the supply of market treats.

Conclusion

This chapter has shown how the three different case examples each reflect tensions about the ways in which children are seen, and the ways in which this is linked to the provision of services. These pictures lie behind the way services are provided and have great influence on the ways in which children's lives are lived.

The case examples have examined the language, concepts and attitudes of initiatives to consider the pictures of a child that are being created. It has shown how to undertake a critical examination of the languages and concepts embedded within policy and practice to consider what they reveal about contemporary attitudes and debates about children.

The ways in which these implicit pictures have effects upon how the service provision is structured and delivered has been undertaken by examining the ways in which the documents formulate:

- how children relate to their family, the community they live in and to the state;

- how children's relationship to concepts such as need, rights and risk are seen;

- whether and how children are seen as investment; and

- how difference is seen.

The chapter has illustrated that behind or contained within every document are ideas about these four areas. These are often less explicit than the overt focus of any proposal – but, by developing the pictures as shown, we can see them and so begin to understand how they fuel and drive the ideas and approach. The chapter has illustrated why we should never take any proposal relating to children at face value. It is important to learn to see the pictures contained within and behind any initiative, which is what this chapter has helped the reader to do: to begin to identify the pictures of children within such proposals and initiatives and to see how they might affect children's lives.

Annotated reading

Coleman, S. and Rowe, C. (2005) *Remixing Citizenship: Democracy and Young People's Use of the Internet*, London: Carnegie Young People's Initiative Publication

A summary and analysis of young people's ideas about government, participation in democracy and new technology.

Hidden Lives revealed: A Virtual Archive <http://www.hiddenlives.org.uk>

This contains material relating to children in care during the period 1881–1918. It includes a mixture of anonymous case files of individual children along with examples of relevant handbooks and magazines, such as 'Our Waifs and Strays', from the period covered.

The Children's Society website at <http://www.the-childrens-society.org.uk>

The site includes material on the political process from a child rights' perspective. It includes sections on parliamentary lobbying, briefings, current campaigns and on ways of becoming involved.

Service, Provision and Policy

What is the aim of Part II?

Part II of the book contains discussion of diverse areas of provision and policy related to children and childhood, reflecting the multi-agency nature of the services that shape their lives. The critical themes introduced in Part I of the book enable a rich evaluation of children's services. All the themes raised in the first part of the book are drawn on differently by authors in Part II to raise questions about particular areas.

Guide to reading Part II

The chapters in Part II can be read independently or in relation to any of the Part I or Part III chapters. Part I chapters help to identify general questions, and Part II chapters reflect these differently in specific areas of service provision. Reading chapters from both parts together provides a richer picture of the wide range of influences on children's services. Each chapter in Part II has a different emphasis, but read together and alongside Part I chapters they demonstrate a range of rich, diverse and critical questions to draw on when evaluating areas of children's services. Part III can also be read in conjunction with Part II as it provides case examples of policy and practice.

Links To Part I		Links To Part III
	Chapter 6 Education: Service or System?	
Chapter 2 Childhood: Rights and Realities Chapter 3 The Politics of Childhood	This chapter considers how the system in England is organised and why and how this might lead to problems and might be different.	Chapter 14 The Swings and Roundabouts of Community Development Chapter 18 The Venture
	Chapter 7 Youth Services and Provision	
Chapter 2 Childhood: Rights and Realities Chapter 3 The Politics of Childhood Chapter 4 The Social Divisions of Childhood Chapter 5 Pictures of Children	This chapter is about services for young people in the UK and the policies which influence their development.	Chapter 14 The Swings and Roundabouts of Community Development Chapter 17 Educating Refugee Children Chapter 18 The Venture
	Chapter 8 Provision for Child Health	
Chapter 2 Childhood: Rights and Realities Chapter 3 The Politics of Childhood Chapter 4 The Social Divisions of Childhood	This chapter explores service provision for child health in the UK context, exploring different concepts, dimensions and models of health and the factors influencing and affecting the health of children and young people.	Chapter 16 The Anna Rebecca Gray Interviews Chapter 17 Educating Refugee Children
	Chapter 9 Children Who Offend	
Chapter 2 Childhood: Rights and Realities Chapter 3 The Politics of Childhood Chapter 4 The Social Divisions of Childhood Chapter 5 Pictures of Children	This chapter considers services and provision for children who offend, examining how children's behaviour comes to be defined as crime and what factors shape social ideas about crime and childhood.	Chapter 14 The Swings and Roundabouts of Community Development Chapter 18 The Venture

Chapter 10 Safeguarding Children

This chapter examines the notion of safeguarding children within the context of major legislative and policy change.

Chapter 2 Childhood: Rights and Realities

Chapter 3 The Politics of Childhood

Chapter 4 The Social Divisions of Childhood

Chapter 5 Pictures of Children

Chapter 17 Educating Refugee Children

Chapter 11 Day Care Services for Children

This chapter considers what is meant by child care and the thinking underpinning the expansion of child care provision.

Chapter 2 Childhood: Rights and Realities

Chapter 3 The Politics of Childhood

Chapter 17 Educating Refugee Children

Chapter 12 Services to Children's Play

This chapter highlights the importance of play for children and the consequent importance of making adequate provision for children's play.

Chapter 2 Childhood: Rights and Realities

Chapter 5 Pictures of Children

Chapter 16 The Anna Rebecca Gray Interviews

Chapter 13 Children's Experience of Community Regeneration

This chapter explores a central theme of social inclusion: the neighbourhood regeneration agenda.

Chapter 2 Childhood: Rights and Realities

Chapter 4 The Social Divisions of Childhood

Chapter 5 Pictures of Children

Chapter 14 The Swings and Roundabouts of Community Development

Chapter 6

Education: Service or System?

SUE WELCH

Before he was first elected Prime Minister in May 1997, Tony Blair was proud to announce (several times) that 'education, education, education' would be the top three priorities of a New Labour administration.

(Chitty, 2004, p. 1)

We have a bloody state system I wish we hadn't got . . . We've got compulsory education, which is a responsibility of hideous importance, and we tyrannise children to do that which they don't want, and we don't produce results.

(Sir Keith Joseph, former Conservative Secretary of State for Education
in an interview reported in Chitty, 1997, p. 80)

Introduction

These two quotations indicate contrasting commitments to the role of the state in providing education and hint at some of the difficulties that governments that take on this responsibility might face. This chapter is meant to help you to understand some of the decisions that have been made in order to produce the education system that we have and how, as Sir Keith points out, it affects the lives of children. There are many aspects of educational policy that could be covered here: the market-led nature of the education system; the structure of the education system; school starting and leaving ages; the relationship between private and public schooling; the place of religion in education;

whether there should be special schools and what the role of local authorities should be are some examples. While some of these are referred to, the main focus of this chapter is what and how children are taught. This has been chosen because it has the most immediate effect on children's experience and because it serves as an example of the tensions that exist in the system as a whole. It also focuses on the English education system as an example of thinking that can be compared with education systems in other parts of the UK and in other countries.

The whole of this book is concerned with services for children and we often talk about the 'Education Service' which suggests that what is provided for children should serve children by being responsive to their needs and rights. The term used throughout this chapter will be 'education system' as, as the title suggests, it questions whether children or indeed society as a whole, are served by what happens to children in schools.

This chapter considers how the system in England is organised and why and how this might lead to problems by considering the following questions

- What are children's rights to education internationally?

- Why do we need an education system?

- What has shaped the current system in England?

- What view of children and childhood underpins the system?

- How might it be different?

What are children's rights to education internationally?

The importance of education for children is enshrined in the 1989 United Nations Convention on the Rights of the Child. Article 28 identifies children's right to education and this puts a duty on all the states that have signed the convention to provide free, compulsory primary education and different forms of secondary education. Article 29 goes on to identify that this education should be directed towards:

More detailed discussion of children's rights can be found in Chapter 2, Childhood: Rights and Realities.

- the development of the child's personality, talents, and mental and physical abilities to their fullest potential;

- the development of respect for human rights and fundamental freedoms, and for the principles enshrined in the Charter of the United Nations;

- the development of respect for the child's parents, his or her own cultural identity, language and values, for the national values of the country in which the child is living; the country from which he or she may originate, and for civilisations different from his or her own;

- the preparation of the child for responsible life in a free society, in the spirit of understanding, peace, tolerance, equality of sexes and friendship among all peoples, ethnic, national and religious groups and persons of indigenous origin;

- the development of respect for the natural environment.

There are some important indications here of why the UN thinks education is important. First, it is clear from Article 28 that education is important for the individual so he or she can develop fully. However, the points in Article 29 are concerned with the child's place in the family, community and the rest of society and they identify the values that the UN consider important for children to develop. So it is clear that education is important not just for the child but also for the whole of society. In fact it is so important that the convention suggests that it shouldn't be left to parents or family to provide: the state needs to provide education and make at least primary education compulsory. The compulsory nature of this right is unusual. Having a legal right to something means that an individual has an entitlement to access, for example, the service of doctors and hospitals, monetary benefits, adequate shelter. But there is no compulsion to take up this access. The compulsory nature of primary education in the Convention may be there to ensure that parents or caretakers don't prevent children from accessing education. An alternative explanation may be that becoming educated is also seen as a duty because the Convention identifies the benefits to society as a whole, not just to the individual. In either case, this compulsion does create a different context to the idea of education as a right. Chapter 2 emphasised the need to look at the provision of the Convention as a whole and in this circumstance perhaps it is important to remember that under the Convention children have a right to participate in decisions that affect their lives and should therefore be very much involved in decisions about how they are educated when that education is compulsory.

Issues around educational provision and the degree to which the aspirations of the UN are met vary from country to country. Economically developing countries and countries at war struggle to provide free education for all children even at primary level when priority is given to building or rebuilding an economic infrastructure and when children need to work for their own and their families' survival. Figure 6.1 is a graph from Global Education Digest (2004, p. 25) accessed from http://www.uis.unesco.org/ev which shows the inequalities in access to education across the world.

The main barrier to education in these countries is poverty and this is sometimes compounded by cultural beliefs that consider girls and children from particular social and ethnic groups to be of low status and not worthy of being educated (UNICEF, 2003).

Within this context it is easy to think that England is doing well: there is free compulsory education for 5- to 16-year-olds and additionally, free provision for 3- to 5-year-olds and 16- to 18-year-olds who want to take advantage of these opportunities. However, as identified in Chapter 4, The Social Divisions of Childhood, there are children who are excluded from the education system and others who have access to the system but are seen to be failures. It is clear that barriers to education are not confined to developing countries: poverty, gender and cultural background have all been shown to impact on educational attainment.

Figure 6.1 How close is the world to reaching universal primary education? Distribution of national primary net enrolment rates by income group and region, 2001.

UNESCO Institute for Statistics, Table 3.

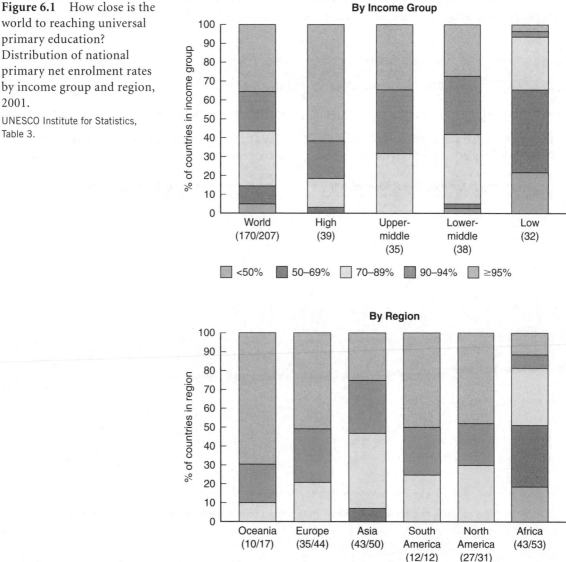

Why do we need an education system?

You might think there is an obvious answer to this question: something like 'to educate children'. However, 'education' in its broadest sense can refer to all the things we learn through interactions with others in our daily activities, such as learning how to talk, how to relate to other people, how to use equipment. What we are concerned about here is why we need to have something that is provided by the state that goes beyond this informal education.

You might have identified a number of things in the 'formal education' column that are to do with subjects such as geography, music or maths that might be difficult to learn through everyday interactions with others. But why are these things seen to be important and who decides what is important to learn?

At the beginning of this section we saw that the 1989 UNCRC identifies the purpose of the education system as two-fold: for the benefit of the individual child and for the benefit of the wider society. This might seem quite straightforward, but there are some difficulties in interpretation. First, there is a tension between the individual child and the rest of society. In Chapter 2, Childhood: Rights and Realities, we found that one of the ways we think about childhood is as a time of preparation for becoming an adult. The education

Reflective Activity 6.1

What happens in the formal education system?

1 Think about learning that takes place within the formal education system and the learning that takes place in everyday life and list the things that occur to you in the table below.

Learning in the formal education system	Learning in everyday life

2 Look at these carefully and think about which things could only occur in the formal education system.

system has to consider the balance between supporting each child as an individual who has unique potential, with its attempts at moulding him or her into the adult that the rest of society needs them to be.

Secondly, there is a difficulty in deciding what sort of society is envisaged so the education system can prepare children appropriately: should we be trying to maintain society as it is or should we be looking for future change? In this section we will look at these tensions in more detail.

Bottery (1990) identifies four different models of education that can help us to think about these issues.

The four models are:

- child-centred model;
- gross national product (GNP) model;
- cultural-transmission model;
- social-reconstruction model.

The main features and criticisms of these are summarised in Table 6.1. You can see that there are good reasons for each model and each has something to offer, but reliance on one would ignore the balance that is needed between the individual and society, and

Table 6.1 Bottery's Models of Education

Model	Main features	Criticisms
Child-centred model	The main concern of education is the individual child. The interests and experiences of children are the starting points of what they should learn. Future society will take care of itself.	Leaving children to develop 'naturally' is irresponsible. Focusing on a child's interests is likely to produce a very narrow curriculum. All children's actions would be seen as equally valuable, e.g. helping others and stealing. It ignores the needs of society.
Cultural-transmission model	A core of beliefs, values and knowledge needs to be passed on to the next generation. Education is the mechanism to make sure that all children learn to appreciate this 'cultural heritage'.	It assumes that beliefs, values and knowledge are unchanging. It assumes that everyone agrees on what beliefs, values and knowledge is important. It assumes the child will passively accept what he or she is taught. It ignores the interests of the child.
Social-reconstruction model	Education should encourage a critical appreciation of current society so it remains stable but also changes. Individuals are active in changing society.	Teachers have a great responsibility because there is no set curriculum. It might encourage too much change. Danger of elitism because teachers have so much power.
GNP (gross national product) model	Education trains individuals into their roles in an industrial, technological, consumer society. Individuals need to be trained to fit into the needs of the economy (some as managers, some as inventors, some as workers, etc.).	Ignores the interests of the individual. Only the values and heritage that advance the economy would be considered to be important. Assumes that we live in an ideal society which needs to be perpetuated.

Source: Bottery (1990).

Reflective Activity 6.2

Trying out the models

1 Look at these statements and identify which of Bottery's models they might be associated with:

A. Pupils must acquire skills that will equip them to earn a living when they leave school.

B. Those in authority in schools should decide how and why pupils are disciplined.

C. In a rapidly changing world there is no point in passing on knowledge and values that have been established in the past.

D. Children should be given their own choice of what to study.

E. Schools should be accountable to society for what they produce. It is possible to measure what is produced objectively.

F. Learning should be an active social process which is guided by teachers.

G. Within school the interests and the needs of children are paramount.

H. Some kinds of knowledge have more value and are more important than other kinds.

A and E are associated with the GNP model

B and H are associated with the cultural-transmission model

C and F are associated with the social-construction model

D and G are associated with the child-centred model

If you got any of these wrong, go back to look at the summaries of the different models or read Bottery (1990) Chapter 1 for further descriptions.

between maintaining society as it is and embracing the need to change.

Each of the models takes a particular view of the child and childhood so, while Bottery advocates an education service that incorporates all models, there may be difficulties in doing this because of the different ways of viewing children.

In Chapter 2, Childhood: Rights and Realities, we considered different ways of viewing children and childhood and within this there was discussion of the child as an agent in shaping his or her experiences. This view of the child is integral to the child-centred model and the social-reconstruction model where children are active in deciding what to study and, in the social-reconstruction model, in shaping society. However, in the other two models the child is seen as passively responding to what is taught.

The different models also have different views about the kind of knowledge that is valued, the type of society that is envisaged and the relationship between school and society. All of these will lead to different reasons for having an education system and this will lead to different ways of designing and implementing the system. The next section draws out some of the thinking behind the current educational system in England.

What has shaped the current system in England?

The current system of education in England has been shaped by what went before so, in this section, we will look at how thinking about education and children has changed, reflecting Bottery's different models.

The key dates and changes can be seen in the Table 6.2.

Prior to 1870, education was restricted to those who could pay for it. The very clear division of society through a hierarchical class system where the lower classes 'knew their place' and respected those in authority needed to be maintained. The poor were uneducated unless they attended voluntary schools, which were run mainly by churches, and, as Chitty (2004) points out, were intended to train the poor for 'industry and piety' (for hard work and goodness) rather than reading and writing. This illustrates one of the tensions that has never been completely resolved: the need to provide education to ensure that children learn the values of society and skills for employment but not 'over educating' them so their raised aspirations lead to social unrest.

Industrial changes and social change during the early 19th century led to the 1870 Forster Education Act where state funding provided a minimal education for as little as possible for the majority of children. At the same time, in contrast, male children of the rich were educated in public schools in the classics and sporting activities, developing qualities that would fit

Table 6.2   Key Dates in the English Education System

Date	Key change	Main effects
Early 19th century	Factory Acts of 1833, 1844 and 1867.	These restricted the use of child labour so children needed to be prepared for the roles they would shortly undertake through a minimal education.
1870	Forster Education Act.	State funding provided minimal education for the majority of children. Children went to school rather than work. Education focused on preparation for their role as workers who would accept the prevailing social order.
1931	Hadow Report.	Suggested education should focus on experiences rather than knowledge. Although there wasn't any implementation at the time this influenced the Plowden Report in 1967.
1940s	Second World War.	Upset the social hierarchy and pointed to the deficiencies in education.
1944	Education Act.	This set up a national system of education for children aged 5–14 with an exam at 11 that determined what sort of secondary education was appropriate: grammar schools concentrated on academic education; technical schools concentrated on preparing students for skilled 'blue collar' work; secondary modern schools prepared children with practical manual skills for work.
1960s	A period of relative prosperity.	More liberal attitudes towards many areas of social life and a weakening in the hierarchical structure.
1967	Plowden Report on Primary Education.	Emphasised the need for a child-centred curriculum that catered for individuals.
Early 1970s	A period of economic decline.	Concern that children were not being educated to prepare them for the needs of the workforce and for their place in society.
1976	James Callaghan's speech at Ruskin College.	Challenged the validity of the curriculum and the degree of control that teachers had over what was taught.
1988	Education Reform Act.	The introduction of grant-maintained schools with funding from the government. The introduction of local management of schools (LMS). The introduction of the national curriculum (NC). Testing of children at the end of each Key Stage.
Post-1997	A plethora of initiatives such as literacy and numeracy strategies; the foundation stage curriculum; revised national curriculum.	Increasing control over what is taught and how it is taught.

them for their roles as leaders and landowners; female children of the rich were privately educated in areas that would prepare them to be wives, managing the household and entertaining husband and guests. Education then mirrored and perpetuated the hierarchical class structure of society and ensured that children were educated for the roles they would be expected to undertake. The academic focus for the rich contrasted with the moral and vocational focus for the poor.

Reflective Activity 6.3

Trying out the models

Which of Bottery's models do you think this approach reflects?

The focus on fitting children for their place in society, both socially and economically, is in line with the cultural-transmission and GNP models of the purposes of education. Education for the needs of individuals wasn't a consideration, although, by the time of the Hadow Report on Primary Education in 1931, there was more of a sense that the experience of education should be positive for the individual as well as for society, and that the curriculum should focus on experiences rather than knowledge and facts. However, these ideas didn't get implemented until much later.

Further changes to the economic and social structure of society, including two world wars and the extension of the vote to the poor and to women, pointed to the need to have educated voters as well as a need for relevant skills for an increasingly technical workforce and national defence. The 1944 Education Act made the assumption that children would have a particular aptitude that could be assessed at 11 and that the different types of education would be 'appropriate to age, ability and aptitude'. While education had been extended into secondary education the belief that children needed to be prepared for their future roles was still very evident. However, the roles weren't to be predetermined by class divisions but by intelligence and aptitude. The distinction between an academic education and a vocational education persisted in the

different types of school. While this system still had a cultural-transmission focus, the GNP model was becoming increasingly evident through the emphasis on preparation for work.

During the 1960s a number of factors contributed to some important changes in the education system. Academic disciplines such as sociology and psychology challenged the validity of a society that was based on a hierarchical class structure and the validity of being able to select students for future roles at the age of 11. An ideal of a society where everyone had an equal opportunity to achieve through the education system became prevalent. Consequently a move towards a single system of secondary education began: the majority of secondary schools became comprehensive and the 11 plus examination was abolished in most LEAs.

Chitty (2004) identifies that the context of economic prosperity and general optimism in the 1960s not only affected the move towards a comprehensive secondary system of education but also affected what was happening in primary schools. The 1967 Plowden Report on Primary Education, strongly influenced by developmental psychology, built on the earlier Hadow Report and took a very child-centred view of what should be happening in schools. It suggested a curriculum that was based on individual needs and interests and more individualised teaching.

The influence of the Plowden Report depended very much on individual teachers, schools and LEAs and it was interpreted in different ways in different schools: many still reflected a more traditional approach to the curriculum and teaching that was more in line with the cultural-transmission and GNP models. However, with the abolition of the 11 plus examination in most areas there was much less pressure in most primary schools to stick to a rigid curriculum that would be tested: teachers were very much in control of the curriculum in primary schools. However, this more child-centred model of education, which was only really implemented in a few areas, was short-lived.

Chapter 3, The Politics of Childhood, explains how economic factors influence policies concerning children.

This was evident in the different economic climate of the late 1960s and the 1970s when there was concern that the more child-centred approach to education wasn't adequately preparing children with the knowledge and skills necessary to work in an increasingly technological and rapidly changing economy, and that respect for authority and moral values was diminishing. This was first indicated in Prime Minister James Callaghan's speech at Ruskin College:

> The balance was wrong in the past. We have a responsibility now to see that we do not get it wrong again in the other direction. There is no virtue in producing socially well-adjusted members of society who are unemployed because they do not have the skills. Nor at the other extreme must they be technically efficient robots.　　(Callaghan, 1976)

He went on to question whether current teaching methods and content of the curriculum were producing what was needed and pointed to the large resources that were going into the education system. These concerns, and concerns about the powerful role of the teacher in deciding what and how to teach without a clear system of accountability, ultimately led to a massive reform of the system in the 1988 Education Reform Act.

The ambivalence of governments towards having a state system of education is clear from Keith Joseph's 1981 comments at the beginning of the chapter and is possibly responsible for the emphasis on accountability that was a key feature of the 1988 Education Reform Act. If the state has to provide education through public funding (and this was increasingly difficult to revoke as the population began to see education as a right, but they also wanted to know how their taxes were being used) then, in order to make sure that money is being used appropriately, there need to be measurable outcomes that can be monitored. The structure of the National Curriculum sets very clear expectations of what children should learn in the form of a ladder of 'levels of attainment'.

Through local management of schools, individual schools took more control of their budgets and budgets were tied to the number of children in the school. In this way schools were intended to become more accountable to parents as parental choice of school would directly influence the school's budget. Through publication of the results of testing children's attainment against the National Curriculum standards parents would have information to guide their choice of school. As parents moved their children away from 'poor schools' to 'better schools' the poor schools would wither away and the better schools would grow. Thus accountability was linked to the idea of a market economy in the education system. The GNP and cultural-transmission models were very much in evidence here.

By 1997 when New Labour came into power these ways of working were entrenched and the new government did nothing to change matters although the rhetoric of the time indicated a much stronger commitment to a state-funded education system and a commitment to social justice through education, emphasising the potential of the education system to diminish the inequalities within society. This might have indicated a move towards a social-reconstruction model of education with education seen to be a vehicle for changing society. However, this would require a much less rigid and centralised curriculum. Since 1997 there have been further indications of central control over not just the curriculum but also the methods of teaching.

Although education now is very different to the system that existed in the 18th century, the tensions that have shaped the developing system are still apparent and continue to be the focus of debate:

- Should education be the same for all children?
- How far should education be for the benefit of society and how far should it be for the benefit of the child?
- What sort of balance should there be between academic and vocational and personal aspects of education?
- Can education solve the problems of society?
- How can the system be made accountable for the resources that are spent?

Although the strong cultural-transmission model of pre-1870 has diminished, this is still an influence alongside a much stronger GNP model. The next section will look more closely at current policy to identify what the current situation is.

What thinking underpins the current system in England?

Nowhere in policy documents does it suggest directly what sort of model is being aimed for in England, but we can find clues in the aims and values outlined in the policy documents, in the content of the National Curriculum and the implementation of the policies. Bottery's models guide us to the sort of things that we can look for: the knowledge that is valued, the society that is aimed for and the role of the teacher and the view of the child.

What do the aims and values of the National Curriculum tell us?

The National Curriculum aims are meant to feed into the aims of the 1988 Education Act. The two National Curriculum aims are:

- The school curriculum should aim to provide opportunities for all pupils to learn and to achieve.

- The school curriculum should aim to promote pupils' spiritual, moral, social and cultural development, and prepare all pupils for the opportunities, responsibilities and experiences of life.   (QCA, 2000, p. 11)

It is clear from these aims that both the individual and society are to benefit from the education system. They suggest that it is trying to provide a balance between supporting the development of each child as an individual (child-centred model) with making sure they will be prepared for life in society as an adult (GNP, cultural-transmission and social-reconstruction models). The further detail of the aims gives indications that the purpose for education fits in with the different models. Table 6.3 gives extracts from the detail of the National Curriculum and identifies how they fit with the four models.

The society that is aimed for is evidently one where there is cohesion and acceptance of difference, where everyone contributes for the benefit of all and where everyone is valued.

While there is a good deal here about passing on values and cultural heritage the values and heritage are very different to the pre-1870 model. They are broader and accept that there might be differences in values. A later section of the National Curriculum goes on to identify the values that the government believe are accepted by all of society under the following main headings.

- *The self*: We value ourselves as unique human beings capable of spiritual, moral, intellectual and physical growth and development.

- *Relationships*: We value others for themselves, not only for what they have or what they can do for us. We value relationships as fundamental to the development and fulfilment of ourselves and others, and to the good of the community.

- *Society*: We value truth, freedom, justice, human rights, the rule of law and collective effort for the common good. In particular, we value families as sources of love and support for all their members, and as the basis of a society in which people care for others.

- *The environment*: We value the environment, both natural and shaped by humanity, as the basis of life and a source of wonder and inspiration.

Similarly the aims associated with the GNP model are not based on a hierarchical system of fitting pupils to different types of job. The difficulty for government policy here is that the comprehensive system of education is meant to enable all children to achieve as much as possible. The government is also viewing education as a key element of its fight against poverty. However,

See Chapter 3, The Politics of Childhood, for further discussion of this.

the economic system needs workers with differing skills and some workers who are willing to do the most menial tasks, which are also low paid and unattractive. As well as passive workers the workforce also requires people who are creative, questioning and flexible to deal with the constantly changing economic circumstances. The current education system is challenged by keeping the principle of equality of opportunity with the idea of achieving such different outcomes. There is clearly a tension between the needs of a market-driven

Table 6.3 Bottery's Models and the National Curriculum

Model	Extracts from the National Curriculum (QCA, 2000)
Cultural-transmission model	Sense of identity through knowledge and understanding of the spiritual, moral, social and cultural heritages of Britain's diverse society and of the local, national, European, Commonwealth and global dimensions of their lives.
	Appreciate human aspirations and achievements in aesthetic, scientific, technological and social fields, and prompt a personal response to a range of experiences and ideas.
	Develop physical skills and encourage recognition of the importance of pursuing a healthy lifestyle and keeping themselves and others safe.
	Develop principles for distinguishing between right and wrong.
	Knowledge, understanding and appreciation of their own and different beliefs and cultures, and how these influence individuals and societies.
	Pass on enduring values.
	Awareness and understanding of, and respect for, the environments in which they live, and secure their commitment to sustainable development at a personal, local, national and global level.
GNP model	Skills of literacy, numeracy, and information and communication technology.
	Creative, innovative, enterprising and capable of leadership to equip them for their future lives as workers and citizens.
	Equip pupils as consumers to make informed judgements and independent decisions and to understand their responsibilities and rights.
	Respond positively to opportunities, challenges and responsibilities, to manage risk and to cope with change and adversity.
	Prepare pupils for the next steps in their education, training and employment.
Child-centred model	Enjoyment of, and commitment to learning.
	Confidence in their capacity to learn and work independently and collaboratively.
	Promote pupils' self-esteem and emotional well-being.
	Respond positively to opportunities, challenges and responsibilities, to manage risk and to cope with change and adversity.
Social-reconstruction model	Enquiring mind and capacity to think rationally.
	Think creatively and critically, to solve problems and to make a difference for the better.
	Develop pupils' integrity and autonomy and help them to be responsible and caring citizens capable of contributing to the development of a just society.
	Challenge discrimination and stereotyping.

economy and the kind of society that is suggested in the aims of the National Curriculum and the government's commitment to reduce poverty. However, nowhere in the aims does it suggest that children should be gaining skills that will enable and encourage them to critically consider alternatives to this current system (social-reconstruction model). While the document acknowledges the changing nature of society, reaffirmed in the foreword to the 2001 White Paper, *Schools Achieving Success*, that education needs to 'meet the demands of a fast-changing world' (DfES, 2001, p. 3), this is in relation to responding to society not being instrumental to that change. The aims that are consistent with the social-reconstruction model are about contributing to the nature of society as it is currently. Similarly, the child-centred elements of the aims don't acknowledge children's agency in determining their own present and future.

So the aims and values can be associated with all four of Bottery's models but in a way that doesn't challenge the existing nature of society in terms of the market-led, consumer-driven economy and the associated hierarchical structure of wealth and status. The situation is further complicated if we look at the content of the curriculum and how this contributes to the expressed aims and values.

What does the content of the curriculum tell us?

Tables 6.4 and 6.5 show what the National Curriculum and Foundation Stage Curriculum require to be taught at different stages.

While all areas are given equal priority in the Foundation Stage there are some subjects, the core subjects of English, maths and science, that are given higher priority in the National Curriculum. It is also interesting that personal, social and health education is non-statutory in the National Curriculum after being an important part of the Foundation Stage Curriculum. Conversely, citizenship, sex education and work-related learning don't have a focus until children are 11 or 14. Only the three core subjects, ICT, PE and religious

Reflective Activity 6.4

The content of the National Curriculum

Look at the table identifying the content of the National Curriculum.

Look at the aims of the National Curriculum.

How far do you think the content of the curricula leads to the identified aims and values?

education continue throughout all four Key Stages with roots in the Foundation Stage Curriculum. These priorities might give some indication of the knowledge that is valued.

One of the early criticisms of the National Curriculum from O'Hear and White (1993) was the lack of coherence between the aims and the content of the National Curriculum. Because there isn't a clear relationship between them there may be mixed messages about what the government believes the education system is for. While the aims suggest a balance amongst the models the content gives a different picture. For example, there isn't a clear association between the subjects studied and the skills needed as an employee: a reflection of the tension between the academic and vocational purposes of education. A further criticism points to the lack of acknowledgement of the broad nature of society in the content of the individual subjects. Later versions have made some attempts to

Table 6.4   The Foundation Stage Curriculum

Area of Learning	Links with NC subjects
Personal, social and emotional development	PSHE, citizenship, religious education
Communication, language and literacy	English
Mathematical development	Mathematics
Knowledge and understanding of the world	Science, DT, ICT, history, geography, religious education
Physical development	PE
Creative development	DT, art and design, music, PE

Table 6.5 The National Curriculum

		Key Stage 1 Reception, Years 1–2 (children aged 5–7)	Key Stage 2 Years 3–6 (children aged 7–11)	Key Stage 3 Years 7–9 (children aged 11–14)	Key Stage 4 Years 10–11 (children aged 14–16)
Core subjects	English	S	S	S	S
	Maths	S	S	S	S
	Science	S	S	S	S
Non-core foundation subjects	DT	S	S	S	
	ICT	S	S	S	S
	History	S	S	S	
	Geography	S	S	S	
	Modern foreign languages			S	
	Art and design	S	S	S	
	Music	S	S	S	
	PE	S	S	S	S
	Citizenship			S	S
	Religious education	S	S	S	S
	Careers education			S	S
	Sex education			S	S
	Work-related learning				S
	Personal, social and health education	N	N	N	N

S = Statutory
N = Non-statutory

address this, but there is still a sense that there is one version of history, art, music, etc., that should be passed on to children in contrast to the aims. The low priority of personal, social and health education and the lack of citizenship at the early stages of education also provide a mismatch with the many aims of the curriculum to do with personal development and becoming part of society. The addition of Citizenship to Key Stages 3 and 4 in 2000 was a response to concerns that young people showed a lack of engagement with the political process and should therefore have a better understanding of the political process and their roles as future citizens. It is noticeable here that the documents talk about children as future not current citizens and children under 11 are not included even in this respect. This is in keeping with the lack of a child-centred approach in the content of the curriculum, which therefore is seen to be more clearly linked with cultural-transmission and GNP models of education and with a focus on specific knowledge rather than the broad aims.

What can the implementation of the curricula tell us?

The implementation of the Foundation Stage Curriculum and the National Curriculum in practice is influenced very strongly by associated policies that stress the accountability of teachers and schools.

The 'ladder' of increasing knowledge and skill is based on the assumption that children, if taught efficiently, will move smoothly up the steps of the ladder. If they don't, then the implication is that they haven't been taught properly or that they are deficient in some way. There is no suggestion that the ladder might be inappropriate or that children might respond in individual ways based on their interests and motivations. Although the National Curriculum only set out to identify what should be taught, not how, pressure on schools and, in particular, teachers of children at the end of Key Stages increased markedly after the introduction of testing and the promotion of league tables. Although the National Curriculum promoted a broad and balanced curriculum, the effects of testing and league tables coupled with parental choice and funding, following children to the school they enrolled in, led to concentration on teaching the core subjects of the National Curriculum and making sure children did well in the tests. The National Literacy Strategy and the National Numeracy Strategy (DfEE, 1998b+c) further restricted decisions that are made by teachers. Foundation subjects in primary schools became squeezed into a small proportion of time and non-statutory elements were virtually ignored. This view of the passivity of children and the role of teacher as implementer of policy are very much in keeping with the GNP and cultural-transmission models of education and at odds with the child-centred and social-reconstruction models. So the aims of the National Curriculum are at odds with the content and structure of the prescribed curricula and the influencing structures around it. How can the centralised system that expects children to climb the rungs of the National Curriculum ladder in the right order at the right time also create questioning, creative flexible individuals?

Chitty (2004, p. 203) summarises Broadfoot's suggestion (2001) that the following current beliefs about the education system need to be challenged:

- Decisions concerning curriculum (inputs), pedagogy process and assessment (outcomes) should be centralised.

- There are standards of 'quality' that can be objectively measured.

- It is necessary and desirable to assess institutional quality according to externally defined 'performance indicators'.

- Punitive use of league tables and other publicly shaming devices will help to drive up educational performance.

- Assessment is a 'neutral' measuring instrument which requires only further technical development to make it more effective.

Current consultation on the future of the curriculum (QCA, 2005) identifies the following changes as being important:

- changes in society and the nature of work;
- the impact of technology;
- new understanding about learning;
- the need for greater personalisation and innovation;
- the increasing international dimension to life and work.

It goes on to identify the challenges:

- How effectively do subjects contribute to the wider aims, purposes and values of education?

- How do subjects need to evolve to respond to the challenges of life and work in the 21st century?

- How well does each subject exploit the potential of technology to support its aims?

- Does its use reflect practice in the wider world?

- How might we organise the national entitlement to deliver the curriculum's aims, purposes and values more effectively?

- Are the flexibilities of the current national frameworks sufficient to guarantee a good match between curriculum aims, design and delivery?

- Do we need to explore new ways of describing national entitlement?

- How can we adequately define future learner needs across subject boundaries?

- While there is broad consensus about the wider aims and purposes of the curriculum, are these aims sufficiently embedded into our accountability and assessment systems?

- How do we ensure that measures of performance are sufficiently wide to guarantee a broad and balanced learning agenda?

- How can we ensure that what we assess keeps up to date with what we want learners to know, do and understand in a rapidly changing world?

- What are the benefits and risks associated with e-learning and e-assessment?

Here there is an indication that the government does accept some of Broadfoot's criticisms and understands the effects that the current 'top down' approach might be having. However, there is no mention about changing views of children and childhood.

What view of children and childhood underpins this system?

In Chapter 2 there were three areas of tension identified in the way we construct childhood and view children:

- Childhood as important in itself versus childhood as preparation for adulthood

- Children as vulnerable people versus children as capable

- Children as victims versus children as villains

Underlying both the GNP and cultural-transmission models, which are very prominent within the National Curriculum and the structures around it, is the notion of the passive child and the view of childhood as preparation for adulthood. As long as children do as they are told they will go through the system smoothly and come out as an acceptable adult.

Linked with this is the assumption that children don't or won't learn unless their learning is clearly directed by adults and they are made to attend school: a view of children as vulnerable but also potential villains.

Other aspects of policy also indicate a perception of childhood as being of low status and a time of preparation for adulthood. Instances of this relate to the relationship that schools have with parents. In the market-led education system devised under the Education Reform Act (1988) focus is on the parent as the consumer of education and schools as the providers of education. Children, who actually experience being in school, are not seen as the consumers! The accountability of teachers and schools, which is such an important feature of the current system, is directed towards parents rather than children, but even then the accountability is on the government's terms as it centres round the testing of the core curriculum.

This view of children is in line with the passivity expressed in the cultural-transmission and the GNP models of education but is at odds with current sociological ideas (e.g. James and James, 2004) about the agency of children and psychological theories (e.g. Bruner, 1996) about how children learn through active participation. There is consequently a dilemma for governments that need to ensure that teachers and schools are accountable and that children learn. If they acknowledge that children learn best when they are engaged and active, the curriculum would need to be flexible to allow for children's interests and motivations. The curriculum would be much more centred on children as children rather than future adults or citizens. In order to teach, teachers would need to understand children and be responsive to their ways of thinking and learning. This would require more autonomy in making decisions about what to teach and how. By going down the 'accountability' route the policy is in danger of confounding its aims.

The perception of childhood and children as passive preparation for adulthood is also at odds with some of the more recent policy initiatives such as citizenship education (although this doesn't start until KS3), *Excellence and Enjoyment* (DfES, 2003d), the *Primary Strategy* (DfES, 2004e), *Every Child*

> Chapter 5, Pictures of Children, will also help you to think about the pictures of children that are seen in these documents.

Matters (DfES, 2003b) and *Every Child Matters: Next Steps* (DfES, 2004c). These identify children as active, creative, capable learners who need to be involved in their own learning as part of a process that takes place in and out of school. There is also an acknowledgement that children are individuals in their own right not just future adults. It seems that another view of the child may be emerging but the ladder still remains and attainment is still measured through narrow tests.

How does this affect children?

The underpinning thinking about the purposes of education and the view of childhood and children affects what happens in classrooms on a day-to-day basis so we will go on to consider what these effects might be.

Many children enjoy going to school and learn and develop through the experiences they have there. Unfortunately this isn't the case for all children and this section looks at how the current education context might be having a negative effect on children's lives.

For teachers to get children to the appropriate level they need children who conform, who will fit into the plans for the day and respond in ways that are expected: the passive children that are assumed in the curriculum structure. James and James (2004) point out that one of the ways children are able to express their agency is by

Reflective Activity 6.5

The child's experience of the curriculum

Consider what it might be like for a child in school where teachers are under pressure to make sure that children meet the required standards in the national tests for maths, English and science.

1   What sort of choice might you have during the course of the day in what you do?

2   How would you feel if you really enjoyed creative things like painting, dance and music?

3   How might teachers respond if you said you didn't want to do maths?

not conforming. Not completing work, not engaging in activities that are unappealing and not attending are all ways of doing this, but these all cause problems for teachers.

Christensen and James (2001), researching children's attitudes to school, found a common feature of children's responses was that school was boring and tiring, captured in this response from a 10-year-old girl:

> 'It's just non-stop working and you're just going like this' (she sighs deeply) 'and just writing every day and it just gets real boring and sometimes you think, God, can't we have a week off or something? Cos it gets really tiring. . . . Sometimes, when it's boring it just feels as though the day's never gonna end'.
> (p. 70)

For children aged 3–5, up to the end of the reception year there is a slightly different picture. The curriculum guidance for the Foundation Stage (QA, 2000) identifies the need for child- as well as adult-initiated activities. However, there are still targets to be met at the end of the Foundation Stage and teachers of children in this phase are often under pressure from colleagues in Key Stage 1 to 'get the children ready' for the more formal approach. This 'top down' pressure is a clear instance of education being seen as preparation for what is to come rather than for the child as he or she is now.

In many schools the result of these pressures is that teachers feel powerless to do anything other than push children through hoops and children feel powerless to have any control over what happens to them.

Chapter 3 identified the danger of thinking about children as a homogeneous group. For some children the difficulties associated with this kind of education system may be even greater. Some of the problems that the current system might be contributing to are:

- underachievement;
- truancy and disaffection;
- bullying and being bullied;
- mental health problems.

The relationship between the current model of education, the perceptions of children and childhood and

these problems will be briefly considered here. None of these problems can be divorced from the wider social and political context so any discussion needs to be tentative.

The first area of difficulty for some children may be the content of the curriculum itself. Children come from a range of different backgrounds, speak a variety of different languages and all have their own identity. It is important for each child to feel that their identity is valued and reflected in school through the formal and hidden curricula. The following is one illustration of how a child might be made to feel as though their identity isn't valued.

> 'My teacher is always telling me that she doesn't see my colour and that she treats all the children the same. If she doesn't see my colour she doesn't see ME'. (cited in Brown, 1998)

You have probably identified some of the more obvious examples such as books and resources representing different ethnic groups and disabled children in positive ways; having notices in different languages and adults who speak a variety of languages; boys and girls being treated differently based on stereotypes. The majority of classrooms do now have multicultural resources and languages other than English are encouraged but there

---

Reflective Activity 6.6

Children's identity in school

1 What other aspects of a child's identity might be ignored or dismissed?

2 Think about the resources that are in classrooms – do they reflect the lives of all children?

3 Think about the language that is used in schools and whether the language children speak at home is represented or acknowledged.

4 Think about the attitudes and values of teachers.

---

are other areas that aren't as obvious. I remember asking my class of 5- and 6-year-olds in a deprived area of London who spoke a language other than English and was surprised when Terry put his hand up. When I asked what language he spoke he said 'dirty' and a broad grin spread over his face. I wonder how much of Terry's lifestyle was reflected in the classroom and how much he felt his identity was valued. Although the National Curriculum can be inclusive of many children, Brown (1998) warns of this being tokenistic and giving the impression of being 'the other' rather than valued as a central feature of everyday classroom life. The pressures referred to earlier make it very difficult for teachers to really get to know individuals and their families in a way that supports an inclusive approach.

As pointed out earlier, while the National Curriculum is meant to be broad, the emphasis on the subjects to be tested means the majority of time in school is spent on these areas. Even in the Foundation Stage, children are expected to be learning sounds and letters and developing skill in writing. Evidence from countries that don't start formal education until the age of 6 or 7 shows that this early emphasis on reading and writing does not give better results by the time children are 15. In fact, for some children, this early emphasis may establish them as failures at a very early age because they don't achieve the targets set for them. Children very quickly learn what is valued by the adults around them and realise that they aren't achieving what is expected.

Reflective Activity 6.7

Becoming a failure

1 Can you think of anything that you're not very good at (e.g. using computers, reading)?

2 What happens when you are faced with having to do something you're not good at?

Most people will avoid these kinds of situation when possible and, when it isn't possible, may approach the task nervously or perhaps voice strongly that this isn't something that they are very good at in order to lower expectations. Children quickly begin to identify themselves as poor readers or writers and it is difficult for teachers to help children to see that they have other strengths and they will be able to do these things in time when it is apparent through the testing that they should be able to do it now.

Children in these situations of not feeling valued or who have defined themselves as failures are much less likely to achieve: self-esteem is crucially important to successful learning. Older children may seek to avoid school by truanting or start to behave badly to help them feel that they can gain some control. Some children may feel under too much pressure and become depressed or even suicidal.

A number of schools have attempted to address some of these problems by involving children more in decision-making. School councils are a means of giving children a voice and where they are introduced in a more than tokenistic way James and James (2004) identify their positive effect on children's self-esteem and behaviour. An adviser to the DfEE was quoted in a *Guardian* report on school councils as saying 'Giving children a voice raises their self-esteem and self-image as learners, which in turn enhances attainment.' He goes on to identify another area of learning that is supported: 'There are some things that can only be learned through participation, and that includes democracy' (Moorhead, 2004).

How might it be different?

More recent documents suggest that policy may be changing to include more child-centred and social-reconstruction models of education. This will be a difficult move to make within the current system and could lead to more fundamental change. This section looks at some examples of more child-centred and social-reconstruction approaches to education from other countries and from within the UK.

A very different approach to early years' education (ages 3–7) can be found in the Reggio Emilia district in Italy. Lori Malaguzzi (1920–1994) was an Italian psychologist and teacher who developed a child-centred and research based approach to educating young children in Reggio Emilia. He based his ideas on theorists such as Dewey and Piaget. The website in the annotated Bibliography gives more background information. After the Second World War, Malaguzzi worked with the community to develop this approach to education to make sure that fascism couldn't develop again by encouraging children to think for themselves, to question and to be an integral part of the community. Here there is no set curriculum: the curriculum is negotiated with children to reflect their interests. There is no system of testing but children's learning is made explicit through a process of documentation. Photographs, children's

Trying out the models

1 Which of the models of the purpose of education do you think are reflected in this approach?

2 What view of children and childhood are implicit?

work and written and oral recordings of what children say are displayed for parents and children. In this way both children and parents are involved in assessing learning and negotiating where this will go in the future. Children are encouraged to take responsibility and to question. The relationship between adults and children is one of working together to gain understanding. The results of this can be seen in the exhibitions of 'The hundred languages of children' that tour the world.

While there is strong emphasis here on child-centred and social-reconstruction models, there is also a strong cultural-transmission element although there is an expectation that children won't accept this passively but will question and be involved in developing the culture of the community. While children may develop skills that are important for the economy this isn't a primary focus. Children are seen as individuals who are an important part of the community, and childhood is valued for itself not just as a preparation for adulthood. They are viewed as capable learners who can negotiate the direction of their learning.

This kind of approach is an important influence on the early years' provision in Stirling. The Foundation Curriculum in Scotland is much less prescriptive than in the English system and there are no goals to be tested at the end of this stage. This allows practitioners to be much more flexible and focus on listening to children to find out what they are interested in and encouraging them to be part of the decision-making process within the settings.

Both these examples focus on children in their early years, before the real impact of the formal education system takes effect and critics point to the impracticality of continuing this approach into primary education. However, there is one example of a private

school in England, Summerhill School, that is based on a child-centred, social-reconstruction model of education. This is a boarding school so children in this setting are part of the school community for much longer periods of time. Staff and children, all of whom have an equal vote in the decisions that are made, develop the rules of the school. There is a curriculum on offer to the children but there is no compulsion for children to attend lessons. A. S. Neill, who started the school in 1921, points to the difficulty of making children follow a particular path in the National Curriculum manner.

> You can't make children learn music or anything else without to some degree converting them into will-less adults. You fashion them into accepters of the status quo – a good thing for a society that needs obedient sitters at dreary desks, standers in shops, mechanical catchers of the 8.30 suburban train – a society, in short, that is carried on the shabby shoulders of the scared little man – the scared-to-death conformist.
>
> (Neill, 1962, p. 27)

Again, a strong child-centred and social-reconstruction focus is present in this approach and children are seen as capable and treated as fellow citizens. There is a total rejection of both GNP and cultural-transmission models as there is no imposed morality or preparation for being part of the economic structure. Critics point to the danger of allowing children to do as they please, but this approach is concerned with the rights of children being equal with the rights of adults: negotiations have to take place and children can only do what doesn't harm someone else.

These instances illustrate that it is possible to accept children's agency and capability and give them freedom to learn. The children identified as having difficulty in the previous section are much more likely to be able to achieve in these sorts of settings although they will not be a panacea for all difficulties. But this does mean that children have to be trusted to learn and teachers have to be trusted to support that learning. This doesn't fit comfortably in a system which has accountability as its main focus.

Conclusion

The questions identified at the beginning of this chapter were

- What are children's rights to education internationally?
- Why do we need an education system?
- What has shaped the current system in England?
- What view of children and childhood underpins the system?
- How might it be different?

We have seen that the UNCRC identifies children's rights to education and what that education should be focused on, but found that the idea of education as a right is confused by making it compulsory. The purpose for having an education system can be seen to be for the benefit of the individual and of society, but these may be in potential conflict and there may be different ideas of the kind of society we are hoping to achieve. These differences are identified in Bottery's four models of the purposes of education.

While there has been a gradual move away from early ideas of education through cultural-transmission and later GNP models, these are still influential but in the context of a society that aims to be more egalitarian. The brief period where a child-centred model was more prominent didn't last long due to pressures to account for the growing cost of education in terms of benefits to society. Although the current aims of the curriculum suggest a continuing movement towards an egalitarian society, the content of the curriculum and the structures of accountability that surround it suggest a much more restricted approach to education. The centralised, prescriptive system gives children little control over their experience in school and expects all children to progress in a similar fashion towards the same goals. While recent policy initiatives are beginning to recognise the agency of children and the necessity for children to have some control over their own learning, these initiatives are undermined by the need for schools to be accountable through a system of testing and public reporting.

The two quotations at the beginning of the chapter indicate that governments are very committed to an education system that will improve lives for children and society, but they are still faced with the difficulty Keith Joseph identified that we are tyrannising many children into doing that which they don't want.

If there is a real commitment to reduce poverty and improve the lives of all sections of society, some radical thinking needs to take place. Education may be a means to achieve this but it is unlikely to happen while there is such a top-down approach to providing education. The challenge for any government is to find ways of involving children, as an important part of not only future society but of society today, in building a system from the bottom up to meet their rights as individuals and help them to understand their place in current society and shape the society of the future. This requires a degree of trust in children, teachers, parents and communities that isn't evident in the current models of accountability.

Annotated reading

Bottery, M. (1990) *The Morality of the School*, London: Cassell, Chapters 1 and 2

This is quite a challenging read, but gives much more detail of the four models of education outlined in this chapter.

Chitty, C. (2004) *Education Policy in Britain*, Basingstoke: Palgrave Macmillan

A very thorough account of the changes that have taken place in educational policy since the 1944 Education Act.

Gearon, L. (ed.) (2002) *Education in the UK*, London: David Fulton

This gives a comprehensive account of the structure and organisation of education in the UK.

Gillard, D. (2004) *Education in England* at <http://www.kbr30.dial.pipex.com/index.shtml>

This site provides access to a brief and very readable summary of educational change since the mid-18th century and gives access to important policy documents.

A.S. Neill's Summerhill School at <http://www.summerhillschool.co.uk/>

This site explains what Summerhill is about and gives access to further resources.

The Reggio Approach An Inspiration for Inclusion of Children with 'Special Rights' at <http://www.milligan.edu/ProfEducation/NMorrison/fpworkshop/dkgreggio200.htm>

This website gives a good overview of the Reggio Emilia approach to early education.

Chapter 7

Youth Services and Provision

MARIAN CHARLTON

Many young people lack, status, rights and power in our society . . . They fall between the two stools of protection and dependence as children, and autonomy and self determination as adults.

(Brown, 1998)

Introduction

Recent research (Jones, 2002) has exposed a growing social divide, changes in patterns of how people live in families and communities, and the extent to which young people are excluded from work, education and employment through barriers related to social divisions. Research indicates that this changing experience of many young people has impacted on their opportunities to achieve (SEU, 1999a) and that a significant minority are not involved in education, training or work (Blanden and Gibbons, 2006).

This chapter is about services for young people in the UK and the policies which influence their development. The chapter addresses four questions:

- What is meant by youth policy and youth services within the context of social policy?

- How are concepts such as youth, young person and teenager used to describe young people?

- Why is it important to consider the international frameworks for youth policy?

- What influences the provision of services for young people: social welfare, social control, social justice or employability?

The chapter opens with an explanation and discussion of the ways in which society views the status and significance of youth within an environment of competing social and political expectations and demands. It goes on to consider notions of youth and examines how these vary with time and place within an historical national and international context. The chapter then considers the influences on provision of services, including political ideology, economic conditions and cultural expectations. In conclusion the chapter identifies the constraints and opportunities for the services identified as young people's services, for the professionals working within them and for the young people at the receiving end.

What is meant by youth policy and youth services within the context of social policy?

This section develops the perspective that youth policy and services need to be understood within a social policy framework. It draws on the theoretical perspective that government policies aim to meet competing demands and that there are a range of discourses often based on vested interest and professional power (Davies, 2005). Social policies and services are shaped by competing pressures which include:

- citizen's demands that needs are met through services and social welfare;
- the economic need for a viable labour force and social stability;
- government's wish to remain in power through balancing these.

The Bridging the Gap (SEU, 1999a) exposed the fact that a significant minority of young people had 'disappeared' and were not involved in education, employment or training. This is the group that is referred to by professionals as disengaged and hard to reach. It is also

Reflective Activity 7.1

Personal experiences of youth

Brown (1998) suggests there is a recurring theme and ongoing preoccupation with the perceived threat to social stability posed by unregulated, undisciplined and disorderly youth. Yet there is increasing evidence to suggest that young people are largely conformist in their behaviour and aspirations (Jeffs and Smith, 1998; Williamson, 1997).

Think about your experience as a young person and the experience of other young people you know.

1 Are young people conformist? Give examples.

2 Are young people a threat? Give examples.

3 What are the implications of such stereotyping for young people?

the group that recent evaluations suggest that services have continued to fail to engage. Their needs have been defined by the government and the lack of response has indicated a further social policy review, with respect being a primary focus. The then Prime Minister, Tony Blair, stated on 6 May 2005 on his re-election:

> But I want to make this a particular priority for this government, how we bring back a proper sense of respect in our schools, in our communities, in our towns and our villages.
>
> And rising out of that will be a radical programme of legislation that will focus exactly on those priorities: on education; on health; on welfare reform; on immigration; on law and order.
>
> <http://www.number10.gov.uk/output/Page7459.asp>

Services for all people, including young people, are organised within a social policy framework. Social policy has two aspects: practical politics and decision-making and analysis. Governments make decisions about providing services for individuals and communities. Decisions are influenced by costs, competing demands and the political beliefs of the government of the time. Academics, civil servants and others study the implications of those decisions: who wins and who loses. Discourses may be based on vested interest, professional power, demands from campaigning organisations and the needs of the economy.

The policy process is complex and services often undergo radical changes from conception to implementation. As a consequence the resulting provision of services may not meet the expectations of practitioners or service users. An example of this is the *Transforming Youth Work* (DfEE, 2001) and *Resourcing Excellent Youth Services* (DfES, 2002). This agenda initially appeared to create opportunities for youth work and for young people. However, it also introduced new pressures such as standards and measures (Ofsted) in the form of recorded and accredited outcomes. These were introduced without resources for training in new approaches, such as accreditation.

Youth services in the UK have spanned 150 years with considerable state involvement over the past 50 years, as is the norm across Europe. Traditionally, services for young people in the UK have spanned government departments and have over time evolved professional identities, codes of ethics and ways of working.

Services for young people in Britain have their roots in voluntary work in 19th century philanthropy. Elementary education was made available, child labour was banned in the 1830s and informal educational opportunities were developed for young people by the churches and other organisations. In the 1870s, compulsory elementary schooling was in place. This extended the period of dependency of young people, and was not universally popular with parents who had to meet the costs of extended child support. It did, however, meet the needs of the economy for a better educated labour force (Kincaid, 1976).

Following the First World War, there was an increase in services provided by the state for young people in the form of schooling, child care and the development of non-formal education for young working-class people. By the 1930s, the need for more state intervention in leisure activities and improved formal and non-formal educational opportunities for young people was slowly being recognised so that services were poised for expansion by the start of the Second World War in 1939.

War is recognised as having a huge impact on the development of services. In the UK, children were evacuated from big cities, separated from families and returned to war-torn cities. This level of disruption created the need for post-war services. In December 1942, Beveridge published a report proposing that all people of working age should pay a weekly contribution in order to pay benefits to people who were sick, unemployed, retired or widowed. Beveridge argued that this system would provide a minimum standard of living 'below which no one should be allowed to fall'. These measures were eventually introduced by the Labour government that was elected in 1945. This report was a significant part of the war effort and aimed to create feelings of social solidarity at a point of time when the country was under threat. The proposed reforms covered five evils of British society: want, disease, squalor, ignorance and idleness, and gave a commitment to universal welfare from 'the cradle to the grave'.

The 1944 Education Act saw the development of services for young people including the development of

a youth service and secondary education for all. In addition a child-care service for children and young people in public care was developed. This was integrated into social services in 1971 following the Seebohm Report (Seebohm, 1968) and the Local Authority Social Services Act, 1970.

Discussed in more detail in Chapter 6, Education: Service or System?

Since then formal schooling has been extended and consequently the period of dependency of young people on parents and carers. This period of time in the life course between childhood and adulthood has become known variously as adolescence, youth or the teenage years, and it has varied by chronological age at different time and place.

Services continued to develop and grow through the post-war years until the policies of the Conservative governments 1979–97 led to the cutback in many services and a much stronger emphasis on social control. The 'New Right' philosophy was based on market principles and not on the principles of universal social welfare and social democracy established in 1945. Prior to 1979 the Conservative Party had justified inequality as part of the natural order, but the New Right differed from this view and believed in change through the operation of markets, an increase in state control and cutbacks in social welfare spending. Cutbacks in public

Further discussion in Chapter 3, The Politics of Childhood.

expenditure led to the steady erosion of the welfare responsibilities of the state and contributed to an increase in poverty and inequality. This has led to the view that young people of this period are characterised as a lost generation. More than 25 per cent of young people in the 1980s were on Youth Training Schemes for the unemployed and it may be significant that this is the generation who are now parents of many of the young people we now refer to as disengaged and socially excluded.

As part of the New Right strategy, the Government sold council houses, by giving people the right to buy without replacing the stock. This was popular with existing tenants, but has contributed to a lack of affordable housing for young people today. School exclusions rose three-fold and it has been suggested that the Prime Minister's view on youth justice at the time was to 'understand a bit less and condemn a little more' (Williamson, 2005). These policies led to an increase in poverty and inequality and the UK became a two-track society. On coming into office in 1997, New Labour coined the phrase 'social exclusion' to describe the experience of poverty and this was the focus of their agenda until 2006.

Chapter 9, Children Who Offend, discusses youth justice.

In 2006 the evidence is that the youth divide continues to grow despite the government agenda of tackling social exclusion. The focus of New Labour social policy is to challenge the social exclusion of the young through widening participation in education, training and employment. The facts are, however, that poverty prevails and the cycle of disadvantage continues (Blanden and Gibbon, 2005). That the youth divide continues and poverty persists indicates that policy needs to be reviewed and that the state needs to go beyond the recent emphasis on education and training and look more broadly at supporting routes to independence. An example of these approaches is evident in Norwegian and Swedish youth policies (Hammer, 2000). Norway and Sweden have retained a social democratic approach to government. Inequality is seen as a problem which can be addressed through some redistribution of income and wealth through the provision of state services. Social rights for young people continue to include affordable housing, a living wage, leisure activities and respect for and action on issues raised by young people.

Discussed in Chapter 4, The Social Divisions of Childhood.

A national and coherent youth policy? Where is the youth work?

Traditionally youth policy in the UK has not been coordinated and has been reliant on the shaping of existing institutions through funding mechanisms. Under New Labour a coherent policy for young people has been developed but not with the Youth Service at the centre. A Minister for Youth Affairs and a Children's Commissioner are now in place and the Children Act 2004 has five identified criteria against which the welfare of children and young people under 18 are to be judged. Services for young people will be coordinated by children's trusts and professional autonomy will be replaced by multi-professional teams.

This legislation is outlined in Chapter 10, Safeguarding Children.

The Youth Service was at it most optimistic point in the 1960s when the Albemarle Report (1959) was published and responded to. Since that point, the Youth Service has been campaigning for an integrated youth policy with the Youth Service at the centre. The Youth service is now at a crossroads. Work with young people is a major policy issue. Youth work skills are heavily promoted and are in demand, yet the Youth Service remains accountable to local authorities and the children's trusts for funding. The Youth Service has been headed up by the National Youth Agency since 1991 but, despite this, it has not achieved full recognition as a statutory service. It continues to be a service which

Reflective Activity 7.2

Services for young people

- Sport, arts and leisure
- Somewhere to meet and chill out
- Supporting young carers
- Supporting young people in public care
- Crime prevention
- Advice and information
- Extended schools
- Learning mentors

1 Which services for young people would you prioritise?

2 Think about and justify the reasons for your choice.

3 What shaped your decisions?

actively promotes young people's personal and social development and a just society. It is also the service that has been drawn on to develop voices of young people and the youth work skills needed in multi-professional and partnership working.

Levels of funding have been affected by the development of new areas of provision and the high priority given to the under-5s (the government allocated £570.9m for youth and community services and £2,886m to education for the under-5s (Local Government Finance Report, 2005/6). The Youth Service is concerned that, despite the rhetoric, young people may be forgotten or resources may go to problem and preventative issues in the multi-agency world of children's trusts.

How are concepts such as youth, young person and teenager used to describe young people?

This section examines a range of concepts such as youth, teenager, young person, transition and the youth divide. It will consider how the meaning of concepts such as 'youth' and 'young people' varies by time and place.

Youth as a stage in the life course

The various transitions through which individuals pass during their lives look to be biologically fixed. But the human life course is more complicated than this as we are social animals and strongly influenced by the cultures in which we live. Stages of life such as childhood and youth have cultural meanings but these meanings are open to interpretation and variation over time and place.

Childhood and youth as separate phases of development are fairly recent concepts. Until the 1830s, children worked full time in the UK and continue to do so in parts of the world. Youth and adolescence is recognised as a phase of transition from childhood to adulthood and adolescents are often stereotyped as difficult and moody.

> Chapter 2, Childhood: Rights and Realities, examines the Convention.

In Europe childhood is regarded as a protected period of life and this is supported by legislation and the United Nations Convention on the Rights of the Child. The Children Act 1989, the Leaving Care Act 2002 and the Children Act 2004 are all examples of UK legislation demonstrating the shift towards a discourse of rights

and protection for children. More recently this has included the right to voice and influence.

Mark Smith argues that the term 'youth' is unhelpful as it gives negative stereotypical views of young people, who are ascribed characteristics which may equally apply to adults. For example he argues that,

> going AWOL is the same as truancy . . . implicit in the terminology is a belief that growing up is a one-way journey, a process of moving on from adolescent ignorance to adult wisdom; from teenage trivia to adult seriousness; from youth training to adult employment. The adult, we are being told, is the finished product, the young person the incomplete prototype. This essentialism built around age, like the equivalent discourses constructed around, for example, gender or 'race', provides a foundation for almost all the literature.
>
> (Jeffs and Smith, 2005)

There are also gender and race issues at play. Angela McRobbie (1994) first put the view that the concept of 'youth' is male and that softer terms such as teenager are often used to refer to girls and young women. This view is now mainstreamed to the extent that the term 'young person' is now preferred and used in preference to the term 'youth' which retains connotations of disaffection and anti-social behaviour.

Further discussion in Chapter 4, The Social Divisions of Childhood.

See Chapter 5, Pictures of Children.

The concepts of children as victims or villains are considered in depth in Chapter 2, Childhood: Rights and Realities.

Phil Jones explores in Chapter 5 the power of such pictures to shape policy against the interests of children. There is also a fear that the negative stereotyping often applied to young people may extend to the services that focus on their needs. In support of this perspective, Mark Smith goes on to develop the view that,

> politicians and policy makers in Britain and Northern Ireland currently tend to talk about young

people in three linked ways – as thugs, users and victims. As *thugs* they steal cars, vandalize estates, attack older (and sometimes, younger) people and disrupt classrooms. As *users* they take drugs, drink and smoke to excess, get pregnant in order to jump the housing queue and, hedonistically, care only for themselves. As *victims* they can't find work, receive poor schooling and are brought up in dysfunctional families.

(Jeffs and Smith, 2005)

If the terms 'adolescent', 'teenager', 'youth' and 'young person' are unpicked it is worth looking at the meaning and interpretation behind the concepts. For example, 'teenager' is a softer term but patronising, while 'youth' is almost exclusively linked to social problems and negative behaviour such as street crime, binge drinking and yob culture.

Youth: a period of transition

In addition to being described as a stage of life in the life course, young people are described as being in a process of transition moving from dependence to independence. The traditional process in the UK has been from schooling into further and higher education to the labour market, or from school to work, from living in the parental home (or in care) to living independently, from economic dependence to economic independence.

Beck (1992) supports the view that this is no longer the pattern and that young people move in and out of work, leisure and education, maintaining a state of semi-financial dependence until a much later age. The argument is that this trend has been an outcome of social policies and changes in the labour market. Wider opportunities for participation in education have been created but, at the same time, access to independent financial support in the form of grants or social security entitlements has been cut back. In comparison, social policy in Norway and Sweden continues to give this support. The UK perspective has been recently evidenced by comprehensive research undertaken by the Joseph Rowntree Trust (2002) and the ESRC research programme: Youth Citizenship and Social Change. Examples of the research are:

- transitions made by young people in public care;
- young people's views on changing family structures;
- relationships between school, families and communities;
- the experience of school.

These reports cover a diverse range of findings relating to young people's experience at work, in their communities and at home. They include information on young people's transitions into adulthood, the transition to fatherhood in young men, the marginalisation and resistance of vulnerable youth, transitions to citizenship and teenagers at risk due to family disadvantage.

Chapter 19, Searching and Researching Childhood: Making Full Use of Libraries.

Young people's experience of growing up has changed in recent years. The period of dependence has been extended. The increased dependence on families has increased the need for positive family relationships and support and educational advice. However, formal education cannot always overcome the effects of early disadvantage and the influence of families and communities. There is an increasing social divide between those who stay on in education and those who leave without qualifications and a divide between those who have children in their teens and those who defer parenthood. This social divide is linked to social class but also to gender and ethnicity. There is an expectation that white middle-class patterns of extended transition and parental support are available and that other alternatives are wrong.

The conclusion of the Joseph Rowntree Trust and ESRC research was that there is a growing youth divide.

Reflective Activity 7.4

Consider personal transitions to adulthood

Consider your movements from school to further education or work or unemployment; the movement from your childhood home to your adult housing and the new relationships and living arrangements you developed.

1 Were there critical moments?

2 Was it a smooth path?

See Chapter 4, The Social Divisions of Childhood.

This is based on diverging paths to adulthood linked to social class, gender and ethnicity, and through experiences such as teenage parenthood, parents' understanding of the importance of education qualifications and parents' ability and willingness to support the cost of an extended period of dependence.

The fact that the youth divide is growing may indicate that policy needs to be reviewed and that the state needs to go beyond the emphasis on education and training and look more broadly at the routes to independence as in Norwegian and Scandinavian youth policies discussed earlier in the chapter.

Why is it important to consider the international frameworks for youth policy?

As identified in the previous section the meaning of concepts such as 'youth' and 'young people' vary by time and place. In the contemporary world these are underpinned by the United Nations Convention on the Rights of the Child and European Union youth policy. An outcome of this international and global dimension is that policies about and for young people are not developed in isolation. Policymakers

See Chapter 2, Childhood: Rights and Realities.

visit projects worldwide looking for innovations that are effective. International agreements relating to issues such as human rights are also significant so that, for example, across Europe trends such as 'listening to the voice of the child' are shared.

This global dimension also includes massive differences in wealth, political ideology and social structure. In Europe, young people are protected in a way that is inconceivable in poorer countries where child labour is more common. Yet young people are a long-term resource for all economies as populations age. This is not always recognised and young people continue to be perceived as a problem, as a group to control and bring to order.

The United Nations proclaimed 1985 as International Youth Year. This laid the foundation for social and political thinking on youth matters. It was ten years later that a global youth policy was drafted, 'The World Programme of Action for Youth to the Year 2000 and beyond' (UN, 2007). The aim of this programme was to influence governments and to create opportunities for young people to become active on the issues that mattered to them. Ten priority areas were identified in 2000 as key for youth development and are evident in UK policy:

- poverty;
- education;
- employment;
- health;
- environment;
- drugs;
- juvenile delinquency;
- leisure;
- gender;
- participation in decision-making.

In 2003 the following were added:

- globalisation;
- information and communication technologies;
- HIV/AIDS;
- youth in armed conflict and intergenerational relations.

These areas are organised in three clusters and report back biennally in the World Youth Report:

- youth in a global economy (hunger and poverty, education, employment, globalisation);
- youth in civil society (environment, leisure, participation, information and communication technologies, intergenerational relations);
- youth at risk (health, drug abuse, delinquency, conflict, HIV/AIDS).

Within the European Youth Programme nation states shape their own policies and services and there is a variation in options and choices. The European Union's focus has been on fostering youth exchanges between members so as to support active youth participation across shared social issues, for example employment and racism, the role of women and minority rights. Across Europe there continues to be variation in relation to service delivery, but in European youth policy there are four perspectives which are shared:

- young people as a resource;
- young people's rights to leisure and care;
- young people's rights to independence and self-reliance;
- to value diversity and difference.

In the UK the Department for Information and Development (DfID) is committed to increasing an understanding of global issues for every child and young person so that they can understand the global considerations which will affect their lives (DfID, 1997).

What influences the provisions of services for young people: social welfare, social control, social justice or employability?

The themes of social welfare, social control, social justice, the labour market and employability are explored in this section in relation to youth policy and services. In some cases the focus of policy is clear. For example the main focus of the New Deal (DWP, 2004) is training, employability and the labour market. The main focus of the anti-social behaviour measures and the 'Respect' agenda is social control and social order but both these policies also have a welfare element. The welfare element of the 'New Deal' lies in the fact that the New Deal supports young people into work through the Gateway Scheme and the welfare element of anti social behaviour orders is concerned with those people who have felt themselves to be harassed by young people. In other cases the focus of policy is not clear and this applies to a number of initiatives relating to young people. For example, Connexions as a service is about supporting young people through advice, but in order to pay for it the government has taken resources from the Youth Service. The theoretical perspective in social policy drawn on in this section reflects these contradictions and the implications for the services.

This is discussed further in Chapters 9 and 10, Children Who Offend and Safeguarding Children.

In 1997 one of the first acts of the New Labour government was to set up the Social Exclusion Unit (SEU). This unit was closed down in 2006. The aim of the unit was to challenge the marginalisation and social exclusion of people living in poor communities. The philosophy of New Labour emphasised citizen rights and responsibilities, challenged market individualism and aimed to distance the Labour Party from its social democratic past and its commitment to universal social welfare.

Young people have continued to feature highly in the New Labour agenda, with the first five reports of the SEU, in 1998–9, dominated by youth policy issues. These were:

- Truancy and Exclusion;
- Rough Sleeping;
- Bringing Britain Together: A Renewal;
- Teenage Pregnancy;
- Bridging the Gap.

These reports were commissioned in the context of an increase in permanent school exclusions of 450 per cent in seven years and the evidence that school exclusion was shown to correlate to youth crime (Graham and Bowling, 1995): that Britain with 90,000 teenage conceptions in 1997 (8000 of them under 16) was identified as having the highest teenage pregnancy rate in Europe with a rate twice that of Germany, three times that of France and six times that of Holland, and that an estimated 160,000 16–18-year-olds (around 8 per cent of the age group) were not in any form of education, employment or training.

The aim of the SEU was to bring young people and adults living on the margins of society into the mainstream. The reports and the philosophy underpinning them have set the scene for a shake up of services for young people as discussed earlier. The speed of legislative and administrative change between 1997 and 2006 put considerable pressure on practitioners, such as careers officers, teachers, social workers and youth workers, to review their practices in line with the government's commitment to multi-professional, inter-agency and partnership working. They have raised concerns relating to professional status and power and illustrate the competing pressures identified at the beginning of the chapter. New occupations such as early years' teachers, learning mentors and classroom assistants have been developed and new forms of provision such as Connexions, behavioural units, New Deal, Sure Start and youth offending teams have been piloted and mainstreamed.

Changes created by the Children Act 2004 and the Children's Workforce Strategy (DfES, 2006a) are contentious if looked at from a youth perspective. The emphasis on children to the exclusion of young people created tensions across the youth work sector and the specific inclusion of young people was eventually explored in the Green Paper, Youth Matters (DfES, 2005g). A significant response was received from youth organisations and young people demonstrating a strength of feeling on the issue.

Social welfare

While working with a group of youth work students in 2006 the following statement was made:

We are inside the building working with achieving young people while the ones we really need to reach are climbing the roof outside.

This statement is an illustration of a practitioner's view of some of the changes in service delivery and the impact on the 'hard to reach'.

The social welfare approach to youth policy is in the tradition of provision for need and social justice. The emphasis on need itself has been contradictory. People in need and suffering oppression have often triggered fear, anxiety and guilt: in the 19th century fear of the mob; in 1960 fear of youth culture; in the 1980s fear of race riots; in 1997 fear of a dispossessed underclass; in 2006 fear of radicalised Asian youth.

The government's belief is that the cycle of poverty and disadvantage can be challenged by social inclusion through education. The report *Bridging the Gap* (SEU, 1999a) together with the Command Paper *Learning to Succeed* (DfEE, 1999) brought in a new strategy in the form of the Youth Support Service, better known as Connexions.

The idea behind Connexions is that all young people have access to a personal adviser and that the young people with the greatest need would be given intensive support. Funding was redirected from the Youth Service and the Careers Service and practitioners were recruited from a range of professional backgrounds. The partnerships were set up in 2002 but by 2006 the service had been disbanded with evaluations showing that the service had failed to make a difference with the 'hard to reach' and disengaged. At the time of writing, a rethink is taking place and personal advisers have now been directed towards working with 16–25s. The fact that the hard to reach have not been reached may not link to the service but to the fact that the cycle of poverty and disadvantage is structural and therefore in need of a different approach (Battsleer and Humphries, 2000).

Social control

All governments have policies and services which enforce the law and maintain social control 'in the national interest'. In the UK that has been the traditional role of the police force but social welfare provision has always had a social control element.

New Labour with election to Government in 1997 inherited heavy crime statistics, with the evidence that much of which was youth crime linked to unemployment and non-attendance at school as highlighted in the Audit Commission Report (1996) *Misspent Youth: Young People and Crime*.

Schools now have the role of challenging truancy and non-school attendance and this is further increased by the Education and Inspection Bill 2006. Schools are required to retain and manage difficult young people. Exclusions must be justified and parents are now made responsible for school attendance. Schools have responded by developing 'behavioural units' and by monitoring truancy and school attendance. This has led to new roles in schools such as learning mentor, personal adviser, classroom assistant and to the need for schools to work much more closely with parents, carers, families and communities.

> This is explored in Chapter 9, Children Who Offend.

In addition to changes in schooling, youth justice reforms were instituted in 1998. These have been criticised as introducing a new authoritarianism and surveillance (Pitts, 2003) and have been referred to as the criminalisation of welfare. There is a public perception that young people are a threat and in need of control and management. This perception needs to be challenged but the reality is that surveillance has increased enormously over the past five years. The use of cameras and security patrols has spread to school playgrounds and shopping precincts. Homework clubs, extended services in schools and summer schools are all examples of the ways in which the leisure time of young people is coming under closer supervision. In some cases the emphasis on safety, child protection and risk assessment is seriously limiting developmental opportunities and activities. These, combined with the common assessment framework and the increased use of accreditation, pose challenges for the ethics and processes of youth work.

Jeffs and Smith argue that

Communities require ways of curbing anti-social behaviour if they are to be places where people can flourish. Individual young people do sometimes behave as thugs, users or victims, but it is not the young who solely need to be restrained. There can be no acceptable reason for controlling people on the grounds of their age any more than on the basis of their race or gender. It is even unacceptable to restrict the movements of young people and children on account that they are in greater risk of becoming victims. Those who perpetrate the crimes should lose their freedom, not potential victims. (Jeffs and Smith, 1999)

He reminds us from a youth service perspective that the tension between policing and advising individuals is often at the expense of group and associational provision. Young people continue to need places where they can meet and socialise with friends under the support of a youth worker.

Social justice

Social justice is a core theme in the United Nations and the European agendas for young people. It is also one of the planks on which democracy has been built. Justice implies fairness. The social justice agenda for young people in the UK is an agenda around human rights, citizenship, participation and involvement in decision-making, rights to welfare and to a voice and influence. It is also an educational issue as young people learn about global inequalities.

> ASBOs are explored in Chapter 9, Children Who Offend.

The majority of young people take their responsibilities and rights as citizens seriously and this is essential if the UK is to retain belief in freedom and rights. Unfortunately, some of the policies related to social control and social welfare undermine the principles of rights and justice and this is not lost on young people. The most blatant example of this is the use of ASBOs.

Paul Thomas (2003) suggests that the issue of civil, social and economic rights is a key issue for young people from diverse cultural communities. This presents significant challenges for policymakers and service providers. One example is the threat to social cohesion of 'Islamophobia' in the wake of the war on terror and responses to the serious scenes of violent disorder in Bradford, Burnley, Leeds and Oldham in the summer of 2001. The outcome of the radicalisation for young Muslims is a live issue and may be an outcome of

Reflective Activity 7.5

Radical youth

Facts: www.peacedirect.org from Young People Now 2006

There are 1.6 million Muslims living in the UK of whom 46 per cent are second generation, 33 per cent are under 16 and 31 per cent leave school with no qualifications (compared with 15 per cent of the total population).

1 Have you thought about why young people become radicalised?
  • beliefs?
  • self-esteem?
  • feelings of injustice?
  • anger at political events?

2 Explore these ideas and add other reasons that you might think of.

feelings of oppression and frustration and the course of social justice.

At the present time a number of national and local projects are focusing on 'making a difference' for young people. Youth parliaments and youth forums are now national policy and local projects such as the 'Voice and Influence' project in Barnsley and the 'Youth Involvement Project' in Kensington <http://www.nya.org.uk/hearbyright/viewindicator.asp?cid=1174> are very successful in getting young people involved. This direction is evidence of the influence of European Policy, but success is patchy and reliant on funding priorities.

Labour market and employability

The labour market approach to youth policy has focused on the needs of the UK economy to compete in global markets. This, alongside social inclusion, is why more resources have been put into education and training. The future labour market needs to be flexible and those entering or about to enter it can no longer hold the expectation of a job for life. New Labour's approach has been to revive the work ethic

Reflective Activity 7.6

Young people and decision making

One way of countering negative images of young people and encouraging them to take on the responsibilities that go hand in hand with their rights is to actually involve them in decision-making processes. Not as many young people are as apathetic towards politics and democratic processes as many assume, and when issues are decided that can affect their own lives and community young people have a right to be consulted. (Voices of young people – British Youth Council Online Survey response to the Green Paper, Young People Now 2–8 Nov 2005) http://www.byc.org.uk/

1 Read this statement and identify the extent to which you agree with it.

2 How do you think young people should be consulted?

amongst young people in an economic climate where the more traditional jobs for males have gone and where expectations of mobility and flexibility have increased employment opportunities alongside reduced employment rights and security. The growth in service industries has led to great differentials in pay with unqualified young people often being caught in low-paid work of a transient nature.

In order to support the development of skills for employability, current educational policy is focused on skills for learning, skills for achievement, and life and social skills. Further and higher education now aims to prepare young people for lifelong learning and the skills required for employability.

The New Deal and New Start were launched in 1998 and was closely followed by the reform of the youth justice system. These changes also followed the Audit Commission's 1996 Report, *Misspent Youth*, which made links between family and parental support, school truancy, low educational achievement and criminal behaviour. The focus of these initiatives has been on the skills and educational needs of young people rather than job creation services. The changing labour market has led to more limited opportunities for young men. The demise of heavy and manufacturing industry and its replacement by high tech, administrative and service sector work, such as elderly care and contract cleaning, has created a low-paid sector with poor conditions of work. The traditional roles of men and women have been transformed and young people now aim to obtain well-paid work through higher education. This, combined with a lack of affordable housing, has created the stage of prolonged semi-dependence on parents identified above, which leaves young people without parental support seriously disadvantaged and is a factor in the continuing youth divide.

Conclusion

In this chapter you have been introduced to the social, political and historical context of youth policy in the UK as well as international influences on policy and practice. The chapter raised important questions regarding the relative influence of different agendas in shaping future policy. For example, what relative influence the drive for full employment and social inclusion has in the face of growing social divisions; the need to incorporate young people into childhood policy in order to create a coherent and developmental youth policy; and, most importantly, will justice- and welfare-based approaches survive in the face of the drive for social order.

Services for young people have undergone a radical change in the period at the end of the 20th century and the first decade of the 21st. Traditional services for young people have been developed, have been subject to cutbacks and finally have been put under pressure through workforce reform and a government commitment to social inclusion, a common assessment framework and multi-professional working. The external environment has also been subject to change as

▶

new concerns have emerged and old certainties have been challenged. Heading up the debate on the future of services for young people is the National Youth Agency, which profiles the interests of youth work and of young people aged 13–25.

A major concern identified by the National Youth Agency is that the integration of young people's services under the Children Act 2004 may disadvantage young people as the protected status given to children may result in an allocation of resources by children's trusts towards the needs of children and away from the needs of young people. The Youth Service position is that young people's services need to retain a recreational, developmental and rights approach to working with young people and youth work, and that services do not become totally problem and care oriented and that opportunities remain for developmental and creative work with young people such as those provided by the Youth Service and developmental youth work.

The future is open and may depend on the forces identified in this chapter. The fact that the youth divide is growing and that the identified hard-to-reach groups are not being reached indicates that policy ought to be reviewed and that the state needs to go beyond the emphasis on education and training and look more broadly at the routes to independence as in Norway and Sweden.

Annotated reading

Barry, M. (2005) *Youth Policy and Social Exclusion: Critical Debates with Young People*, London: Routledge

The book addresses the overarching predicament of youth generally, and then devotes a chapter to the many specific themes and problem areas they confront. Part 1 contains the chapters relating to the wider social issues of youth policy and the social inclusion of young people. These are social inclusion, citizenship, social rights, education, youth transitions and leisure. Part 2 focuses on specific issues such as unemployment, homelessness, youth justice and young mothers. Each chapter is backed up by a postscript from a young person giving a youth perspective.

Davies, B. (2005) 'Youth work: a manifesto of our times', *Youth Policy*, Leicester: National Youth Agency

Bernard Davies has written consistently on youth policy from a youth work perspective. His work spans 30 years and records with careful analysis the detail of youth policy in the UK.

DfES (2002) *Resourcing Excellent Youth Services*, London: The Stationery Office

The DfEE and the DfES have published various government papers relating to young people. These have been extensive throughout the terms of office of New Labour and indicate the priority given to young people by the government. They also indicate the direction of government policy, which has been to support work with young people on the basis of innovative approaches.

Jones, G. (2002) *The Youth Divide: Diverging Paths to Adulthood*, York: Joseph Rowntree Foundation

This report should be of interest to anyone who works with or for young people as it addresses many general concerns for policy and practice. At a time when the major policy thrust is to combat social exclusion, the report shows how difficult this will be. The overwhelming finding from the studies cited is that, far from being a homogeneous group ('youth'), young people are becoming more and more sharply divided between those who have and those who have not.

National Youth Agency website <http://www.nya.org.uk>

The National Youth Agency supports those involved in young people's personal and social development and works to enable all young people to fulfil their potential as individuals and as citizens through informing, advising and helping those who work with young people in a variety of settings, influencing and shaping youth policy and improving youth services nationally and locally.

Youth and Policy

The journal devoted to the critical study of youth affairs, youth policy and youth work. It is the key journal for reading about youth work, youth policy and services for young people.

Young People Now

This is the weekly magazine devoted to detailed information on the range of work developed with young people and youth work. It is practical and is packed full of up-to-date practice issues.

Chapter 8

Provision for Child Health

RUTH CROSS

'Children . . . are a country's best investment and need the very best services and resources, not only for health but also for their well-being'.

National Service Framework for Children, Young People and Maternity Services (DoH, 2004b)

Introduction

The aim of this chapter is to explore current service provision for child health in the UK context. It begins by looking at what we mean by 'health', considering different concepts, dimensions and models of health drawing on relevant theory and research. It then goes on to consider the range of factors that impact on child health illustrating the complexity of the issue under discussion. Current issues for child health are examined before considering briefly the history of service provision for child health. This sets the context for current policy and delivery and the key legislative and policy frameworks are considered. The impact of these on provision for child health is reviewed and consideration is given to how service provision for child health may be improved. Unless otherwise stated the chapter refers to UK-wide policy.

The chapter addresses the following questions:

- What is health and what are dimensions and models of health?

- What are perceptions of health?

- What are the major health issues and influences affecting children and young people?

- What aspects of the history of service provision for child health set the context for current policy and delivery?

- What are the key legislative and policy frameworks and how do these impact on service provision for child health?

- How can service provision for children's health be improved?

What is health and what are dimensions and models of health?

Health is a very individual and subjective concept. It is influenced by many factors – the word 'health' means different things to everyone and its meaning is dependent on a wide range of things. It is therefore difficult to create a satisfactory, all-encompassing definition of what health actually is. 'Health' may include many concepts including physical, mental, social or emotional health. It may also be conceptualised as the absence of disease, quality of life or even as a 'commodity' – something that can be bought and sold. As Pridmore and Stephens state

it is difficult for us to define any universally acceptable conceptualization of health. Health is

What is health?

Take a few moments to reflect on the following. What do these words mean to you? Write down your thoughts.

- **health**

- **being healthy**

You may also want to talk to others about their own concepts of health (e.g. friends, family, colleagues) and see how their ideas differ from, or are similar to, your own and each others'.

Consider also the following:

Health is not, in the minds of most people, a unitary concept. It is multi-dimensional, and it is quite possible to have 'good' health in one respect, but 'bad' in another.   (Blaxter, 1990, p. 35)

He who has health has hope and he who has hope has everything.   (Arabian proverb <http://www.heartquotes.net/Hope.html>)

1 Can you find any other comments on, or definitions of, health?

2 How do they compare with your own ideas?

interpreted in very diverse ways by the different populations of the world and understanding of health is always evolving.   (2000, p. 30)

The World Health Organization (1946) defines health as 'a state of complete physical, mental and social well-being and not merely the absence of disease and infirmity'. This is commonly referred to in health-related literature, although it is often criticised for being idealistic and unattainable. Is anyone ever truly healthy by this definition? In contrast, consider the following definition:

Health is a blessing. A desirable quality, but one which we are often told money cannot buy; health can be bought, sold, given or lost – bought (by investment in private health care), sold (via health food stores), given (by surgery and drugs) and lost (following accidents or disease).
     (Aggleton, 1990, p. 15)

You will come across other definitions of health in the wider literature and have defined it for yourself in the first exercise (Reflective Activity 8.1). However, for the purposes of this chapter a *'holistic'* concept of health will be used. Rather than health being seen in 'positive' (i.e. a sense of well-being) or 'negative' (i.e. an absence of ill health or the presence of disability) terms, health viewed 'holistically' means that 'separate *influences* (on health) and the interaction of different *dimensions* of health have to be taken into account' as argued by Naidoo and Wills (2000, p. 6).

Models of health

It is important to consider models of health in particular relation to children and young people. Two predominant models of health will very briefly be looked at – the *medical* model and the *social* model.

The *medical* model is sometimes also called the 'western scientific medical model' this focuses on a scientific, objective view of health and the physical body – the sick child, the pathological breakdown of body systems, diagnosis, prescription and treatment. Service provision within the framework of this model would therefore be in the form of clinics, hospitals and/or 'delivered' via health-care professionals

Reflective Activity 8.2

Dimensions of health

- **Physical**
- **Mental**
- **Social**
- **Emotional**
- **Spiritual**
- **Sexual**
- **Vocational**
- **Environmental**
- **Cultural**

(adapted from Naidoo and Wills, 2000, and Ewles and Simnett, 2000)

Take a few moments to see if you can think of any other 'dimensions' of health.

1   How would you argue the case for including these dimensions of health?

2   Choose three of the dimensions presented above. How do you think they are related? How do they impact on each other in terms of health experience?

(i.e. doctors, midwives and nurses). The medical model focuses on a more negative, individualistic view of health and gives very little attention to the wider social and environmental determinants of health. However, this model has been of significant influence as it has provided the basis for the culture of health-care professionals' training and has therefore heavily influenced provision for child health in the past.

The *social* model of health views a child's health as being influenced by social causes. It considers causes of ill-health to be outside of the physical body itself. It is also sometimes referred to as an 'ecological' or 'environmental' model of health. The social model relates to a variety of factors including lifestyles, housing, food, water, alcohol and drug use, the environment, policy (for example economic, transport) and employment. It acknowledges that differences in health experience (inequalities) exist between different groups of people and seeks to determine why. One of the major factors

that impacts negatively on health is poverty. The effect of poverty on health cannot be understated. This is strongly evident (Ball, 1996; Roberts, 2000). In both the UK and the global context the relationship between poverty and ill health is supported by empirical research. The social model allows for factors such as this to be considered when exploring health. Provision for child health within this framework is as varied as the factors influencing health themselves and covers a wide range of services and activity. Therefore the people involved in service provision for child health are not confined solely to health-care professionals.

Disability in childhood is a good example with which to illustrate the differences between these two opposing models of health. The medical model of disability locates the disability within the child and views the child as 'disabled'. Children with disabilities have to adapt to fit into a majority able-bodied world. The child with the disability is seen as the 'problem'. Conversely the social model views disability as a product of society, of societal norms and values which result in discrimination against children with disabilities. Children with disabilities are *dis*-abled by the society in which they live. Society must adapt to the needs of children living with disabilities and not vice versa. The way that society is structured is seen as the 'problem' and not the child themselves.

See Chapter 16, The Anna Rebecca Gray Interviews, for the account of her childhood by a disabled young woman.

You will see that service provision for child health is presented within this chapter in relation to both the medical and the social models of health. For further information on these two models you will need to read more widely (Aggleton, 1990; Blaxter, 2004).

Reflective Activity 8.3

Models of health

Return to the notes you made for the exercise in Reflective Activity 8.1.

1   What model of health is reflected in what you wrote? Medical or social?

What are perceptions of health?

Calnan (1987) carried out a study exploring laypeople's (non-professional) concepts and ideas of health and illness and found that definitions were given in the following ways:

Being healthy is:	Not being healthy is:
Getting through the day	Below normal continually
Never being ill	Poor lifestyle
Feeling strong	Lack of energy
Feeling fit	Being ill/having something wrong
Being active/energetic	Having a serious illness
Getting plenty of exercise	Having a long-term illness
A state of mind	Having an incurable illness
Not being overweight	Going to the doctor
Being able to cope with life's stresses	Being depressed/unhappy
	Not coping with life
	Losing weight
	Unable to work
	Being in bed/hospital

Different writers in the field have come up with alternative ways of conceptualising health. These include,

- Health as *balance,* illness as *imbalance.*
- The body as a *machine,* illness as 'malfunction' of the machine.
- The perception of the degree of control an individual has over their own health (also called 'Locus of Control').
- Health or illness as a result of *fate* or *divine will.*
- Health as providing the means to do what one likes or as the ability to carry out key roles (e.g. home maker, employee).

- Health as *resilience* against infection or hazards.
- Ideas about access to the *means* necessary for good health (e.g. health care, reasonable standard of living). (Curtis, 2004)

Several studies have been completed exploring children and young people's concepts of health. In one study, Chapman et al. (2000) found that younger children (5–11 years old) defined health in terms of diet, exercise and rest, hygiene and dental hygiene. They also described health negatively in terms of illness, smoking, drugs and the environment. Some children included terms referring to emotions and mental health, illustrating what is increasingly becoming apparent – that children face mental health difficulties as well as adults. When asked what makes people healthy or unhealthy positive responses were given in terms of nutrition, exercise, medical check-ups and interventions, safety and hygiene. Negative responses referred to sickness and diseases, poor diet, lack of exercise, smoking, drinking, dirt, germs, abuse and depression. Young people (over 12 years) said that a balanced diet, taking exercise, not smoking or drinking (often) and a healthy mind were important for their health and they also highlighted the importance of looking good. They identified alcohol, smoking, bad diet and junk food, pollution, lack of exercise, stress and depression as issues that put their health at risk. They emphasised the importance of a positive state of mind, being happy and confident about yourself and 'learning to accept who you are' (p. 11).

When asked if health is a matter of luck, Brynin and Scott (1996) found that younger children are more likely to accept this, but that this belief tends to decline with age. They also found that older children believe that health is under their own control (or not a matter of luck). Brannen and Storey determined that

> few children perceived their health in definitively positive terms – 34 per cent good, 48 per cent fairly good, 9 per cent not good and 9 per cent unsure. Children frequently link their health status to eating healthy or unhealthy food or to eating in excess. (1996, p. 25)

Research carried out by Pridmore (1996) in Botswana exploring Botswana children's perceptions about what made them healthy revealed that the children thought drinking clean water, playing, eating good food and keeping clean kept them healthy. Things that made them unhealthy were believed to be fighting, being hungry, drinking alcohol, smoking, dirty water and sugary foods. Some similarities are evident in the findings of the studies discussed.

What are the major health issues and influences affecting children and young people?

In the context of the UK at the current time (spring 2006) there is overwhelming evidence that there are specific and significant health issues affecting children and young people.

A major issue affecting the health of children and young people in the UK at the current time is accidents and unintentional injury. These include road traffic accidents, poisonings, falls, drowning and burns. Research shows that accidents and unintentional injury are the single most important cause of death for children. They kill more children than disease or any other way of dying. Accidents are the commonest cause of death in children between 1 and 15 years old (RoSPA, 2006).

Reflective Activity 8.4

What are the current health issues for children and young people?

Take a moment to consider the issues that you think affect the health of children and young people in the UK at the present time. Think about what information is presented to you in the mass media (i.e. TV, newspapers, radio, Internet).

- What causes childhood deaths?
- What causes child disability?
- What causes child ill health?

Think of some specific examples and write them down.

1 What were the factors influencing the 'health outcomes' for the children and young people involved in your examples?

2 Try to think of health in a 'holistic' way when you do this and try also to consider the notion of health using a social model. What did you find?

About 1000 children die each year from accidents and half of these deaths are from road accidents (Thomson et al., 2000). Accidents also cause non-fatal injuries and account for approximately two million hospital attendances by children each year (Avery and Jackson, 1993; Towner et al., 1993; RoSPA, 2006). It is of significance that the degree of accident and unintentional

> For more discussion of social divisions and children's lives, see Chapter 4, The Social Divisions of Childhood.

injury is related to deprivation relating to social divisions in society. This problem is identified in the government health strategy *Saving Lives: Our Healthier Nation* (DoH, 1999a) which prioritises accidents and unintentional injury as a major public health issue, as does the public health White Paper *Choosing Health: Making Healthier Choices Easier* (DoH, 2004a).

Another major issue affecting the health of children and young people is the increasing numbers that are overweight or obese. Recent studies suggest the levels of childhood obesity within the UK have more than doubled within the last decade (Ebbeling et al., 2002). This reflects similar trends in other high income countries (Dehghan et al., 2005). Being overweight and/or obese has direct links with lack of physical activity or exercise. Obesity in childhood most likely results from an interaction of nutritional, psychological, familial and physiological factors (Kidsource, 2002). Thirty per cent of UK children are overweight and approximately 17 per cent are clinically obese. This has major implications for health, both in the short term and the long term (Sahota et al., 2001).

What are the key factors influencing child health?

The biggest influences on child health and disparities in child health experience are poverty, deprivation and disadvantage. As has been discussed, 'health in childhood is affected not only by biological factors but also by the lifestyle and problems of the parents, including unemployment, low income and poor housing' (Ball, 1996, p. 10). Children in the lowest income circumstances are most at risk of experiencing poor health in childhood. They are more likely than children in better

economic situations to:

- die in the first year of life;
- be born small, be born early, or both;
- be bottle fed;
- die from an accident in childhood;
- smoke and have a parent that smokes;
- have poor nutrition;
- become a lone parent;
- have or father young children;
- die younger.

<http://www.barnardos.org.uk/resources>

A child in the lowest social class is twice as likely to die before the age of 15 as a child in the highest social class.

A child from the lowest social class is nine times more likely to die in a house fire than a child from a well-off home.

(<http://www.barnardos.org.uk/resources>)

Children in low income families are approximately 3 times more likely to have a mental health problem than children from better off families.

(<http://www.statistics.gov.uk/children>)

The existence of inequalities in child health is of paramount importance to service provision for child health. Facts and figures such as those above cannot be ignored by policymakers, stake holders or service providers. Factors such as these impact on the health of children and young people and have to be taken into account. This inevitably leads to a complex arrangement for service provision.

What aspects of the history of service provision for child health set the context for current policy and delivery?

When considering service provision for child health it is important to bear in mind that this includes provision for promoting good health as well as preventing, and providing for, ill health.

Who is responsible for child health?

Most people would agree that the weight of responsibility for child health lies with a child's parents or caregivers. Mayall and Foster (1989) did a study which found that parents believed that child health services should be parent-led and that the responsibility for their children's health was primarily their own as the children's parents. It is interesting to see that recent changes in policy over the last decade have led to child health services being child-led as much as parent-led with the increased focus on children's 'voices'. Most care for sick children is undertaken by parents and caregivers in an informal environment, usually the home. However, as Macfarlane and Mitchell point out,

> every child has some needs which are beyond the capacity of the parents to meet unaided. Some children have special needs over and above these. Services must therefore be flexible and responsive to a wide range of individual demands. Statutory and voluntary services are intended to help parents in their task. (1988, p. 153)

As a result, as well as parents and caregivers, there are a whole host of agencies with responsibilities for child health which requires multi-disciplinary and inter-agency working. In addition, when health is viewed in its widest sense (i.e. holistically as previously discussed) and covers the range of dimensions introduced it can be seen that wider public health measures (e.g. sanitation, safe food, water supply) will significantly benefit child health and the eradication of disease brings in the responsibility of governments in terms of policy development and consequent service delivery. For example, parents and caregivers are relatively powerless when it comes to ensuring cleaner air and yet the environmental policy agenda of national government and cooperation of international governments can make a positive difference in reducing polluting emissions. This clearly has implications for children's respiratory health.

Why is provision for child health important?

It is important to invest in, and provide for, child health for many reasons. First and foremost children are the future of the country. As stated in the National Service Framework for Children, Young People and Maternity Services (DoH, 2004b) 'children . . . are a country's best investment and need the very best services and resources, not only for health but also for their well-being'. Similarly Aggleton (1996) argues that it is important to lay solid foundations for future health during childhood. Health in childhood, and even *in utero,* has an impact on health for adulthood. The evidence strongly suggests that ill health breeds ill health. Here the view of the child as an investment for the future is apparent. However, investing in child health should also be about improving the health experience for the child themselves – investing in the child now, a notion strongly linked with the rights of the child.

Key policy developments in child health over the last 150 years, and especially in the last 10, have transformed service provision. From the introduction of the 1834 Poor Law Act to the numerous policies of the past decade significant changes have taken place. The pace at which this has occurred has increased dramatically in recent times with major developments in policy since 1997. Services have evolved in line with policy recommendations to encourage the involvement of children and young people much more than previously. However, a great deal of this has been reactionary rather than proactive and has occurred in direct response to what has been described by some as significant failings in the UK health and social care system, some of which have resulted in causing children considerable harm.

What are the key legislative and policy frameworks and how do these impact on service provision for child health?

As pointed out in the *National Service Framework for Children, Young People and Maternity Services* (DoH, 2004b), the management of health-care issues of children and young people is almost always more complex than is usually imagined. Many people, structures and systems are involved, from children and young people themselves through to professionals and non-governmental agencies. Services for child health cannot be considered independently of other factors such as these because provision for child health is such a complex, multi-faceted issue. For example, as argued by Macfarlane and Mitchell (1988, p. 177), 'the interdependence of health and social circumstances and the complexity of the interaction between them mean that virtually all social support has some implication for health'.

The government is a key player and partner in provision of services for the health of children and young people (see Figure 8.1). Government action to enhance children's and young people's health takes place across all sections of government at local, regional and national levels. As we have seen, health is affected by many complex factors and therefore the sectors involved are varied – from education to housing to environment to the Home Office. This is illustrated through the work of the Department for Education and Employment, which has been instrumental in leading the development of the National Healthy School Standard. In addition, the Department of Work and Welfare has been responsible for raising the levels of benefits

> See Chapter 3, The Politics of Childhood, which covers the political and economic context of childhood and children's services.

and targeting them at some of those most in need, particularly families with young children as the Acheson Report recommended (Stretch, 2002) and we have already seen the importance of economics on health outcomes. It should be noted, however, that this has had mixed results. Difficulties have been encountered with take-up of benefits and out-of-work benefits have been insufficiently addressed to date.

The impression, therefore, is of a complex picture for service provision for child health involving a wide range of people which requires multi-disciplinary and inter-agency working. However, the main purpose of this is to support and enable families to carry out their role in caring for their children's health wherever possible. As stated by Macfarlane and Mitchell (1988) one aim of health services is to aid parents as the primary protectors and managers of their child's health. Only in certain circumstances should any service itself take on this role: 'one of these is child birth, for in this country almost all pregnancies and deliveries are supervised by the obstetric services and all resulting new-born infants receive some care from health service staff' (p. 158). This is followed up by visits from health visitors and visits to child health clinics which takes place through primary health-care services.

Reflective Activity 8.5

Health Service responsibilities

- Health promotion
- The prevention of ill health
- Protection
- Detection
- Management of acute illness and injury
- Management of chronic illness
- Management of mental health problems
- Management of children with disabilities
- Management of vulnerable children

(Adapted from Hamilton, 2003)

1 Can you identify the potential members of a National Health Service primary care team who would be involved in provision for child health? You can find out from your local primary care trust, GP surgery or health centre, or by using the Internet. Make a list.

2 How does each member of the PCT contribute towards the health and well-being of children?

Primary health-care services for children and young people

Primary health care has become increasingly significant in line with changes in government policy over the last couple of decades. The majority of care is

Figure 8.1 Current government policy context of current service provision for child health.

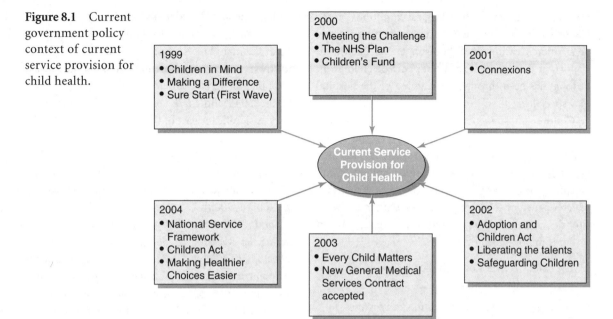

undertaken by parents. Due to the changing face of health service provision over the last couple of decades children, as with all age groups, are spending less and less time in hospital. General Practitioners (GPs) have responsibility for all the children in their practice. The Primary Care Team carries out preventative work for child health. This includes child health surveillance, a programme of routine child health checks and monitoring in the first five years of life which includes screening, immunisations, developmental checks and advising parents and caregivers. This work is extremely valuable since prevention of childhood illnesses are an important factor in providing better health. Specialist members of staff include personnel such as community paediatric nurses.

Community NHS Trusts provide services for children and young people and include child protection, chiropody, continence and dental services, early years screening, family planning, health visiting, HIV/AIDS services, immunisation and vaccination, liaison work with local authorities, school nursing, special needs services, speech and language therapy, audiology and community paediatric services. Of particular significance is health visiting which, Mayall and Foster (1989) argue, is the face of health service provision for younger children.

One of the key targets of *Saving Lives: Our Healthier Nation*, the government health strategy, is to focus on healthier schools. School nurses promote the health of the children and give help and advice to pupils, parents and children. Each school has a named doctor and nurse who visit the school regularly and refer children to other community services such as child guidance, physiotherapy, speech therapy, audiology, dentistry or the enuresis service (bed wetting).

It is important to determine whether measures such as these have positively impacted on the child health experience. While the range of services appears wide-reaching and comprehensive critical concerns over provision are still raised over issues such as, for example, accessibility of services for hard-to-reach or marginalised groups. At the time of writing service provision for child health in primary care is undergoing significant change and the future of some key roles, for example health visitors, is unclear.

Secondary health-care services for children and young people

Secondary health care is provided in hospitals. Approximately half of all children treated in hospital are referred for injuries or other surgical conditions. In the UK one child in four attends accident and emergency departments each year (Thomson et al., 2000). An important development in the support of children in hospital has been through the training of the hospital play specialist.

Children's hospitals existed as one of many different kinds of hospital at the birth of the NHS and recent policy trend has seen a return to specialist hospital provision for children. An example is Bristol Children's Hospital (Bristol Royal Hospital for Sick Children), which opened on 22 April 2001. According to the website (details below) the vision for the hospital is based on three important things:

- the child's eye view of both the physical surroundings and how the place feels
- the need for a relaxed, interesting and secure environment to reduce fear and tension for the child and for the family as a whole
- recognising the vital role that the family plays in the treatment and recovery of their child, so aiming to meet the needs of the whole family. <http://www.ubht.nhs.uk/BCH/BCH/newhosp. htm>

While the Bristol Children's Hospital is an example of good practice for secondary health-care provision for children, there are still many ways that children and young people have identified that health services can be improved. Chapman et al. (2000) found that children wanted services to be more child friendly and accessible, shorter waiting times, more doctors and nurses, and better information. Older children and young people wanted to be listened to and to receive more information.

Health service provision

Some of the key areas of legislation and policy in affecting provision of services relating to the health of children and young people will now be discussed in more detail.

Saving Lives: Our Healthier Nation is the health strategy released by the government in 1999. The strategy proposed to tackle the root causes of ill health – including air pollution, unemployment, low

wages, crime and disorder, and poor housing encompassing a social model of health. It focused on prevention of the main killers: cancer, coronary heart disease and stroke, accidents and mental illness and included a wide range of service providers including local councils, the NHS and local voluntary bodies and businesses. A significant part of this strategy in terms of the health of children and young people is the aim to eliminate child poverty by the year 2020. However, while this is an admirable aim there is evidence to show that some of the inequalities seen in child health are widening (Roberts, 2000).

Working Together to Safeguard Children: A Guide to Inter-agency Working to Safeguard and Promote the Wellbeing of Children (DoH, 1999b) is a government document setting out how all agencies and professionals should work together to promote children's welfare and protect them from abuse and neglect. It is aimed at people in a variety of roles – any job that brings someone into contact with children and their families, from the police and social services to health-care and educational professionals. It is also relevant to non-professional roles such as those that exist within the voluntary sector. *Working Together* impacts on service provision for child health and aims to promote concepts such as working in partnership. However, working in multi-agency and inter-disciplinary ways is not without its challenges and requires time and energy. In practice difficulties can arise around resource allocation, lack of commitment, differing agendas. For more information please see the Department of Health website <www.dh.gov.uk>.

> For more discussion of *Working Together to Safeguard Children* see Chapter 10, Safeguarding Children.

The NHS Plan (2000) is the government's policy paper which outlined its intentions in modernising the NHS. It aims to tackle the health inequalities that divide Britain and sets national targets for tackling health inequalities with the relevant supporting investment. Priorities identified for children's services in the NHS Plan are to:

- improve children's health and address health inequalities;

- maximise NHS and social care input to cross-government programmes to children;

- develop child and adolescent mental health services;

- improve safeguards for children;

- improve adoption services;

- improve services for disabled children.

In November 2000 the children's taskforce, which was created to advance the NHS Plan for children, came into being. Specifically, the taskforce was to address health inequalities in order to promote the health and well-being of children and young people. The National Service Framework discussed previously is key to taking forward the NHS Plan in terms of provision for child health.

Children's rights and health

The United Nations Convention on the Rights of the Child (UN, 1989) is an international human rights treaty which introduces the concept of children as subjects with rights of the same inherent value as adults. Encompassed within it is 'the child's right to the best possible health'. Children have the right to life and the best possible health and access to the best possible health-care services. There are two key principles in the Convention which address children's health rights – Article 6 and 24. Article 6 states 'the right to life and optimal development' and Article 24 states 'the right to the best possible health and access to health care'. It can be seen from earlier discussion in this chapter that the UK has a long way to go in meeting children's rights in this regard especially when inequalities in health are considered. The global picture for child health is even more stark. These two articles specifically set out the standard for prioritising child health services and are underpinned by other articles within the Convention.

> See Chapter 2, Childhood: Rights and Realities, for in-depth discussion of children's rights.

Children are therefore entitled not to be discriminated against and to be listened to, taking an active involvement in their own health care. This means listening to the views of children and young people and doing something about what they say they want. The implication of the Convention is that health-care service for children should be children-centred. The Convention also has implications for staff training and provides a guiding framework for changes in practice in child health services in order to promote child-friendly and child-centred health services. As evident by the example given earlier of the Bristol Children's Hospital, good things are happening in this regard. However, we still have a long way to go. Children and young people still have to be content with a variety of issues when they come into contact with health-care services including non-child friendly environments in secondary (acute) services.

The Convention has been an important signpost in the development of services for child health in the UK. *Every Child Matters* was a government response to this. The Convention followed the Human Rights Act 2000 and relates to issues such as confidentiality, consent and participation. As a result of this Convention, children and young people have a right to have their views elicited on 'all matters affecting the child'. Therefore, children and young people should be involved in consultation and decision-making about their own personal health services.

Every Child Matters (Green Paper, 2003) and the Children's Act (2004) was a government consultation exercise for a framework which sets out to,

> improve outcomes for all children and their families, to protect them, to promote their well-being and to support all children to develop their full potential.
>
> <www.dfes.gov.uk/everychildmatters/>

One of the main intentions of the Green Paper is children 'being healthy, enjoying good physical and mental health and living a healthy lifestyle'. It is hoped that this can be achieved through strong links between mainstream services with long-term emphasis being placed on the creation of children's trusts. The consultation exercise found that most children and young people thought it was important to be as healthy as possible and choose a healthy life.

The National Service Framework for Children, Young People and Maternity Services

The National Service Framework (DoH, 2004b) has an overall aim to improve the lives and health of children. It aims to set the philosophy and the health-care agenda for children for the next decade or so. It sets standards for the community health and social care that children should receive. Its creation was prompted by the Kennedy Report on the Bristol babies' heart cases and the Laming Report on the case of Victoria Climbié, both of which revealed significant shortcomings in how health-care services for children were organised and carried out. Dr Simon Lenton, vice president of the Royal College of Paediatrics and Child Health, said of the Children's NSF,

> this is the first time anywhere that there has been a comprehensive review of children's health services, and standards set for them. It is the greatest opportunity to improve children's services since the establishment of the NHS.   (Lenton, 2004)

The Children's NSF has five core standards:

- promoting health and well-being, identifying needs and intervening early;
- supporting parents and carers;
- child, young person and family-centred services;
- growing up;
- safeguarding and promoting the welfare of children and young people.

The Children Act 2004

Following the consultation exercise *Every Child Matters,* the Children Act came into effect in November 2004. This Act sets the scene for the wider implementation of children's trusts. The long-term aim is to integrate children's services under the umbrella of children's trusts and children's centres which will combine nursery education, family support, employment advice, child-care and health promotion on one site.

Reflective Activity 8.6

The Children, Young People and Maternity National Service Framework

Refer to the executive summary of the Children's NSF, which can be found at <www.dh.gov.uk> using the search facility.

Consider Hallden's (1991) two views of the child:

- The child as 'project' – the child is seen in terms of the future or as an investment; adults are seen as the experts or instructors
- The child as 'being' – the child develops independently; adults are seen as supporters

According to Hallden's theory what view of the child is reflected in the NSF?

The long-term strategy and vision for children's services is to ensure that 'all children are given every opportunity to stay safe, be healthy and reach their fullest potential through enjoyment, achievement and contribution' (DfES, 2003b).

The public health White Paper published in November 2004 (Choosing Health: Making Healthier Choices Easier) proposed to prioritise action to ensure that children have the 'healthiest possible start in life' and included the voluntary restriction of advertising, promotion and sponsorship of unhealthy foods, children's 'personal health guides', a new child health promotion programme, the modernisation and expansion of school nursing services in association with the national healthy school programme, which aims to encourage schools to foster better health, provide free fruit and vegetables to all children aged 4 to 6, improve school meals in order to increase their nutritional value, support cycling to school and promote sport in school. In addition to healthy schools the White Paper also focuses on underage tobacco sales and the issue of teenage pregnancy.

Chapter 3 of the White Paper, entitled 'Children and Young People – Starting on the Right Path' laid out specific recommendations regarding the delivery of services for children and young people, including further information about children's trusts designed to integrate service delivery in one location in all areas by 2008 and to bring into existence 2500 children's centres by March 2008.

Due to the complexity of service provision for child health it is clear that one single organisation cannot provide for child health nor deal with child health inequalities single-handedly. In addition to the work of the National Health Service, cooperation and commitment is required from a range of other services and sectors including statutory, voluntary and private organisations as well as informal care. Different sectors working together will effect optimum impact.

Hamilton (2003) identifies six major themes applicable across all forms of service provision for child health. These are children's rights, participation and partnership, health outcome monitoring and information technology, workforce issues and clinical governance, partnership with Government, inter-agency and multi-disciplinary working and inequalities in health status and access to care.

Provision for child health through voluntary services (non-governmental)

Numerous voluntary services impacting on the health of children and young people are in existence. New societies appear on a regular basis and are often started by concerned and affected parents.

> The strength of voluntary effort is that private agencies can act as quickly as need is perceived, can alter direction rapidly, and are not as bound

by rigid conditions and restrictions. All too often acceptance of what has been achieved in the same field . . . prevents the adaptation at which the voluntary sector should excel.
>
> (Macfarlane and Mitchell, 1988, p. 157)

Voluntary services can often fill a gap in service provision or provide for a need where governmental services have failed.

How can service provision for child health be improved?

Macfarlane and Mitchell observe that

> financial stringency and changes in political philosophy have resulted in a slowing-down in the development of the child health services and have placed a greater emphasis on parental responsibility and while this had had little difference for families with adequate resources, it bears heavily on the increasing number of parents who are unable to meet the basic requirements of their children because of poverty and unemployment, social deprivation, disintegration of family life, or, in some cases, a disinclination to acknowledge their responsibilities . . . statutory services, whether provided by central government or local authority,

Reflective Activity 8.9

Improving service provision for child health

Take a few moments to reflect on your childhood experiences of health provision (or find out about the experiences of a child or young person that you know), for example, being in hospital, visiting the GP or dentist.

1 Describe this experience. What was good about it? What could have been better?

2 As a result of this experience how would you suggest improving services for children's health?

tend to develop gradually in response to the recognition of deficiencies, public demand, and political pressures.

(Macfarlane and Mitchell, 1988, p. 156)

They conclude that it is often only when service provision becomes inadequate or major system flaws or abuse is uncovered that legislation is introduced. Stark examples of this in recent times are the Bristol heart enquiry and Victoria Climbié cases which have effected significant changes in policy and subsequent provision.

Chapman et al. (2000) found that many children wanted more information directly from health professionals and to be spoken to directly, not through their parents ('doctors should tell children first or at the same time', 'children want to know what is happening'). They advocate that doctors and other health professionals need help to see their actions from a child's perspective – this doesn't necessarily come easily to everyone and requires training and education – 'the GP is not always attentive and generally the NHS response is not appropriate to my needs' (p. 10). Attempts have been made to do this through *Every Child Matters* and, as illustrated by the Bristol Children's Hospital, children's voices are being heard and their ideas and opinions acted on.

Roberts (2000) argues that the biggest differences to child health will not be made by the National Health Service, but by changes in other sectors – as we have seen. He also discusses how inequalities in child care have even worsened in some cases. The consequent effects on child (and indeed adult health) are evident. Roberts argues that a minimum income standard is needed to maintain good child health and well-being and that the most effective time to intervene to reduce inequalities in health is in early childhood. She goes on to state that child public health is potentially the most important and effective activity in health and social care because it combines interventions in health, education, housing and public policy. A health service for children and young people should:

- Provide for the child as a whole (for their complete well being not just the condition for which they are receiving treatment or care).

- Be child and family centred so that children, their families and their parents/carers experience a 'seamless' web of care treatment and support. (Hamilton, 2003)

Child-centred health services require new policies and personnel. Radical changes in policy require radical changes in service provision and working practices.

Changes in service provision and the new multi-agency approach being adopted across the sector have meant many more roles have been, and are about to be, brought into existence across local authorities, the police, education and the health service. These range from directors of children's services to children's centres and extended schools development managers, children's rights officers and healthy schools co-ordinators.

(Johnson, 2004, p. 4)

This professional diversity emphasises the need for inter-agency and multi-disciplinary working and cooperation and involves many different professionals. For example, with the concept of extended schools becoming more of a reality the class teacher's role in child health is increasingly key and is broadening beyond education in its traditional sense. It is often the teacher who notices if a child is unwell or experiencing difficulties and who refers this to the parents/guardians or to other outside agencies as necessary.

Conclusion

This chapter has introduced you to the complexities of the concept of health and challenged you to consider health within different dimensions, particularly in relation to children and young people's health, through addressing the question 'What is health?' The factors affecting health have been considered in specific relation to the health issues affecting children. It has provided a brief history of recent service provision for child health and set the context for present policy and existing and planned service delivery. Key legislative and policy frameworks have been discussed and the impact of these on service provision for child health have been illustrated providing specific examples of current services for child health. By engaging with the material and the activities in this chapter you should now:

- be able to discuss the meaning of health, and different definitions/dimensions of health;
- have a greater understanding of the factors affecting the health of children and young people and the health issues they face;
- be familiar with legislative and policy frameworks affecting service provision for child health;
- appreciate how legislation and policy is linked to the provision of services for child health;
- understand, and be able to describe, specific examples of service provision for child health, both governmental and non-governmental;
- appreciate how health services for children may be improved.

Annotated reading

Blaxter, M. (2004) *Health*, Cambridge: Polity

Clearly written and accessible text exploring concepts of health. A must for readers interested in exploring the complexities of defining health in more detail.

MacFaul, R. et al. (2004) *The health of children and young people.* National Statistics http://www.statistics.gov.uk/children/downloads/ prov_use_services.pdf

A useful website for further information about acute service provision for child health.

Maynard, T. and Thomas, N. (2004) *An Introduction to Early Childhood Studies*, London: Sage Publications

A clearly written and useful edited volume on childhood studies incorporating a chapter on early childhood policies and services by Sonia Jackson (pp. 91–107) which has direct relation to the issues around policy and provision raised in this chapter.

http://www.health-for-all-children.co.uk

This website has the 4th edition of the publication of the same name with supporting references and information and links to futher sources. It provides up-to-date information about child health.

The Internet is perhaps the best source of up-to-date information in this rapidly developing area.

Chapter 9

Children Who Offend

DOROTHY MOSS

10-year-old 'yobs' to be named. The naming and shaming of 'yobs' as young as 10, who are made the subject of antisocial behaviour orders will be the norm, the Home Secretary, Charles Clarke, announced yesterday.

(*The Guardian*, 2, March 2005)

Introduction

This chapter explores four critical questions in relation to services and provision for children and young people who offend:

- How does children's behaviour come to be defined as crime and what factors shape ideas about crime and childhood?

- Which particular groups of children come into contact with the criminal justice system and why?

- What debates related to childhood, crime and the state have shaped provision?

- What about justice for children?

Nacro (2005) drawing on the Crime and Justice Survey (a national survey of self-reported offending by people aged 10 to 65 years) point out that offending peaks among younger people and that 32 per cent of 10- to 17-year-old males admitted offending within a twelve-month period. In the main these offences were relatively minor and related to property. Crimes of violence and sexual offences are less common but many crimes go unreported. Crimes of a sexual nature (less than 1 per cent of youth crime) are less likely to be reported and attrition rates in relation to sexual offences, that is, where charges are dropped or modified prior to or during a prosecution, are also very high (Lees, 1997).

However, it must be stressed that the majority of crime committed in childhood is relatively minor and does not involve violence of this sort. Those under 18 are more likely to break the law than adults, but the majority of crimes are committed by adults. 'During 2003, children and young people under 18 years of age accounted for less than 11 per cent of all detected crimes, while adults, aged 21 years of age and over, were responsible for 77 per cent of all such offending' (Nacro, 2005, p. 2). There is no evidence to suggest youth crime is increasing.

As well as being identified as a high offending group, children and young people are vulnerable to crime. For example, evidence shows that 7 per cent of children experience serious physical abuse from their parents or carers (Faux, 2004). Children are also at risk of crime from other children. Their perceptions and experience of crime affect their confidence and ability to participate in society (Morrow, 2002). They adapt their behaviour to avoid actual and perceived threats. They speak of their fears in relation to racist neighbours, vandalised houses, violence, gangs in parks and streets, drugs and needles, drunks and pubs, and harassment from police: 'I like singing and dancing . . . but I don't go to the club after school because it finishes quite late and I have to walk home on my own' (girl quoted in Edwards and Hatch, 2003, p. 21). There is evidence that some children and young people, particularly girls, gay and lesbian children and black and minority ethnic children restrict their movement around the community because of fear, experience and expectations of abuse and/or harassment (Lees, 1997; Webster, 1994; Stonewall, 1996).

Children and young people can also be vulnerable to crime where the perpetrators may operate at a corporate (business) level.

It is well known that children's health and well being can be harmed by various forms of environmental pollution, such as from concentrated pesticide use, air pollution from industrial sites and high environmental concentrations of heavy metals, notably lead.

(Montgomery et al., 2003, p. 15)

Children as victims of crime gain far less media attention than children as perpetrators of crime. It is only the very extreme cases of child abuse or killing that get sustained media attention. Public attention in relation to crime in childhood more often focuses on 'disorderly youth'. The

See Chapter 5, Pictures of Children.

images of threatening youth influence general perceptions of young people. An important study by Pearson (1983) points out that this attention to youth is not new. He argues that each new generation of young people is viewed as more disorderly, rebellious and dangerous than the previous one. Although levels of child offending fluctuate and change in nature in relation to social and cultural change, fears of youth crime as new and expanding are distorted. Each generation searches for the causes of crime and finds the explanation in a perceived deterioration in behaviour. The focus may be children themselves, their families, the media or the state.

Reflective Activity 9.1

Popular views of children who offend

The historical view, in relation to youth crime has been that,

generation by generation, crime and disorder increase by leaps and bounds. Parental care plumbs increasing depths of irresponsibility, while the shortage of authority in the home is said to be mirrored by the excessive leniency of the law and the interference of the sentimentalists. As the rising generation soars to new heights of insubordination and depravity, working mothers are reliably identified within this otherwise predominantly masculine discourse as the primary cause of these 'new' outrages – whether by reference to the mill hands of the 1840s, the deterioration of motherhood in the Edwardian years, or the careless guardians of the 'latch-key' kids in the post-war years. Abuse is piled against mass education from it's beginnings in the Ragged Schools, via the 'Board Schools' of the early 1900s, to the 'permissive' jungle of the modern comprehensive system. Spectator football is also associated with violence, rowdyism and unsporting behaviour from its inception, while on a wider front; popular entertainments of all kind have been blamed for dragging down public morals.

(Pearson, 1983, p. 208)

Think about the way children who offend are viewed today and consider some of the explanations for their behaviour you have heard.

Do you feel Pearson's views still apply (that one generation sees the behaviour of the next as worse than their own) or do you feel children's behaviour is actually deteriorating? Try and think of some evidence to back up your position.

As the following headline from the Daily Mail in February 2001 suggests, there is still a general popular view that children's behaviour is deteriorating, 'The breakdown of the family was last night blamed for the shocking numbers of teenagers abusing hard drugs, alcohol and cigarettes.' The explanation for child offending is far more complex

See Chapters 2 and 4, Childhood: Rights and Realities and The Social Divisions of Childhood.

than this. However, such views of young people (for example, as 'out of control' and as 'threatening') have an impact on their self-esteem. Children talk about their exclusion and labelling in the world of adults: 'They just think we're thugs,' 'We're like the lower class people' (Edwards and Hatch, 2003, pp. 24 and 25). These perceptions can turn into self-fulfilling prophecies for some young people.

How does children's behaviour come to be defined as crime and what factors shape ideas about crime and childhood?

The nature of crime and punishment in childhood is continuously redefined; although 'disorderly youth' is a common theme, new offences are identified, new explanations given for children's criminal behaviour and new remedies pro-

See Chapter 10, Safeguarding Children.

See Chapter 6, Education: Service or System?

moted. For example, in the early 21st century there has been a developing emphasis on children's misbehaviour as 'anti-social' and new forms of intervention in the form of 'anti-social behaviour orders' (ASBOs) have been taken out against children. These were introduced in the Crime and Disorder Act 1998 and enable police and other authorities to ban children (and adults) from certain behaviour or from going into particular areas. At the same time there has been more emphasis on the importance of children's moral and social education and their education for citizenship. Both these

developments seek to alter behaviour and attitudes amongst young people. It could be argued they draw attention away from the wider inequalities that surround youth offending.

As a result of this policy, there has been increased media attention on children's offending behaviour, in particular because ASBOs permit the naming and shaming of offenders. Children as young as 10 and 11 have had their names and photographs published in newspapers. The promotion of ASBOs has also led to more children being imprisoned for relatively minor offences. ASBOs are civil orders and a lower standard of proof is required for them to be imposed. However, their breach is a criminal offence and has led to a recent surge in the numbers of children in prison. The Howard League for Penal Reform (2005) point out that in April 2005 there were 2500 boys and girls held in prison (including on remand), double the numbers held in 1993.

There has been a steady rise in the number of ASBOs issued to children as you will see from Table 9.1. The practice of publicly naming and shaming children not only makes them vulnerable to vigilante groups (people who want to take the law into their own hands) but also means the faces and names of particular children who have offended become widely known and remain in the community memory for many years. Media coverage of children and crime must be treated with some scepticism because of the way it may distort perceptions of the amount of crime committed by children and the nature of the offences they commit. The focus on extreme and rare cases for example misleads

Table 9.1 ASBOs Issued in England and Wales (45 per cent juveniles)

Year	Number of ASBOs issued (England and Wales)
2001	323
2002	403
2003	1035
2004	1826

Source: Home Office Information Services (2005).

us into thinking such examples are more common than they are. In addition, media reporting may reflect a change in the system of recording and punishing offences rather than an actual change in the type of offences committed by children (Farrington, 2002). For example, 'Among boys under 14 years of age . . . the increased use of formal caution is enough to account for the whole of the increase in recorded crime for this age group during the 1970s' (Pearson, 1983, p. 217). It is very important to critically question material in the newspapers, particularly the tabloid press.

Foucault (1977) discusses the history of crime and punishment and stresses the importance of understanding the process whereby some behaviours come to be defined as crimes and also the purpose of punishment. His insights cast light on the children, crime and justice system. Foucault argues that although we may believe that systems of crime and punishment are concerned only to repress 'wrong' behaviour, in fact they are as much concerned to develop and define what should be considered morally right in a given society. Debate about crime and punishment is shaped by people who have access to considerable power to influence policies. Many voices are excluded (in particular the voices of children themselves). We also know that children are one of the least powerful groups in society. Their voices are rarely heard and their views not taken into account. Politicians, the media, religious and professional interests shape the development of our ideas about crime. In addition, many voters who have

> See Chapters 2 and 3, Childhood: Rights and Realities and The Politics of Childhood.

Reflective Activity 9.2

Anti-social behaviour orders (ASBOs)

The Howard League for Penal Reform Calls for the Abolition of ASBOs

The Howard League for Penal Reform today called for the abolition of anti-social behaviour orders (ASBOs) for children. The charity said that when ASBOs were introduced it was intended they would rarely be used against young people – but children have become the focus of the orders. In its submission to the House of Commons Home Affairs Select Committee inquiry into anti-social behaviour, the Howard League for Penal Reform suggested that to tackle anti-social behaviour resources should be put into activities for children that engage them in positive and constructive ways rather than using ASBOs that isolate, exclude and stigmatise them. ASBOs exacerbate social exclusion, compound problems; and increase social tension. Some local authorities are putting children at risk by publishing leaflets with the names and photographs of children alleged to be involved in anti-social behaviour. Excessive and inappropriate use of ASBOs has resulted in significant numbers of children being imprisoned . . .

The order contravenes the government's commitment to the UN Convention on the Rights of the Child.   (Howard League for Penal Reform, 2004)

Boy, 11, confined to his own street

After a two month trial period, magistrates agreed that the 11 year old tear away who cannot read or write and has been excluded from every school he has attended, should be barred from his local town centre and every road but his own on three large housing estates. Standing under 5ft but already a criminal veteran with 13 convictions on top of ten offences when he was under 10 and could not be charged (name and photograph of child) must stay indoors between 7pm and 8am unless accompanied by a legal guardian or social worker.   (*The Guardian*, 7 December 2004)

Newspaper articles where children are 'named and shamed' as a result of ASBOs are more frequent.

Consider the impact of the process of 'naming and shaming' on the children involved, both in the short and long term.

concerns about youth offending, because they have experienced the consequences of it or because their fears have been magnified by media coverage, want politicians to put youth crime high on the political agenda. The definitions of childhood criminality that emerge relate closely to the definitions of normality such people want to promote in a particular community. For example, are teenage girls who behave 'yobbishly' viewed as more problematic than boys because they breach socially stereotypical ideas about how girls should behave? It is not always clear why some behaviour comes to be defined as criminal and other behaviour (which we might personally feel should be criminalised) remains unpoliced.

An action in itself is not a crime unless the society in which it is committed defines it as such. What actually

Reflective Activity 9.3

Constructing crime in childhood

Carrabine et al. (2002, pp. 3–14) discuss the power relations involved in the social construction of crime. For example, they raise questions about different behaviours and explore the points at which they have been considered to constitute criminal offences. I have adapted and modified some of these examples in view of the focus here on childhood in the list below.

Consider each in turn. At what stage do you feel these behaviours should be criminalised?

- A child taking a life
- Consensual sex at 16 between gay young men
- Children's art
- Children's music
- Children's street play

Now read the discussion below and see if your views have changed.

A child taking a life

The assumption would probably be that a child taking a life has committed a crime, yet taking a life may be viewed as self-defence; or a child may be seen to be under the age of criminal responsibility. Media representation of children involved in killing tends to underplay such issues.

Consensual sex at 16 between gay young men

Consensual sex between 16-year-olds is currently not a crime in England, Scotland and Wales. However, this was not the case for gay young men until 2001 and is still not the case in many parts of the world. Many young people find themselves at risk of prosecution.

Children's art

Those involved in graffiti art may be subject to criminal charges.

> I started writing graffiti like every kid did that I was hanging around with. If you couldn't talk over a record very well then it was the other thing you did . . . Some people do say that graffiti is ugly. Well a lot of graffiti is ugly . . . it's a product of society so it's bound to be pretty ugly. Some people want to make the world a better place I just wanna make the world a better looking place. If you don't like it you can paint over it.
> (Banksy in Squall, 2002)

From Banksy's perspective, graffiti art is socially useful. From another, it may be viewed as criminal activity.

Children's music

There are many occasions when children (and adults) gather in groups to listen to loud music. When such an event is licensed it is not an offence, but the unlicensed playing of loud music may be a public order offence. The disturbance to the local community may be no different.

Children's street play

The majority of children play in the streets near their homes. Young people in particular tend to gather in groups within their communities, particularly when more formal leisure facilities are not available. The introduction of curfews and the dispersal of young people has meant that the police now have powers to remove young people to their homes even where no offence has been committed. This has been successfully challenged by a 15-year-old boy in the courts (BBC, 2005).

influences the definition and construction of child-hood crime? At a basic level one might say

- the context of the behaviour;
- the motivation and intention of the child;
- the consequences of the child's behaviour;
- the risks involved if such behaviour was permitted;
- the age and understanding of the child.

However, those studying crime in childhood (Muncie, 2004; Goldson, 2002; Scraton and Haydon, 2002; Goldson and Muncie, 2006) would also point to the influence of

- current ideas about what is appropriate and 'normal' behaviour for a child;
- the status and rights of the child in a given society;
- the political and professional interests of those involved in making decisions about children, crime and punishment;

- critical events, in particular those related to children in society (for example, the very rare cases of children killing children);
- the broader political, economic, social, environmental and cultural context.

The combination of this wide variety of influences will be different in different communities. This leads to very different approaches to children who may commit relatively similar crimes. Look at the examples in Reflective Activity 9.4.

Such childhood crimes are rare and extreme but serve to show how societies and communities can approach and deal with crime in very different ways. Collective cultural values and mores, such as reform rather than revenge and belief systems that consider childhood as 'innocent' are likely to generate a remedial approach such as that taken by Norway; whereas those with a desire for retribution rather than

See Chapter 2, Childhood: Rights and Realities.

Reflective Activity 9.4

Different responses to children who kill children

'In 1993 a 2-year-old boy (Jamie Bulger) was killed by two 10-year-old boys in Merseyside, England. The toddler was taken by the older boys from a shopping centre and later killed. There was public outrage and the older children were portrayed in the media as monsters and brutes. They were named in court and were sentenced to fifteen years' detention. Underpinning the approach to them was the view that they were a danger to society, that they were criminally responsible and that they deserved to be punished as adults would have been. Their sentences were later reduced on Human Rights grounds and they were released after eight years.

'In 1994, in Trondheim, Norway, a 5-year-old girl was killed by two 6-year-old boys. Although the crime was very similar (except for the age of the offenders) the children concerned received no punishment. They were considered under the age of criminal responsibility. Even had they been 10 years old, they would

have been treated in the same way as the age of criminal responsibility in Norway is 15 years (not 10 as is currently the case in the UK). The Norwegian children were intensively supervised and rehabilitated. They received psychological and emotional support. They were not named at any stage and they were reintegrated back into their original school, the same school that their victim had attended.' (BBC News, 2000).

1 Why do you think the child offenders were treated so differently?

2 In both cases the offences were particularly extreme. Was it just the age of the offenders that made a difference?

3 Consider some of the influences on the definition of crime and punishment discussed previously. What questions are raised in relation to these two case studies?

remedy and views of children as villains are likely to adopt the stance taken by much of the British media.

Severe punishment of the young has been shown to be relatively ineffective in reducing reoffending rates, for example reoffending rates on leaving a Secure Unit are 70 per cent to 80 per cent (Muncie, 2004). Nevertheless, punitive approaches to the young persist in the UK and in many other parts of the world. Why? Foucault would argue that the purpose of punishment is not solely to repress 'wrongs' but to define 'rights' or 'the moral good' and send a message to the wider community:

> Penalty would . . . appear to be a way of handling illegalities, of laying down the limits of tolerance, of giving free rein to some, of putting pressure on others . . . In short, penalty does not simply 'check' illegalities; it 'differentiates' them.
>
> (Foucault, 1977, p. 272)

The way that 'moral good' is defined may reflect some interests more than others, for example it could be argued that the increased punishment of graffiti artists serves the interest of property owners rather than children.

There is no doubt that crime and punishment is of great concern to the community as a whole. Many victims of crime in particular lack a voice and have little influence. Victims of crime are more likely to be from working-class, black and minority ethnic communities (CRE, 2002). Some children are victimised on the basis of age (including childhood), gender, sexuality, mental health or disability (Lea and Young, 1993). It is important to understand where powerlessness shapes the experience of the victim as well as the offender. Some people do not even report crimes because they fear they will not be believed.

It is strongly argued that crime and punishment of the young is an electoral issue and in the run up to any election, crime and punishment issues are amplified in the media and political debate, 'Being "tough on crime" leads to punitive "solutions" in which a fearful public may be persuaded that "something is being done"' (Muncie and Hughes, 2002, p. 12). 'Media grabbing headlines about law and order win votes' (Goldson, 2002a, p. 133). These writers raise important questions

about the political motivations, rather than genuine concern for both victims and offenders, that has led to an era of 'new punitiveness' towards children (discussed later in the chapter).

Which particular groups of children come into contact with the criminal justice system and why?

Those who come into contact with the children crime and justice system are disproportionately boys from low-income households or looked-after situations, and disproportionately from some black and minority ethnic communities (Muncie, 2004). Although the numbers of girls going through the courts has increased there is little evidence to suggest the numbers actually offending have increased, just that more are being taken to court (Nacro, 2005). There has been long-standing debate on how accurate statistics are in reflecting the relationship between class and crime. As early as 1958, Short and Nye argued that middle-class boys were engaged in as many criminal acts as working-class boys but they were less likely to end up in the criminal statistics (cited in Maguire, 1994). Although this argument has been challenged there is a general consensus that the offences of middle-class young people are underestimated.

In relation to 'race' there is evidence that black young people are over-represented within the youth justice system and generally treated more harshly:

> According to Youth Justice Board data, for instance, children classified as black or black British made up 6.2% of the youth offending population during 2003/4. At the remand stage, such children were less likely to be granted unconditional bail than their white counterparts, and more likely to be remanded to secure facilities . . . black or black British young people constituted 12.2% of those receiving a custodial sentence. (Nacro, 2005, p. 6)

Many different sociological and psychological theories have been developed to explain child offending.

Muncie (2004) provides clear summaries and overviews of these theoretical perspectives in his book *Youth Justice*. In this case I discuss his critiques of three: these are the *positivist*, *radical* and *realist* approaches.

The first questions asked by *positivist* theorists exploring crime are can we find 'scientific' explanations for the behaviour of children and therefore help prevent reoffending? Such explanations might focus on the individual offender, for example their personality and psychological makeup and experience. In the 19th century even their body type was seen as relevant; in fact Lombroso thought that child criminals could be detected because of their large jaws and strong canine teeth! But such approaches give limited insight into the wider social context of crime in childhood. More convincing positivist explanations focus on social factors that might shape child offending. Factors such as poverty, poor housing, the influence of peers, exclusion from school and lack of play space are seen as relevant.

See Chapter 14, The Swings and Roundabouts of Community Development, and Chapter 18, The Venture: Case Study of an Adventure Playground.

The *radical* approach ponders to what extent we should consider childhood crime in relation to social inequality and social division. How relevant are the wider inequalities of class, gender, race and ability to both the definition and the practice of crime? Crime in childhood may be a product of inequalities and also may reinforce social divisions. What power and influence do children have access to? What background are they from and would they be policed differently according to their background?

See Chapter 4, The Social Divisions of Childhood.

The *realist* may give as much attention to the victims of crime as well as the offenders. In the 1990s, new thinking about crime drew renewed attention to the experience of both victims and offenders. Emphasis on particular issues varied according to the wider political perspective of the researcher. For example, people writing from a politically right-wing perspective, such as Charles Murray, emphasise moral decline in society, and the negative impact of state welfare in eroding individual independence and creating an 'underclass' where children are more liable to offend (Murray, 1990). Those writing from a socialist and social-democratic perspective draw attention to the lack of adequate welfare support, lack of social justice for both victims and offenders, and the experience of relative deprivation. This is where people perceive themselves to be unfairly disadvantaged in relation to others (Lea and Young, 1993). Renewed attention to the victims of crime also produced evidence that some groups were particularly vulnerable to victimisation and inadequate protection.

The murder of Stephen Lawrence, who was killed solely on the grounds of his colour and whose killers have yet (at the time of writing) to be brought to justice is a case in point. The Macpherson Report (1999) drew attention to the pattern of institutionalised racism evident in the way this case was handled that led to Stephen's killers going free. More recently, research has demonstrated that young people in prison have been on the receiving end of racist treatment (Wilson, 2003). Webster (2006) discusses the absence of local research into the interaction of social class, place and race in bringing children into contact with the criminal justice system.

These different perspectives on childhood crime do not always contradict each other. Each offers a partial view, a particular angle on child offending. Each draws attention to different factors and influences. Some, however, do directly oppose each other, being fundamentally shaped by different underpinning theories and beliefs about children and society.

What debates related to childhood, crime and the state have shaped provision?

Solutions to child offending represent conflicting ideas about childhood and crime as well as areas of consensus and agreement about what is best for children and the wider community and 'what works'. Clearly a major influence on a given system is the agenda of the politicians of the day and the resources they are willing to commit to this area of public spending.

Historically, in particular since the early 19th century, two key debates have influenced the pattern of provision. One focuses on the welfare and needs of the child, and the social factors that give rise to offending, the other on community justice and law and order, the experience of victims and the need for punishment and deterrence. These perspectives have shaped approaches to children who offend. Contemporary policy is informed by competing debates about the interests of victims and offenders, pragmatic measures concerned to reduce offending and overarching political agendas concerned with maintaining political support. Muncie (2004, pp. 247–95) provides summaries of five approaches to youth justice.

Child welfare

The child welfare perspective is evident in moves that try to treat children differently to adults and take into account the status of the child as 'vulnerable'. Such moves reflect recognition of the social context of criminal behaviour in childhood and that crime in childhood could be a result of the conditions in which children live. The emphasis is on reform, diversion and rehabilitation (Goldson, 2002a, p. 122).

Youth justice

Emphasis here is placed on the rights of victims and the ineffectiveness of welfare approaches in reducing offending. The importance of disciplinary intervention and the need for 'the punishment to match the crime' and fairness and equity in relation to sentencing are emphasised.

Restorative justice

The emphasis here is on the importance of a strong community-based solution to childhood crime. For example, offenders are expected to 'repay' both victims and the wider community. The victim, for example, may be involved in deciding the sort of reparation the offender should make. Restoration may be achieved through, for example, repairs to damaged property, direct apologies to the victim and voluntary work of benefit to the community at large. Failure to cooperate with such measure may lead to more punitive sanctions. This approach draws attention to the rights of the victim and the community to redress, to the responsibilities of the offender and the responsibilities of the community to help the fight against crime.

What works (risk management)

Muncie (2004, p. 277) discusses the 'risk management' approach, termed 'the principle of "what works"'. In the mid to late 1990s, this approach gained popularity. Measures may include, at the level of the individual, the identification of and intensive work with potential persistent young offenders (youth inclusion projects). At a wider level, agencies, such as the Connexions service, are set up that attempt to track and support 13- to 19-year-olds who may be at risk of offending (because, for example, they are not in school, training or paid work), attempts are made to reduce levels of school exclusion, and attempts are made to encourage all children to stay on at school beyond the age of 16 (through, for example, educational maintenance allowances). The aim is to reduce the risk factors that give rise to child offending. The practical, moral and political problems with this approach are discussed by Smith (2006), for example the attempts to identify 'risk factors' may be simplistic, overgeneralised and undermine human rights.

Authoritarian

In the early 1990s and continuing to this day, a more authoritarian and interventionist approach in relation to child offenders has developed in the UK. Initially this was characterised, under the Conservative government of the early 1990s by an emphasis on morality and family values and more recently, under New Labour, by an emphasis on community and citizenship (Goldson, 2002a). Criminal justice legislation has seen an increase in the range of punitive penalties, treatment measures and surveillance related to children and young people. Measures introduced range from secure training centres for 12- to 14-year-olds in 1994 (Goldson terms these 'children's jails'), to the introduction by New Labour of the Crime and Disorder Act 1998, '. . . an extraordinarily wide-ranging and intrusive piece of legislation which is substantially weighted to "tackling" youth crime' (Goldson, 2002a, p. 132) and includes measures such as curfews to enable the dispersal of children and young people who may have committed no offence.

Consider these and other approaches to child offending in relation to the case study in Reflective Activity 9.5 below.

Current approaches to child offending are a mixture of welfare, preventive, justice and risk management measures within an authoritarian framework (Muncie, 2004). Systems vary in different parts of the UK (for example, children's hearings are a feature of the Scottish system alone) but the political need to be seen to be doing something strong about youth crime has led to some highly moralistic and punitive sanctions. Even though many measures are intended to prevent and reduce child offending, in reality many more children are currently caught up in the system. It is well known that the majority of children grow out of criminal behaviour and it is important to give them time to do this and perhaps avoid over-intervention (Goldson, 2002a, p. 128). However, the opportunities to 'grow out of crime' are under threat because of the strong negative labelling of young offenders.

Reflective Activity 9.5

Approaches to Child Offending

Case Study

You are a youth justice worker, working with Adam and Shireen. Adam is 17 and Shireen 13 years old. They were involved breaking into a cricket club. Shireen climbed through a window and took some bottles of whisky and Adam was look out. Both of them tried to sell the whisky and someone informed the police. Both have been in trouble with the police before.

1 Consider the different approaches to interventions drawn from Muncie (2004) and Goldson (2002a) above and the case study.

2 Imagine you are making recommendations for how Adam and Shireen should be dealt with.

3 Consider the different perspectives in turn and in each case draft recommendations for how the children should be dealt with.

4 It may help you to add a bit more detail to the case, such as family circumstances, environment, schooling, etc.

5 Finally, consider what your own personal position is in relation to all the approaches discussed.

What about justice for children?

The following questions emerge from the material discussed so far in this chapter. Some related issues to stimulate your thinking and discussion follow each question.

- Is the context of childhood offences such that children from low-income groups are more likely to offend? Consider lack of space for play and leisure; lack of access to consumer goods; homelessness; racism; school exclusion; and childhood poverty levels. These are the product of profound inequalities in childhood and have all been linked to offending behaviour. Clearly many children on low incomes are not engaged in crime and it is important not to stereotype them in this way. In addition it is important to ask whether those that do get caught up in the criminal justice system are treated differently to children from wealthier backgrounds.

- Is the policing and visibility of some groups of children higher than that of others leading to some groups being policed more than others? Consider, for example, the 'anti-social behaviour' of better-off children, or children living in the leafy suburbs rather than inner-city areas. Consider the activities of students in the evenings in high-density student areas. Consider the crimes that occur behind closed doors. Consider all these factors in relation to patterns of policing and surveillance in different communities.

- Are children policed differently to adults? For example, ASBOs are used against both children and adults (see Reflective Activity 9.2). But what sort of behaviour is penalised? Consider the consequences of the actions of adults for children, such as dangerous driving. Might more of this adult behaviour warrant the use of such orders? Why were 45 per cent of ASBOs in England and Wales given to young people (see Table 9.1)? Do you feel that this is an accurate reflection of child versus adult anti-social behaviour?

- To what extent is the children, crime and justice system institutionally racist? Does the system fail to provide an appropriate service to children and young people from black and minority ethnic groups (MacPherson, 1999)? Young people from some black and minority ethnic communities are stopped and searched far more often than their counterparts. Such groups are also more likely to be victims of racially aggravated crime (CRE, 2002). There is also evidence of different sentencing (Nacro, 2005; Allen, 2003).

- How does crime in childhood relate to the consumer culture in which children live with wide advertising to children of goods they cannot afford? How do we interpret a child stealing, for example? Advertisers target children who cannot afford the goods they advertise. What are the consequences of this? The experience of inequality in a consumer society has a profound connection to childhood offending (Bauman, 1998). Piachaud (2005, p. 9) cites the Treasury's child poverty review, 'Child poverty damages childhood experience through limiting access to activities, services and opportunities, increasing exposure to risks, and diminishing access to the resources and support that increase resilience.'

- How do ideas about gender identity and sexual difference help us understand crime in childhood? Feminists have argued that boys are socialised into masculine roles that encourage aggression against each other and against women and girls (Lees, 1993, 1997). Ideas about gender may shape both our ideas about crime and the nature of punishment of both boys and girls (Hudson, 2002). The common belief is that girl offending is on the increase; in reality it is the response of the youth justice system in relation to girl offenders that seem to be shifting as more girls are being taken to court. The percentage of offenders who are girls has however been stable over the last eleven years; fluctuating between 20 per cent and 23 per cent between 1992 and 2003 (Nacro, 2005).

- What about the rights of those children at the extreme and punitive ends of the youth justice system? To what extent have the rights of such children been eroded? We have discussed children subject to ASBOs above. Also consider children's experiences of racism, bullying and inhumane treatment in prison (Goldson, 2002b). Wilson, a former prison governor, researched experiences of children in young offender institutions and found evidence of overt racist abuse of inmates, articulated by one young person as follows, 'I've been called a "chimp" before. I was also called a "golliwog" by one of these officers. I ended up getting into trouble for that and I was put on adjudication' (Wilson, 2003).

- To what extent do measures in the children, crime and justice system impact on the rights of all children? Increased powers to move children on and the imposition of curfews (introduced in 1998) are examples to consider. Graham Duffy (Children's Society, 2003), aged 16, says of curfews,

> The majority of young people don't hang about because they want to cause trouble; they do so because there is little else for them to do. The

police in my town are already moving young people away from the local 'hangouts' but they only end up further down the town in even larger numbers or go to quieter places which are less safe.

Such measures put all children under suspicion if they gather in groups, thus reducing the status of children and their rights of free movement in the community.

Non-governmental children's organisations such as the Children's Society, UNICEF and Save the Children have been campaigning with children to further their rights in relation to systems of crime and justice. Nevertheless, children and young people are relatively silenced and have limited access to justice. However, they have demonstrated that

See Chapter 2, Childhood: Rights and Realities.

Reflective Activity 9.6

The case of Euan Sutherland

'A sixteen year old boy had a sexual relationship with an eighteen year old boy. Both were committing a criminal offence until the law was changed in Britain in 2001. Both would still be committing an offence in at least 70 countries of the world that bar same-sex relationships at any age.' Euan Sutherland (aged 16) successfully challenged the law through his Human Rights application to the European Commission on Human Rights as this extract shows:

'The applicant became aware of his attraction to other boys at about the age of 12. As his contemporaries became more interested in girls he became more aware that he was sexually attracted to boys. From about that time he felt sure that his sexual orientation was homosexual. He tried going out with a girl when he was 14. They are still friends but there was no sexual attraction with her, and the experience confirmed for the applicant that he could only find a fulfilling relationship with another man.'

A result of this application and the associated campaign was the equalisation of the age of consent in Britain. (Stonewall, 2004)

Euan Sutherland faced criminalisation as a young gay person and took his case to the European Commission on Human Rights. At the time of this case, it was a sexual offence to have gay consenting sex until 21 years. Heterosexuals were legally permitted to have consensual sex at 16. The impact of this for young gay people beginning to develop loving relationships was very destructive. Not only did they face prejudiced attitudes, but their actions could be criminalised. Euan Sutherland was brave enough to challenge this situation in the European courts.

1 Review the key learning in this chapter so far including the material on popular views of children who offend; news and political coverage of child offending; definitions of crime in childhood; social explanations for child offending and different policy approaches. It may also help to return to some of the material in Chapter 4, The Social Divisions of Childhood.

2 What popular assumptions about children who offend are challenged by the case of Euan Sutherland?

they have the capacity to resist and transform existing practices that they feel are unjust. This may be at the everyday level of adopting strategies to avoid surveillance (Children's Society, 2003), but it has also been evident at a national and international level (see Reflective Activity 9.6). Scraton and Haydon (2002) make an excellent case for a rights-based approach and the decriminalisation of children.

Conclusion

This chapter has introduced you to some of the key areas of academic research in relation to children who offend. Questions about the way childhood crime is defined, measured and reported have been raised. Some of the main social theories about child offending and different policy approaches to children who offend have been introduced. Finally, critical questions have been discussed which relate to social justice for different groups of children.

We raised four key questions in this chapter:

- How does children's behaviour come to be defined as crime? The chapter pointed to the powerful actors involved in constructing definitions of crime and how such definitions relate to the normative social expectations of children and young people. In Reflective Activity 9.6 the significance of ideas about sexuality is given as a further example of the shifting nature of what is considered crime in childhood. Dominant beliefs that same sex relationships were sinful led to many societies outlawing loving and consensual relationships.

- Which particular groups of children come into contact with the criminal justice system and why? The vulnerability of particular children related to their class or colour or minority status was discussed. Again, Reflective Activity 9.6 provides a further example of a group of children and young people who have been criminalised in relation to their social status, in this case because of their sexual identity.

- What debates related to childhood, crime and the state have shaped provision? We explored different approaches to intervention, ranging from those that put child welfare first, to those that emphasise the old adage, 'Spare the rod and spoil the child'. The material in Reflective Activity 9.6 further demonstrates the shifting legal context of intervention.

- What about justice for children? We discussed the rights of particular groups of children in relation to the youth justice system. The material in Reflective Activity 9.6 demonstrates that the pursuit of justice for children has sometimes been led by children and young people and this has led to some major shifts in practices related to 'offending'.

Annotated reading

Carrabine, E., Cox, P., Lee, M. and South, N. (2002) *Crime in Modern Britain*, Oxford: Oxford University Press

An overview of research evidence relating to crime in modern Britain; it is clearly written, informative and accessible: with some focus on young people.

Goldson, B. (2002a) 'Children, crime and the state', in Goldson, B., Lavalette, M. and McKechnie, J. (eds) *Children, Welfare and the State*, London: Sage

A very useful overview of the welfare and justice debate and the way that these have historically shaped the children, crime and justice system in sometimes unexpected ways.

Goldson, B. (2002b) *Vulnerable Inside: Children in Secure and Penal Settings*, London: Children's Society

Detailed and moving material concerned with the experiences, perceptions and rights of children in prison.

Goldson, B. and Muncie, J. (eds) (2006) *Youth Crime and Justice*, London: Sage

A range of authors consider historical and social-structural contexts (including class, race and gender); different rationales and approaches to intervention and future directions.

Lees, S. (1997) *Ruling Passions: Sexual Violence, Reputation and the Law*, Buckingham: Open University Press

A powerful text giving detailed insight into the legal and social response to sexual violence; the focus is mainly on the experiences and perceptions of women and girls.

Muncie, J. (2004) *Youth and Crime*, 2nd edn, London: Sage

An essential guide for anyone concerned with the history and practice of the youth justice system; it contains excellent theoretical overviews and summaries of research.

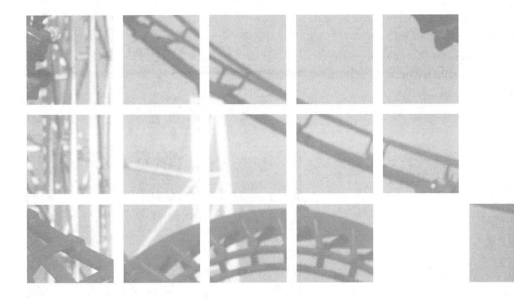

Chapter 10

Safeguarding Children: Visions and Values

GARY WALKER

We will be called upon to make common cause across professional boundaries and with reformed structures and services to create the means by which the needs, interests and welfare of children can be better protected and advanced. Underpinning this must be not just the resources but an attitude that reflects the value that our society places on children and childhood.

(Paul Boateng, Chief Secretary to the Treasury, UK, Introduction to *Every Child Matters*, DfES, 2003b)

Introduction

This chapter explores the notion of safeguarding children within the context of major legislative and policy change. It is important to reflect in some detail on major changes in child welfare policy in order to understand the debates shaping children's policy. How are the tensions between the interests of the state, professionals, the family and children resolved? How do we begin to evaluate how policy rhetoric (in this case related to child welfare) matches the reality of legislative proposals? Policy in relation to children (in particular concerned with their protection) continuously changes and the purpose of this chapter is to both introduce contemporary debates about safeguarding

children as well as deepen understanding of the processes of policy development involved and the implications for children's rights. The chapter includes consideration of not only the changing emphasis of legislation and guidance on protecting or safeguarding children in England since 1991, but also the *Every Child Matters* (DfES, 2003b) strategy as a broad vision for change in children's services. The following key questions are examined:

- What visions of the relationship between the family and the state are apparent in the legislation and guidance relating to safeguarding children?
- How are the rights of children and those of parents to be balanced?

- Is the vision for safeguarding children matched by values that always place children at the centre?

- What are the values and attitudes towards children and childhood that are reflected in the legislation and guidance?

What visions of the relationship between the family and the state are apparent in the legislation and guidance relating to safeguarding children?

The Children Act 1989, which came into force in October 1991, marked a significant watershed in social care legislation. It brought about a 'fundamental change of child law' (White et al., 1991, p. v). This section is going to focus on those aspects of the Act which relate directly to the protection of children. It will track the changes in emphasis, particularly with the accompanying guidance, since 1991.

> For further discussion of this change see Chapter 2, Childhood: Rights and Realities.

Familiarity cannot only breed contempt, but also scotoma, or blind-spots. It is therefore useful to remind ourselves of some of the fundamental principles of the Children Act 1989, which, of course, still applies to child-care decisions. These are:

> For further discussion on these principles see Chapter 3, The Politics of Childhood.

- The child's welfare is paramount. Briefly this means that what is in the child's best interests should guide decisions about that child.

- Parents have responsibilities as well as rights. The concept of parental responsibility is a fundamental one which reinforces the relationship between the family and the state. Parents are seen, generally speaking, as the ones who know best how to raise their children.

- The family is the best place for children to live. This reinforces the concept of permanency. Every effort should be made to try to ensure children can live with birth parents. If this is not possible, every effort should then be made to find them an alternative permanent family as quickly as possible.

- Children have the right to be protected from 'significant harm'. Where families may need support, they should be offered appropriate help, if the child has been assessed as being 'in need' of services, as defined in Section 17 of the Act.

The date of this Act is crucial in locating it in terms of the political and philosophical landscape. Coming

Section 31 of the Children Act 1989

This does not provide a definition of 'significant'; however, 'harm' is defined as follows: 'harm' means ill-treatment or the impairment of health or development; 'development' means physical, intellectual, emotional, social or behavioural development; 'health' means physical or mental health; and 'ill-treatment' includes sexual abuse and forms of ill-treatment which are not physical.

Section 17 of the Children Act 1989

This states that a child is 'in need' if a) he or she is unlikely to achieve or maintain, or have the opportunity of achieving or maintaining, a reasonable standard of health or development without the provision of services by a local authority; b) his or her health or development is likely to be significantly impaired, or further impaired, without the provision of such services; or c) he or she is disabled.

Neglect and emotional abuse: definitions

Neglect is the persistent failure to meet a child's basic physical and/or psychological needs, likely to result in the serious impairment of the child's health or development.

Emotional abuse is the persistent emotional mal-treatment of a child such as to cause severe and persistent adverse effects on the child's emotional development.   (DfES, 2006c)

squarely in the middle of the eighteen years in which the New Right were in government, and following the publication of the Cleveland Report in 1988, which crit-icised Social Services for perceived over-intrusiveness in

See Chapter 7, Youth Services and Provision.

family affairs, it reflects the thinking of that time, with its emphasis on minimal state intervention.

Section 47 of the Children Act 1989

Where a Local Authority have reasonable cause to suspect that a child who lives, or is found, in their area is suffering, or is likely to suffer, significant harm, the authority shall make such enquiries as they consider necessary to enable them to decide whether they should take any action to safeguard or promote the child's welfare.

The Act makes it clear that the state should only intervene if necessary to safeguard and promote the welfare of the child. Intervention should be evidence-led, and should amount to the minimum required to protect the child. Burden (1998) places this in the context of political the-ory, explaining that this approach, also known as Neo-Liberalism, per-ceives the state as capa-ble of violating individual rights if it is not limited in its function. An illustration of this can be found in the government guidance accompanying the publication of the Children Act 1989. It is interesting that very early on the point is made, in a section headed 'Protection from Protection' that

Neo-liberalism is discussed in Chapter 3, The Politics of Childhood.

> potent powers, if misdirected, may themselves cause harm to a child by enabling the state to intervene in his or his (sic) family's life when it should not.
> (An Introduction to the Children Act 1989, p. 6)

In other words, the state should only intervene if and when it can demonstrate that there are grounds to do so, and that it is in the best interests of the child. If it cannot do so, it should leave well alone and allow fami-lies to parent children without interference. The atti-tude towards children that is exposed here is that they

Chapter 2, Childhood: Rights and Realities, discusses this aspect of the approach to children's rights.

are effectively the private property of parents and their welfare is only of concern to others if these parents fail to deliver safe outcomes.

How are the rights of children and those of parents to be balanced?

There are clear tensions here. Not all instances where children need protecting are easily demonstrable, for example children at risk of neglect or emotional abuse. By definition, these two categories of abuse are complex, long term and difficult to quantify precisely. Identification often requires intervention and assessment over a period of time, something which the current legislation only allows for if parents consent. The Act therefore appears to limit opportunity for agencies to work with families with some statutory support in order to promote the child's welfare.

This is further reinforced by the fact that support offered to families under Section 17 is of course entirely voluntary. Families can reject this support, even where professionals judge that lack of such support could compromise the welfare of the child. Only if this leads to them having reasonable cause to suspect the child is suffering, or is likely to suffer, significant harm can they use the statutory duty to investigate.

If the Children Act 1989 is the umbrella, the guidance document *Working Together* (DfES, 2006c) tells those working beneath it to implement its principles, how to behave. It sets out the duties and responsibilities of all agencies in the child protection process, which all agencies are expected to follow. There have been four versions of *Working Together*, and each version supersedes the previous one.

The first dates back to 1988, and reflects the Cleveland enquiry, dealing mainly with sexual abuse. The second version corresponded with the implementation of the Children Act 1989 (DoH, 1991). The third version was published in 1999 (DoH, 1999b). The fourth version was published in 2006 (DfES, 2006c) and reflects the context of multi-agency working within the *Every Child Matters* agenda.

Reflective Activity 10.1

When is harm 'significant'?

Jake is a 3-year-old white British boy living in England with his mother, a lone parent. Household income is via state benefits. Jake does not attend any playgroup or nursery provision, and has limited scope for playing outside because he lives in a local authority flat with no safe outside play area. When the health visitor visits, she notices that the flat is untidy, with dirty clothes strewn around the floor of most rooms. Jake's mother does not own a washing machine. There are only a few toys available, and some of these are broken, with sharp edges. Jake's language development is delayed. On her latest visit, the health visitor weighs Jake, and he has lost 3lbs so that his weight is now less than it was four months previously. She informs Jake's mother that she is going to make a referral to Social Services as she believes Jake is suffering, or likely to suffer, significant harm.

1 Do you think the Health Visitor is justified in her actions?

2 Do you think Social Services would be justified in responding to this referral by launching enquiries under Section 47 of the Children Act 1989?

3 Can you think of other approaches or actions which may help to ameliorate this situation, using Section 17 of the Children Act 1989?

4 Do you think Jake is suffering, or likely to suffer, significant harm?

It is interesting to compare the last three documents in terms of their emphasis, and there is no better place to begin than their subtitles. The 1991 version was called *Working Together Under the Children Act 1989: A guide to arrangements for inter-agency co-operation for the protection of children from abuse.* In contrast, the 1999 and 2006 versions are both entitled *Working Together to Safeguard Children: A guide to inter-agency working to safeguard and promote the welfare of children.*

We can immediately see the shift – from narrow 'protection' following the principles already described above of minimal state intervention, towards a broader approach to promoting children's welfare. This depicts a change from the view of state intervention as being something to be wary about to it being welcome, if it is supportive. Some of the circumstances for this are laid out in the 1999 and 2006 versions as 'sources of stress' on families, although, curiously, these appear as early as page 8 in the 1999 version, but not until page 158 in the 2006 version. The identified factors are domestic violence, substance abuse by parents, mental illness in parents, social exclusion and (in the 2006 version) parental learning disability. Here appropriate support services are seen as important elements in the prevention of abuse as well as providing much-needed services to address the issues. And, in acknowledging social exclusion, the New Labour government has dramatically separated itself from the proclamation of the former New Right Prime Minister, Margaret Thatcher that 'there is no such thing as society' (Woman's Own, 1987). The links between such social ills as poverty, racism, lack of educational opportunity and child welfare are made explicit, recognising the impact of some of the social divisions explored in Chapter 4. This illustrates a significant change of emphasis between 1991 and 2006, which has seen a change in government, from New Right to New Labour. Through these changes, the New Labour government claim a supportive and benign role for the state, if conducted in a sensitive manner.

The difficulty here is that the tensions remain – particularly between parents' right to self-determination and the provision of support for vulnerable children. It is one thing stating that agencies should offer services to promote children's welfare; it is quite another thing to encourage a reluctant parent to accept support. The state can only be helpful if parents allow it to be, and the parents' position is reinforced by the principles of the Children Act 1989 and the underlying presumption that parents have the right to bring up their children as they wish, up to the point where the children are at risk of suffering actual or likely significant harm.

Whether by design or accident, these tensions go some way to being addressed in the 2006 version of *Working Together*. The move towards safeguarding and promoting children's welfare and away from mere protection is an attempt at a holistic approach to the child. Intervention should not just be focused on the specific concern or incident, but should assess the full circumstances in which the child is living, and see where support can be offered and provided. There is, or should be, therefore, a continuum of a child being 'in need' to potentially (or actually) being 'in need of protection':

> Effective measures to safeguard children are those which also promote their welfare. They should not be seen in isolation from the wider range of support and services already provided and available to meet the needs of children and families.
> (DfES, 2006c, p. 3)

This suggests, too, that services should seek to work preventatively and intervene early when approached by parents to support them with child rearing. Inherent in this is the development of non-stigmatising services, so that parents feel comfortable in asking for, and receiving, help: 'Asking for help should be seen as a sign of responsibility rather than as a parenting failure' (p. 1). Nevertheless, there remain some echoes of the minimalist intervention position. The document goes on to say that, 'Only in exceptional cases should there be compulsory intervention in family life' (p. 1). This refers to the necessity to protect a child from 'significant harm', a concept explained earlier in this chapter.

So the most recent position, at the time of writing, appears to be this: agencies can, indeed should, respond positively and supportively if parents request support, but agencies cannot intervene without parental agreement unless it is necessary to protect the child from significant harm. The underpinning attitude towards children and childhood appears to contain, therefore, a somewhat mixed message: child rearing is the responsibility of us all, but people other than parents can only exercise this responsibility without parental consent if the children are in danger. The government's vision for the future of services for children and families, *Every Child Matters,* takes forward this position. The next section examines this in depth.

Is the vision for safeguarding children matched by values that always place children at the centre?

Every Child Matters (DfES, 2003b) was published as a government green paper. It sets out the UK government's vision of reform for services working with children and families, and is backed by the Children Act 2004 and further enhanced by the follow-up publication *Every Child Matters: Change for Children* (DfES, 2005c). A key impetus for the production of this programme is identified at the outset, in the Prime Minister's foreword to the green paper: the inquiry headed by Lord Laming into the death of Victoria Climbié, who died in London at the age of eight after suffering months of abuse from her carers – an aunt and her partner. Lord Laming's report made 108 recommendations as to how to improve the safeguarding of children, many of them detailed suggestions for producing better quality guidance, training and practice. The following sentence in this report appears to explain the reason for the introduction of such a wide-ranging vision for children and families as *Every Child Matters*: 'It is not possible to separate the protection of children from wider support to families' (Laming, 2003, p. 6). However, given that we have seen that as early as 1999, the government were making the link between safeguarding children and family support, one wonders whether Lord Laming's report provided a timely hook on which they could hang their considerable plans for the future of service delivery to children and families.

Five desirable outcomes for all children and young people are identified as the main elements of *Every Child Matters*. These are:

- Being healthy
- Staying safe
- Enjoying and achieving
- Making a positive contribution
- Achieving economic well-being

It is immediately apparent that the document's proposals go far beyond that which would normally be associated with safeguarding children. Therefore while the starting point may well have been Lord Laming's report into the death of Victoria Climbié, the final destination is an altogether broader and more radical place: an ambitious programme of change claiming to improve outcomes for all children and young people. It is difficult to believe that Lord Laming had such a vision in mind when he wrote that sentence about the link between family support and child protection.

The proposals for the delivery of the five outcomes are described in some detail across four areas. It is only necessary here to provide the key proposals in each area.

Area 1 Supporting parents and carers

- Universal services such as schools, health and social services providing information and advice and engaging parents to support their child's development.
- Targeted and specialist support where needed.
- The use of compulsory parenting orders as a last resort where necessary.
- Extended schools or children's centres offering on-site child care from 8.00am to 6.00pm.

Area 2 Early intervention and effective protection

- Improving information sharing, including the possibility of a national database of all children.
- Developing a common assessment framework.
- Developing multi-professional teams based in and around schools and children's centres.
- Establishing a lead professional where children are known to more than one agency.

Area 3 Local, regional and national integration

- The development of children's trusts to integrate key services.

- The creation of a director of children's services to lead local action.

- Requiring agencies to work closely with one another to improve outcomes for children and young people.

- The development of local safeguarding children's boards to replace the current area child protection committees.

- The establishment of a Children's Commissioner to act as an independent champion for children and report to Parliament.

Area 4 Workforce reform

- Implementing a strategy to improve the skills and effectiveness of the workforce.

- Improved training and development of common occupational standards children's practice.

These serve to illustrate how broad the vision stretches. Safeguarding children is superseded by a quite conscious effort to go further for children, to 'maximise the opportunities open to them – to improve their life chances, to change the odds in their favour' (DfES, 2003b, p. 1). Lord Laming's synthesis of child protection and family support is taken to new heights and lengths, and yet it is interesting to note that there is a failure to fully incorporate children's rights, an omission that has been noted in various pieces of legislation affecting children (Freeman, 2002).

At this point it is necessary to pause and reflect on these aims. The rhetoric may be very appealing, and yet fundamental questions and issues arise. Let us begin with the five outcomes for children. Some of the questions that need asking here are laid out in the activity boxes below to encourage further reflection.

There is a final issue about the way the proposals appear to view children and young people as malleable.

Reflective Activity 10.2

Being healthy – who decides?

Being healthy includes physical, mental, sexual health and avoiding illegal drugs.

The following case studies are taken from *Every Child Matters: Change for Children in Health Services* (DfES, 2004a).

The Tuck Shop at Wolsey Junior School in Croydon has a Healthy Tuck Shop. It stopped selling crisps and instead provides fruit for the children. Pupils currently consume 2 to 4 boxes of satsumas, bananas and apples a week and staff have noticed a difference in children's behaviour and concentration levels. The initiative has had a beneficial, calming influence across the whole school.

Southend has 12 Walking buses, enabling children to walk safely to school. Each bus includes at least two parent/volunteers, acting as a 'driver' and a 'conductor' and the children pick up passengers at pre-determined 'bus stops' along the way. Walking Buses ensure regular daily exercise and an opportunity for social interaction among children. The scheme is cutting car journeys to school and reducing traffic congestion near the school entrance. It is also encouraging greater independence among children.

1 What underlying attitudes and values towards health and exercise do you think are present in these examples?

2 Who do you think might have decided to implement these activities?

3 To what extent do you think children might have been consulted or involved in planning and organising them?

4 Do you think they had a right to have been?

5 What do you think the evidence was for some of the claims e.g. that the Tuck Shop had a 'beneficial, calming influence'?

Reflective Activity 10.3

Staying safe – from what, and how?

Staying safe includes being safe from abuse, accidents, injury, bullying, discrimination, anti-social behaviour and instability.

1 Can you think of any other dangers or risks you would want to add to this list?

2 How realistic do you think it is for all children to be free from bullying or discrimination?

3 How do you think children might be kept safe from them?

4 Do you think there might be discrepancies in what some children perceive as bullying or discrimination compared with others?

5 If so, who should decide whether an action against a child amounts to harm?

Reflective Activity 10.4

Enjoying and achieving – how should this be measured?

Enjoying and achieving includes being ready for and getting the most out of school, achieving personal and social development, and taking part in leisure activities.

1 Do you believe school is always a positive experience for children?

2 Can you think of examples where it may be a frightening, or negative place for children?

3 Should children's success be mainly measured on the exam results they achieve?

4 If not, what other success criteria would you impose?

5 Where do you see children with profound and multiple disabilities fitting in with this?

6 Should enjoyment be linked to leisure pursuits?

7 What other activities can you think of, that may not be labelled as 'leisure', that children and young people may enjoy doing?

Reflective Activity 10.5

Making a positive contribution – who decides what is positive?

Making a positive contribution includes taking part in decisions and supporting the community, being law-abiding, developing positive relationships with others, being self-confident and able to deal with challenges, and developing enterprising behaviour.

1 Do you think making a positive contribution means fitting into existing social norms and values?

2 How do you think children and young people can take part in decisions that affect their lives?

3 Who should decide what a positive relationship with others is?

4 Who should be responsible for discouraging or forbidding relationships perceived to be negative?

5 What would you describe as enterprising behaviour?

6 Can you think of enterprising behaviours by children and young people that may be perceived by others to be a nuisance or harmful to the children or adults?

Reflective Activity 10.6

Achieving economic well-being – whose definition?

Achieving economic well-being includes going on to further or higher education, training or employment after leaving school, living in decent homes, having access to transport and material goods, avoiding poverty.

1 Do you think being ready for work should be the aim of school?

2 Can you think of other ways that young people might achieve economic well-being other than those described here?

3 To what extent do you think there is a danger that over-concentration on 'fitting in' with the work ethic may stifle creativity or other less conventional lifestyle choices?

4 If this does happen, does it matter?

It seems to suggest that if they can be coaxed, supported, tweaked, or pushed then they will do as the state wishes. Individual agency of children appears to be absent, as if what will be rewarded is behaviour that reflects, or fits in with, the prevailing values and norms of adults. Here the underlying attitude appears to echo the view of childhood as preparation for adulthood, or as conduits for replicating society's ideologies. See Part I, Chapters 2–5, for further discussion of this perspective.

A similar argument about malleability could be made in respect of parents. Take the proposal to provide universal advice and support through schools and health centres. While this sounds wonderful, it immediately raises a tension between voluntary support and the parents' right to reject that support (unless the consequence is significant harm to children). There still has to be a balance between professionals offering advice and support, and allowing parents to choose their own destinies, and those of their children. *Every Child Matters* does not resolve this

See Chapter 5, Pictures of Children.

tension. The proposals here appear to reinforce one of the guiding principles of the Children Act 1989 – that parents know what is best for their children – and yet there appears to be a hint of coercion in expecting professionals to dish out advice and support when parents drop their children off at school or attend a medical appointment. As the questions above have highlighted, there is a debate to be had about whose values or world view should or should not be accepted as the template for action and decisions about children.

This issue of individual, not to mention civil, rights is further highlighted by the proposal for an electronic information system in every local authority, based on national standards, and capable of interaction with other data sets. In effect, this would be a national database of all children. Each child would have a unique identification number so they could be tracked anywhere in the country. Lord Laming's original recommendation was to *explore* such an idea – clearly he was aware that it was fraught with difficulties. For instance, *Every Child Matters* states

> there is a strong case for giving practitioners the ability to flag on the system early warnings when they have a concern about a child which in itself may not be a trigger to meet the usual thresholds for intervention. (*Every Child Matters*, 2003, p. 53)

Certainly the civil rights organisation Liberty is concerned about these matters. They question whether a national database is a sensible use of resources and advocate instead the targeting of efforts on those clearly at risk, and better training for workers. They believe this would avoid the risk that 'supposition piled upon rumour and supplemented by wild guesswork will be the new way of trying to guarantee our children's safety' (Littlewood, 2003). While this may be a little colourful, the point is well made: is this an example of the government using a sledgehammer to crack a nut? With the apparent lack of choice as to whether a child's name appears on the database, the assumption here, it could be argued, is that the state knows best how to support children, a neat reversal of one of the basic tenets of the Children Act 1989 which presumes that families know best how to achieve this.

Reflective Activity 10.7

A national database of all children

The proposal for such a database raises some deep ethical questions which can be articulated in the form of questions as follows:

1 Who do you think should have access to input data?

2 Who should ensure the data is accurate?

3 Who should decide whether the quality of the information inputted is sufficiently robust to merit entry onto the database?

4 Should parents have the right to see what is recorded?

5 Should children have the right to see what is recorded?

6 If children are going to be tagged as 'at risk' or 'in need' is this labelling them in a simplistic fashion?

The deficit model

The Plowden Report of 1967 advocated a policy of positive discrimination in favour of children from poor areas of the UK. As a result large-scale programmes of compensatory education took place across the country. The evaluation concluded that, while such programmes could not fully compensate for social deprivation, they could improve cognitive and linguistic abilities. The mixed success of such programmes, in the US as well as in the UK, led to the development of a 'difference model', whereby social and cultural differences from the prevailing norm are seen as valid within certain limits, for example extreme child-rearing practices would need challenging (Smith et al., 2003).

The proposal for all day child care also raises some concerns. While not wanting to assume that every parent would send their child to such provision for ten hours a day, there are some questions to be asked here. Is the motivation for providing such provision to support parents' ability to work, to enhance both the work ethic and tax revenue for the government? Perhaps it is instead, or additionally, about providing children with as much 'positive' experience as possible during their waking day, in reflection of a deficit model of development (see Smith et al., 2003). If this is so, who decides which experiences are 'positive'? Is it in the interests of children to be in a structured environment for up to ten hours a day? Clearly these are not new questions, but these proposals have resurrected them.

These are further explored in Chapter 11, Day Care Services for Children.

Two other elements of *Every Child Matters* are presented as new, and yet on closer examination do not appear to be so. The duty upon agencies to cooperate with one another was, and of course still is, present under Section 27 of the Children Act 1989. Admittedly, the wording of the duty under the Children Act 2004 is stronger. The emphasis has shifted from agencies having to respond if approached by another agency to having a duty to actively make arrangements to promote cooperation. It seems that agencies cannot be trusted to cooperate without specific requirements being placed upon them to do so. Neither is there any mention of how agencies are to overcome some of the long recognised difficulties and barriers in working effectively together, such as different core functions of agencies that may clash and compete; different values, cultures and practices between agencies; lack of clarity in boundaries between agencies; lack of clarity in lines of authority and decision-making between agencies; historical or current jealousies or rivalries between agencies; different and conflicting social policy or legislation under which different agencies may be labouring; and lack of clarity about why agencies are involved (Stainton Rogers, 1989).

Secondly, the establishment of local safeguarding children's boards (LSCBs) which are heralded as the body which will 'co-ordinate the functions of all partner agencies in relation to safeguarding children' (DfES, 2003b, p. 74). The rationale for the change from area

Figure 10.1 Lord Laming's vision for new arrangements for safeguarding children.

Parliament

↑

Children and Families Board (Govt. level)

↑

National agency for Children and Families
(led by Children's Commissioner, to advise on policy, scrutinise new legislation, agree national outcomes for children and how to achieve them)

↑

Committee for Children and Families (local level)

↑

Management boards for Children and Families
(local level to ensure strong local partnership work, training, shared budgets)

child protection committees (ACPC) is two-fold: we are told that in some areas ACPCs are 'not working well' (p. 74), and the establishment of LSCBs will be a legal duty for all local authorities. The proposed remit of LSCBs is very similar to that of ACPCs, although the boards are perceived to have a broader role, including one of prevention as well as traditional narrower child protection. Additionally, they will have a duty to investigate *all* child deaths in the area, including accidental deaths, in order to prevent future deaths.

There does not appear to be a direct line of accountability established from LSCBs through regional bodies to central government. *Every Child Matters* states that they 'may have responsibility for current ACPC responsibilities as set out in *Working Together to Safeguard Children* (1999)' (p. 74). The accountability referred to in *Working Together* is that 'The Secretary of State for Health may seek comments or information from ACPCs on child protection matters from time to time' (DoH, 1999b, p. 34).

In the 2006 version of *Working Together* (DfES, 2006c), however, accountability is via an inspection and review framework. Each local authority, and therefore each LSCB, will be subject to a joint area review (JAR), which will 'assess how children's services, taken together, contribute to improving outcomes for children and young people' (p. 64). Should shortcomings be identified, it will be for the local authority to lead in taking action, if intervention is necessary.

This is interesting, because one of Lord Laming's central recommendations was to improve accountability from local to national level. When he spoke about the need for new arrangements for overseeing child protection work to replace ACPCs, Lord Laming had a much more radical solution in mind from that with which we appear to have ended up. He envisaged the new local boards having a clear reporting responsibility which can be represented as in Figure 10.1.

Contrast this with Figure 10.2, the position of Local Safeguarding Children Boards (LSCBs) as outlined in *Every Child Matters*.

At this point, it is worth reminding ourselves of the reasons behind Laming's vision of change to safeguard children. Refreshingly, he avoided merely lambasting

The Secretary of State for Health

↑

Joint Area Review Inspections (national level)

↑

Director of Children's Services (local level)

↑

Local Safeguarding Children Boards
(local level coordinating the functions of partner agencies, allocating any pooled funds)

Figure 10.2 *Every Child Matters'* vision for new arrangements for safeguarding children.

the poor practice of front-line professionals, whom he acknowledged work in challenging circumstances. He saved some of his fiercest criticism for the senior managers who allowed the 'organisational malaise' (Laming, 2003, p. 4) to spread. He is rightly indignant at the finding, after Victoria Climbié's death, that while junior staff were suspended, some of their senior officers were promoted. As he concludes, 'This is not an example of managerial accountability that impresses me much' (p. 4). The impetus for his new model of accountability is therefore clear: to try to ensure that in future there is management accountability in a direct relationship between local and national bodies, which would be tested through joint inspections. This level of accountability, in relation to local safeguarding children's boards, appears to be absent in *Every Child Matters*. Are we then to believe that, while it is not possible to separate the protection of children from wider support to families, it is possible to separate it from central government accountability?

A further point needs to be made about legislation. Laming concluded in his report that, in his opinion, 'the legislative framework for protecting children is basically sound' (p. 6) and that the failures in Victoria Climbié's case were not a matter of law but the implementation of it; in other words professionals did not follow basic procedures set out in various statutes and guidance documents. *Every Child Matters*, on the other hand, has the Children Act 2004 to give it the powers it requires for implementation. This is obvious at one level – given it has a more wide-ranging remit than protecting children it needs new legislation to carry this off. However, a question remains as to the extent to which this represents a fundamental shift in the relationship between the state and the family – one where the former has a more powerful and active role in the name of family support, which emotively cannot now be separated from the protection of children. In saying this, it is not to argue that state intervention in family life is inherently negative; it is merely to point out that to uncritically accept all forms of state intervention as beneficial and liberating carries its own dangers. It is a question of balance – between the rights of parents and children to choose their own destinies and the role of the state in determining and executing what it sees as positive outcomes for families.

What are the values and attitudes towards children and childhood that are reflected in the legislation and guidance?

In addressing this question, the contradictions between the rhetoric of *Every Child Matters* and other government legislation need teasing out a little more. Three examples are going to be used to illustrate them. First, the government that promulgates this apparently child-centred programme use the same legislation to maintain the position that 'reasonable chastisement' (Children Act 2004, Section 58) of children is acceptable (that is, physical punishment which does not leave visible injury). Surely this leaves their credentials somewhat tainted. If every child does really matter, should we leave them at the mercy of a rather muddled piece of legislation, in which smacking is allowed, as long as it is not too hard, and where the smallest and most defenceless members of our society are the only ones who remain open to being assaulted without protection of the law? To use Paul Boateng's own words, does this reflect the 'value that our society places on children and childhood' (DfES, 2003b)?

For further discussion of this issue see Chapter 3, The Politics of Childhood.

Secondly, the area of youth justice is riddled with inconsistencies. The government has produced five additional documents designed to supplement the green paper with more detailed information. These are *Every Child Matters: Change for Children*: in health services; in schools; in social care; young people and drugs; and in the criminal justice system.

The publication *Every Child Matters: Change for Children in the Criminal Justice System* (DfES, 2004b) is interesting for what it omits as much as what it contains. The document provides a short summary of aims and action for this group of children. It is a fairly bland account of responsibility and action plans for various agencies to prevent and address offending running only to seven pages compared to the document on health which runs to 69 pages. Two important omissions are anti-social behaviour orders and a change in the law regarding the presumption that, unless the prosecution proves otherwise, a child aged between 10 and 14 does not know the difference between right and wrong.

Anti-social behaviour orders (ASBOs) were introduced by the New Labour government from 1 April 1999 as part of the Crime and Disorder Act 1998. They were ostensibly devised to tackle behaviour which 'caused or was likely to cause harassment, alarm or distress'. The local authority or the police may make an application for an ASBO with respect to any person aged 10 or over. If approved, the Order prohibits the named person from doing anything proscribed in the order. While being subject to an ASBO itself is not a criminal offence, breach of it is. ASBOs last for a minimum of two years and breaching it can lead to a fine or imprisonment. For young people aged 12 to 14, the latter can mean a secure training order; for 15- to 18-year-olds it could lead to a six-month custodial sentence.

A key difficulty appears to be in the wording of the Act whereby ASBOs can be issued. The language is so broad – 'behaviour which caused, or was likely to cause harassment, alarm or distress' – as to allow for some absurd interpretations of it. Foot reveals that under the 'frightening vagueness' (Foot, 2004, p. 2) of the definition there have been orders banning children from playing football and an 87-year-old grandfather from being sarcastic. As he concludes, the definition could, in principle, include having an affair with a married partner.

A further difficulty is that, because of the way ASBOs are issued, they deny people the right to have a jury hear evidence and decide on guilt or innocence, and they allow unsubstantiated hearsay evidence to be heard (Foot, 2005). Ten young people a week are being jailed as a result of ASBOs (ibid), a far cry from the aim stated in the *Every Child Matters* publication on the Criminal Justice System to 'minimise the use of custody' (DfES, 2004b, p. 3). Set against this, however, is evidence that ASBOs do not 'appear to be bringing a whole new group of young people into the offending environment' (Brogan, 2005). This conclusion is based on 43 cases, where 42 of them had been prolific offenders before breaching the ASBO, and the report itself acknowledges the limitations in size and methodology of the study. The report further concludes that where ASBOs are issued in the civil court, young people involved do not have the benefit of referral to the youth offending team for oversight, and are therefore unlikely to receive the support and intervention necessary to assist them in complying with the terms of the order. Once again, this seems to contradict the message in *Every Child Matters* stressing the importance of 'services and agencies continuing to move towards prevention and early intervention' (DfES, 2004b, p. 4).

There is a further issue here which seems to oppose the apparently child-centred vision contained in *Every Child Matters*. The legislation on ASBOs makes no distinction between a 10-year-old child and an adult in the terms for issuing an order. Children are therefore at the mercy of potentially over-zealous local authority officers, police or magistrates who may wish to make a point, or make an example of a particular child. If every child really does matter, can it be right that a 12-year-old boy can be held to account for, say, playing football which 'alarms' a neighbour, in a manner which could lead to him being given a custodial sentence in a secure training centre if he continues to kick a football in the wrong place? And, if this is so, what does this say about the value our society places upon children? That they are as culpable, as responsible, and as accountable for their actions as adults? While I do not want to subscribe to the view that children display the opposite of these attributes, a distinction needs to be made between 10-year-old children and adults in terms of levels of understanding, liability and realising the consequences of their actions.

Yet here is another rub – the Crime and Disorder Act 1998 made two further changes to the way children who offend are dealt with in criminal law. Section 34 of the Act abolishes the rebuttable presumption that a child over 10 is 'doli incapax' or incapable of committing an offence. In other words, where before the prosecution had to prove that a child aged between 10 and 14 knew that what they were doing was wrong, this is now no longer the case. The presumption now is that the child did know it was wrong, that a 10-year-old is capable of making such a distinction. This is quite explicitly laid out in the consultation document prior to the Act receiving royal assent, which states in the paragraph

> For other discussion of the attitudes to children related to crime and justice, see Chapter 9, Children Who Offend.

introducing this change that 'the Government proposes to reassert responsibility' (Home Office, 1997, p. 1). Macauley (2003) suggests that one might have expected such a change to coincide with a rise in the age of criminal responsibility, but this is not the case.

Section 35 of the Crime and Disorder Act 1998 is concerned with the effect of the defendant's silence at a trial. Where before, a child under 14 was exempt from the clause that it would be permissible for a court or jury to 'draw such inferences as appear proper' from such silence, this is now not the case. In other words, children aged 10 and over now risk their guilt being inferred by not giving evidence in court. What this fails to take into account is the potential stress and trauma to a child of giving evidence in open court, and being subject to cross-examination. Once again, we see the removal of the distinction between children and adults in terms of responsibility and actions.

For further discussion of children and youth justice, see Chapter 9, Children Who Offend.

The final area to illustrate the contradictions between *Every Child Matters* and other legislation is child poverty. Figures for 2005 show that 3.6 million children – one in four – live in low-income households (CPAG, 2005). The official measure for poverty in 1999 was defined as households with incomes below 60 per cent of the median after housing costs (Flaherty et al., 2004). The government has pledged to halve child poverty by 2010, and to eradicate it by 2020, an ambitious target. By 2004, consensus seemed to be that the government were on target to reduce child poverty by a quarter (Lohde, 2004). However, there is equal consensus that the next stage, to halve child poverty by 2010, will be much more difficult (Piachaud, 1999; Lohde, 2004). The reasons for this are thus: direct benefits and other policies to help poor families are relatively simple ways of assisting families just below the level of official poverty, in order to lift them out of poverty. Much more difficult to access are those households in deeper poverty. This is not merely because these families need more resources and assistance; it is also a political consideration. Piachaud (1999) and Lister (2001) explain that there is a taboo by successive governments on overtly redistributing wealth to the poor, as this may be perceived as reducing the incentive to work and encouraging dependence upon the state. One of the fundamental principles of UK society is that where people do not contribute to the economy, they have to been seen to be treated more harshly than those that do so, in order not only to 'punish' them and make it uncomfortable, but to set an example to others. In other words, the government could end child poverty at a stroke by guaranteeing a minimum household income for every family; however, to do so may incur the wrath of those in work who may well demand more pay to maintain the income differential – a recipe for potential economic and political disaster. To put it bluntly, no government in the UK seems prepared to take the risk of self-destruction in order to end poverty for a quarter of children (Jones and Novak, 1999).

For further discussion on poverty, see Chapter 3, The Politics of Childhood, Chapter 4, The Social Divisions of Childhood, and Chapter 8, Provision for Child Health.

An even more cynical manoeuvre by the New Labour government appears to be the change in the way poverty is measured. There are two elements here. The 1999 measure for eradicating child poverty was no child living below 60 per cent of median income. In 2003 this changed to having a poverty rate that is among the best in Europe where children are not experiencing material deprivation (Lohde, 2004). The difficulty with this is that the government is yet to define what 'among the best' means. Secondly, the exclusion of housing costs from the measure of child poverty allows more children to be lifted out of official poverty, and therefore allows the government to claim more success in eradicating child poverty. In reality, housing costs account for a substantial proportion of poorer families' budgets and therefore there is a hidden group of children who will continue to experience poverty (ibid).

The then Chancellor of the Exchequer, Gordon Brown, has said of children 'they are 20 per cent of the population but they are 100 per cent of the future' (Piachaud, 1999). This upbeat rhetoric does not appear to be fully matched by the government's actions on child poverty, which could leave around a quarter of children – 5 per cent of the population – living in conditions which impede their health, development and life chances. For it is worth reminding ourselves what the effects of poverty are. We are not talking here about some intangible state where people – children – merely feel less well off or somehow estranged from society. We are talking about the following: poor diet and nutrition, increased risk of sickness and ill health in childhood, debt and exclusion from social activities (Flaherty et al., 2004). Children are twice as likely to die within their first year if their parents are from unskilled manual rather than professional classes (ibid). For these children, poverty can literally be a matter of life or death. If every child matters, and if the government is serious about children being 100 per cent of the future, are children not owed a more robust and secure future than the present approaches seem to provide?

These three illustrations – physical chastisement, youth justice and child poverty – can lead to the conclusion that, while the government do indeed believe, on the one hand, that every child matters, on the other hand, perhaps certain groups of children – those at the mercy of parents who choose to use physical punishments, those who are perceived to cause alarm or distress, or who offend, and those who are poor – matter less than others.

Conclusion

This chapter has charted the journey of child protection legislation and guidance in England since 1991. In doing so, it has attempted to address the key questions posed at the outset. What has been demonstrated is that the philosophy and practice of the Children Act 1989, based on minimal state intervention and the sanctity of the family, has given way to a new approach. This change began with the publication of the third version of *Working Together* in 1999. This introduced the notion of safeguarding and promoting the welfare of children as set against a narrow concept of protecting children. In other words, the child's broader lifestyle and circumstances need to be taken into account when planning interventions and services. The journey was completed with the publication of *Every Child Matters* and the Children Act 2004 which takes the vision for successful outcomes for children and families to new heights.

Indeed, at one level it is difficult to argue against this vision. Of course every sensible minded person wants children to grow up free from ill health, danger, ignorance, social exclusion and poverty. However, beneath the rhetoric there are some fundamental questions about the relationship between children and families, and the state, and about the values and attitudes towards children contained within the vision and in other legislation affecting children. There seems to be a palpable shift towards assuming all state interventions and ideas are sound ones, yet there is a case for pausing and questioning this. For instance, as we have seen, certain groups of children appear to have less currency than others, despite the headline focus on the good of all children.

If the aim of *Every Child Matters* is to try to eradicate risk to children, by closely linking their welfare to family support, then is the price for this – a vast programme of state intervention – worth paying? The answer may be 'Yes', but it is worth asking the question to ensure we are not merely seduced into accepting it on the basis that to reject it would be to place children in danger.

Safeguarding children is a complex business. It clearly involves putting resources into supporting families as well as ensuring professionals who work with them are motivated, well-trained and effectively managed. While the proposals for the future of this work appear to go some way to address these, there is some justification for concluding that they do not fully reflect values that place children at their centre. Inherent tensions and contradictions remain. These tensions can be summarised as follows: those between the rights of parents and children, between voluntary support and statutory intervention, and between the role of the state and the right to self-determination. These, and the inherent contradictions in government legislation and guidance – in how children are viewed and treated – may well serve to ensure that there will continue to be children whose childhoods reflect a different societal value from the child-centred, children-as-precious view put forward in the official vision for the future of safeguarding children.

Annotated reading

Foot, M. (2004) 'Asbo absurdities', *The Guardian*, 1 December, available at <http://society.guardian. co.uk/societyguardian/story/0,,1362899,00.html> accessed 27 May 2005

Matt Foot's article highlights some key problems and contradictions in the legislation surrounding Asbos. This movement to address the inequity and at times sheer absurdity of Asbos has gained momentum such that a campaign group, Asbo Concern, was launched in September 2005. See <http://www.asboconcern.org.uk>.

Freeman, M. (2002) 'Children's rights ten years after ratification', in Franklin, B. (ed.) *The New Handbook of Children's Rights*, London: Routledge

Freeman's chapter explores the position of children's rights in England ten years after ratification of the UN Convention on the Rights of the Child. He suggests that in spite of the commitments made in this document, children's rights are palpably absent from key legislation, including divorce, education and even child protection. He concludes that we have no basis for being complacent about the status of children's rights.

Smith, P., Cowie, H. and Blades, M. (2003) *Understanding Children's Development*, 4th edn, Oxford: Blackwell Publishing

This now classic child development textbook explores many relevant and interesting areas. Key research in child development is summarised and critically evaluated, providing the reader with a balanced view of the issues.

Stainton Rogers, W. (1989) 'Effective co-operation in child protection work', in Morgan, S and Righton, P. (eds) *Child Care: Concerns and Conflicts*, London: Hodder & Stoughton

Although this chapter pre-dates the Children Act 1989, it nevertheless provides a stimulating and still relevant contribution to the debate on multi-agency cooperation, including potential barriers and principles of good partnership to help overcome these.

Chapter 11

Day Care Services for Children

CHRISTINE HINES

Early childhood is a time of vital importance in children's development. Children's experiences in the earliest years of their life are critical to their subsequent development – quality early education is the most important factor 'bar none' in determining a child's life chances.

(Childcare Bill Summary, 2006)

Introduction

The past twenty years has seen a growth in all types of child-care provision with an increasing emphasis on early years. This support has been through a range of financial schemes, from vouchers to help with some of the costs of purchasing provision to tax credits for working families. These developments are shaped by various sectors and interests: public, private, voluntary and family-based, including education, health, social welfare and employment. It would appear that families have a wide range of provision to choose from and that they are able to access funding to help them purchase this provision. However, in reality it is not that simple and this chapter will explore the issues relating to the range of provision available and equality of access to this. It will also seek answers to why there has been such growth in child-care provision – is the Government concerned with the holistic development and

well-being of children or are there other motives underpinning this?

In an attempt to find answers to these questions this chapter will consider the following questions:

- What is meant by child care?
- What thinking underpins the expansion of child care?
- What issues stem from the move towards more integrated child-care provision?
- Is there equal access to 'quality provision'?
- What is meant by 'quality provision'?

What is meant by child care?

During the 20th century, there was a growth in the provision of services for children. Some of this growth was connected to economic need. For example, during the Second World War when women, regardless of their marital status, were required to work to keep industry moving in a time when men had been recruited into the forces, the government introduced state-run nurseries to care for children below school age. However, the majority of these disappeared when the war ended and women were no longer required by industry as men who had been drafted into the armed forces returned home and to the jobs they had left some years earlier (Harding, 1996). In the years immediately after the war there were two pieces of legislation that changed child care in different ways. The first of these

See Chapter 6, Education: Service or System?, for further discussion of this.

was the 1944 Education Act, which for the first time provided free education for all children aged 5–15 years. The

See Chapter 8, Provision for Child Health, for further discussion.

Act also established a number of support services, for example dental and medical

check-ups, recognising the significance of health to learning. The second piece of legislation was the Children Act 1948. This Act, combined with the growth of child psychology, represented, as Cameron (2003, p. 89) states, 'a much more inclusive approach to care in child care legislation'. There was an emphasis upon the 'care and welfare' of children up to the age of 18, especially those who were without parents or guardians. This was further progress in the idea that society should take more collective responsibility for children. Although both these pieces of legislation were concerned with children, the responsibilities for the education of children and the care and welfare of children lay with different government departments and a third department was concerned with health. This division has impacted on the way provision has developed. Later parts of the chapter will consider this development.

During the second half of the 20th century the terms 'welfare' and 'care' were often used synonymously when discussing children's needs. However, we need to be clear what the terms mean in the context of this chapter. When referring to 'children's welfare' we are discussing children's physical well-being – health, food, shelter, etc., whereas 'child care' refers to who is looking

after them – parent, family member or foster carer, for example. We need to be mindful of this when looking at provision for children and be very clear about what we mean by the term 'child care' as it has different meanings to different groups and historically the phrase has changed its meaning. The 1948 legislation for the regulation of nurseries and child minders referred to children

See Chapter 10, Safeguarding Children.

who attended such settings as being 'looked after' rather than 'cared for'. Today the term 'looked after' refers to children under the jurisdiction of the state through the local authorities, mainly in foster homes, whereas 'child care' covers the spectrum of services on offer to families. This chapter will be concerned with the latter. The range of child-care provision is wide and many families select more than one option depending on their domestic circumstances, financial situation, the age of their children and the number of children they have. The next section will look at the key factors underpinning the need for child care.

What thinking underpins the expansion of child care?

Historically, child-minding outside the home for working-class children evolved during the Industrial Revolution, especially in areas where there was a high demand for women's labour such as at the Lancashire cotton mills. As many had moved into these 'new towns' from more rural settings, often they had no relatives to call upon to provide child care so they sought to pay someone for this service. The service, like many in those times, was unregulated so it was common to find one woman looking after 15–20 (or more) children of varying ages in a tiny terraced house with little in the way of facilities. Apart from the period of the Second World War, little changed in this situation until the 1960s.

Broad social, political and economic forces shape the amount, type and quality of child-care provision and the relationship with changes in the structure of employment are as evident in the Industrial Revolution

as they are in more recent developments, discussed below.

This section will explore the Government's economic agenda and the social changes that occurred during the latter half on the 20th century as key principles underpinning the need for the expansion of child care at the beginning of the 21st century. The Labour government, at the time of writing, has made a long-term commitment to child care with its Ten Year Strategy for Childcare (HM Treasury, 2004).

Debates concerning the relative benefits of early years provision outside the home and care within the home are ongoing and complex. Moss and Penn (1996) point to the potential benefits for children, parents, families, providers, employers and society of 'good quality' provision but also point to the costs of providing this. Since 1997 there has been an increasing emphasis on early years provision. Why has there been this sudden interest in the early years? There are economic and social explanations for this.

One economic explanation relates to the workforce: we have an aging population. After the post-war baby boom in the 1950s the number of children being born in the UK has been in decline. Therefore, we have fewer numbers in the workforce group of 16–65 years and the government needs women to fill this shortfall if it is to

maintain its standing on the global economic stage. In order to achieve this a system of regulated child care needs to be in place in order to provide a 'quality service'. Hence, the growth of nursery classes for children over 3 and the extension of the hours they may attend by 2010.

While the Government may have an economic agenda for the extension of child-care provision, we cannot ignore the changes that have occurred socially during the past 50 years and the impact of these upon the demands for child care. The Second Wave women's movement (1960s onwards) sought to free women from being financially dependent upon men and achieve equality in the employment market (Harding, 1996). New social movements at this time were concerned to gain equality and political and economic change for women, people from black and minority ethnic groups, and other socially oppressed groups. One strand of their demands was for equal access to high-quality child care.

It was extremely difficult in the 1960s for a woman to obtain a mortgage or loan on her own despite her independent earnings. In the workplace women were generally paid less than men for similar work and access to promotion was blocked because companies denied women the same training opportunities as their male counterparts. Women took major responsibility for domestic labour including looking after children. Some of these inequalities still exist (Equal Opportunities Commission, 2006). However, much has changed since the 1960s and there are more opportunities for women in our society to have careers alongside motherhood. The majority of women now work in paid employment, though there is evidence of a slowing down in men's involvement in domestic labour, possibly because of increased labour demands on them as well as attitudes (Crompton et al., 2005).

All these developments have had a tremendous impact upon the demands for child care as parents require services that are open before and after the traditional 9–5 working day. Even with school-aged children, services before and after school and during the holidays are needed. These demands are further impacted by another social factor – the decline of family-based networks of care in some local areas. The decline of traditional manufacturing and industry in the UK alongside the increased numbers of graduates has changed the labour market and people need to move around the country, either to find work or keep their existing job. Thus, many no longer live near their parents or siblings, people who in the past might have provided child care.

In addition to this the single-parent family has become much more commonplace within our society. One in four children lived in single-parent households in 2004 compared with one in fourteen in 1972 (ESRC Society Today, 2006). The majority of single parents rely heavily on having access to extended care for their children so they can go out to work. For many the option of paid work remains unrealistic; just over half are in paid employment (ibid).

Thus it could be said that the main factors underpinning the growing need for child care relate to wider social, political and economic changes. These include changes in the structure of employment and labour-market needs; changes in the welfare benefits system where incentives and sanctions are increasingly built in to enforce and encourage the employment of people on benefits (CPAG, 2006); and the struggle for equal rights for women. Clearly those professionals and parents more directly concerned with the

well-being, education and healthy development of children from all social positions and class backgrounds have also been central to developments and improvements in provision. Many have recognised the inherent value of the experiences that child care can provide. Child care is seen as a way of enhancing social interaction, language acquisition, physical and creative development, and so forth. As research into the benefits of children's play and social interaction have emerged over the past few decades so the demand from parents and professionals has grown.

See Chapter 12, Services to Children's Play.

The way in which this service area has developed is also influenced by economic, social and political factors. The emphasis now is on the development of children's centres. Currently these centres are being established in areas where it is felt there is most need, such as inner cities. The *Every Child Matters* (DfES, 2003b) agenda argues the importance of children:

- being healthy – physical and mental health and emotional well-being;
- staying safe – protection from harm and neglect;
- enjoying and achieving – education, training and recreation;
- making a positive contribution to society – support for the vulnerable and positive outlooks;
- social and economic well-being – parents in employment.

At the time of writing, where established, these integrated services include:

- early years provision – an integrated child care and education service;
- social services – social workers, family officers;
- relevant health services – e.g. pre- and post-natal care, health visitors;
- services provided by Jobcentre Plus to assist parents to obtain work;
- information on other services available to families.

The establishment of these centres, it is argued, will provide much-needed support for many that are regarded in socio-economic terms to be the poorest families in the UK. However, the inclusion of Jobcentre Plus at the centres underlines the Government's drive to lower unemployment numbers so the agenda is not quite as straightforward, nor as positive for children as it might appear. Developments in the US (Link and Bibus, 2005) demonstrate the difficulties and welfare penalties faced by the poor and, in particular, single parents when the emphasis became welfare to work (albeit that some child care was provided for the latter).

It is also suggested that children's lives will be improved, not just through access to care within the centres, but also through the support and training that is given to parents and carers. This has both social and economic motivations. Children in families and communities where there is a high level of unemployment may sometimes find it difficult to see education and work as important. It is intended that children's centres will influence the whole community in a way that encourages children to value work and to become better citizens in the future. It is argued that this social aspiration will also have economic benefits as they will be contributing as adults to the economy of the country and will make fewer demands on services. The realities of lack of access to quality work in particular areas may be underplayed in this perspective.

What issues stem from the move towards more integrated child-care provision?

The main focus for child care in Britain is in the area of pre-school. Moss and Penn (1996) identify the range of services available to young children and their families towards the end of the 20th century. Table 11.1 below (adapted from Moss and Penn, 1996) shows that the funding, staffing ratios, qualifications of staff and aims of the provision varied considerably. Moss and Penn emphasise the ad hoc nature of the development of these services which was determined by the different government departments responsible for the provision. Major changes to this provision have been taking place since 1997 to coordinate both provision and the way it is delivered and inspected.

For children of school age there is another layer of provision most of which is in the private sector.

- Childminders offer care before and after school. This service involves taking and collecting children from school. Childminders will often offer some provision during the school holidays.

- Before- and after-school clubs are generally based on school premises, but operated by private companies or voluntary agencies who rent space from the school. They provide a range of supervised activities for children. The age range is generally 5–11. Some of the clubs provide breakfast (cereal, toast, juice); nearly all provide a snack and a drink in the after-school session. There is often no provision during the school holidays.

- Holiday clubs operate during the school holidays and provide day care, through a range of sporting, art and educational activities, for children up to the age of 12 years. This service is provided by various sectors: schools, private businesses, health clubs, local authority leisure centres and charitable trusts.

The overall picture of child-care provision at the end of the 20th century was fragmented and uneven in quality and provision. In 1998, under the auspices of Sure Start, the first attempt to have a more coordinated approach to service provision was implemented through Early Years Development and Childcare Partnerships (EYDCP) that were set up regionally. These bodies consist of representatives from all providers and those concerned with child-care provision in the locality. They work together to identify child-care needs in the locality and plan to improve this and ensure that appropriate training is provided for all those involved in child care. The work of Sure Start and the EYDCP provided the basis for *The Ten Year Strategy for Childcare* (HM Treasury, 2004) that intended to ensure 'that every child gets the best start in life and to give parents more choice about how to balance work and family life' (p. 1). This was to be addressed through four main themes:

- choice and flexibility: parents to have greater choice about balancing work and family life;

Table 11.1 Services Available to Young Children and their Families

Type	Administration	Values–philosophy	Staffing	Ratios	Charge
Publicly Provided Services					
Nursery schools	Education	To enlarge a child's knowledge, experience and imaginative understanding and thus his or her awareness of	Nursery teachers degree/PGCE	1 to 23 (teaching)	Free
Nursery classes (attached to primary schools)	Education	moral values and capacity for enjoyment: and . . . to enable him or her to enter the world after formal education is over as an active participant in society and a responsive contributor to it	Nursery nurse	1 to 13 (overall)	
Reception classes	Education	Introduction to formal schooling	Primary teacher degree/PGCE	1 to 30/40	Free
Day nurseries	Social Services	Day care services emphasising the care and protection of vulnerable children	Nursery nurses (NNEB)	Recommended 1 to 5 (2–5 years)	Usually means tested
Family centres	Social Services	Emphasis on a programme of work involving parents and children. Usually compensatory		1 to 3 (0–2 years)	

Type of provision	Responsible body	Description	Staff	Adult:child ratio	Cost
Combined nursery centres	Social Services/Education	Vary widely in their emphasis and approach, but usually include a combination of care and education	Nursery teachers and Nursery nurses	1 to 3 (children with special needs) 1 to 2 (0–2)	
One O' Clock Club Playcentres	Leisure/Social Services	Recreational emphasis – frequently non-directive play, with mothers or carers present	Play Leaders, often qualified	2–?	Covers food costs
Voluntary Services					
Playgroups (may also be private)	Registration and inspection duty of Social Services Majority affiliated to Pre-School Playgroup Association (PPA)	Loosely modelled on nursery education. Parents committees manage the groups and parents often help on a rota basis. The emphasis is on *play* as the tool for learning. May provide opportunity groups for children with disabilities. Emphasis on parental development and support	Play Leaders PPA trained Volunteers	1 to 8	Average £7.50/ 2.5 hour session
Voluntary nurseries	Registration and inspection duty of Social Services	Centres generally established by voluntary child-care organisations focusing on community development or 'self-help' centres that have grown out of voluntary community groups	Social workers Nursery nurses (NNEB)	Recommended the same as for day nurseries	Minimal charge to cover costs or free
Family centres Family support centres			Volunteers		

(continued)

Table 11.1 (continued)

Type	Administration	Values–philosophy	Staffing	Ratios	Charge
Voluntary Services					
Specialist resource centres Toy Libraries	Play Matters National Toy Libraries Association	Lend toys at minimal cost to children and families	Volunteers	N/A	Minimal charge for toys
Out of school (may also be private)	Kid Club Network (Education/Youth service/Leisure) Registration and inspection duty of Social Services for 5–8	Promotes play-care services for children before and after school and during school holidays	Play leaders / Volunteers	1 to 8	Varies
Parent–toddler groups	Often supported by the PPA	Often self-help initiatives that offer a drop in service to parents to meet and toddlers to play. Parent must be present	Volunteers	Varies	Minimal to cover costs
Private Services					
Childminders	Registration and inspection duty of Social Services	A private arrangement between parent and childminder offering full day care in a childminder's home. Emphasis on 'extension of home' and individual care	Women at home may have short occupational training	Registration generally 1 to 3 under 5 years inc. own children	National Childminder's Association Guidelines £50–70/week

Nannies	Private or registration duty of Social Services if carer is involved with 3 families or more	Day care for children within their own homes provided by a carer who comes to the home. Emphasis on individual care	Nursery nurses or untrained	Varies according to family size	Varies
Nurseries	Registration duty of Social Services	Day care for working families or students. Educational content and quality of care can vary enormously. Emphasis on group care. Profit driven	Nursery nurses PPA or untrained	1 to 3 (0–2) 1 to 4 (2–3) 1 to 8 (3–4)	£50 to £200/week
Nursery schools	No requirement to register nor inspection necessary, other than school inspection if part of a school	Varies. Often emphasis on formal education, the 3 Rs. Profit driven	Teachers Nursery nurses	Varies	£50 to £200/week

- availability: for all families with children aged up to fourteen who need it, an affordable, flexible, high-quality child-care place that meets their circumstances;

- quality: high-quality provision with a highly skilled child-care and early years workforce, among the best in the world;

- affordability: families to be able to afford flexible, high-quality child care that is appropriate for their needs.

These stated aspirations reflect the economic and social changes highlighted in the earlier sections of this chapter. The government has the challenge of how to make child care accessible and affordable at the same time as improving the quality of provision. The following two sections will look at these issues in more detail.

Is there equal access to 'quality provision'?

Stanley et al. (2006) have written an excellent paper that identifies and discusses inequalities in access. This section summarises some of the key issues covered in their paper.

Historically, state-funded child care has been described as 'patchy', and the contemporary position reflects 'all the ambivalences and contradictions of a century of weak policy making' (Penn, 2005, p. 124). As described earlier, such care has often been created as a national response to specific events such as the labour crisis as a result of the Second World War or local authorities have responded to demands in the local labour market. Since 1997 the Labour government has been seen by some to make moves to embrace a more coherent child-care agenda, not only with policy but by actions such as the doubling of the number of child-care places available (Stanley et al., 2006). However, this does not mean that access to child care has ceased to be a problem; the reality is that there are substantial restraints relating to geographical location, affordability and appropriateness.

For those families living in urban areas, many primary schools have a nursery class or foundation stage unit and many have seen the introduction of children's

centres. The question of access would not appear to be a problem, until the situation is examined more closely and it is seen that many of the private nurseries are located in the more affluent areas of our towns and cities. Some may argue that this is a response to the fundamental economic laws of supply and demand, but research by Sylva et al. (2004) has shown that the children from disadvantaged backgrounds can benefit significantly from good quality pre-school experiences, but geographically are unable to access a large proportion of it.

In rural areas the situation is worse as many of the schools cannot support running a nursery class so there will be one nursery class for a cluster of schools. This means families will have to travel to access this. For many, this is not an option as public transport is very limited and the family car is used by the main wage-earner to get to work, thus excluding another section of society from accessing what is available.

The creation of policy in this area needs to address the complexity of the ways in which many different issues combine to restrict access. Government policies, such as the Labour goal that by 2010 there should be 3500 children's centres, that is one for every community, would seem to remove the geographical barriers referred to above. Yet even so there is a more fundamental barrier for families in accessing child care: financial constraints.

Stanley et al. (2006) in their report *Equal Access? Appropriate and Affordable Childcare for Every Child* highlight the plight of families on low incomes. They argue that there is no equal access to provision as those who stand to gain the most are most often the least able to benefit from what is available due to the costs involved. See Table 11.2 for child-care costs.

As Table 11.2 illustrates, child care is expensive, even for families on above-average incomes. However, the government has introduced Working Tax Credit (WTC) to ease some of this burden for low-paid working adults, but this is not as straightforward as it may appear due to restrictions that apply. Only families where one adult works at least 16 hours per week may claim WTC. Families only receive 80% of child-care costs up to £175 for one child or £300 for two or more children. Eligibility is means tested and as household incomes rise there is a steep decline in the level of support (Stanley et al., 2006).

Table 11.2   The Average Cost of Child Care

Service	Age range catered for	Cost per week*	Type of provider
Registered childminders	Children aged 7 or under	£90–£140 for a full-time place	Private
Day nurseries	0–5 years	£100–£170 for a full-time place. Costs are reduced for 3- and 4-year-olds who claim their free entitlement in such provision	Private, public or voluntary
Pre-school playgroup	2–5 years	£3–£6 per session	Private or voluntary
Early education & nursery classes	3–4 years	Free through the universal part-time entitlement	Public
Out of school clubs	5–14 years	£41	Private, public or voluntary

*typical rate per week, according to Daycare Trust 2006 annual survey of child-care costs.
Source: Stanley et al. (2006).

Yet even with this level of support, low-income families find it difficult to access the provision available. Bryson et al. (2005, cited in Stanley et al., 2006) state that only 25 per cent of lower-income families find affordable provision in their area, compared with 45 per cent of those on higher incomes. In addition, 11 per cent of families not using child care cite affordability as the main reason for not doing so.

The WTC further emphasises the points made earlier regarding what is underpinning the expansion of child-care provision – the need to get adults into the job market. But what about those children who live in workless households? Some may argue that these families have no need for child care, but surely linking employment to access to quality child-care provision only further disadvantages the already disadvantaged. Penn has raised important issues regarding political and cultural attitudes towards child care, poverty and economics,

> Some economists . . . routinely calculate the financial trade-off between investment in childcare and outcomes for children. If investing in childcare makes little difference to how children perform later in life, it is not worth making the investment. Poor childcare is 'good enough'. It does not matter if many young children are cooped up together

> with bored caregivers. The quality of children's lives in the here and now, and the pleasures they might get from their daily life are of no consequence in this economic reckoning.   (Penn, 2005, p. 116)

According to the Department for Work and Pensions (DWP) (cited in Stanley et al., 2006) 1.8 million children lived in families where no one is in paid work, and around half of children in poverty live in workless households. Without access to high-quality child-care provision how can these children improve their life chances and break the cycle of poverty that surrounds them? Moreover, how can the government achieve Article 4 of the 1989 UN Convention on Children's Rights to eradicate child poverty?

Many of the objectives of the Childcare Bill (2005) are due to be delivered after 2007/8 and the future of the crucial aspects of the bill relating to the development of child care is dependent on the future and nature of government investment. Without a commitment to funding, all sectors involved in providing child care will be unable to make long-term plans and build upon what has been achieved over the past decade. This could have a profound impact upon the types of care available and the quality of the services provided.

Therefore the financial restraints surrounding child care have an impact upon all those concerned, from government ministers to the families who have to make the choices of which option to take – work or stay at home? Yet, even if all the services were free and easily accessible, the complexity of issues relating to provision, referred to earlier, means that for some families there would still be problems regarding access to child care. These 'problems' surround the appropriateness or nature of the provision available.

For some groups within our society the lack of appropriate high-quality child care is the real barrier to access. This is especially true for families from black and minority ethnic communities and from families and children with disabilities. Stanley et al. (2006) effectively argue that the levels of use of formal child care differ markedly by ethnicity. This is indicated in Table 11.3.

They point out that while these figures indicate overall trends, they do not reveal the 'true picture'. Research by the National Centre for Social Research (2005, cited in Stanley et al., 2006) found that within these broad groups there were certain sections who were accessing child care much less than others. These were mainly two groups, Pakistani and black African. But why is this?

The reasons surrounding this are complex and require a number of cultural and social factors to be taken into account. Bryson (2005, cited in Stanley, 2006) suggests the following:

- High levels of child-care use among white families may reflect their higher incomes and the relatively high proportion of mothers in paid work (both full- and part-time), while high usage among black Caribbean families is thought to be linked to lone parenthood and full-time maternal employment.

- Relatively low levels of use among Pakistani and black African families may reflect both circumstances (low maternal employment, low levels of lone parenthood, tendency to have other adults living in the household) and preferences (such as for parental/familial child care based on cultural or religious factors).

Alongside this a number of issues are identified by reports and research. These include:

- access to information about child-care services: research has indicated that more black than white families experienced difficulty accessing information about child care;

- 96–98 per cent of the child-care workforce are white and this may act as a barrier to usage amongst black and ethnic minority groups in respect to areas such as culture and language (Daycare Trust, 2005; Stanley et al., 2006);

- a lack of appropriate child-care provision to meet the needs of children with a disability or who have a special educational need (SEN). Research carried out by the Daycare Trust (2004) found that 69 per cent of families with children in these groups found it difficult to access appropriate child care. There are approximately two million children in England and Wales with SEN, with 1 in 30 entitled to additional support (Payne, 2004, cited in Stanley et al., 2006);

- The National Centre for Social Research (2005, cited in Stanley, 2006) reported that parents of children with a disability or SEN found it difficult to obtain information about appropriate provision. They also revealed that, even if provision was found, access to transport to and from the setting was another difficulty. In addition, evidence suggested that these children were subject to active discrimination from both carers and other parents creating yet another barrier to accessing child care.

These highlight specific points regarding access to facilities or appropriate kinds of care. Further factors

Table 11.3 Use of Formal Child-care Services by Ethnic Groups

Ethnic group	Percentage of parents who use formal child care %
White	87
Black	81
Asian	70
Other	71

(Daycare Trust, 2003 in Stanley et al., 2006)

impact upon such children and families. For example, the lack of appropriate places for children with a disability or SEN is further compounded by the fact that approximately 55 per cent of their families are living in poverty (Joseph Rowntree Foundation, 1998, cited in Stanley et al., 2006). This is due to the high costs of caring for these children and the high levels of care required, both physical and emotional, often acts as a barrier to parents seeking employment. Thus, they are unable to access the additional funding that the WTC offers.

So, despite the substantial investment that policy demands, and the actual financial commitment, the complexity and inter-relationship of different factors which combine to create barriers to access need to be recognised and addressed for there to be equity in child care. There are still many barriers for sections of our society in accessing what is on offer. One can only hope that these issues surrounding equality of access, geographical, financial and appropriateness, are addressed and that all our children can benefit from the rich experiences that the spectrum of child care offers.

Reflective Activity 11.1

Improving children's quality of life

Prout makes similar points to Penn (2005) regarding the problem of policies that focus primarily on children as an investment for the future, rather than an adequate acknowledgement on improving children's quality of life in the present:

> A focus on futurity is unbalanced and needs to be accompanied by a concern for the present well-being of children, for their participation in social life and for opportunities for human self realisation.   (Prout, 2000, pp. 305–6)

How do Prout's points relate to access to good child care for children from homes affected by poverty, or whose access to quality child-care provision is affected by the lack of government policy addressing issues concerning race or disability discussed in this chapter?

What is meant by 'quality provision'?

Throughout the chapter so far there have been numerous references to 'quality provision' but we may all have different ideas about what this means.

Dahlberg et al. (1999) identify two broad ways of thinking about quality. The first of these, 'the discourse of quality' (p. 87) considers quality to be associated with particular outcomes and the structures that support those outcomes being met. Chapter 6, Education: Service or System?, discusses how this approach to identifying quality is value driven and what is deemed to be quality provision will be influenced by the values and priorities of those who decide what the outcomes and the structures will be. This has clearly been the case in the education system, but we are now seeing prescribed outcomes for young children in the curriculum documents that chart progress from birth. The government's social and economic agenda identified earlier in the chapter means that quality of provision is assessed by how well children are prepared for the next stage, in this case for compulsory school. The quality of provision is also determined through

See Chapter 2, Childhood: Rights and Realities, and Chapter 3, The Politics of Childhood, for further discussion of the implications of seeing children as an investment.

Reflective Activity 11.2

What is 'quality provision' in the early years?

1   How would you make judgments about the quality of provision for children who are being cared for and educated?

2   Are there specific things you would want to see happening? What would these be? Why?

3   Would you want to make judgments by looking at what children had gained from being in the provision? What sort of things would you want them to gain from the provision?

Ofsted inspections that identify how well a setting meets identified standards of provision (Ofsted, 2006). This clearly focuses on seeing children as an investment.

A very different approach is described by Dahlberg as a 'discourse of meaning making' (p. 105). This focuses on trying to gain a deeper understanding of practitioners' work with children so all those involved can be involved in discussions about the value of what is happening to children in settings and what might need to be changed. What is considered to be quality provision would therefore be a focus for debate rather than a static set of requirements and outcomes.

A government that has clear economic and social targets may have difficulty with a 'discourse of meaning making' because the outcomes would not be measurable. However, the measurable outcomes that exist are not always meaningful to the lives of children and their carers. The vision of 'quality' that is embedded in the Ofsted frameworks and the outcomes for children may not be shared by all families because of the variety of social and cultural backgrounds. This vision of quality may not improve access for these groups unless they are part of the discussion of what provision should be like.

What is acknowledged by the government is that, in order to improve quality in the care and education of children, the staff need to be well educated and has pledged that by 2015 every full day care setting will have a specially trained early years professional. This will be a graduate profession equivalent in status to qualified teacher status and will lead and support the practice of a team of qualified staff (CWDC, 2006). This is a high-cost initiative, not just in terms of training, but also in terms of providing pay and conditions of service that will be needed to attract more highly qualified staff into settings. At the time of writing, decisions about pay and conditions have not been made and, as can be seen in Table 11.1, there are many discrepancies that need to be sorted out across the sector. If pay and conditions reflect the importance of the role, the real cost of child care will increase enormously and the financial barriers to provision may increase. However, although the initiative to improve the education of staff stems from a 'discourse of quality', it may facilitate a move towards a 'discourse of meaning making' as practitioners become more knowledgeable and critical in their approach to working with children and carers. This may result in settings being able to work with families and children in ways that break down some of the cultural and social barriers.

Reflective Activity 11.3

What is 'quality'?

Think about these two approaches to evaluating provision. The current system is based on 'the discourse of quality' through setting targets for the service as a whole that filter down to individual settings. For example, one of the targets for 2008 is

> Improve children's communication, social and emotional development so that by 2008 50 per cent of children reach a good level of development at the end of the Foundation Stage and reduce inequalities between the level of development achieved by children in the 20 per cent most disadvantaged areas and the rest of England.
>
> A 'good' level of development is defined as a score of 6 points or more across all 7 assessment scales in Communication, Language and Literacy and Personal Social Emotional Development. We will be looking for stronger progress in the 20 per cent most disadvantaged areas as children's centre services are rolled out. (Sure Start, 2006)

A 'discourse of meaning making' would emphasise the need for practitioners to be constantly improving their knowledge of children and the effects of their interactions. This would then be discussed with other practitioners and parents and carers as well as the children.

1 What do you see as the positive features of each of these discourses?

2 What do you see as the negative features of each of these discourses?

Conclusion

The chapter has identified that changes in the provision for the care of children have developed and are continuing to develop in ways that are influenced by economic, social and political factors. Although provision is increasing there are difficulties in some groups accessing provision through geographical, financial, cultural and social barriers. Attempts to integrate and improve services are part of a much broader agenda of getting parents into work and developing children into socially and economically prepared adults. This means that ideas of what is thought of as quality provision is identified in terms of these outcomes. However, these ideas about quality may reinforce some of the barriers that groups of children and their carers experience in gaining access to provision. Financial barriers may also increase as the cost of child care increases. The government may be faced with a dilemma: improving the quality of child care may make it unaffordable for many families so the 'getting parents into work' agenda may be compromised by the 'preparing the next generation for work and social roles' agenda.

The future of these services appears to depend very much on the economic and social agenda. If the government continues with its commitment to spending in this area it is unlikely to move away from a measurable target-driven approach to provision. The definitions of quality are likely to remain as outputs and standards rather than more flexible debates about the experiences and wishes of the children, their carers and those who work with them.

Annotated reading

The Children's Workforce Development Council, <www.cwdcouncil.org.uk>

This gives access to the most current initiatives in the children's workforce.

Moss, P. and Penn, H. (1996) *Transforming Nursery Education*, London: Paul Chapman Publishing

This was written before many of the recent attempts to provide a more unified approach to child-care provision but it gives a very good summary of the difficulties associated with the fragmented provision in the UK and identifies barriers that needed to be overcome. You might like to consider how far these have been overcome through initiatives that have occurred since Moss and Penn were writing.

Penn, H. (2004) *Understanding Early Childhood: Issues and Controversies*, Maidenhead: Open University Press

Contains an effective review of the development of policy and services for children. In the chapter 'Past, Present and Future' the book looks at the history of child care in the UK and offers challenges to government initiatives such as Sure Start.

Services to Children's Play

FRASER BROWN

Play is so critically important to all children in the development of their physical, social, mental, emotional and creative skills that society should seek every opportunity to support it and create an environment that fosters it . . . The child's capacity for positive development will be inhibited or constrained if denied free access to the broadest range of environments and play opportunities.

(Welsh Assembly, 2002, pp. 2–3)

Introduction

This chapter explores aspects of play provision and seeks to answer the following questions:

- What is play?
- Why should we spend money on play provision?
- How has the nature of play provision in the UK developed in the last 50 years?
- What are the implications of this piecemeal approach?
- What might the future of play provision be?

The quotation at the beginning of this chapter highlights the importance of play for children and the consequent importance of making adequate provision for children's play. It is not unusual to hear the value of play described in terms of education, socialisation,

therapy, and much more (Brown, 2003a). Moreover, during play, things are often not as they seem, which led Bateson (1955, p. 51) to talk of the 'paradoxical' nature of play. This multiplicity of purpose, and general 'ambiguity of play' (Sutton-Smith, 1997), makes it hard to define. It has been argued for hundreds of years that play has widespread relevance for human development (Hughes, 1999) and that it should be regarded as a fundamental human right. Indeed, that right was enshrined in Article 31 of the United Nations Convention on the Rights of the Child (UNICEF, 1991), but what should societies do when opportunities to play are restricted? Unfortunately, there is no real agreement about how to make adequate provision for children's play. It is not possible to pigeonhole the purpose of play into a single aspect of development, which means supervised play provision may be found in settings as diverse as adventure playgrounds, after-school clubs,

168

hospitals, schools, prisons, etc. (NPFA, 2000). Unsupervised play areas are not only found in parks and recreation grounds, but also in shopping centres and public houses.

The funding of unsupervised provision has remained fairly secure in recent years. The same cannot be said of supervised play provision, the funding of which has been largely dependent on the vagaries of government policy. It is generally accepted that the best way for play projects to safeguard their future is to secure public funding. However, the multi-faceted nature of play makes it largely unsuited to the essentially compartmentalised nature of that form of funding. The issues that create this inherent contradiction were introduced in Part I and will be explored later in the chapter:

- the need to keep children safe, secure and free from danger, set against the need for children to experience challenges and develop an understanding of risk (Hughes, 2001);

- the expectations of parents when they leave children in the care of playworkers, set against the freedom of children to explore their environment (McKendrick et al., 2000);

- the income generated by charging for the service set against children's freedom to come and go as they please (Brown, 2003b).

You might find it useful to look at Chapter 2, Childhood: Rights and Realities, for further discussion of the relationship between parents and the difficult balance between children's participation and protection rights. Chapter 3, The Politics of Childhood, considers economic aspects of provision and Chapter 5, Pictures of Children, explains how all these tensions are underpinned by the images of children that we develop.

This chapter also contains reference to a number of very successful play projects that have closed as a result of the vagaries of government funding. However, on a more optimistic note, it refers to the case study in Chapter 18, The Venture, an adventure playground in Wrexham where the organisers have tapped into successive incarnations of government money to create a highly successful play project that is now used as a prototype for new projects throughout Wales, and the rest of the UK.

What is play?

Children's play is a complex phenomenon, with wide-ranging benefits including the development of cognitive skills (Fisher, 1992), motor skills (Johnson et al., 1987), imagination (Singer, 1995) and socialisation (Yeatman and Reifel, 1992). It has a significant role in the development of communication skills (Handelman, 1992), and, according to Freud (1974), enables human beings to attain and retain emotional equilibrium. Bruner (1972) suggests that play is at the very heart of our capacity to develop flexibility and adaptability, and so may be the driving force that underpins human evolution. The last 150 years have seen a great many writers trying to define play. In particular, there has been a lot of interest in why children play, and what role it may have in human development. With a few notable exceptions (e.g. Spariosu, 1989; Sutton-Smith, 1997), most of the relevant and substantial underpinning work appeared much earlier in the 20th century. Towards the end of his classic text, *The Ambiguity of Play,* Sutton-Smith (1997, pp. 219–20) identifies 110 credible attempts to explain the phenomenon of play – and there are doubtless many more. In fact, there is such a diverse array of play theories that most writers have tried to simplify matters by creating some sort of classification system into which each theory can be accommodated. For example, Hughes (1999) identifies five major groupings: classic (biogenetic); psychoanalytic; cognitive development; arousal modulation; and contextual. My own approach to analysing the value of play was to classify the theories under nine headings: arousal seeking – fun and enjoyment; freedom to act independently; flexibility; socialisation and social interaction; physical activity; cognitive development; creativity and problem solving; pursuit of emotional equilibrium; and self-discovery (Brown, 2006).

Garvey (1991) suggests the most effective way to explain play is to identify common threads within the leading theories. This is not simple since some of those theories are directly contradictory. For example, play has been seen as both the consumer of surplus energy (Spencer, 1873) and the recreator of lost energy (Lazarus, 1883). Theories cover a wide range of disciplines: behaviourism (Berlyne, 1960), cognitive development

(Piaget, 1951), psychoanalysis (Axline, 1969), etc. It was that wide array of ideas that led Huizinga (1949) to conclude that play 'is not susceptible of exact definition either logically, biologically, or aesthetically'. Nevertheless, Garvey (1991) identifies five commonly accepted characteristics of play:

- Positive effect means that play is pleasurable and enjoyable. Even when it is not actually accompanied by signs of mirth, it is still positively valued by the player.

- Intrinsic motivation means that play has no extrinsic goals. Those involved in play aren't playing for anything other than the pleasure of play.

- Free choice means that play is spontaneous and voluntary. It is not obligatory but is freely chosen by the player.

- Active engagement means that play involves some active engagement on the part of the player.

- Non-literality means that play has certain systematic relations to what is not play.

The main themes of Garvey's view have become deeply ingrained in the philosophy of playwork, as expressed in the 'Playwork Principles' (Play Wales, 2005), which were developed after extensive consultation with the profession.

Reflective Activity 12.1

Features of play

1 Think about a particular example of play you have seen or experienced when children are playing in a playground. Which of Garvey's features of playful activity do you think were apparent?

2 Sluckin (1981) says the most important freedom in play is freedom from adults. Think about another example of play you have observed or experienced where adults were present. How do you think the play was affected?

- All children and young people need to play. The impulse to play is innate. Play is a biological, psychological and social necessity, and is fundamental to the healthy development and well-being of individuals and communities.

- Play is a process that is freely chosen, personally directed and intrinsically motivated. That is, children and young people determine and control the content and intent of their play, by following their own instincts, ideas and interests, in their own way for their own reasons.

Thus, it is generally accepted that the value of play is wide-ranging, with significance far beyond the simple exercise of motor skills. It has developmental impact, in terms of intellect and socialisation. It is at the root of individual personality and our sense of self. It drives the creative process, and the growth of problem solving skills. It helps us attain, maintain, and retain emotional equilibrium, and it facilitates the development of skills that enable us to interpret the meaning of other people's actions. Play is clearly a serious business.

Why should we spend money on play provision?

British society has long recognised the need to provide play opportunities that both enable and encourage children to play. In a personal letter to the inaugural meeting of the National Playing Fields Association, Lloyd George said,

> The right to play is a child's first claim on the community. Play is nature's training for life. No community can infringe that right without doing deep and enduring harm to the minds and bodies of its citizens.
>
> (National Playing Fields Association, 1926)

As recently as 2004, the Dobson report *Getting Serious About Play* stated,

> From an early age, play is important to a child's development and learning, it isn't just physical. It can involve cognitive, imaginative, creative, emotional and social aspects. It is the main way children express their impulse to explore, experiment and understand. Children of all ages play. (DCMS, 2004a)

The quotation at the beginning of the chapter also emphasises the importance of play for children's development. Lloyd George's view was actually quite enlightened for the times. In between the two world wars, play provision was generally justified in paternalistic terms. For example, the NPFA's Royal Charter of Incorporation charged the organisation with extending 'the benefits of . . . playgrounds . . . to the poorer members of the community' (NPFA, 1933, p. 4). There is no precise statement of what those benefits might be, but the same objective also mentions 'promoting the physical and moral welfare and the safety of the population'. This may have had more to do with the mores of a patriarchal society than any deep understanding of the value of play. Given the social context of the time, the reference to safety of the population may have been more concerned with protecting the general public from unruly elements than with promoting the rights of children. Nevertheless, there is a clear implication that playgrounds offer benefits of a spiritual and psychological nature as well as the more widely understood physical benefits.

For around fifty years the National Playing Fields Association was the only organisation in the UK that made any substantial attempt to promote children's play provision. In a conference report, Bob Gooch, NPFA's assistant technical director, is quoted as recommending local authorities to install a range of equipment (NPFA, 1954). It appears the organisation's thinking was that *variety* made good playgrounds, and that equipment was the answer to the lack of recreational opportunities. This was usually justified in terms of frequency of use rather than any concept of child development.

In the late 1960s, with the appointment of Drummond Abernethy as director of the children and youth department, the NPFA began to take the message about child development more seriously. Abernethy was an educationalist, who had been involved in drafting the 1944 Education Act. In a booklet entitled *Playgrounds*, he suggested play consists of a compound of fantasy, imitation, adventure, physical development and coordination. Thus, 'play in all its aspects is as essential to a child as food' (Abernethy, 1973, p. 6). However, Abernethy was predominantly an evangelist for the adventure playground movement, and so when, in the same booklet, he gave his observations on conventionally equipped playgrounds, he saw them as offering 'little challenge to either initiative or imagination' (p. 38). Thus, on the one hand, NPFA was for the first time recognising the wide-ranging nature of play, on the other, they were dismissing fixed equipment playgrounds in favour of 'leadership' (as playwork was then called).

In the mid-1970s, the NPFA had begun to reflect the development of this new philosophy through its appointment of staff; regional officers were appointed on the basis of their experience and expertise in playwork. In general, the appointees were from a background in adventure play. They saw children's play in terms of its substantial developmental value, but tended to regard fixed equipment playgrounds as a waste of money.

Subsequently a number of playworkers have developed their own theoretical justifications for playwork. Hughes (2001) sees the issue in terms of human evolution and the survival of the species. My own approach is grounded in a child development perspective (Brown, 2003a). Else and Sturrock (1998) focus on the psychotherapeutic potential of playwork. Each theorist sees playwork as being concerned with the correction of 'developmental imbalance' (Abernethy, 1968, p. 20), albeit their description of that imbalance takes a variety of different forms. Each one is rooted in its own quite distinct rationale, but they all ultimately focus on the negative outcomes of a failure to provide appropriate play opportunities for the nation's children. All three approaches see the play process as infinitely more important than any product that might result. Hart says the children agree:

> The only time playgrounds in the USA are really
> exciting for children seems to be when they are
> being built for there are lots of materials for
> them to work with. Once they are finished
> the playgrounds quickly become boring.
>
> (Hart, 1995, p. 21)

Playwork seeks to restore the missing play opportunities, and so enable children to achieve their full developmental potential. As a result, after a lengthy consultation with the profession, the recently agreed playwork principles include the following statement about playwork: 'The role of the playworker is to support all children and young people in the creation of a space in which they can play' (Play Wales, 2005). This is achieved by identifying and removing barriers to the developmental process, and enriching the child's play environment (Brown and Webb, 2002). However, unlike all other professions in the children's workforce,

playwork takes the child's preference as its starting point. Thus, playwork is necessarily reflective, non-judgemental, non-prejudicial and generally non-directive. Rather than taking control of children's lives, it instead relies on appropriate responses to children's play cues to set the agenda. In a previous book I described playwork as follows:

> Playwork may be seen as a generalised description
> of work that includes adventure play, therapeutic
> work, out-of-school clubs, hospital play,
> environmental design, and much more, i.e. all
> those approaches that use the medium of play as a
> mechanism for redressing aspects of developmental
> imbalance caused by a deficit of play opportunities.
>
> (Brown, 2003, p. 52)

There is obviously no reason why a healthy well-adjusted child should not also be able to enjoy a variety of playwork opportunities, but the question that provides the heading for this section of the chapter is, 'why should we spend money on play provision?' Clearly it would be difficult to justify public spending on play provision if it were simply about entertainment. Even 'keeping the kids off the streets' would not really be a sufficient argument. However, the concern at the heart of the playwork philosophy harks back to the Lloyd George quote mentioned above, that if we infringe the child's right to play, we risk 'doing deep and enduring harm to the minds and bodies' of our children (NPFA, 1926). Unfortunately, that is exactly what we are doing. For a variety of reasons, including those cited by Hughes (2001) and mentioned previously, children's freedom to play has become increasingly curtailed over the past 30 years. Children are less free to explore their local neighbourhoods nowadays. Their world is ever more restricted by adult agendas, albeit sometimes for the best of motives.

Thus, children in the UK today are predominantly experiencing a form of play that does not contain two elements that most play theorists argue are fundamental to the nature of play. First, they are seldom free to engage with their environment in an exploratory way. There are few challenges in their play experience, and hardly any opportunity to take risks. Secondly, they are unable to exercise control over their environment.

Most play environments are relatively inflexible, and so the opportunity for children to experiment is increasingly restricted. According to Sutton-Smith, one of the main functions of play is 'the potentiation of adaptive variability' (1998, p. 231). In my own terms, play is right at the heart of the developmental link between the degree of flexibility in a child's environment and the extent to which the child develops flexibility in their decision-making and problem solving. This ideal developmental cycle, which I characterise as 'compound flexibility' is struggling to run its natural course because of the inflexibility of the modern world (Brown, 2003). Thus, the role of the playworker is to restimulate the developmental process. This is done by working to each child's agenda and adopting non-judgemental stances, coupled with a non-directive approach.

These are just a few of the many arguments that have been used by playworkers in recent years to justify spending public money on play provision. It is a measure of the developing confidence of the playwork profession that it is now beginning to move on to develop theoretical analyses of its day-to-day work – for example, the 'BRAWGS Continuum' (Sturrock et al., 2004), which is a development from the 'Colorado' paper (Else and Sturrock, 1998). There are also sociological models (Brown and Cheesman, 2003); process models (Lester, 2004); and spatial models (Brown, 2007). Whether we see playwork as an evolutionary process (Hughes, 2001) or a developmental stimulus (Brown, 2003), there can be little doubt that the playwork profession is increasingly seeking official recognition for the value of its work. For 50 years the UK Government took little notice. However, more recently there are signs that they are beginning to respond, as we shall see in subsequent sections.

How has the nature of play provision in the UK developed in the last 50 years?

The general depiction of the exercise of power in the market place provides an interesting example of society's misconceptions about childhood and these are discussed in Chapter 3, The Politics of Childhood. Children are often perceived as 'gullible' and susceptible to innovation rather than being seen as 'movers and shakers' or participants in the process of change. Little worth is attributed to the child as an innovator, an inventor or a controller of social movements within the experience of childhood. It may be true that children had Power Rangers and Pokémon thrust upon them by the toy industry, and that adults were responsible for the development of computer games. However, the recent Harry Potter phenomenon was unquestionably child-led in the first instance, which suggests that children may be more significant actors in the market place than previously thought, i.e. not just passive recipients, but also proactive participants. For McKendrick et al. (2000, p. 297) 'the key issue with respect to "children as a market" is the extent to which children are active agents'.

See Chapter 2, Childhood: Rights and Realities, for further discussion of participation in decision-making.

One such market, where it might be assumed children have the opportunity to be active agents, is play provision. After all, play is one of the few areas of activity where it is generally accepted that children should be free to exercise choice. As we have already

Reflective Activity 12.2

The role of playworkers

Playwork is a generic term for a profession that encompasses those occupations where the medium of play is used as the major mechanism for redressing aspects of developmental imbalance. Playwork is rooted in an understanding that children learn and develop through their play. Playwork involves identifying and removing barriers to that process, and enriching the child's play environment. Playwork always seeks to take the child's agenda as its starting point.   (Brown and Webb, 2002)

1 To what extent should playworkers take an active role in child development?

2 Consider the value to both the child and to the wider society.

seen, most discussions about children's play assume it is freely chosen, personally directed and intrinsically motivated behaviour, undertaken for its own sake (Play Wales, 2005). Play is the child's vehicle for moving, shaping, altering, manipulating and controlling their social, personal and developmental experience (Garvey, 1991). A child's playing, and his or her play culture, is able to maintain traditions while subtly enabling change, innovation and creativity. How does this process work, and in particular, what is the significance of play provision in the child's world? To what extent does that provision address the real needs of children? To what extent does it relate to the true value of play? These questions are highly pertinent to the following discussion of the development of play provision over the last 50 years.

In 1993, Burton reported on research that explored the role and function of local government in supporting children's play. It found that recognition of the importance of play and the development of both policy and practice is inconsistent across the UK. Burton (1993) suggests that local authorities have the potential either to boost or suppress the range of play opportunities available to children, and that, while an officially recognised play policy may support the development of good quality play facilities and opportunities, policies alone are no guarantee of good practice. In this new millennium, most towns and cities in the UK offer a wide range of facilities for children to play, including both supervised and unsupervised provision. However, that provision does not necessarily reflect the play needs of the child. Moss and Petrie (2002) suggest the Western world has come to regard provision for children in terms of the outcomes it is likely to produce. These outcomes derive from an adult rationale, expressed as targets, outputs, etc. They argue it would be preferable to view such provision as 'children's spaces' rather than 'children's services' – places where children are able to escape from adult attention, experience risk and develop their own culture. Moss (2002, p. 437) says children's spaces should be regarded as 'places for provocation and ambivalence, wonder and amazement, curiosity and fun'.

History shows us that successive governments have not known where to place play provision in the bureaucratic structure. In fact they have never placed local authorities under any obligation to provide for children's play. However, starting with the penny rate, local authorities have been legally able to provide for children's play for over 100 years. The 1944 Education Act was the first piece of legislation specifically to mention the subject. Since then, there have been a number of social programmes that have impacted upon play provision, albeit none of them was solely targeted at children's play.

> Chapter 13, Children's Experience of Community Regeneration, identifies and discusses other initiatives that impact on children's play.

They include: post-war slum clearance programmes; preventative care initiatives, such as the Intermediate Treatment programme; Section 106 agreements (under the terms of the Town and Country Planning Act 1990); GIAs (General Improvement Area) and HAAs (Housing Action Area) (established by various Housing Acts); the Urban Programme, in all its guises; the Inner Area Partnership programme; City Challenge; Single Regeneration Budgets. In the 1970s and 1980s the Manpower Services Commission was responsible for a number of employment schemes that resulted in the temporary expansion of supervised play provision, including YOPs (Youth Opportunities Programme) and STEPs (Special Temporary Employment Programme).

This array of programmes has its roots in education, health, housing, social services, the environment, urban regeneration, employment, youth crime, and so on. In fact, nearly every aspect of public spending (central and local) has at one time or another been used to improve children's play opportunities. Play providers have a long history of piggybacking their projects onto the funding streams offered by these programmes. Since the benefits of play are many and varied, it is not surprising that the funding for play projects has been derived from such a wide range of sources. It is also not surprising to find that play provision takes many forms.

The largest proportion of UK spending on children's play goes on fixed equipment playgrounds, with swings, slides, roundabouts, etc. Traditionally these have been sited in parks, but they may also be found in housing estates, public houses, shopping centres, etc.

By their very nature such facilities are relatively inflexible, and so the last fifty years has seen the development of a different approach to play provision: playwork. As we have already seen 'playwork' is a generic term for a number of approaches that seek to address the child's developmental needs through the medium of play. The following examples are not intended to be read as comprehensive portraits of the specific type of provision being described; nor do they offer a complete overview of play provision in the UK. They are offered here in order to illustrate the diverse and varied nature of supervised play provision in modern day Britain.

- *Adventure playground* – an enclosed 'open access' play area, supervised by qualified playworkers, in which children are able to seek out opportunities for creative activity often not available elsewhere. Use of the play facility is free of charge. The age of users may vary widely, but the main focus tends to be on school-aged children. 'Adventure' in this instance is not a reference to the 'assault course' look of many playgrounds; it has much more to do with the idea that this type of provision stimulates the sense of 'adventure' in the child's mind. The modern adventure playground is the descendent of Sorensen's (1931) original concept of a junk playground, where children used scrap materials to create their own play space.

- *After-school club(s)* – a 'care'-based scheme, for which children have to be registered. A lot of play activity takes place, but children are generally not free to leave until collected by their parents or carers towards the end of the session. It is a form of provision that aims to benefit working parents, as well as their children. Some playwork theorists argue that this is not strictly playwork, since there is an adult agenda and the children are not free to come and go as they please (Hughes, 2001); however, all play provision has adult-imposed boundaries to a greater or lesser extent, and within the after-school setting there is no intrinsic reason why the club cannot be characterised by 'fun, freedom and flexibility', which some regard as the essence of playwork (Brown, 2003).

- *Holiday playschemes* – supervised play opportunities during school holidays, especially during the summer period, offering a range of activities for all ages. The focus tends to be more on entertainment, and 'keeping the kids off the streets' than other forms of provision, but this is not always the case. Holiday playschemes have often been the forerunner of permanent provision.

- *Hospital play* – to some extent a response to the recognition that sick children recover much more quickly when they have access to good quality play opportunities. The full-time workers may be qualified hospital play specialists, or sometimes nursery nurses. In the US hospitals have taken this to heart with the 'Child Life' approach, where the child's life in hospital is approached holistically by a team of workers including doctors, nurses, social workers, child development workers, etc.

- *Play therapy* – usually one-to-one sessions run by therapists who are specialists either in the field of child psychology, or in children's social work. It is based on the twin ideas that: a) children will reveal their problems in the nature of their play (Klein, 1955); and b) children can come to terms with their problems through play (Axline, 1969). There are several postgraduate courses in play therapy in the UK.

- *Playrooms in prisons* – preferably sited near the 'visits room' – a recognition of the fact that children visiting their parents in prison can find the experience quite disturbing, and possibly even traumatic. It also allows the adults time together. When attached to waiting areas in prisons they are less satisfactory.

- *Pre-school playgroups* – an indoor facility, usually for 3- to 4-year-olds, supervised by at least one qualified pre-school playleader (usually with a PLA qualification). These are not the same as nurseries, since play is seen as having its own value, separate from education.

- *Mobile provision* – intended to bring play opportunities to areas with a high level of need, combined with a low level of provision, often in the form of a playbus, but could be a van, or other mobile vehicle. They sometimes offer additional community activities, e.g. book club, drama workshops, craft work. The playworkers are peripatetic, often called 'play rangers'.

- *Toy libraries* – originally intended to serve the needs of the parents of disabled children. A variety of toys (usually approved by the Good Toy Guide) may be hired or used on site. Many toy libraries also serve the general play needs of their local community.

Chapter 11, Day Care Services for Children, discusses how all provision for young children is becoming more concerned with education through play.

Playwork also takes place in a variety of venues whose central focus is not necessarily play. For example city farms, special schools, adventure holidays, etc.

What are the implications of this piecemeal approach?

As we have already seen, play is a complex subject which is hard to define and has benefits so varied that they are impossible to pigeonhole. This makes it difficult for play providers to make a clear and concise argument for government funding. It also makes it hard for governments to allocate funds effectively, since they are much more comfortable with neatly compartmentalised approaches to funding. Consequently, in the second half of the 20th century, services to children's play were not only characterised by their diversity (which is no bad thing), but also by their lack of staying power (which is a thoroughly bad thing). The vast majority of government funding schemes have been short term in nature, which has made it extremely hard for play providers to plan ahead, with the result that a number of well-managed and altogether effective projects have collapsed under the strain. Most play projects have gained their impetus from a particular funding stream, and then struggled to survive once the funds dried up. On the other hand the organisers of The Venture in Wrexham have been very successful in their applications to a wide range of government funding schemes. As a result they have managed to create a highly successful play project that is now used as a

See Chapter 18, The Venture: Case Study of an Adventure Playground.

prototype for projects in Wales and elsewhere. However, for most play projects this approach has been neither feasible nor realistic. The following section provides three examples of the way in which potentially successful projects have suffered as a result of the vagaries of government funding.

- *Stenhills adventure playground* began in the 1970s on the site of an old council tip in Runcorn. It was funded by a five-year urban aid grant, but the limited funds only allowed for the employment of one playworker on a relatively unattractive salary. The management committee were initially able to recruit an extremely committed individual who ran the adventure playground effectively. This was a traditional adventure playground where the children were able to use scrap materials to develop their own playspace, to destroy it if they wanted to and to recreate something afresh. The playground was a constantly changing space, very much in the mould of playwork pioneers such as Sorensen, Abernethy, Benjamin. However, this solitary playworker very soon reached 'burn out', and had no option but to leave. Subsequently, it became harder to recruit effective playworkers and so the pace of change on the playground began to slow. Consequently, when the money ran out, there was no longer any ground swell of local support to lobby for its survival and the playground closed. If the funding had been adequate to begin with, it would have been possible to employ more than one playworker, and the project would not have been so dependent on the commitment of a single individual.

- *Islington summer playschemes* lost 505 playscheme places in 2003 when the council heavily cut its holiday grants fund. Schemes either did not run or catered for fewer children. A further 203 places ran for fewer days, and 396 places cost more. Alan Sutton, who co-wrote a report into these events, commissioned by Islington Children's Fund, suggested that funding problems faced by community-led play services were compounded by a government shift away from informal, free-at-the-gate playschemes, run by local volunteers, to formal parent-focused child care, staffed by professionals and reliant on parental fees. 'The move towards paid-for child care has made services less affordable for those most likely to be already socially excluded.' Of the six playschemes that serviced ethnic minority communities, all closed because of the loss of the council subsidy. According to Adrian Voce, then director of the Children's Play Council, local authorities in many parts of the country appeared to withdraw funding from playschemes in the expectation of forthcoming lottery money. This illustrates the way in which play services throughout the country are impacted by the lack of statutory support for their work (*The Guardian*, 2005).

- *Keynsham community playscheme* won a government 'partners in excellence' award in 2005, but was threatened with closure by the local authority and its partners because an older funding stream was drying up and the new source was yet to arrive. According to a newspaper report, 'even on a freezing cold day, children are playing in the local park after school, climbing trees, running up hills and splashing in mud. In summer, their number doubles' (*The Guardian*, 2005). In the previous year the park was largely empty because children were afraid of being bullied by older children or being attacked by a stranger. However, the presence of two community play rangers eased those fears and reclaimed the park for school-aged children. The scheme proved extremely popular with the result that several councillors wanted it extended into their wards. Nevertheless, with the winding up of the Children's Fund, hundreds of community playschemes throughout the country faced closure (*The Guardian*, 2005).

- *Playwork in Northern Ireland* has not benefited from lottery money in the same way as their counterparts in England. When challenged about this, the Northern Irish branch of the lottery said their consultations didn't show play as a need, therefore they did not allocate any money to that area, despite the recommendations of the Dobson Report (DCMS, 2004a). Eva Kane, who is regional manager of Fit for Play in PlayBoard Northern

Ireland, says that merely shows how weak the play sector is in Northern Ireland. Far from being evidence of a lack of need, it is in fact evidence of the extent to which the sector needs help (Kane, 2005). What this demonstrates is the way in which decisions that affect children's play opportunities are made by people who have little understanding of the subject.

This section has explored the varied nature of children's play and the way in which that has led to confusion over responsibility for play provision. Successive governments have made funds available, but usually with highly restrictive criteria regarding the way the money should be spent, and always with a time limit. Because of the multi-dimensional nature of play, most play projects fail to satisfy the criteria. Those that do struggle to survive beyond the time limits of the funding. As a result, the past 25 years has seen many good projects disappear.

What might the future of play provision be?

In recent years the government has introduced a number of new programmes that have been used by play providers to good effect. The first of these was the National Childcare Strategy, which was introduced in a green paper, *Meeting the Childcare Challenge* (DfEE, 1998a). The proposals were presented jointly by Ministers with responsibility for education, employment, social security and women. This indicated the government's recognition of the multi-dimensional impact of such measures. At the same time, it illustrates both the varied nature of the subject and the difficulty politicians have in locating responsibility for provision. In 2000, the DfEE issued guidelines for out-of-school care schemes for school-aged children which contained small sections on anti-sexist play, anti-racist play and learning through play. However, the document focuses far more on the practical aspects of setting up and running such schemes. For example, it offers advice on management, legal issues, finances, premises, staffing, school collection and transport, and the countdown to opening (DfEE, 2000). This advice was subsequently updated by Kids Clubs Network (2002), but without much fundamental change. The guide is just one of twelve in the DfEE's Good Practice in Childcare series – none of which focus on children's play. Despite this apparent lack of interest in children's play, hundreds of imaginative providers have used the complex legislation to establish child-care projects with a playwork focus.

Subsequently we have seen play providers making use of finance provided by Best Play, and the New Opportunities Fund. The Children's Fund was launched in November 2000 as part of the Government's commitment to tackle disadvantage among children and young people. This has led to the development of children's centres, which have received substantial short-term funding. It is hoped there will be a children's centre in every local authority area. Most of these centres incorporate some form of dedicated play provision. However, as with so many of these schemes, there is no guarantee of long-term sustained funding and it is not clear what will happen when the money runs out.

It is only very recently that the government has started specifically to mention children's play in its legislative programmes, albeit sometimes only after intense lobbying. For example, the government has recently announced that £155m will be made available in England to improve children's play provision. This was eventually confirmed after five years of continuous pressure from the playwork field. In the run-up to the 2001 election, Chris Smith, the Minister with responsibility for children's play, stated that a future Labour government would set aside £200m from the New Opportunities Fund for play provision in the UK (CPC, 2001). He also challenged those working in this field to identify the outcomes of play so that the money could be well spent. Following a two-year research programme on play and play provision for school-aged children in England, the Children's Play Council concluded that play opportunities for older children are often restricted (Cole-Hamilton and Gill, 2002). The report argued for improved public funding and strategic planning for the development, support and maintenance of good play opportunities, and made detailed recommendations aimed at all levels of government. Despite the fact that the research had been funded

by the Department for Culture, Media and Sport (DCMS), the government failed to act upon any of the recommendations.

Instead, they initiated a further study (DCMS, 2004a), under the guidance of Frank Dobson. The Dobson Report, like the earlier CPC report, was also based on consultation, commissioned research and a review of existing evidence. The report concluded that the additional £200m should concentrate on areas and groups with the poorest access to good play opportunities, with particular focus on inclusion of disabled children and young people. The majority of the funding should support projects that follow existing good practice, and the rest of the funding should be earmarked for innovative projects. In particular it recommended the revival of the open access approach to play provision – an approach that had generally fallen out of favour since the 1970s with the expansion of after-school clubs, fears of litigation, etc. On this occasion, DCMS even offered feedback to children and young people on the Internet (DCMS, 2004b).

The money finally came on stream in April 2006, when it was confirmed that The Big Lottery Fund would set aside £155m over five years for children's play. The money, at the time of writing, is being used to fund three distinct strands of work. Around 10 per cent is available for innovative projects that use novel methods to address identified needs within the field of children's play. A further 10 per cent is being used to fund the Play England Project, which is implementing a national and regional support and development infrastructure for children's play projects in England. The bulk of the money, around £124m will be allocated to the Children's Play programme. This places funds in the hands of local authorities to be spent according to a set of criteria developed in consultation with the playwork field. Local authorities will not be allocated any funds until they have developed a local play strategy and can show how they are engaging with the local community in the form of 'play partnerships' (BIG, 2006).

By the time the Big Lottery Fund programme was launched, the Greater London Authority had already responded to the funding criteria by commissioning Adrian Voce, then director of London Play to produce a practical guide outlining how local authorities could best plan to provide children with accessible play spaces, offering free, high-quality and inclusive play opportunities (GLA, 2005). The speed of their response provides an interesting demonstration of the influence that funding can have on local authority practice. The guide includes chapters on: play and its benefits; play provision; the policy context for play; the methodology and stages to preparing a play strategy; and implementation of the strategy. An earlier example of this is provided by Hayes (2002) who describes how the 'Best Value' review for the play service at Nottingham City Council resulted in a new play policy, increased funding and improved pay and conditions for staff.

In more general terms the government says they view the development of children and young people's plans as a significant element in its reform of children's services (DfES, 2005h). The guidance notes associated with these CYPPs recommend that local authorities develop a 'single, strategic, overarching plan for all services which affect children and young people in the area', including 'play and leisure services' (DfES, 2005i). The guidance note points planners in the direction of the outcomes framework included in *Every Child Matters: Change for Children* (DfES, 2005c), which sets out five high-level outcomes of importance to children and young people:

> These outcomes are considered in some depth in Chapter 10, Safeguarding Children.

- Being healthy
- Staying safe
- Enjoying and achieving
- Making a positive contribution
- Achieving economic well-being

These outcomes are broken down into 25 more specific aims, one of which has to do with 'recreation'. As a result, Ofsted's *Inspection Framework for Children's Services* (2005, p. 20) includes the statement that one of the key judgements relating to the 'Enjoying and Achieving' outcome, is that 'all children and young people can access a range of recreational activities, including play and voluntary learning provision'. However, this statement was not included in the original draft and was only introduced after considerable lobbying from the playwork field. Of course there is a strong argument that

Reflective Activity 12.3

Playwork and *Every Child Matters*

Guidance provided on the relevant website (DfES, 2005c) states,

> play organisations have a unique role to play in helping to deliver *Every Child Matters: Change for Children* agenda, by:
>
> - delivering the five outcomes – particularly enjoying and achieving and making a positive contribution;
> - being key partners in children's trusts and contributing to children and young people's plans;
> - supporting families and promoting diversity;
> - reaching millions of children and young people through positive out-of-school activities.

Playworkers have argued that their profession has the potential to address all five outcomes, not just the two highlighted by the government (enjoying and achieving and making a positive contribution).

How do you think services to children's play might be said to address each of the five outcomes?

playwork has the potential to impact on all five outcomes, not just one part of one outcome.

A third, and largely distinct area where the government has recently shown more interest in children's play provision is that of parks, play areas and green spaces. In 2002, the Department of Transport, Local Government and the Regions (DTLR) conducted a review of both the users and uses of parks, play areas and green spaces. Their report also looked at innovation and good practice in management, with an emphasis on partnerships and community involvement. The report includes material about children's play, and makes links to Local Agenda 21 and to the relationship with other urban regeneration initiatives, thus recognising the multi-faceted nature of play provision. One major outcome of this was the 'Parks for People' programme, which is jointly funded by the Heritage Lottery Fund and the Big Lottery Fund (to the sum of £90 million over three years), and which espouses a long-term vision that 'every community should have access to a well-designed and maintained public park with opportunities for enjoyment and recreation for all'. Among other things, the programme offers funds for 'recreational and play activities', and seeks to encourage 'structured play activities or after-school activities' (HLF, 2006).

Set against these promising developments, when the government issued its Children's Workforce Strategy (DfES, 2005i), playwork was not mentioned at all – despite the fact that Skills Active (2005) calculated the playwork workforce in the UK to be 132,730 with a gross value added output of £1.5 billion. Other countries have a slightly more positive record when it comes to national governments taking a lead in the field of children's play provision. For example, the national play policy for Ireland aims to create better play

opportunities for all children. It sets out a number of principles and objectives, and provides an overview of the current levels of play provision. It looks at a range of issues, including a partnership approach between the statutory, community, voluntary and private sectors, the development of a play infrastructure, safety and funding. It also identifies responsibility for implementation and sets target dates for the achievement of actions (NCO, 2004). In Wales, the Welsh Assembly Government has produced its own Play Policy (Welsh Assembly, 2002), and subsequently constituted the Play Policy Implementation Group, which in turn made 24 specific recommendations for future action. Significantly, their report was substantially focused around open-access playwork, and included reference to such fundamental playwork concepts as adventure play, self-directed learning, play deprivation, risk, community involvement; home zones.

Conclusion

This chapter has explained the importance of play for all aspects of children's development and the role of playworkers in supporting children in their play. However, the importance of the child's right to play has generally gone unacknowledged in the policies of successive governments, possibly because the benefits of play are so wide reaching and cut across the boundaries of government departments. This is reflected in the variety of provision and the different funding arrangements that have been outlined in the chapter. While this may be problematic for many play projects, the example of The Venture illustrates that it is possible to overcome these barriers. Unfortunately the future may be equally problematic as the positive developments in The Children's Fund, *Every Child Matters* and Parks for People are so far not supported through the Children's Workforce developments. The hope for the future may be seen in the models of playwork in other parts of the UK.

See Chapter 18, The Venture: Case Study of an Adventure Playground.

Annotated reading

Brown, F. (ed.) (2003) *Playwork: Theory and Practice*, Buckingham: Open University Press

Presents a range of theoretical and practical perspectives of playwork, with examples of playwork in practice, including adventure playgrounds, establishing play in a local authority, and a therapeutic playwork project with abandoned children in Romania.

DCMS (2004) *Getting Serious About Play: A Review of Children's Play*, London: Department for Culture, Media and Sport

The report of the government's review of children's play chaired by the Rt Hon Frank Dobson, MP. Sets out how to best invest the £200 million from the New Opportunities Fund, pledged in 2001, for improving children's play opportunities.

Garvey, C. (1991) *Play*, 2nd edn, London: Fontana

Analyses the way in which play helps the child to learn about the self, about others and about the world. Describes the various manifestations of play, and looks at their origins.

Hughes, B. (2001) *Evolutionary Playwork and Reflective Analytic Practice*, London: Routledge

Explores the complexities of children's play, and its meaning and purpose. Considers the fundamentals of evolutionary playwork, and looks at some key theoretical concepts underlying playwork.

Sutton-Smith, B. (1997) *The Ambiguity of Play*, London: Harvard University Press

An examination of play which suggests that play theories are rooted in seven distinct rhetorics: the ancient discourses of fate, power, communal identity and frivolity, and the modern discourses of progress, the imaginary and the self.

Children's Experience of Community Regeneration

JANE KETTLE

'In the future, I would like to see more people happier and full of joy.'

(Angelina, age 8, from the Gipton area of Leeds)

Within 10 to 20 years, nobody should be seriously disadvantaged by where they live.

(Neighbourhood Renewal Unit, 2005)

Introduction

This chapter explores a central theme of New Labour government policy to promote social inclusion: the neighbourhood regeneration agenda. Some children are excluded from service provision for a range of reasons. One of the factors is concerned with where children live and the experiences they have within their communities. The quotations at the beginning of the chapter suggest that both government and children have aspirations for this to be improved, and this chapter discusses the work being undertaken in the UK and how effective this is.

See Chapter 4, The Social Divisions of Childhood, for discussion of exclusion.

The built environment in all its forms has been the focus of social, economic and political concern for decades. Over recent years there has been an increased understanding of the need to address the problems facing poor and sometimes alienated communities. Working for better communities has become a political imperative through neighbourhood regeneration. Children live, work and play as part of these communities, and this chapter will identify how neighbourhood regeneration can affect the lives of children and how children can be part of neighbourhood regeneration. The key questions to be considered are:

* What is the impact of living in a poor neighbourhood?

- What do we mean by community regeneration and who runs it?

- How and why are space and place important for children?

- What is the relationship between community regeneration and children?

- To what extent are children involved in community regeneration?

A crucial part of the government's reform agenda is that 'active citizenship' is central to creating sustainable communities. Local communities facing renewal require diverse and sophisticated skills and understanding of the concepts of citizenship, leadership, empowerment and regeneration. The regeneration of spaces and places can foster important skills and knowledge including an understanding of planning, an awareness of partnership working, engagement with financial planning and an awareness of politics (McInroy and MacDonald, 2005). These concepts may well be new and not yet developed in children. They relate to complex and detailed activities that require a level of confidence and in some cases experience that children may not yet possess. Building this capacity in children is sometimes ignored. However, a recent review of a social action group that worked with children and young people perceived to be at risk of offending in Nottingham in the 1970s described the participants' lasting sense of pride and achievement. The participants spoke of the skills they had retained over years (public speaking, running meetings, producing newsletters and looking after budgets) as well as the physical legacy of a flourishing youth centre (*Communities Today*, 2005). So, although the government's vision of active citizenship and a holistic approach to community regeneration is both radical and ambitious, and the reality of the regeneration context is problematic and complex, there is robust evidence that when young people are valued as equal citizens and work in partnership with adults and professionals, there can be inclusive results. The notion of active citizenship is applied with varying degrees of sophistication in 'circle time' and personal social and health education (PSHE) in primary schools and through a more formal approach in citizenship classes at secondary level.

This does need great care in the planning and allocation of resources. At the time of writing the latest response by the government has been to launch the Academy for Sustainable Communities, a new national skills organisation supporting the creation and renewal of local communities that are vibrant, prosperous and attractive to live in. At its launch in the summer of 2005, the chair, Professor Peter Roberts, set out an ambitious goal: He said that the

> goal is to ensure that there are sufficient people with the right skills and knowledge to deliver and maintain sustainable communities across the country. The academy also aims to foster cross-occupational learning and understanding, and learning between communities – inspiring and enabling people across different fields to work together in a coherent, farsighted approach to creating and renewing places where people want to live, work and play. (Roberts, 2005)

Inclusive language, but to what extent is this invitation to be involved extended to children?

To respond to some of these issues we need to understand the way children perceive and value neighbourhoods and how they can become involved. Are there any trigger points for involving children in regeneration activity and how might professionals engage more effectively with children in neighbourhoods? Matthews (2002) has noted how children have been both misunderstood and dismissed as a resource for regeneration. He states that

> The involvement of children and young people in decision-making in their neighbourhoods, and their involvement in community regeneration, is inevitably limited. Despite the proclaimed wish of New Labour and many local authorities to involve them, attempts to do so are fraught with difficulties, and are in many cases half-hearted. The societal tendency to view children simultaneously as demon and angel, demeaned and ennobled, is clearly seen in neighbourhood strategy where efforts to provide for children (often without meaningful consultation with the children

themselves) are counter-balanced by containment strategies for controlling the 'delinquency' of children and young people. (Matthews, 2002, p. 265)

It would appear that there is often more political mileage in criticising and condemning young people rather than using their achievements as a building block to success, but children can be a force for change where neighbourhoods are in conflict. Ted Cantle, chair of the Community Cohesion Review Team (CCRT) said after the Bradford Riots in 2001 that, while the team was inspired by many of the children they spoke to, these young people were participating in regeneration against the odds and with fragile resources. They actively wanted to break down the barriers between different community groups and to work together to build a more harmonious future (CCRT, 2001).

> For further discussion on these themes see Chapters 7 and 9, Youth Services and Provision and Children Who Offend.

What is the impact of living in a poor neighbourhood?

Poor standards of housing and living environment exert a major influence over a range of other issues affecting disadvantaged neighbourhoods. Children who live in problematic environments (such as poor or inadequate housing, run down estates with little or no provision for play or leisure) experience everyday tensions and difficulties. There is considerable evidence that children living in deprived neighbourhoods face a wider range of problems than their contemporaries elsewhere. This is described amply in a range of government reports and publications generated over recent years by, for example, the Social Exclusion Unit (SEU) and the former Office of the Deputy Prime Minister (ODPM). The evidence demonstrates that deprived neighbourhoods have a lot in common. They are characterised by poor housing, poor health, poor

> Chapter 7, Youth Services and Provision, explores other aspects of this trend.

education, fewer job opportunities and higher crime rates than in other areas. There is likely to be inadequate public transport, poor leisure and sports facilities and few shops; in other words, a degraded infrastructure. Young people now depend on their families for longer. A recent survey by the Office for National Statistics, revealed an increase in the number of adults living at home with their parents. Some young people may be delaying leaving home because of economic necessity, such as difficulty in entering the housing market. Others may simply choose to continue living with their parents or return to the family home after struggling on their own. In spring 2004, 58 per cent of young men (aged 20 to 24), and 39 per cent of young women of the same age lived at home with their parents. This puts additional pressure on families living in degraded areas that may be less able to cope with these pressures than those in thriving communities.

Young people in deprived neighbourhoods face a particular but wide range of problems. Compared with people of the same age in other areas they are more likely to:

- have difficulties in education and in finding a job;
- experience conflict at home;
- become homeless;
- suffer from health problems, particularly mental health problems;
- become involved in crime or drug misuse, and also more likely to be a victim of crime;
- experience racism <www.renewal.net>.

The factors that lead to declining neighbourhoods are multiple (unemployment, poor educational attainment, family breakdown, crime, poor quality housing, for example), but it is important to note that many of the problems facing children in these areas have been made worse by the public services' failure to address them effectively. Generally, policy and delivery have been fragmented and uncoordinated, with services tending to follow crises rather than preventing them. Responsibility for problems in deprived neighbourhoods at both local and national level until recently lay with no single organisation or government department, creating confusion over priorities and roles (SEU, 1998a).

Analysing community advantages and disadvantages

Drawing on the discussion of what leads to declining neighbourhoods consider your home community or the community in which your university is located. What contributes to the advantages or disadvantages it faces?

The need to regenerate and renew neighbourhoods is central to the government's agenda, as both published research and crises such as urban rioting and racial tensions have highlighted the social and economic implications of communities in crisis. There is a renewed emphasis on community participation and this is where problems occur surrounding the role that children can or should be expected to play in determining what regeneration activities should take place, and where Britain lags behind other parts of Europe. For example, in countries like Sweden, Denmark or Germany there are well-equipped community centres and facilities for children on most social housing estates (the areas where regeneration is often focused in the UK). Policymakers in these countries do seem to understand that for children to be active citizens they have to be a part of the community throughout their lives (*Communities Today*, 2005). To build sustainable communities all sections of the community must be involved.

What do we mean by community regeneration and who runs it?

Regeneration of particular neighbourhoods is a complex and expensive process, and has a mixed track record in terms of the success of its different intended outcomes. Improving the conditions (physical, economic, social and environmental) of people living in poor quality neighbourhoods has been a matter of concern (but not always action) of successive governments throughout the 20th century, and regeneration as a phrase was coined in the US in the 1970s. In the UK we have been talking about 'regeneration' since the 1990s, in a more expanded context than the economic, investment-based process that predominated in the US (where regeneration focuses on change of use and development of neglected localities, mainly ex-industrial or commercial settings, for example mixed-use brownfield development and adaptive reuse of street-level storefronts).

At the beginning of the 21st century, regeneration has become big business. Many built environment professionals are associated with the regeneration business. Architects, urban designers, planners, housing workers, surveyors, construction managers and developers all need to operate in this quickly moving arena. We have urban, rural, coalfield, cultural, neighbourhood and community regeneration all competing for funding and prominence. The organisation that steers the regeneration agenda in England was, until spring 2006, the Office of the Deputy Prime Minister (ODPM), and its overarching mission was to create prosperous, inclusive and sustainable communities for the 21st century, places where people want to live, that promote opportunity and a better quality of life for all (<www.odpm.gov.uk>). The ODPM was replaced by the Department for Communities and Local Government (DCLG) and this entity is carrying forward and developing this theme.

What is especially significant is that over recent years there has been a sea change in how policymakers talk about community and the role of community in regeneration. One of the reasons for this has been a growing awareness of the urgent need to address holistically the problems faced by the poor and alienated communities that exist across many parts of the UK. In 1997, the Prime Minister established the Social Exclusion Unit to find out what were workable solutions to the problems of, in the first case, the worst housing estates. (Since then it has been acknowledged that deprived neighbourhoods are not confined to inner urban council estates.) He described these as crime, drugs, unemployment, community breakdown and bad housing. By 1998 the Social Exclusion Unit had produced an initial report which examined what the problems were and it was found that they went far deeper than the superficial list outlined above. The report, entitled *Bringing Britain Together: A National Strategy for Neighbourhood Renewal* (SEU, 1998a), focused on the new geography of poverty, acknowledged the limited success of previous regeneration activities and stressed the urgent need to involve communities.

Essentially, the social inclusion/exclusion debate and the concept of regeneration are closely related and it is important to note that regeneration and renewal in some form (slum clearance programmes in the 19th and 20th centuries, for example) have existed in one form or another for many years. However, the plethora of initiatives has been variously described as a patchwork quilt (Means and Smith, 1996) and bowl of spaghetti (Hall, 2003). Having one department concerned with regeneration may alleviate some of this fragmentation, although a common problem of coordinating roles and departments is that they have little control over financial planning and spending and, as ministerial roles are mostly advisory, they are relatively powerless in decision making.

Between 1999 and 2000, within the remit of the Social Exclusion Unit, eighteen Policy Action Teams (PATs) were set up to examine detailed aspects of social exclusion. They were all related, and one of them, PAT 12, was specifically about young people. The team's central tenet was that young people should be put at the centre of policies that affect them and services should be organised around the needs of young people. Emerging from this was the *Learning to Listen: Action Plan for Children and Young People* (ODPM, 2003), which makes a visible commitment to involve children and youth, to value their involvement and to evaluate and improve participation policy and standards. The PAT report highlighted a number of indicators that the country's children are not thriving when compared with their European neighbours. One in five children were growing up in workless households, a higher figure than any other OECD member country. One in five also had special educational needs but, of that 20 per cent, only one in six had statements detailing their support requirements. One in 16 school leavers had no educational qualifications and almost 10 per cent of 16- to 18-year-olds were outside education, training or employment. Teenage pregnancy rates were twice that of Germany, three times that of France and six times

that of the Netherlands. There were more 15- and 16-year-old drug users in the UK than in any other EU country.

Government scrutiny of deprived neighbourhoods has not been confined to that carried out by the Social Exclusion Unit. There has been a plethora of reports and recommendations to address the regeneration agenda in a holistic and joined up way. One such influential example was the White Paper on urban regeneration, *Our Towns and Cities: The Future – Delivering an Urban Renaissance* (ODPM, 2000). This was published in November 2000 and it raised challenging questions about how to reverse the decline in Britain's urban areas and to make towns and cities spaces that were attractive to live in.

Although the incoming government in 1997 put regeneration high on its agenda, there was a watershed in 2001 when the National Strategy for Neighbourhood Renewal was launched. The National Strategy set out a clear approach to renewing neighbourhoods under stress. The aim was to be holistic and not just to focus on physical problems such as poor quality housing (many of the slum clearance programmes of the 1960s and 1970s which only dealt with physical problems are deemed to have failed).

The key principles that appear to be pulling together the profusion of initiatives and funding streams all operating locally in parallel, together or independently, without any sort of coordination are that:

- this far-reaching strategy now acknowledges that there are hundreds of severely deprived neighbourhoods;

- the visible impact of deprivation is only the tip of the iceberg; neighbourhoods are affected by poor schools, worklessness, bad transport links and a lack of social and cultural facilities;

- dividing money up into particular pots is not really effective; to be effective it is important to harness all the different mainstream funding sources to target.

Most importantly, neighbourhood renewal cannot work if residents, including children, are not on board.

Four years after the launch of the National Strategy, an interim report called *Making it Happen in*

Neighbourhoods: The National Strategy for Neighbourhood Renewal – four years on (Neighbourhood Renewal Unit, 2005) revised and reported on what was the most holistic regeneration strategy developed in the UK. Emphatically, the focus is on putting local communities at the heart of the decision-making process, drawing on the strengths of the public, private and voluntary sectors. It is central to regeneration policy, and part of the government's agenda to promote fair and equal opportunity, now that all groups within a community should be involved in the regeneration of that community.

The Neighbourhood Renewal Unit runs a number of the government's cross-sector regeneration programmes, including: *New Deal for Communities*, partnerships tackling the five key themes which all impact upon children:

- poor job prospects;
- high levels of crime;
- educational under-achievement;
- poor health;
- problems with housing and the physical environment.

Reflective Activity 13.2

Redressing deprivation

The Government states that people living in our most deprived areas experience these five circumstances:

- poor job prospects;
- high levels of crime;
- educational under-achievement;
- poor health;
- problems with housing and the physical environment.

1 In what ways do National Strategy for Neighbourhood Renewal themes impact on children?

2 Consider the connections between these circumstances (or themes) in children's daily lives, for example the links between poor housing and health. What other connections can you make?

This applies only to England but there are parallel strategies in development for Scotland, Wales and Northern Ireland.

How and why are place and space important for children?

The relationship between children and the built environment is a complex one. There is no clear definition of children's environmental rights as there is when it comes to, for example, work or education. As a nation we make assumptions about what it means to be a child, but in reality children's interpretations of places are different; what may go unnoticed by an adult may well be perceived as a threat by a child. For example, busy roads with inadequate crossing spaces, ill-placed public seating or poorly sited bus shelters can be problematic to children. (Conversely bus shelters where youths congregate become spaces of danger for adults who fear the menace of congregating youths.) Recent research confirms children's fears of dangerous strangers in urban neighbourhoods (Wells, 2005). And while children and adults may well express shared concerns about urban danger, children demonstrate a greater vulnerability to attack. Children living in areas in need of renewal may well experience 'environmental chaos', that is, high levels of noise, overcrowding and a lack of safe public gathering spaces. This can impact on their motivation and capacity to concentrate and learn (Save the Children Sweden, 2002).

> See Chapter 2, Childhood: Rights and Realities.

Children from all social groups are different from other marginalised groups (such as men and women from black and minority ethnic backgrounds, or women in general) because they are not often in a position where they can have any dialogue with professionals about what they want in a community, or about what concerns them about their environment. Matthews and Limb (1998) consider that children will remain marginalised in society until it is recognised that they experience the environment in different ways to adults. They are particularly vulnerable to crime and

Children's concerns in neighbourhood design

The evidence shows that children's concerns were more universal than personal when designing their neighbourhoods.

1 Why do you think that might be?

2 How do you think children's perceptions of space and place diverge from adults' perceptions?

and competent visual and spatial thinkers (Gallagher, 1997). Gallagher evaluated a project called 'Our Town' where twenty children aged 8–9 from Pittsburgh, Philadelphia, designed a fictitious city. This was followed by an assessment of their actual built environment. When the two were compared the children identified needs in their own space and suggested interventions. The roles of the adults (planners, architects, educators, residents) were supposed to be that of a 'collaborative design group' but the adults soon assumed the role of facilitators and data-gatherers. However, 'the adult assumption that children would design exclusively for themselves was proven to be unwarranted. Their concerns were more universal than personal' (Gallagher, 2004, p. 256).

> Chapter 5, Pictures of Children, offers further discussion of how adult images shape provision of children.

threatening behaviour. The increase in traffic in recent years has made local neighbourhoods dangerous for even the most 'streetwise' children, and the emphasis is on the child's behaviour rather than on the car driver to respond to the presence of the child. This can also be seen in the increasing intolerance to children's activities in what are public places, 'no ball games' and 'no cycling' notices are now being joined by 'no skateboarding' warnings where children may want to engage in this activity. Children's activities are being constrained in places designed for public use; witness the banning of youths wearing 'hoodies' in the Bluewater Shopping Centre. Emphatically, the environment is designed for adults, by adults, and children are obliged to engage with it on these terms (Freeman et al., 1999). This is what Qvortrup (1994) calls the 'adult praxis at work'. There is, however, considerable evidence that children can be both perceptive observers

What is the relationship between community regeneration and children?

As well as the umbrella programmes (the Communities Plan and the National Strategy for Neighbourhood Renewal) discussed in this chapter, there are a range of nationwide government initiatives to support children in struggling neighbourhoods. It is these nationwide, government-funded initiatives provided by or involving mainstream services that have the greatest potential to make a large-scale difference to children and young people in deprived neighbourhoods. There is a wide range of programmes at this level. These include,

- ConneXions – a youth service that provides information and advice for young people;

- Sure Start – the government programme set up with the aim of delivering the best start in life for children in disadvantaged communities. The project brings together early education, child care, health and family support;

- National Family and Parenting Institute – an independent charity working to support parents in bringing up their children, to promote the well-being of families and to make society more family friendly.

There are also many projects operating at a local level. These hinge on the concept of community regeneration or, more specifically, on how practitioners and policymakers actually engage with the communities they are working within. All recent policy initiatives put participation high on the policy agenda. Matthews (2001) provides a comprehensive review of this. There is an emergent interest in the extent to which social capital can be harnessed, in which communities rather than policymakers or practitioners are central to local social change. A working definition of 'social capital' is the 'stock of active connections among people: the trust, mutual understanding, and shared values and behaviours that bind the members of human networks and communities and make cooperative action possible' (Cohen and Prusak, 2001, p. 4). Working with disaffected, disenfranchised communities is hard, but ever since Alexander's calls for local people to be at the centre of design-based decision-making (Alexander, 1977), there has been a steady growth in the appreciation of the principle that the creation of good quality places and neighbourhoods is more likely if those who live in them have a say in how

See Chapter 14, The Swings and Roundabouts of Community Development, for an example of this.

Reflective Activity 13.4

Involving children in neighbourhood renewal

Marshmont is a vibrant neighbourhood renewal project with extensive involvement of the residents of the local community. It is planning to develop more activities for children and young people and wishes to involve them in planning, design and management of the projects.

How might this be achieved?

they are planned, designed and managed. There is considerable guidance on what constitutes good practice.

David Wilcox in his work on effective community participation suggests that there are five levels or stances which offer increasing degrees of control, or of shifting the balance of responsibility for decision-making from professionals to residents, depending on the circumstances:

- *Information*: the least is that people can be told what is going to happen;

- With *consultation*, a number of options are put forward and feedback is sought;

- In *deciding together*, communities are invited to make suggestions, put forward ideas and options, and join in deciding the best way forward;

- *Acting together* requires different interest groups deciding what is best and forming a partnership to carry it out;

- *Supporting independent community initiatives* means helping others to do what they want, usually within a financial or legal support framework (Wilcox, 1994).

Although there is a growing literature about how to involve children in making public decisions about regeneration, there is little evaluation of what is effective. The ways in which different organisations, agencies and professionals approach community involvement varies, as do the ways in which power and the opportunity for decision-making vary in how participants are able to access these. However, there is a wealth of research which indicates that children are more often than not sidelined in these activities (Henderson, 1997; Fitzpatrick et al., 1998; Freeman et al., 1999). The impact of youth involvement on regeneration strategies has been limited. Indeed, youths and adults have a different perspective on what form 'regeneration' should take, while at the same time successful youth in-

> For further discussion of these 'sanctions' see Chapter 9, Children Who Offend.

volvement also requires the commitment of adults. Children have been disproportionately affected by emergent 'sanctions' designed to curb social unrest, such as anti-social behaviour orders (ASBOs), acceptable behaviour contracts (ABCs) and youth curfews.

Matthews (2002) groups the reasons why this is so into three broad categories. These are:

- the nature of regeneration schemes;
- the attitudes of adults;
- the characteristics of young people.

The nature of regeneration schemes

Barriers to involving children in area-based regeneration would appear to include formality, complexity and bureaucracy. The very nature of regeneration activity means that it is complex and multi-faceted. Many different professionals and agencies are involved and the planning and financial appraisal is both time consuming and intricate. In addition, the nature of governance structures means that boards and committees must be established and terms of reference agreed. The length of time that these processes can take may mean that children who have been consulted don't see the effects of the consultation.

For example, the Swarcliffe PFI (Private Finance Initiative) in East Leeds was approved in the late 1990s. The scheme involved the regeneration of a large area of 1960s and 1970s council housing on a peripheral estate, including the demolition of tower blocks and some low-rise housing. At the inception and design stage Banks of the Wear Housing Association, which has

skills in the engagement of children and young people, undertook close consultation with young residents, arranging focus groups at local fast food outlets. The response rate was good

> Chapters 7 and 14, Youth Services and Provision and The Swings and Roundabouts of Community Development, explore this theme further.

and young people expressed their ideas and vision for the future of their home. Over five years later, the final details were approved and the physical regeneration started. Many of those children who took part in the consultations will have passed into adulthood without seeing a tangible impact from their involvement.

The regeneration process is also difficult to understand if a person is not closely or directly involved. The complexity described above is added to by the volume of formal and jargon riddled language. The general process whereby different schemes or agencies are required to bid for resources means that consultation is of necessity brief, and, as Fitzpatrick et al. (1998) note, the complexities of consulting with children mean in these instances that children are by-passed. If it is difficult to involve the most active and engaged young people, then the possibility of involving 'hard to reach' young people, those that PAT 12 are most concerned about, poses severe problems.

People, including children, need support in developing the capacity to become involved in this kind of decision-making. There are a range of skills required for working with children in what is often an open-ended situation. The Social Exclusion Unit identified a perceived shortage of skills in institutions at neighbourhood level (SEU, 1988) and the national evaluation of the late 20th-century City Challenge initiatives highlighted significant barriers to community involvement, together with personal barriers to effective participation at individual level. There was also evidence of marginalisation of community interests in the Single Regeneration Budget Challenge Fund round 1 and round 2 schemes. Research carried out in Leeds on the impact of demolition during regeneration activity (Kettle et al., 2004) suggested that the organisational cultures of the agencies involved did not really facilitate *participation* and that this lack of direct engagement with residents

Reflective Activity 13.5

Case study of consultation

'The aim was to encourage young people outside of formal education to visit museums and galleries and use the resources they offer. The involvement of young people varied from project to project, some were accessed through the youth service, recruited through New Deal and existing partnerships with organisations supporting young people.

'Each project was planned by the museum leading that particular project and reflected the interests and needs of the particular community within the museum's catchment area. Youth workers tended not to become involved in museums as many youth workers felt their young people would not be interested in museums. Where youth workers did become involved, i.e. our Leicester City Museum project, it was very successful. Each museum evaluated their own project and collated a report from information gathered, an independent evaluator was also commissioned to undertake specific areas of evaluation.

'This was a good piece of work for young people and museums. Two groups which tend not to have a lot to do with each other. Both groups discovered that actually they had a lot to offer each other. Museums weren't just dusty archives or irrelevant objects and young people brought energy, new ideas, enthusiasm, new technologies, etc. The programme opened a lot of eyes and broadened a lot of minds and it wasn't just those of the young people.

'This was a very long and complex project running over three years. We learnt a lot, we made lots of mistakes, sometimes the mistakes worked better than what we planned, some parts of the project went well and some didn't. We encouraged our museums to report the bad bits alongside the good bits.'
(Create-Scotland, 2005)

1 Why do you think this project worked?
2 What are the essential elements for success?

diminished the effectiveness of the programme. The Egan review of skills concluded that built environment professionals needed a broad range of generic skills to build sustainable communities. This backs up the assertion of the ODPM (now DCLG) that professionals engaged in community regeneration lack skills in partnership working, consultation, valuing diversity and working with communities (ODPM, 2002). However, Kirby with Bryson (2002) note that, although facilitating children's participation in decision-making and planning is both challenging and demanding, very few practitioners receive specific training.

Even if children do want to get involved in regeneration activities, one barrier is the lack of awareness or understanding on the part of organisations about how they can actually be engaged. Hart (1997, p. 63) points out, 'community based organisations need help in recognising the capacities of children and how to involve them'. Although some regeneration organisations have now employed youth workers to help achieve key performance indicators in relation to

inclusive consultation, Jeffs (1997) suggests that it is difficult to achieve involvement that will lead to children being able to influence and develop. There are a number of reasons for this including:

- Regeneration takes places within structures that are predominantly adult and there are barriers (time, finance) associated with designing participative structures that are appropriate to children;

- The regeneration industry is somewhat risk averse; full involvement of children does involve an element of risk, for example giving children the opportunity to make mistakes and learn from them.

However, there are examples of projects that are focused on involving children and young people in regeneration. 'Young Voices in Regeneration', a partnership between Groundwork, Save the Children and other local organisations, aims to involve young people in local decision-making to improve public open space and reduce conflict. The Young Voices programme started in April 2003 and during its time it has worked with over 80 young people in areas of deprivation in Coventry. Young voices has helped young people apply for funding to pay for activities of interest and environmental projects related to local issues, identified by individual groups. As well as working with young people Young Voices involves parents and other adults in the community in environmental projects with the hope of forming youth clubs and youth projects led by local people. Another project, 'People Making Places', is a programme of education and learning to help people to have the knowledge, confidence and understanding to become involved with the future shaping of where they live. An important aspect of the programme is working with young people, giving them the opportunity to work alongside built environment professionals and to help them get more of a sense of ownership. This work is focused on areas undergoing regeneration, and this is intended to give an increased feeling of relevance to those getting involved (Powell, 2004).

Attitudes of adults

Adults too often regard young people with suspicion, contempt or fear. But young people today also show good manners (often in the face of incivility from their elders and supposed betters), respect, energy, commitment enthusiasm, skill and enterprise. All too often, the measures introduced to control or penalise the few, punish or disadvantage the many.   (NYA, 2004, p. ii)

The attitudes of adults to children are both complex and perplexing. There are tensions in both the way children are perceived by adults and how they are conveyed in the media. Typically, children are stereotyped as being incompetent, unable to participate with adults on an equal footing and in need of protection from the harsh realities of life. Children's input is often regarded as too immature for consideration and the behaviour of urban youth is sometimes felt to be anti-social. The

See Chapters 2 and 3, Childhood: Rights and Realities and The Politics of Childhood, to identify the tensions in more detail.

Chapters 4 and 9, The Social Divisions of Childhood and Children Who Offend, identify ways in which this can disadvantage children.

needs of children and adults are seen as mutually exclusive and adults feel qualified, having been young once, to make decisions on behalf of children. Willow (2001) suggests that, in the UK, adult-based expectations are adept at making children feel and appear incompetent.

At the same time, there has been a series of so-called moral panics over the last fifty years about the state of the country's youth, from mods and rockers to glue sniffers and joy riders. Children in deprived urban areas are easily stereotyped and the correlation between regeneration areas and high concentrations of 'dysfunctional families' will only further stereotype and stigmatise them. There is evidence that older members of communities do not recognise that certain behaviours (such as hanging around street corners or bus shelters) is normal adolescent activity. Recent work by Millie et al. (2005) revealed that anti-social behaviour involving teenagers being noisy or rowdy is perceived by many to be the worst sort of incivility.

Consequently, as Freeman et al. (1999) note, there is a perception that it is children who need to change their behaviours to suit their existing environments rather than adults, whether practitioners, professionals or residents, looking at ways in which environments can be adapted to enhance children's well-being, both physical and emotional. The power relationship between adults and children is important here in thinking about how and why adults impose their views on children. This can be exemplified through consideration of a regeneration scheme on a Leeds council estate where there was provision made for children's play space. Something seemingly straightforward revealed tensions and conflicts with community consultation and these are identified in Reflective Activity 13.6.

These are identified in Chapters 2 and 3, Childhood: Rights and Realities and The Politics of Childhood.

Play is acknowledged in the United Nations Convention on the Rights of the Child (UNCRC, 1989) as being a right for all children. It has a central role in health and well-being and access to leisure and open space is a feature of liveability. Children need play spaces with clear spatial and social identity. Physical environments are in a constant state of change, especially when regeneration is taking place, and this can have a negative impact on access to play, particularly for older children. Adults often prefer safe play spaces for under-8s. These users are more likely to be supervised and engage in less 'dangerous' play than skateboarding or football. Attitudes to the latter are often tempered by fear of children, especially when play is less local and more physical. The combination of seeing children as both vulnerable and as villains can restrict children's rights to play:

See Chapter 2, Childhood: Rights and Realities.

> Unsupervised play enables children to take risks, to think through decisions and gain increased self-confidence and greater resilience. However, as a result of parental fears, and the seeming priority given to cars over the needs of children, many children's ability to play has been severely curtailed.
> (Mental Health Foundation, 1999, p. 36)

Characteristics of young people

While adult perceptions of children may be a barrier to participation, children's perceptions of the community can also be problematic. McGillycuddy's (1991) work suggested that a lot of urban children experience feelings of alienation and hostility towards their communities. This may be because of feelings of helplessness or fear. By creating opportunities for involvement in the positive transformation of the built environment we could facilitate children in becoming agents of change rather than victims. However, attitudes expressed by young people themselves can hinder their involvement in community regeneration. They may have ostensibly better things to do and peer pressure may channel them into other activities. Young people are territorial and protective of their immediate neighbourhoods. Those living in deprived neighbourhoods

or those teetering on the brink will be less mobile and more restricted to this space. A lack of confidence in their ability to participate and a suspicion and anxiety about formal decision-making structures may form an obstacle. Kirby with Bryson (2002) note that the reasons why children choose not to become involved with community regeneration are under-researched, but suggest that cynicism about how much adults will listen may be a factor.

The voices of children have great significance for the regeneration agenda. The urban summit youth fringe event in 2002 indicated that children wanted more education on drug abuse, a firmer stance on disruptive school pupils, more community-centred house design, an increase in the number of street wardens to deter crime and anti-social behaviour, and effective and affordable public transport (Communities and Local Government, 2004). Co-chairs Phil Hope MP and Amar Abass (youth representative, Blackburn) hosted a lively debate involving 100 young people, youth workers and adult delegates, including ODPM Ministers, Jeff Rooker and Tony McNulty. The debate focused not only on how to improve life in towns and cities, but also wider questions about the role of young people in society. The strongest messages for local and central government were articulated in an impassioned plea from one young Blackburn delegate for government to listen more closely to young people and their ideas if it was to expect young people to listen to them.

Recent work by Burke and Grosvenor (2003) demonstrates that children do have the capacity to assess their environments and to propose change. Research into the effects that demolition of housing has on people's communities was carried out by the Centre for Urban Development and Environmental Management (CUDEM) at Leeds Metropolitan University in 2003–4. There was clear evidence that children had a strong feeling of what a cohesive community should be like. One young girl was worried by drug users, rough boys and outsiders, and from perceptions that the area was 'rough and there are too many people causing trouble'. All the young people interviewed had plenty to say about their neighbourhood and how they engaged with their communities. Teenagers, often perceived to be the problem, shared similar concerns with adults about the negative impact of drug abuse in particular. But

Reflective Activity 13.6

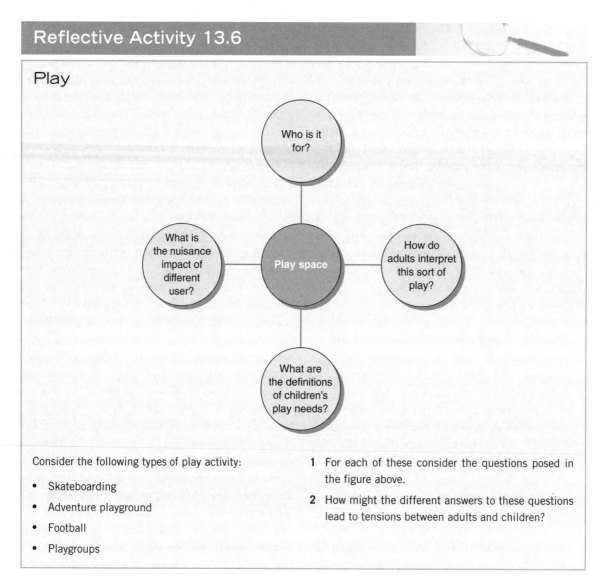

Play

Consider the following types of play activity:

- Skateboarding
- Adventure playground
- Football
- Playgroups

1 For each of these consider the questions posed in the figure above.

2 How might the different answers to these questions lead to tensions between adults and children?

intergenerational suspicions and a mistrust of adolescent males across the community meant that there was little perception by adults that children and young people could be a valuable resource for regeneration if consultation was meaningful. A lack of involvement did not mean a lack of interest: 'if I thought they was going to do something I would go to a meeting' (Kettle et al., 2004). The impetus for children to be involved in regeneration does appear to be an adult-led agenda and there is little research examining how and why children might want to be involved. The case studies in Chapters 14 and 18 provide insights into different approaches involving the participation of children and young people.

In 2001, Perpetua Kirby consulted with 50 young people who had become involved in environmental regeneration projects in the Birmingham area, about why they had got involved. All these children were from disadvantaged areas where there was a lack of youth facilities. Most just wanted to have fun (68 per cent). Some wanted to improve their environment (36 per cent). But very few wanted to learn about how decisions are made or to meet adults who make those key decisions (Kirby, 2001).

To what extent are children involved in community regeneration?

The chief executive of the Groundwork Trust, Tony Hawkhead, said, in 2004, that too many young people these days are treated as an 'environmental problem, to be swept off the streets like litter' (The Highland Council/NHS Highlands, undated). But his experience shows that, given the right support and skills, young people can be a powerful and positive force for improving the quality of community life.

The key concepts for involving children at neighbourhood level are participation and empowerment, both of which are highly compatible with community development objectives and which need to be given higher priority. The evaluation of the New Deal for Communities (NDC) found that, in terms of youth involvement, all the NDC projects in the case study areas had at least one member of staff with responsibility for youth inclusion, and they all had dedicated youth projects. The numbers of specific projects ranged from seven to thirty, with the average being around fifteen. These projects did not appear to be targeted at sub-age groups although some appealed to particular groups. But the awareness of the young people themselves about what was going on was limited (ODPM, 2006). The issues that bothered the young people in the NDC areas were

- crime/fear of crime;
- people viewing children as criminals;
- the physical environment;
- houses being used by 'smack heads' and drug dealers;
- the community.

The researchers from Sheffield Hallam University asked the children in the Coventry project what they would like their local NDC to achieve. Not many respondents were very forthcoming. But the things they did come up with were an improvement to the physical environment, the provision of facilities to relieve boredom (and consequently minimise the risk of anti-social behaviour), the creation of a safe environment that is accessible at any time and the removal of drug dealers and 'smack heads' (ODPM, 2006).

Overall, however, it does appear that a lot of evidence about good practice in involving children and young people in regeneration is anecdotal. In Kirby's extensive survey about the effectiveness of children's participation, she reports that, where there have been detailed studies of regeneration schemes, children and young people have had little impact on creating change (Kirby, 2002). This assertion is supported by the influential Fitzpatrick et al. (1998) study, which concluded that children had a minor impact on regeneration activities and where they did have influence it tended to be sidelined towards 'youth specific' issues. Children only succeeded in impacting on the strategic focus of regeneration in two out of the twelve initiatives reviewed. This may be because children living in areas that experience regeneration tend to be relatively disadvantaged anyway. But Kirby (2002) argues that, in such areas, relations between children and adults tend to be poor to begin with, and that there is evidence that some project work alleviates conflict and helps relations to improve. Adults do appear to be prescriptive in their assessments of children's needs and their capabilities. It may well be that children might wish adults to be less able to control their environments.

Conclusion

This chapter has assessed how and why space and place are important for children within the context of regeneration activity in the UK. Government policy has made much of neighbourhood renewal as a means of tackling social exclusion and a number of national initiatives for community development have been implemented. These include community warden schemes and Sure Start projects, amongst others, which have a strong focus on supporting children. Conversely, government has taken some draconian measures to restrict and curtail children's activities, such as the introduction of curfews, thus contradicting its approach to investment in childhood and reinforcing children as villains of the piece.

In particular we have considered how regeneration affects children and the extent to which children are able to have a say in what happens to their neighbourhood. Discussion has focused on the impact of living in poor neighbourhoods and raised important questions as to the additional barriers children in such areas face due to disadvantage and deprivation. Within this context we have considered the extent to which children are involved in community regeneration. It would appear that children ultimately express similar hopes and fears for the future of where they live to those expressed by adults. They have different ways of expressing their feelings and traditional ways of community consultation have led to their exclusion, along with a lack of support and development for those wanting to shift the agenda.

There are a number of opportunities presenting themselves as regeneration activities intensify during the early part of the 21st century. Those running local strategic partnerships could go some way to ensuring that young people have a voice in determining the allocation of regeneration resources. The Academy for Sustainable Communities could initiate training programmes for professionals and community representatives to teach them how to involve young people in their work. There could be a greater role for non-governmental organizations (NGOs) to act as mediators or 'honest brokers' between young people and those in authority. Underlying this is a need for a more rigorous approach to incorporating the United Nations Convention on the Rights of the Child into UK Law and having a Commissioner for Children who has responsibility for monitoring the implementation of children's rights. These are crucial if we are to change the status of children as decision makers in their communities and consequently their opportunities for contributing to the regeneration of these communities.

Annotated reading

Freeman, C., Henderson, P. and Kettle, J. (1999) *Planning with Children for Better Communities*, Bristol: The Policy Press

Uses examples and case studies from a variety of professions and disciplines in order to explain different methods which can be used to support children's participation in decision-making processes. Contents: Setting the scene; The contemporary context; Children's rights; Children's participation and the political agenda; Children in the community; Children and professionals; Involving children in regeneration; Children's physical environment; Planning with children.

Hart, R. (1997) *Children's Participation: The Theory and Practice of Involving Young Citizens in Community Development and Environmental Care*, London: Earthscan publications

This text is designed to be a reference manual about some of the ways in which children can be both empowered and take direct involvement in their communities. The argument behind this (apart from the obvious aspect of the UN Convention on the Rights of the Child) is that if we want tomorrow's environment to be sustainably managed we need to train today those people who will carry out the tasks tomorrow, i.e. children.

Matthews, H. (2001) *Children and Community Regeneration*, London: Save the Children

This text identifies major social and political barriers to the involvement of children in community regeneration. It presents new research on how the community interests of both children and adults can be met. At the policy level it identifies positive changes in approaches to regeneration and the potential of inclusive local strategic partnerships. It also looks closely at good practice, describing a wide range of neighbourhood initiatives in which children and young people have been heavily involved.

ODPM (2005) *Making it Happen in Neighbourhoods: The National Strategy for Neighbourhood Renewal Four Years On* (Neighbourhood Renewal Unit), London: The Stationery Office

A progress report against the aims set out in the National Strategy for Neighbourhood Renewal demonstrating progress made in neighbourhoods and a summary of new funding and high-level government targets announced as part of the Spending Review, 2004. The report suggests that the government has set out an ambitious vision for narrowing the gap between deprived neighbourhoods and the rest of the country and discusses common elements of these communities, including poor housing, poor health, poor education, few job opportunities and high crime rates – what has been called 'postcode poverty'.

Services in Action: Case Studies

What is the aim of Part III?

Part III of the book contains case studies that are examples of children's services in action. They reflect the constraints and limitations of services as well as imaginative ground level approaches to addressing children's needs and furthering children's rights. Some of the services that form the focus for Part II are reflected in the case studies and the issues that are highlighted in Parts I and II can be seen across the case studies.

Guide to reading Part III

The chapters in Part III can be read independently or in relation to chapters in Parts I and II. Activities at the end of each case study refer back to questions in Part I and help you to identify some of the influences on children's services that are occurring in the case studies. Reading these case studies in conjunction with some of the chapters from Part II, which focus on specific areas of service provision, will help you to identify some of the realities of individual services for service users and those working in the services. The case studies also illustrate the ways that services impact on each other and inter-relate and the importance of inter-agency cooperation.

Chapter Map Part III

Chapter 17 Educating Refugee Children: A Class Teacher's Perspective

This chapter illustrates some of the difficulties associated with the prescribed curriculum and raises questions about government policy in relation to children's rights to care and protection as well as to education.

Chapter 3 The Politics of Childhood

Chapter 4 The Social Divisions of Childhood

Chapter 12 Services to Children's Play

Chapter 13 Children's Experience of Community Regeneration

Chapter 18 The Venture: Case Study of an Adventure Playground

This chapter shows how a successful adventure playground was set up and identifies some of the factors that have made it successful. It illustrates that it might be possible to work with children who are 'difficult' in positive ways.

Chapter 2 Childhood: Rights and Realities

Chapter 4 The Social Divisions of Childhood

Chapter 6 Education: Service or System?

Chapter 7 Youth Services and Provision

Chapter 9 Children Who Offend

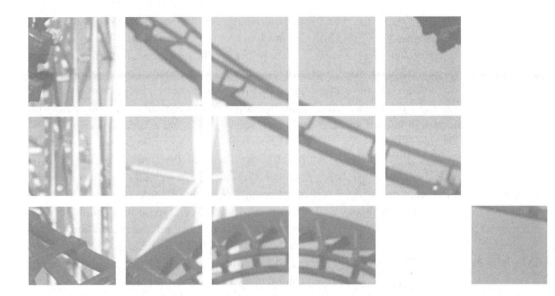

The Swings and Roundabouts of Community Development

ROS CHIOSSO

I like the slide best 'cos me and my friends can shelter under it when it rains.

(Matthew, aged 9)

Introduction

Any community work text will inform you that community development is a multi-layered and time-consuming process that involves skills and persever-ance. What is less commonly available are 'warts and all' accounts documenting the difficulties and setbacks. For those who engage with community development, the process can be intensely frustrating and brilliantly rewarding in equal measures. The purpose of this chapter is to provide insight into this complexity by telling a story about a community group that wanted to provide local children with a playground.

This chapter considers a working definition of community development

- The political context in which it is currently used
- The experience of building a children's playground and the particular problems encountered with

intergenerational community development work

- Intergenerational community development
- Sustaining collective engagement
- Continuing professional support.

Defining community development

Community development has a multiplicity of mean-ings. The term is most commonly used in its literal sense, namely to support the development of commu-nities particularly those in disadvantaged neighbour-hoods. Within the community regeneration 'industry', community development has a particular resonance and is more commonly understood as a process of change and development that occurs in communities

For further discussion of regeneration see Chapter 13, Children's Experience of Community Regeneration.

(Henderson and Thomas, 2002). This understanding is underpinned by an explicit set of values and principles captured in the working statement produced by The Community Development Xchange (CDX):

> Community Development is about building active and sustainable communities based on social justice and mutual respect. It is about changing power structures to remove the barriers that prevent people from participating in the issues that affect their lives. (SCCD, 2001, p. 1)

At the heart of the community development process is a commitment to challenging discrimination and oppression, a commitment to working together, valuing the skills, knowledge and expertise of all, including those with least power and formal education. It draws on a rich and eclectic theoretical base that includes the work of education for liberation theorists Freire (1970), Alinsky (1971), Fanon (1986) and the stories of many less well-known community activists. The theoretical and ideological perspectives that underpin community development are grounded in the concept of reflective practice and this is key to understanding the links between theory and practice.

To be engaged in community development work inevitably means taking a particular stance – one that is unlikely to be neutral or involve 'sitting on the fence'. It is almost always discussed as a positive and enabling process and the evidence to support its effectiveness is extensive and well documented. The Community Development Xchange and others (Community Development Foundation, Development Education Programme, Hope and Timmel, 1995) have published a substantial body of excellent literature that explains, theorises and provides practice guidelines that support the community development process (Gilchrist, 2004; Barr and Hashagen, 2000; Wilson and Wilde, 2000; Hope and Timmel, 1995). It is therefore not my intention to add to this; my contribution is to analyse and reflect on some of the difficulties and complexities of using a community development approach

particularly where children, young people and adults are involved.

The principle of inclusiveness, the full and active participation of all, is at the heart of community development, yet there is comparatively little published material that explicitly refers to community development with children, young people and adults. Henderson (1995) makes the point that policymakers have done little to build bridges between the generations and yet it is children's interests that frequently inspire community involvement – especially of women. I would further add, perhaps contentiously, that youth and community work practitioners can also find intergenerational work 'challenging'. The Hirst Wood playground project was an all too familiar example of this, despite a genuine commitment from the organising group to be inclusive. It highlights the very real difficulties of trying to engage with different constituencies, who invariably had differing needs and agendas and few resources – both human and financial. Much of the case study material that documents and evaluates community development projects fails to explore the difficulties, setbacks and complexities of the processes involved and even fewer discuss intergenerational work. For example, the case studies cited on the renewal net website <www.renewal.net> focus almost exclusively upon successful community development initiatives and highlight the creative and innovative practices deployed. The brief summaries, all of which follow a standard format, provide the reader with clear objectives and glossy snapshots of 'what works'. However, I have a strong sense that only half their stories have been told. Some of the interventions that were needed to assemble and sustain the work are overlooked, inadequately evaluated or perhaps conveniently forgotten. It would be helpful to hear these stories – to discover the 'glue' that held these projects together (or not!) and to analyse those messy bits that people on reflection would perhaps prefer to keep quiet. The glue that is absent is perhaps more familiarly known as reflective practice.

Case studies of projects all too frequently appear in a sanitised format, beautifully presented with slick evaluations that lack warmth, humour and personal insight. They are invariably policy focused, with checklists or good practice guidelines attached that purport to promote 'what works'. Clearly more thoughtful and

grounded (qualitative) accounts do exist. Hulyer's (1997) neighbourhood community development work on estates reflects with honesty, humour and compassion the difficulties of trying to practice community development in a neighbourhood where children, young people and adults have different and competing agendas. Amongst his conclusions he identifies the time-consuming nature of this work and the need for ongoing professional intervention from trained community development practitioners. Another is Bob Holman's (2000) *Kids at the Door Revisited*. This publication was a follow-up study to *Kids at the Door* (1981) that documented the experiences of a community project located on the Southdown council estate near Bath. This community development project offered a whole range of services to families and children. The more recent study evaluates the long-term impact of the Southdown project and records the experiences and stories of adults with whom Holman worked when they were children and young people. Holman, a community development worker, kept a detailed diary during the period 1976–86. He argues that central to the project's usefulness were the individual relationships that were established, the fact that workers lived locally and that the project received support from all constituencies.

A more recent locally produced publication (Writing Renewal 2, 2005) uses the skills of creative writers to tell the stories of communities engaged in neighbourhood renewal, for example creative writers worked with Frizinghall residents to tell their stories about growing flowers, fruit and vegetables in their gardens – Frizinghall is a culturally rich and diverse neighbourhood close to Bradford city centre. The stories are inspirational and feature ordinary people (professional workers and community activists) doing extraordinary things. This publication is a welcome addition to the glossy snapshot 'what works' approach adopted by the national renewal website. Placing a favourable 'spin' on work produced is an imperative, particularly if future funding for increasingly target-driven work is to be secured. In addition, there is a need to send out positive, policy-driven messages as funding bodies are very in tune with 'what works' and with approaches supported by concrete evidence and achievable outcomes. However, transparency is also vital and the stories attached to community development are fascinating. To focus predominantly on 'what works' belies the complexity and serendipitous nature of much community-based activity. While the principles and values of community development offer clarity, vision and purpose, the broad cross-section of people involved sets in motion processes that are multilayered and unpredictable. Setbacks can seem insurmountable. To read other people's 'stories' can offer hope, inspiration and encouragement – even those where the 'outcomes' were disappointing. They also contain important learning for policymakers, politicians and practitioners. This chapter tells the 'story' of the Hirst Wood playground development.

New Labour and community development

In recent years, particularly since New Labour was returned to second and third terms of office, there has been a significant growth in literature to support the community regeneration 'industry'. Community work in general and community development in particular foundered in the wilderness for much of the 1980s and 1990s. The investment in 'community' by New Labour, particularly since the establishment of the Social Exclusion Unit in 1997, has spawned a diverse and extensive number of initiatives most of which implicitly, if not explicitly, support the CDX concept of community development. For example, the regional government office, Yorkshire Forward, in partnership with the consultancy COGS (1999) produced a good practice framework for evaluating community participation.

The Sure Start programme is part of a wider government agenda to reduce the social exclusion experienced by families with pre-school children in disadvantaged neighbourhoods. A commitment to community development principles

See Chapter 8, Provision for Child Health, for a fuller discussion of Sure Start's objectives.

is evident in the Sure Start approach as illustrated by Attree's (2004) study of the Sure Start programme in Barrow.

> it seeks to provide the supportive community context that empowers its members by stimulating involvement in community activities and ideally employment. (Attree, 2004, p. 155)

As the value and effectiveness of community development as an approach has come to be realised and embedded into social regeneration programmes there has been a significant growth in publications to support this. These publications are to be welcomed and are valuable resources, particularly for poorly supported community groups. The shortcomings of some

See Chapter 13, Children's Experience of Community Regeneration, where this literature is discussed.

of these texts are that the realities and complexities of community development processes are inadequately discussed.

My contention is that, at the heart of most community development-based initiatives, a combination of approaches are likely to have been involved, including strategies that do not sit comfortably with the values and principles of community development. These approaches include those that are government targeted, non-participatory and professionally driven. In addition, there is an absence of qualitative material that explores community development work with different constituencies, in particular, children, young people and adults. In our case, the difficulties of trying to support an inclusive agenda was at times overwhelming and the part played by chance and serendipity in determining the final and successful outcome should not be overlooked. To understand this, some explanatory background to the development of the Hirst Wood playground is required.

Hirst Wood 'community'

Hirst Wood is located in Shipley, West Yorkshire and is currently home to some 1200 people amongst whom approximately 25 per cent are children and young people. It is an almost exclusively white area, with approximately 70 per cent owning their own homes and the remaining 30 per cent in social housing. The total area comprises only a few streets and a small industrial site. The majority of houses were former Bradford Council properties that were sold off to existing tenants in the 1980s. In the 1990s two small housing estates were added (built by a Housing Association) and these include both owner-occupied and rental properties. Hirst Wood is located in the Aire Valley, close to beautiful countryside, the Leeds–Liverpool canal, the river Aire and local woods. It is also geographically isolated from the rest of Shipley and is surrounded by large, stone-built Victorian houses in the more middle-class areas of Saltaire and Nab Wood. These factors are significant, for Hirst Wood has generally been viewed by its residents as a neglected back water, too small to attract significant resources from Bradford Council, and too well located in lovely surroundings (see above) to gather much support for neighbourhood play facilities.

In the early 1990s a group of local residents (myself included) came together, without external professional help, with the vague purpose of wanting to bring about improvements to the area. Hirst Wood had something of a reputation in the 1980s as a tough place to live where 'problem families' were once housed. This reputation still persists today, despite the influx of new residents. This legacy can be attributed to the behaviour of a small minority of local young people and their families. This factor was the impetus for the community group coming together. The group was mostly comprised of parents and older people with grandchildren. One of the objectives was to look at creative ways of tackling the boredom and lack of facilities for children and young people in the area. From the outset, however, it was only adults that were involved in the meetings. A few tentative attempts were made to include young people, but these were broadly unsuccessful. Young people, understandably, did not want to come along to 'boring' meetings dominated by adults. This factor was important since in later years, as the group became more established and active, the voices of children and young people were largely absent.

The group met on and off throughout the 1990s (usually in people's houses) and was most useful as a meeting point and information exchange for residents. It also, with support from local councillors, brought in occasional youth service interventions, although with no meeting place this rarely happened outside the summer months. The Hirst Wood Regeneration Group (HRG), as it is currently known, was relaunched in the late 1990s and for the first few years received good support from local residents. The much-needed involvement of new residents was, in part, initiated and supported by a community development worker from the Shipley Area Committee of Bradford Council. Her role was highly influential in encouraging and sustaining new membership. She ensured Hirst Wood had a voice at the twice-yearly neighbourhood forums (opportunities for residents to articulate their views to the local authority) that had previously been dominated by residents from more affluent areas. Once residents found their feet at these meetings, a separate

annual neighbourhood forum focusing on the needs and interests of Hirst Wood was set up in addition to the other forums in the area. Apart from boosting the morale of residents by regularly attending Hirst Wood meetings, she also encouraged local ward councillors to come along and acted as a conduit through which information could be passed between the council, Hirst Wood and other voluntary and statutory projects in the area.

She was able to support the group in many practical ways, for example in helping to establish a constitution, acting as a sounding board for new ideas, supporting applications for small sums of money to develop community projects. Her interventions were often small and seemingly insignificant. She would take time out both before and after meetings to listen to people and to ensure we were well informed about new developments in the area. For example, when a Sure Start initiative was established in Shipley, Hirst Wood, despite meeting many of the government's social deprivation indicators, was deemed too small to be included, especially as it was some distance away from the other estates covered in the proposals. After persistent lobbying one of the roads was eventually included and this was a valuable addition since, later on, Sure Start became one of the playground's funders. It was these small-scale interventions, taking time out to listen to people, to empathise with our concerns, to share aspects of herself that made the difference – it provided some of the social glue that sustained the group.

See Chapter 3, The Politics of Childhood.

One of the first successful initiatives of the HRG was to bid for funds from the Community Chest (funds held by the local authority) for a set of goal posts for the small grass recreation ground in Hirst Wood. This request came from local children and young people who, with help, wrote in support of the application. Hope and Timmel (1995) cite a similar example and make the point that communities, at least initially, need to set and achieve their own goals and that these should take precedence over those prioritised by outside agencies. This small success boosted our confidence and encouraged the HRG to apply for neighbourhood renewal funds when the government's Neighbourhood

Renewal Strategy was launched in 2001. With the help of the local authority we applied, and were successful, in securing funding to support youth work in Hirst Wood. The funding paid for two part-time youth workers for six months and covered the rent on a small youth base housed in a unit on the industrial site. One of the outcomes of this youth work project was to give Hirst Wood children and young people an independent voice, to express their own needs and interests. They would come along to occasional HRG meetings and express their views, although not always with tact and diplomacy. Their top priority was for play and sports facilities. They persuasively argued that the 'lovely surrounding countryside' was unsafe, that their parents would not allow them access unless accompanied by adults and that a designated play area would allow them to hang out and keep them gainfully occupied. The playground project was launched.

Hirst Wood playground project

At the outset the playground initiative attracted universal support from all constituencies. Children and young people who had been campaigning for years for local play facilities were delighted and keen to have a say in the design and equipment to be provided. At the local neighbourhood forum, attended by residents, Councillors and other voluntary sector agencies there was general agreement that this would be a useful resource, not only for Hirst Wood but for other families in the area who pass through on their way to the woods and the canal. However, despite this universal support and expressions of interest from residents and voluntary and statutory sector projects, there were few offers of practical help. When the final funding application was despatched in the summer of 2003 only a handful of people were involved. These included a few local residents, one local councillor and a local authority community development worker.

Initially, the playground project got off to a flying start. The local Sure Start offered to give £10,000 if this could be matched by another partner organisation. After discrete lobbying by local authority workers in the area and with the help of a local councillor, Bradford Council agreed to provide a further £10,000. Thus,

within a few months, we had £20,000 towards the projected total of £40,000 with comparatively little effort. Initial costings, equipment and design suggestions were given to us by a play development worker from Bradford Council, and she offered guidance on suitable equipment for disabled children and those with sensory impairments. With this information we were able to move the project forward and with the help of the part-time youth workers we set about engaging the support of local children and young people.

See Chapter 4, The Social Divisions of Childhood, where issues related to the exclusion of disabled children are discussed.

The youth workers at this time were running two groups, one for younger children aged 12 and under, and another for young people aged 13 and over. Despite our hopes that the playground would appeal to 5- to 13-year-olds, those over 10 quickly lost interest when they saw the proposed designs, the limited range of equipment that was available and, more to the point, affordable. The under-10s happily selected the items they wanted and were then anxious to know how long it would take to construct. Their expectation was that the playground would be installed in a matter of months and they too gradually lost interest. The older youth group started to lobby for more facilities appropriate for their age group. Their requirement was for an all weather, illuminated, multi-purpose, enclosed sports area. They thought we could fundraise for this alongside fundraising for the playground. When the realities of such a venture were discussed the young people became increasingly frustrated. The behaviour of a small minority of young people, for some time, had been a matter of concern, and the playground project, instead of forging alliances, appeared to be creating even more disillusionment on all sides. From this point onwards, their involvement with the playground was, at best disinterested, at worst actively destructive. This reinforced youth worker concerns that integrated children's services may target younger rather than older children. The situation was further exacerbated by the youth work project coming to an end with

See Chapter 7, Youth Services and Provision, for further discussion.

little prospect of more funding or the statutory youth service filling the gap.

In addition to this setback, the impetus to gain additional funding for the playground had hit an impasse. Applying to the Community Fund appeared our best way forward, but the application process, we soon discovered, was daunting, requiring specialist knowledge and skills. A great deal of the group's energy had been diffused and sapped with the management of the youth work project. Two relatively inexperienced 'youth' workers had been appointed and on reflection the HRG was neither sufficiently experienced nor resourced to take on employer responsibilities. The £20,000 sat in a bank account for the next few months with offers of practical help in short supply.

Eventually, the newly elected chair, with the help of a community development worker, agreed to take it on and they embarked on a time-consuming, painstaking, bureaucratic process. In addition, planning permission was needed for use of the recreation area and this too involved a complex legal process. The application gave the impression that all constituencies were actively involved, whereas in reality this was a distorted and misleading picture. The project was reliant on a handful of committed individuals. When the application was eventually refused (our constitution was considered insufficiently charitable) the few individuals involved were exhausted and deflated. The playground project was shelved.

We were galvanised into renewed activity, when, a few months later, we received a letter from Bradford Council, to the effect that we would lose the local authority funding if it was not spent in the current financial year. It could not be held over to the next financial year. If we lost the local authority funding we would also lose the Sure Start funding, we would be back to square one. The HRG chair was, understandably, not prepared to launch another funding bid, yet her skills, particularly in IT, had been invaluable in the previous application. Furthermore, at this juncture involvement from the local authority in HRG was limited. The remit for community development work in Shipley is extensive and we had received a great deal of support as a fledgling group. HRG was now an active, legally constituted and thriving community group and we had accepted the need for the local area office to

redirect their limited resources towards others in the area. Nevertheless, a small group of us came together (the result of a chance meeting with our dogs in the local woods!) and with advice and support from the local area office, decided to seek funding from WREN (Waste Recycling and Environmental Network). With the help of a newly appointed community development worker who also had good IT skills and using much of the material cited in the Community Fund bid, a new application was put together. This application was successful and in the autumn of 2003 a further £20,000 was added to the playground fund.

With the funding secure, the motivation to tackle all the other issues such as planning permission, site maintenance and disabled access was rediscovered. Construction work started a few weeks before Christmas 2003, but then stalled due to poor weather. The playground site encased behind steel barriers became a magnet for local young people. They were keen to try out the newly installed play equipment despite pleas from local residents to keep away until completion. The most difficult time was when the plastic surface encasing the equipment was being laid. The surface needed to be left undisturbed for a day or so in order to set. It survived unsullied largely due to the fact that it was winter and that I lived directly opposite the playground and could keep the area under surveillance. The playground finally opened in Spring 2004.

The playground consists of the following play 'furniture': two sets of swings, one for juniors, the other for toddlers; a multi-unit comprising a slide/climbing frames; a springie tractor; a springie bulldozer; a merry-go-round; a long metal seat; a 'talking bob' interactive unit.

Eighteen months on the playground has survived unscathed and is well used by a mixed constituency of children and young people in the neighbourhood. Younger children accompanied by their parents or child-care workers from the local nursery use it during the day. It has become a stopping off point for older primary school children on their way home from school. Young people in the area use it as an occasional place to hang out and meet friends in the evenings. It also serves as an all weather football pitch and occasional cycle track. It is also well used by the families of walkers, cyclists and day trippers on their way to the

Leeds–Liverpool canal and woods. There is a strong sense of ownership that it belongs to Hirst Wood and this, in part, is evidenced by the fact that the sign erected by the HRG at the opening ceremony is still intact and has not been vandalised.

So what is there to conclude from this? The playground project raises a number of key issues including: the complexities involved in intergenerational community development; the importance yet frequent absence of collective engagement of local people; the significance of ongoing professional support, especially where large capital ventures are involved. Each of these issues merit further consideration.

Intergenerational community development

On reflection, the playground objective to provide a safe play facility that would meet the needs and interests of local children and young people was accomplished only in part. Our well-meaning attempts to engage a wide age range of children and young people in the project were unsuccessful. In fact, these were counterproductive as we unwittingly raised hopes and expectations and thus the disillusionment was even more acutely felt. There was a need for transparency right from the outset. The members of HRG, mostly women with young children, grandchildren or caring responsibilities, were primarily interested in providing a play facility for small children. Few of the members had teenage children and, in fact, several had been the target of anti-social behaviour from young people.

Motivation for community activity is a key element and one that has been analysed by Chanan (2000). He persuasively argues that community activity (which he distinguishes from volunteering) is inspired by a degree of self-interest coupled with the desire to tackle shared problems and meet joint needs. Chanan's research further identifies caring responsibilities as a key indicator of community involvement. Anecdotal evidence (grounded in my own practice experience and that of others) would suggest that women's and men's nurturing instincts have a significant part to play and

the roles of 'mothering' and 'fathering' are issues, in themselves, deserving further research and discussion. Furthermore, it is predominantly older women that demonstrate a collective responsibility and an interest in children's welfare and this is evidenced in their relationships and knowledge of local children. Young children in the area had consistently requested play facilities and thus the playground provided an ideal opportunity to meet an explicit need and, arguably, fulfil a 'mothering' role. The idea that children and young people should be active partners in this venture was in reality an overly ambitious expectation, considering our resources.

The desirability of community projects which can promote intergenerational involvement and weather the inevitable conflicts is self-evident, but the motivation, needs and interests of all participants have to be explored from the outset. As Driskell (2002) argues, the genuine participation of children and young people in community-led projects is likely to be elusive, and it will be adults' needs and interests that will primarily be served. Christensen and O'Brien (2003) remark that children's and adults' participation in the creation and sustainability of 21st-century cities (and communities) involves a complex and fraught process of negotiation. Furthermore it requires a sophisticated level of skill, knowledge and experience on the part of the facilitators – an additional resource few community-led projects can afford or access. Hart (1997) suggests that children do not have to be operating at the highest level of participation for this to be meaningful and, perhaps more to the point, ethical. As long as children are not manipulated, used to decorate or promote a cause they know little about, or used as tokens to elicit the 'youth vote', then their participation can be supported (Hart, 1997). In terms of the playground project we did our 'incompetent best' to promote opportunities for children and young people's involvement and, in the final analysis, the choice not to do so was theirs.

The reality of inclusive community engagement is further hampered by a policy agenda awash with initiatives that are predominantly community- or youth-focused (Neighbourhood Renewal Strategy 2001, DFEE, 2001). However, as Chawla and Malone (2003) argue, the needs of young people do need to be seen in context with community needs. To separate youth from community, which is the policy and practice of both central and local government, fosters social division and marginality. It is easier to restrict the funding for generic youth work (young people initiated and led) as opposed to targeted, problem-focused youth provision, when the constituency involved has no electoral clout. It will be interesting to see the extent to which there is a paradigm shift once the new policy agenda that underpins *Every Child Matters* (2003) and *Youth Matters* (2005) embed themselves into local governance (DfES, 2003b; 2005g). Both these agendas explicitly refer to the importance of community engagement. Intergenerational community development work in the meantime will remain firmly as a good idea, only very occasionally glimpsed in successful practice.

See Chapter 3, The Politics of Childhood.

Sustaining collective engagement

Lack of engagement with the HRG and the playground project was not confined to local children and young people. Nevertheless, the mantra of community participation is articulated at every opportunity by regeneration projects even though the practice is far more illusory and elusive. 'Community' and 'participation' are complex and problematic concepts and attempts to define, analyse and prescribe practices that will invoke their success are well documented (Driskell, 2002; Yorkshire Forward, 1999; etc.). It is easy for groups to lose heart when having followed all the good practice guidelines establishing a welcoming culture at meetings, using an accessible venue, encouraging neighbours to come along, negotiating agendas, offering lifts to those with a disability, publicising achievements via a newsletter, on the Internet, organising social events, the failure to attract new membership persists.

Chapter 13, Children's Experience of Community Regeneration, also discusses this issue.

The above strategies have occasionally worked for the HRG in the short term. A few new faces have come along, motivated, as Chanan (2000) identifies, by a mixture of self-interest and public spiritedness. Sustaining this involvement, however, has been more problematic and the life cycle of HRG has mirrored that of many other similar community groups. The one constant has been the involvement of older women, particularly those with caring responsibilities. Some of these women have drawn strength and gained personal empowerment from the group and become semi-detached, choosing to invest their newly found confidence, self-esteem and capabilities in other projects, including paid work. They have, in effect, fulfilled the community regeneration agenda. For, as Attree (2004) theorises, the objective of community empowerment is to enhance the capacity of individuals to undertake projects that promote the economic and social well-being of their communities. However, less attention has been given to the flipside of empowerment for local neighbourhoods, that newly empowered individuals, quite understandably, have a tendency to move on, or even out of their local area, thus reducing the stock of experienced community activists and reserves of social capital.

Looking back over the minutes of HRG meetings from the past 10 years, over seventy residents (including young people) have participated in meetings and neighbourhood activities. It is helpful, perhaps, to take the long view and recognise that all groups experience periods of expansion and contraction and that group processes are notoriously difficult to predict or control. Group involvement is a practical impossibility for many (for all the known reasons) and, for the vast majority, of no significant interest. Research by Chanan (2000) investigating levels of community involvement in different European areas found only 5 per cent of the sample was highly active, 9 per cent were moderately active and 86 per cent were not active at all. The HRG would appear to reflect a more European-wide experience of community involvement where minimal numbers of activists sustain community development. Nevertheless, the community regeneration 'industry' has a tendency to make huge assumptions about the individuals that make up communities and the preferred methods for collective engagement of meetings, groups, forums, 'have your say' sessions will inevitably attract only an exceptional and unrepresentative minority.

Continuing professional support

One of the significant issues to emerge from the Hirst Wood project is the need for continuing professional support for community groups, even where the motivation and skill base of participants is high. The handful of active members involved with the project were, with one exception, well-educated professional men and women or those who had retired from professional careers. Turner and Martin (2003) argue that the success of community-based projects is largely determined by the skill base and motivation of participants, but in the final analysis it is the quality of the 'project manager' that is the key determining factor. Their view is that there should be less pre-occupation with institutional 'capacity building', but more focus on identifying, nurturing and supporting key individuals in communities. This highlights the need for ongoing community development even in the strongest and most vibrant of communities as few groups are capable of sustaining themselves on community activism alone. Hulyer (1997) makes a similar point and says that the biggest mistake made by community workers is to believe that community groups will take over the running of community-based activities. Nevertheless, an exit strategy is generally accepted as good practice for once a community group has been 'empowered' and 'skilled up' there is an underlying assumption that they will be able to move forward independently. This reasoning belies the fact that 'capacity' in communities shifts and is highly variable.

Those who buy into community development as a process recognise that it requires long-term, sustained investment. Synergy occurs where there are positive and constructive working relationships between council officers, council members and local community activists. These relationships founded on trust and mutual respect can bring about radical change.

Reflective Activity 14.1

Reflecting on play provision in Hirst Wood

You might find it helpful to reflect on this case study and devise an action plan for the new multi-use games area project (see p. 211). The following guidelines are designed to support you through the reflective process and to enable you to explore the importance of this to professional practice.

Analysis and reflection

1 What personal and professional issues did this case study raise for you? For example, consider how you might feel if you were a resident as opposed to a worker.

2 What local and external factors influenced the attitudes and behaviour of the different groups within Hirst Wood, for example younger children; young people; adults?

3 What factors supported/hindered their participation?

4 Should the views of children and young people be respected, listened to and acted upon, even where these conflict with other community members?

Learning

5 What have you learnt about community development processes?

6 What have you learnt about 'participation' and those who 'participate'?

Future Action

7 What factors should be considered in the planning, design and installation of the new project?

8 Who should be involved with the new project and how do you promote 'genuine participation' that is representative?

9 What 'support' might be needed to sustain this project? Whose support might you enlist?

10 How should conflict between different interest groups be resolved? For example, if a vocal group of adults living in close proximity to the Multi-Use Community Area (MUCA) are opposed to this venture should their views be respected?

Reflective Activity 14.2

Linking this chapter with Part I

This chapter describes the difficulties in involving children in the process of developing local play facilities. Part I explains how the status of children and young people in society affect their participation and how images of children and young people affect their status.

1 What pictures of children are created in this chapter?

2 Look for pictures, within the descriptions, of very young children and older children. How are they different?

3 Chapter 5 will help you to identify words to describe these pictures. How might these different pictures affect the level of participation of the children and young people?

4 Chapters 2 and 3 will help you to think about the way in which we think about children and how the pictures we have of children affect the level of participation they are able to have in decision-making.

The HRG continues to this day to receive support from local councillors and local council officers. They regularly attend meetings and are willing to get involved in all manner of activity including picking up dog dirt on the local recreational ground before a community fun day.

The idea that local people should develop their own strategies for local problems and issues is persuasive and resonates in government neighbourhood renewal policy. The difficulty with this approach is that it rarely works in practice. For example, fundraising for capital items (of any size) may be practically feasible for an experienced community group, but professional support can fast-track the process. Running a community fun day and completing the required 'risk assessments' is far less time-consuming if you can use a proforma already devised for this purpose. Finally 'Community problems', on closer analysis, are rarely confined to a particular locality but are in fact structural, complex and increasingly global. As Bauman (2004) comments the 'think global act local' mantra is dangerously misleading as comparatively few problems can be resolved at local level.

This experience coupled with many others has led me to conclude that community development, as defined by Community Development Xchange and others, is most useful as a set of visionary principles underpinned by an ethical value-base, but, in all honesty, relatively few community-led projects are able to deliver and sustain the process. Community development is more likely to be a messy, difficult and flawed process that at times will need to engage with other less-empowering approaches including those that are professionally led, externally driven and with poor representation from local communities, especially children.

Finally, there is a postscript to this story. At the time of writing, the HRG (with the support of council members, council officers, young people and the youth service) is about to embark on a community consultation for a multi-use games area. This would be situated on the same recreational space as the Hirst Wood playground. It is a resource that local young people have requested. As to whether this gets approved, funded and built will depend on all the issues discussed above and others yet to unfold!

Annotated reading

Chanan, G. (2000) 'Community responses to social exclusion', in Percy-Smith, J. (ed.) *Policy Responses to Social Exclusion*, Buckingham: Open University Press

This chapter highlights the complexity involved in tackling social exclusion and the need for government to inject significant resources into disadvantaged communities. It also examines voluntary/community activity in several disadvantaged neighbourhoods in seven different European states and makes the point that those who are actively involved are an exceptional minority.

Chawla, L. and Malone, K. 'Neighbourhood quality in children's eyes', in Christensen, P. and O'Brien, M. (2003) *Children in the City: Home, Neighbourhood and Community,* London: Routledge Falmer

There are some lovely and insightful accounts in this book about how children from different social-class backgrounds spend their free time.

Driskell, D. (2002) *Creating Better Cities with Children and Youth: A Manual for Participation,* London: Earthscan/ UNESCO

This provides a text book guide to engaging children and young people. It includes some great ideas and strategies and if resources and time are in plentiful supply this shows you how to do it. But if money and time are in short supply . . . you will need to adapt!

Gilchrist, A. (2004) *The Well-Connected Community: A Networking Approach to Community Development,* Bristol: The Policy Press/CDF

Alison spent many years as a community development worker and this book draws on her extensive experience. It is refreshing to read about the importance of building and sustaining informal relationships with people in community groups and partnerships and this book blends theory with practice.

Chapter 15

Mind the Gap: A Multi-Agency Approach to Raising the Educational Attainment of Children in Care

GARY WALKER

Ideologies separate us. Dreams and anguish bring us together.

(Eugene Ionesco)

Introduction

The title of this chapter refers to the gap between the educational attainment of children in care and the attainment of other children. This case study provides a snapshot of an attempt to improve access to services (in this case education) for one group of potentially much-excluded children and young people. It is included to demonstrate the thorough, thoughtful, multi-agency and systematic work involved in improving access to services for specific groups of children who may otherwise miss out.

> See Chapter 4, The Social Divisions of Childhood, for other examples of children deprived of adequate services.

Professional responsibilities evolve over time as a result of changes in the law and guidance, and variations in resource allocation. Professionals from different agency backgrounds may possess diverse cultures and beliefs, yet as the quotation above indicates, they can and do come together for the good of children out of a sense of anguish for the prevailing situation and a desire to improve the lives of children with whom they are working.

This chapter explores

- The work of a multi-agency team in one local authority which developed a distinctly multi-agency approach to try to tackle the educational underachievement of children in care in their area.

Analysis of the projects will illustrate the link between theory and policy, and the daily experiences of children.

- Background information and research evidence on the issues surrounding the educational experiences of children and young people in care. This will include the context of the educational learning of this group of children, and how their progress is measured.
- The child's experience through practical examples of project work undertaken.

The multi-agency team

In the local authority which forms the focus of this chapter, a discrete team was established in 1999 to try to tackle some of the barriers to learning faced by children in care, and to implement some of the solutions. Quite explicitly their remit is to bring the educational attainment of children in care closer in line with their peers by assisting the corporate parent to fulfil its responsibilities. The concept of 'corporate parent' was introduced in the national guidance as a way of trying to ensure that every professional, as well as others involved in the life of children in care, for example local councillors, accepted personal responsibility for trying to improve the situation of children in care (DfEE and DoH, 2000).

This team is multi-agency in its core structure. It consists of two coordinators, one a qualified teacher employed by Social Services, and the other a qualified social worker, employed by Education. The third team member is a support officer (employed by Education) whose brief is to support the education of those children specifically living in children's homes.

The work of the team is overseen by a multi-agency steering group consisting of senior managers from Social Services, Education, Health and the voluntary sector. The coordinators report to this group quarterly, giving a progress report against the major action points in the annual team plan. The steering group may also suggest a new focus for work following some national or local initiative.

The model that the team operates is the distributed model of working (Fletcher-Campbell et al., 2003).

This means that the team retains the overview of the children concerned, but additional teaching or services are provided by the schools or other departments, and are embedded within mainstream provision where possible. One clear aim of the team is to build the capacity of schools, social work teams and carers to support these children effectively. This contrasts with the discrete model, under which one larger team of professionals is not only responsible for tracking the pupils, but also for providing many direct support services. The articulated advantage of the former model (notwithstanding the view that it costs less to have a smaller team) is that long-term success can only be achieved if individual schools, carers and social work teams themselves learn how to support children in care, rather than come to rely on 'experts' being parachuted in to solve the problems on their behalf, a pattern which can come to repeat itself. Before the work of the team is described in detail, some background information is provided to help place their work in a wider context.

Background information and research evidence

There are, at any one time, approximately 60,000 children and young people in care in England and Wales (SEU, 2003). Children in care are also sometimes known as looked-after children or children in public care. The group includes children who are on Care Orders and who are voluntarily accommodated by the local authority.

Concern about their educational performance is not new. The first major study to highlight the poor outcomes for this group of children was that conducted by Jackson (1987a). In the same year, she promulgated the view that this educational failure was due not to the attendant problems these

> Compare the difficulties of these children with the refugee children that are the focus of Chapter 17, Educating Refugee Children: A Class Teacher's Perspective.

children have, but rather to a lack of appropriate support, encouragement and cooperation from those responsible for them (Jackson, 1987b). This challenged the contemporary view, she argues, that one could not expect children in care to fare well in education since they had more pressing issues to deal with, such as emotional trauma, separation and loss, or, worse, that they were delinquent slow learners.

In 1999 the government instigated a national drive to lessen the gap between the educational attainment of children in care and their peers. This was part of the 'Quality Protects' programme that was set up to improve the lives of children in care. These outcomes are measured in terms of the percentage of children who achieve the national average scores in Standard Assessment Tasks (SATs) at the end of Key Stages 1–3, and in GCSE outcomes at the end of Key Stage 4. In spite of the Quality Protects programme, children in care still routinely fail to meet the above required targets in larger numbers than their peers who are not in care (SEU, 2003). This is illustrated in Table 15.1.

The possible reasons for this gap in attainment are now well-documented. They include:

- inflexible or unavailable personal support for children at a time of crisis;

- a lack of training for teachers on meeting the needs of, and responsibilities for, the children;

- insufficient priority given to education by social services staff (Social Services Inspectorate, 1995).

Other causes are:

- a lack of encouragement to attend or do well at school;

- teachers' and carers' low expectations of what children in care could achieve;

- learning being disrupted by frequent moves;

- not having enough space or resources to complete homework;

- being bullied and stigmatised at school;

- poor liaison and collaboration between schools and social services (Borland, 1998).

A final set of reasons include insufficient support in the care setting to help compensate for educational disadvantage and the lack of a single advocate for the children (The Who Cares? Trust, 2003).

The reason why this is seen as a critical issue to address is that there is evidence that poor experiences of education and care can contribute to social exclusion in later life. For instance, between a quarter and a third of rough sleepers have been in care; young people who have been in care are two-and-a-half times more likely to be teenage parents, and around a quarter of adults in prison spent some time in care as children (SEU, 2003).

Chapter 3, The Politics of Childhood, provides more discussion of social exclusion, and inequalities in childhood are further explored in Chapter 4, The Social Divisions of Childhood.

There is, thankfully, available research into what might improve the situation. Borland (1998) argues for collaborative support involving specific education planning. The Who Cares? Trust (1999) articulate this as

Table 15.1   Educational Outcomes for Children in Care Compared with their Peers, 2005

Indicator	Children in care	All children
Percentage achieving Level 2 at the end of Key Stage 1 (7-year-olds)	58%	86%
Percentage achieving Level 4 at the end of Key Stage 2 (11-year-olds)	44%	80%
Percentage achieving Level 5 at the end of Key Stage 3 (14-year-olds)	27%	73%
Percentage achieving at least 5 GCSEs graded A*–C at the end of Key Stage 4 (16-year-olds)	11%	56%

(DfES, 2006).

'personal education plans', a tool which the national guidance identifies as an essential requirement for every child in care (DfEE and DoH, 2000). This personal education plan should contain clear short- and long-term targets together with a description of the support on offer to achieve these. The plan should be drawn up at a face-to-face meeting involving the school, carer, social worker, parent and young person as appropriate.

Other possible solutions suggested include:

- increased awareness of all staff of the issues faced by children in care;
- a designated teacher for children in care (a requirement under the national guidance);
- quick transfer of information when children change school;
- timely assessment of need;
- a system for agreeing with children and young people how information about them is handled within school;
- schools need to be flexible enough to enable young people to access appropriate support (Borland, 1998).

Further suggestions include as few exclusions from school as possible; structured behaviour management; study support where needed; celebrating success; and peer support coupled with anti-bullying strategies (The Who Cares? Trust, 1999).

Hunt (2000) cites some further factors which lead to better outcomes. These include learning to read early (before the age of 8); having a carer/parent who values education; having friends outside care who do well at school; developing out-of-school interests; and having a significant adult who offers consistent encouragement as a mentor, role model or champion. Berridge (2000) emphasises the importance of stability and continuity, concluding that changes of school outside normal transfer 'can be highly stressful, and should be avoided wherever possible' (p. 7).

In their report, Ofsted (2001) interviewed 300 young people in care, and a summary of the findings on what they believed would be helpful suffices here:

- a caring, supportive non-stigmatising school where there is access to an adult in confidence;

- being treated as any young person;
- a consistent social worker who is interested in education;
- commitment and support from carers;
- stability of care placement;
- access to resources for study.

Chapters 14 and 18 also identify the importance of incorporating the views of young people.

The issues raised here have a striking resonance with other research findings. Jackson and Sachdev (2001) are quite explicit about their desire to reflect the views of young people, and in focus groups they discovered the 'huge gap between well-meaning policies . . . and the day to day experiences of young people' (p. 11). They also found that the young people were articulate about the difficulties, and about what did or could help them. This included:

- the use of personal education plans;
- setting and monitoring of targets;
- direct support to young people;
- education training for foster carers;
- appropriate resources in care homes;
- leisure opportunities;
- advocacy for children excluded from school.

This detailed study, which also includes the administering of questionnaires to young people, and a review of previous research findings, has a depth which adds weight to the conclusions, even though they echo many of those encountered already.

The multi-agency approach

The best way to illustrate the work of the team is to describe some examples of their project work. Following this, common themes and issues will be explored.

The partnership with the Early Years Service

It seems appropriate to begin with the development of a discrete Early Years personal education plan, designed to support the early education of children aged 3–5 years. Personal education plans are the key multi-agency planning and support tool for children in care. The national guidance is committed to ensuring that every child has a personal education plan within 20 days of entering care or starting at a new school or educational setting (DfEE and DoH, 2000).

Once the team had decided such a plan was necessary (as distinct from the mainstream personal education plan) they set about consulting with partners in the Early Years Service to design a draft plan. This was the beginning of a very successful partnership, and over a series of five meetings, not only was the draft plan agreed, but a central training programme for all Early Years setting staff was approved and outlined in principle. The two coordinators then produced, still in consultation with the Early Years Service, six central training kits on 'The

Education of Children in Care' (see Figure 15.1). They delivered this to all Early Years settings managers, who then cascaded it to the setting staff. As it is the social worker's responsibility to initiate personal education plans, the draft plan was piloted in three social work area sites before the final version was launched. The entire process, from inception to delivery of all the training to all setting staff, to the implementation of the personal education plan, took a shade over twelve months.

Monitoring of personal education plans

A second example of multi-agency work that the team introduced was the system to monitor both the quantity and quality of all personal education plans. The team devised a two-pronged approach to such

Figure 15.1 Extract from the Early Years Services central training kit on the education of children in care.

Good Practice when a Child Enters or Leaves

When a child attends your setting, ensure that:

- There has been an **induction meeting** attended by the child, carer, the social worker (and if appropriate natural parents) and yourself and/or the setting's Nominated Officer for children in care.

- The setting has obtained **relevant information** from the social worker or carer, but treat personal information as confidential.

- You have **contact details** of the social worker and carer, and if appropriate, the natural parents.

- You have discussed with the social worker who should receive **reports and other communications**, and **who should be invited to parents' evenings**, etc.

- The setting has been informed of when the next **Social Services Care Review** on the child will be taking place so that you or an appropriate person can contribute to the Review either in person or by a report.

- You are aware that children in care may suffer **educational disadvantage** for a number of reasons: for example, disrupted placements; emotional

trauma; unresolved concerns about their families; fears about their future; low self-esteem; being subject to stigmatisation and bullying; unaddressed special educational needs; the lack of a consistent adult to act as their advocate.

- All **individual needs are identified** via the **Personal Education Plan** in conjunction with other agencies, and **strategies are developed** to meet these needs.

When a child leaves your setting, ensure that:

- You **advocate**, where appropriate, on behalf of children when proposed moves of home or educational placement are made by social services to ensure maximum stability and continuity of educational provision.

- All steps are taken to ensure that **good liaison** and **cooperation** exist between yourself and any receiving setting/school. This includes:
  1. Transfer of information
  2. Continuity of programmes and support.

- You support the child through the process, and mark the ending in a positive way.

monitoring. They firstly agreed with the independent reviewing officers (employed by Social Services) a checklist to be used at every child-care review to record the existence or otherwise of a personal education plan, and to record issues related to the quality of such plans (see Figure 15.2). They then undertook six-monthly 10 per cent sample surveys of personal education plans, which necessitated requesting from social workers a copy of the plans for scrutiny. The first of these was very successful, and the independent reviewing officers were very quick and keen to respond to the new monitoring system, faithfully completing and returning the checklists on a monthly basis. These were then summarised by the team, who sent a monthly report to senior managers in Social Services on the state of play, so they could be built into future planning.

Figure 15.2 Sample page from a personal education plan for a Year 5 pupil showing individual targets which were monitored.

School Based Targets

1) SHORT TERM TARGETS (e.g. numeracy, behaviour etc)

AREA	ACTION	BY WHOM	Date Completed
Behaviour	To avoid raising voice or using violence when expressing an opinion	Pupil supported by Class Teacher/other staff	
	To interact with others without threatening or intimidating them	Pupil supported by Class Teacher/other staff	
Attainment	To sustain concentration and motivation to the end of the task	Pupil supported by Class Teacher/other staff	

2) LONG TERM TARGETS

AREA	ACTION	BY WHOM	Date Completed
Behaviour	To forge and sustain positive relationships with staff and peers	Pupil supported by Class Teacher/other staff	
Attainment	To achieve at least Level 4 in English, Maths and Science	Pupil supported by Class Teacher	

Extra curricular activities/sports/study support	Actioned by whom
To be more active in football at school	Class Teacher to arrange support for this

Assessing foster carers' ability to support education

A third multi-agency development of the team was the production of a toolkit for assessing the ability of foster carers to support the education of children in their care. The impetus for this arose out of a recommendation of the Social Exclusion Unit (SEU, 2003) report, which emphasised the positive role that a significant adult who is supportive of, and interested in, education can have. The team drafted the toolkit – a series of statements or questions related to education issues with three columns to tick the response as appropriate (see Figure 15.3). The statements or questions were designed not to test the educational qualifications of carers, but rather to try to ensure they shared positive values about the benefits of education and that they had a basic understanding of what is involved in supporting children's education. This draft toolkit was then shared, discussed and agreed with managers within the fostering section of Social Services before being implemented for all fostering officers to use in assessing new, or reviewing existing, carers. The team, in consultation with the fostering managers, monitors the use of this toolkit at six-monthly intervals.

The leisure card

A fourth example from the work of the team is the introduction of a leisure card for every child in care in the authority. This entitles the child, plus two adults and a further child, free entry into 85 museums and sites of interest across a large geographical region surrounding the home authority. This is an interesting example because the partnership work in setting it up involved the local Museums Council and five neighbouring local authorities. Preliminary discussions took place with representatives from the Museums Council, at which it was agreed that such a scheme was desirable and feasible. Following this, five neighbouring authorities were contacted and it was agreed that all would financially contribute to the cost of setting up the scheme. The funding was used to employ a freelancer (employed through the Museums Council) to liaise with the museums to encourage them to join the scheme and to produce the information booklets and cards. As the museums agreed that the target audience would be allowed free entry, there were no ongoing costs. The scheme has proved to be a great success (see Figure 15.4), and is expanding, in terms of both the numbers of sites and local authorities wishing to join.

The Year 11 Project

The final example is a specific project which provided direct funding to Year 11 children in care and was designed to do two things: ensure entry for GCSE examinations where the young person was at risk of not being entered, and/or help to boost GCSE grades. The team contacted every social worker and school of every Year 11 child in care and asked them to identify those young people who might benefit under the criteria set out above. Once the replies were received and processed, the schools were then contacted and asked to produce a written individual support plan for each young person identified; only if the team agreed with this plan was the funding released to the school. Twenty-six young people were supported in total. Typical plans included paying for extra tuition, attendance at revision classes and purchasing specialist resources. The predicted GCSE grades were obtained to enable comparison with actual grades at examinations (see Figure 15.5). Social workers were contacted again to confirm the young person was to receive the specified support to enable them to monitor this. The project was evaluated by the team as successful. Table 15.2 shows that the percentage of pupils who were entered for a GCSE examination increased by 10 per cent on the previous year, and those achieving one GCSE graded A*–G increased by 13 per cent.

Analysis of the projects

The illustrations below indicate success of the projects, not only in themselves (in terms of the work) but also in positive outcomes and experiences for children. In trying to understand this success, it is possible to identify some common elements.

First, the audiences approached by the team were receptive to the idea of being a good corporate parent, and were very keen to link in with the work of the team. This seems especially true for the Early Years Service,

Figure 15.3 Extract from the toolkit to assess foster carers' ability to support education.

Competence	Appropriate response	Has been discussed	Evidence of working towards	Has knowledge
Has knowledge that some children may have different educational needs and may receive extra support or tuition	Children may have special or additional educational needs e.g. learning disabilities (general or specific), behavioural needs, language, sensory impairment, physical needs			
Understands how these may be addressed	Statement of Special Educational Needs (SEN) or via additional funding in mainstream schools or through special school provision			
Understands the importance of advocacy for children	Is comfortable in challenging schools where appropriate			
Understands the importance of supporting children through specific events	Would be willing to attend parents' evenings, shows and sporting events etc. Expectation for fee-paid carers or agreed with S.W.			
Understands the need to support children's homework	Could provide space, quiet time and practical help and could access extra help if needed			
Understands the need to celebrate children's achievements	Actively rewards children's success in all areas of school life			
Understands basic educational abbreviations (will help clarify roles and info from school)	e.g. SATs, GCSE, GNVQ, SENCO, abbreviations for subjects, EWO, EP, RO, etc. see glossary on next page			
Understands the importance of on-going training	Would be prepared to go to regular training on education issues			
Understands the value of education	Recognises that education is key to life chances and must be seen as a priority for children in care who will need extra support to maximise their potential			

Figure 15.4   Example of use of the Leisure Card, and comments by, two brothers.

John, aged 11, and Mark, aged 10, used the card to visit three attractions with their foster carers. John thought the stately home with lots of different rooms was great, as it reminded him of the *Narnia* stories; Mark liked the armoury.

At a museum for children, John liked dressing up in various costumes, while Mark gave it 10 out of 10 for all-round fun.

When they visited a second large house with a bird garden, John enjoyed the boat ride on the lake, and Mark's favourite birds were the penguins.

the independent reviewing officers, the Museums Council, and schools and social workers involved in the Year 11 project. There was a shared philosophy and understanding between the team and the Early Years Service of the importance of supporting a good educational foundation for young children in care, which was seen to promote future learning and build resilience for dealing with later setbacks. Furthermore, their own model of training for staff fitted in very well with the proposed training – it was seen as sound staff development that settings managers delivered training as part of their remit, and so they were very willing to use the central resources to do so. The independent reviewing officers already used checklists for other matters, such as health, and the introduction of another one, especially one produced in consultation

Figure 15.5   Example of Year 11 plan and subsequent outcomes for a pupil.

Simone was consulted about and agreed with the following support plan to assist her with GCSEs:

• additional tuition time using teachers at the school for all subjects

• extra support from teachers to enable completion of homework

• mentoring support to help keep her focussed

• transport and tuition costs to enable Simone to enter Italian GCSE at another centre, as the school did not offer this

• specialist input from an artist in Textiles

Simone's predicted and actual GCSE grades are shown here:

Subject	Predicted	Actual
English Language	E	D
English Literature	E	D
Maths	G	F
Science	F	D D (entered for Double exam)
Italian	-*	B
ICT	G	C
Health and Social Care	C	D D (entered for Double exam)
Textiles	F	C
Total score**	**17**	**42**

*No prediction available as school could not assess progress.
**GCSEs are scored as A* = 8, A = 7, B = 6, C = 5, D = 4, E = 3, F = 2, G = 1

This shows considerable progress, even if Italian is removed from the comparison.

Table 15.2 Outcomes from the Year 11 Project

Indicator	Year 1	Year 2
Percentage entered for a GCSE or equivalent exam	57%	67%
Percentage achieving 1 or more A*–G grades	52%	65%
Percentage achieving 5 A*–C grades	5%	5%

with them, was not taxing. The idea of the leisure card dovetailed with the social inclusion agenda that museums now have, and this encouraged the Museums Council to participate. Clearly, schools and social workers wanted the best possible outcomes for the young people in their care, and were more than willing to cooperate with customised plans to boost GCSE outcomes through the provision of additional funding. In short, the propositions from the team fell on fertile ground.

Secondly, the built-in consultation initiated by the team. From the very beginning of each project, the team ensured that partners were at the centre of decision-making so that they did not feel 'done to' but rather that they were an equal partner, sharing in, and contributing to the joint development of, a piece of work with clear objectives. For instance, the Early Years Service managers were able to bring their expert knowledge of the Foundation Stage curriculum to bear in designing the Early Years personal education plan.

Thirdly, it is important to acknowledge the energy, commitment and personal qualities of the team coordinators, which ensured that each project was completed on schedule. Part of the reason for this was that one coordinator used his existing contacts and relationships within Social Services to carry workers along with him on the projects. This personal element cannot be underestimated as it involves a level of trust and familiarity which can be vital in ensuring that the other party makes a positive contribution. Furthermore, the team itself, being a living exemplar of a sound multi-agency approach, modelled good practice to others,

a fact that must have been a contributory factor in the successes.

Stainton Rogers (1989) has described the factors more likely to foster a positive rapport between agencies. We can recognise some of them here: all workers appeared to understand their own roles and those of others; there was good common understanding of the goal of the work; and there were good channels of communication based on previous contact and experience. Similarly, the positive factor of an open culture between agencies about the issues involved, as identified in a recent inspection of eight local authorities also appeared to have been present here (DoH, 2002).

Of course, not all the project work described was successful. In particular, the team only received about 40 per cent of the six-monthly sample personal education plans requested, leaving questions about whether the remaining 60 per cent existed. Furthermore, the early evidence on the foster carers' assessment toolkit is that its use by fostering officers is piecemeal and not yet embedded into ongoing practice. One reason for this may be that 'education' is not yet in the forefront of social workers' or fostering officers' work so does not get prioritised in the work or assessments they carry out, the focus of which is 'care'. Here we see reflected some key barriers to effective multi-agency cooperation: differing functions of agencies which clash and compete; different values and ideologies of agencies; and conflicting social policy and legislation (Stainton Rogers, 1989; David, 1994; Sutton, 1997). This last point is crucial and should aid understanding of the complexities of the process. Workers are forced to adhere to the legal requirements and priorities of their own agency, and so cannot be blamed if they subsequently fail to perform additional duties which fall outside these demands.

A second explanation for the difficulties encountered may be that the underlying culture within Social Services appeared to include a sense, or even a reality, of being overwhelmed by work, of treading water, and lacking energy to push through new initiatives. This contrasted sharply with that of the team whose culture was permeated with a positive, 'can do' approach. Roaf (2002) refers to these tensions between agencies in the form of jealousy (not relinquishing areas of work), inertia (constant movement and change in organisations) and tension between preventive and crisis-led work. This is not intended as a criticism of the former. It can be irritating (not to mention debilitating) to be approached by bright-eyed workers from another team asking one to put effort and energy into a new piece of work when one feels overworked. One manifestation of this appeared to be a tendency by social workers to deflect responsibility away from themselves. For example, despite it being the social workers' role to ensure personal education plans are completed for every child in care, some of the reasons given for non-completion stretched credulity and appeared to be aimed at providing excuses beyond the control of the worker concerned. For instance, that children were not on the roll of a school, that schools were unwilling to engage in planning, or that the personal education plan form itself (piloted by social workers) was unhelpful.

The child's perspective

A key theme for the team, in developing the various projects, was trying to ensure that the child's perspective and voice were represented. The child's perspective has been threaded through, in this chapter, using the illustrations of practice. Nevertheless, it is possible to identify some further examples of how the team integrated the child into the work.

> The importance of this is discussed further in Chapter 2, Childhood: Rights and Realities.

Reflective Activity 15.1

Key issues raised in this chapter

Jenny is 11 years old, white British and is in Year 6 at school. She has been in foster care for about a year after sexual abuse by her father came to light. She is on a Care Order, and has contact with her mother about once every 2 months. She cannot live with her mother because her mother has not fully accepted the extent of the abuse and continues to see Jenny's father. Jenny has no contact with her father, who was not convicted by the criminal courts. Jenny has also witnessed violence by her father towards her mother. Jenny has one pre-school sibling who is also in care, but in a different placement from Jenny. She has contact with him once a fortnight.

Jenny has continued to go to her existing primary school using Social Services transport. There are some very difficult times in school when she exhibits violent and unpredictable behaviour. She is of average ability, and achieved Level 2 in Key Stage 1 SAT tests. She has special friendships in school, but occasionally falls out with other children.

It is January. Social work managers have decided that they want Jenny to move to a new school at Easter to be nearer the foster placement as the transport is proving too costly. The social worker is unhappy with this, and would like her to remain at the school until the end of the year. The school is also concerned that a move of schools at Easter would disrupt preparations for the forthcoming SAT tests in May, and that a July leaving date would much better facilitate a move to High School.

1 Who do you think the 'corporate parents' are in this scenario? Think about professional roles as well as others who may be involved, directly or indirectly.

2 What issues might be involved for Jenny in this situation? Think about emotional factors such as stress and uncertainty, as well as broader issues such as her response to ongoing contact with her mother and brother, possible onset of puberty, etc. Think about how these might act as barriers to learning for Jenny.

3 What can or should the social worker and other corporate parents do to support Jenny? Think about Jenny's rights to be consulted and involved in decisions, about how the social worker can work creatively to try to secure ongoing transport, what the school could do to advocate for Jenny, what the role of the foster carer might be and what senior managers in all services should consider when making decisions.

The Early Years personal education plan contained two 'child-friendly pages', the first of which depicted a hippopotamus with a very large open mouth, out of which arose a huge speech bubble for the child's views to be recorded, in writing or by drawing. The second such page consisted of a series of smaller speech bubbles containing questions such as 'What do you like doing best?' or 'Is there anything you don't like?' designed to elicit views from the child about their educational setting.

All personal education plans are monitored in respect of the extent to which they demonstrate consultation with, and involvement of, children and young people.

The leisure card scheme is very popular with children (see Figure 15.4); in particular, the fact that it is their card (as opposed to, say, the carer's) gives them kudos with peers and it has been said that this is a boost to their self-esteem.

Finally, the Year 11 project involved the schools and social workers consulting with young people over what type of support they would find most useful in assisting them with examinations. This ensured that when the plan was implemented, the young people felt they co-owned it and had investment in it. This too, may help to explain the success of the project.

Reflective Activity 15.2

Linking this chapter with Part I

This chapter considers how to improve the access that children in care have to the education system to improve their life chances. Part I chapters consider the political and economic reasons for providing services for children and the barriers to services that exist for some groups of children.

1 What sort of political and economic motivation might there be for the kind of initiative described in this chapter?

2 What might a successful outcome look like from the point of view of the children in care?

3 What might a successful outcome look like from an economic point of view? Chapter 2 will help you understand some of the differences in motivation.

4 What other barriers to provision might children in care face? Chapter 4 will help you to identify some of these.

Conclusion

The work of the multi-agency team described in this chapter, operating in a positive multi-agency arena, has been shown to yield good outcomes for children in care. This can be measured both in terms of hard examination results and softer indicators, such as involvement in planning, engagement in educational leisure activities, and more effective support from significant adults. The outcomes appear to support a view that concentrating on hard examination results alone is one-dimensional. Other positive experiences children and young people have may be equally significant in terms of improving future life chances. There is an area rich for future research.

The successes shown here, however, must be accompanied by a warning against complacency. Clearly, the many barriers to learning faced by children in care are not going to be removed at a stroke. It will take the continued efforts of all agencies working together to do this, not to mention further and focused resources. Minding the gap between the educational attainment of children in care and that of their peers is a complex business, and necessarily involves minding that other gap that exists between agencies – in ideology, in focus, in culture – to ensure that children do not fall into the cavity it can create. By concentrating on the dream to make things better identified in the quotation at the beginning of the chapter, and by working through the common and shared torment, there is real hope that this can be achieved.

Annotated reading

Department for Education and Employment and Department of Health (2000) *Education of Young People in Public Care: Guidance*, London: The Stationery Office

This national guidance sets out the duties and responsibilities of all agencies in relation to children in care. It introduced the key notion of 'corporate parent' to emphasise the need for anyone working with and for children, from front-line staff to senior managers and local authority councillors to ask themselves how they could support the education of children in care.

Fletcher-Campbell, T., Archer, T. and Tomlinson, K. (2003) *The Role of the School in Supporting the Education of Children in Public Care*, Slough: National Foundation for Educational Research

This research focuses on how schools do and can support children in care. There is a sound literature review, and coverage of the role of the local authority, school policy and provision, the role of designated teacher for children in care, and how schools link with other agencies to support such children.

Jackson, S. and Sachdev, D. (2001) *Better Education, Better Futures: Research, Practice and the Views of Young People in Public Care*, Ilford: Barnardo's

This is an accessible and very readable account of key issues relating to the education of children in care, based on research findings, good practice and, crucially, the views of young people.

Chapter 16

The Anna Rebecca Gray Interviews

ANNA GRAY

Introduction

This chapter is included to provide an individual account of services. The editors approached Anna Gray a young woman with Down's syndrome to write a chapter from her point of view. She decided to interview her parents, and then to ask them to interview her with questions she devised in order to provide an individual view of her own and her family's experiences. This chapter is a transcript of the interviews co-edited by Anna Gray and Phil Jones.

This is my chapter. This is about people and bits and bobs about what people do in services like school. I decided on questions to interview my family about the services at different times in my life, when I was a child and now as teenager. It's how people welcomed us, and how we report about them. With the help of Phil Jones, I wrote questions and asked my dad, Michael, and my mum, Diane. Then they used the questions to ask me what I thought. Then I put some ideas about what I

liked, didn't like and thought the services could improve. In the interviews I can give answers about what's happened to me and what's my opinion and how we think people could be helped more.

We each drew a diagram of the services when I was little and the services now I am a teenager and then did the interview.

Three questions to do with the diagram 'when Anna was little':

- What did the services do for me when I was little?

- What do you think adults and children think of these services?

- How could they do better jobs?

Three questions to do with the diagram of 'Anna now':

- What kind of services do teenagers like, or like to have?

- What effects do these services have on teenagers?

- How can they improve the jobs they do?

Here are the diagrams and the interviews.

Michael Gray interviewed by Anna

Anna: **Draw a diagram of me when I was little. What did the services do for me when I was little?**

Michael: In Leeds I've got Mothers and Toddlers, which was important for you and your mum, Mrs Grady, who you were with in the playgroup and then primary, and Miss Byrne, who was a teacher and a key person wasn't she?

Anna: OK. So what did they do for me when I was little?

Michael: So, when you were tiny you were born prematurely and you were in hospital and the special care baby unit looked after you. They were very good and they used to let me and your mother come in and talk to you and play with you, even when you were first born and you were in hospital for six weeks.

When you were in hospital, for the six weeks, people were doing exercises with you, talking, doing games with you and then you came home and we worked up a programme, things to do with you at home.

Then you started having portage, which is learning at home, like a school at home, and people used to come to the house and help you with your skills, things like grabbing objects and moving objects and then, as you got older, sorting objects and putting them in containers and toys. You used to do that right up to the time when you started going to Mothers and Toddlers.

At Mothers and Toddlers you were playing with other children and meeting other mums and dads and grandmas, aunts – other people. Then you moved on to Mrs Grady's playgroup where they used to do play, and skills like sitting down pretending you were having lunch and then riding trikes and bicycles and make up games, dressing up, listening to music, dancing to music. Sometimes I used to come along and see you, when you did productions which was nice.

Then you went into the nursery at Altown Hall Primary School. They were very good there, and that was when you first met Miss Byrne. We'll come back to school in a

> For further discussion of health services and the medical and social models of disability, see Chapter 8, Provision for Child Health.

> For further material on play provision for children see Chapter 12, Services to Children's Play.

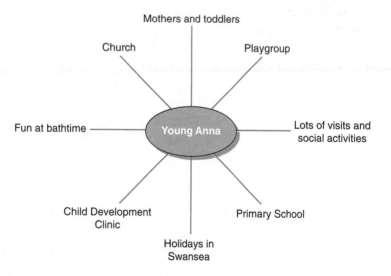

Michael's diagram of services for Anna when she was little.

second. When you were very little, as well, you used to go to hospital to have your ears checked very regularly. They used to syringe your ears with water and you used to giggle. We also went to see a doctor about your eyes. You used to read the chart. Your feet – remember you had an orthotic?

Anna: Yes, that's right, a blue one and you've got one now.

Michael: That's right and that was to try to help your foot not turn in; it was like stiff flour and water. You didn't like that did you?

Anna: No.

Michael: Then at Alton Hall you were in the early years, learning to read and write, number work and skills playing which was good. Is that OK so far?

Anna: Yes. Go back to the Toddlers and the church in Stafford.

Michael: OK. On Sundays you went to church with mum, and there was a Toddlers group and you played games there.

> For further discussion of this area of provision see Chapter 11, Day Care Services for Children.

Anna: And what was the church called?

Michael: Rising Blood Baptist Church, and you had lots of friends there.

Anna: Do we still have friends there?

Michael: Yes, we do.

Anna: There were people there who we know through that group and we still go out for meals with them.

Michael: We still see them once a year. Thank you for reminding me. So from that group you and we still have friends that we see.

Anna: **What do you think adults and children think of these services?**

Michael: When we were in Stafford and you were at the Child Development Clinic your mother and I were pleased. It was good for you because you were doing lots of interesting things, and it was good for your mum to meet other mums and the people who looked after you.

At the Child Development Clinic they had lots of workers, physiotherapy, speech therapy and people who could refer you to the hospital and see about your eyes and ears. That was excellent. The Child Development Clinic was brand new and new to the region. We were very lucky, as with the portage.

Michael's diagram of services for Anna as a teenager.

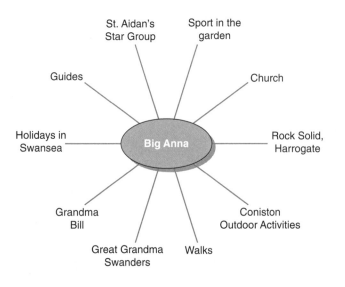

Anna: How could they do better jobs?

Michael: I think the main thing, and I've talked this through with your mum, was the speech therapy. It wasn't very easy to access it, and I don't think they came through into school to see you. Perhaps they should have spent more time with you and followed it up, to get the speech therapy to come to school. All the medical services over all and the Child Development Clinic were mostly very helpful.

Anna: What kind of services do teenagers like, or like to have?

Michael: The first thing would be to have hobbies and activities, so teenagers have youth groups, like some of the ones you go to and ones where you can go away on breaks. Can I give an example of this?

Anna: Go on.

Michael: Like this weekend you went away and you did abseiling. It was organised and it's good, I think, to do things with your friends.

Anna: I was a bit scared about what was happening.

Michael: But you did it, you had a go.

Anna: But I want to keep doing that.

Michael: That was very useful, I think. We can take you to do things individually – but that was more social: sharing, taking turns. So, if I go with you individually to do scrambling up Ilkley Moor, for example, or out walking, then you're just the focus: socially you have all the attention, which is good sometimes but, at other times, it's nice to be in a group: taking turns, walking with others, helping others, which you did. And then in the evening you had a sleepover.

Anna: Keep talking.

Michael: Which was quite exciting I think. You stayed up till three o'clock in the morning.

Anna: Two.

Michael: Which is what teenagers do.

Anna: Well, I had a problem. There was all others talking and someone had sweets. So there were those and we were talking a lot.

Michael: But the activities were structured which was good – so there was some structure and I think you like structure and a clear routine. There was a programme and you had orienteering, following a map with a compass, and the same when you go to family ones at Coniston. A lot of people go.

Anna: There was one person who organised the whole thing.

Michael: That's right, and families go together. There are other services to provide the chance for teenagers to meet in a safe environment – for example, going out. You like dancing – so I'd like to see other places where you can go and meet other teenagers. You're going to go out with some of the students at the university you did work experience at next year when you're old enough.

Anna: What effects do these services have on teenagers?

Michael: I think services for teenagers at school are useful for you to think about the future: setting goals, what you might do, and your vocational work. That's right isn't it?

See Chapter 6, Education: Service or System?, for further discussion of education and vocation.

Anna: Anything else?

Michael: First of all, the medical – if somebody who needs their eyes or ears checking it's important that the services can be accessed regularly or if there's a problem to check – like sometimes if you have a cold your hearing drops off – and its important we can have that checked. It's good as, for example with your walking, if there's a problem they can check the orthotic every so often in physiotherapy. There should be the support of regular checks so that the problems don't get more big or difficult later on.

Anna: If we go to the hospital we go to the cafeteria.

Michael: Yes, when you go to the doctor it's a treat going to the cafeteria.

Anna: Yes, sometimes, but not much!

Michael: So, the other services: the educational provision that's offered by church groups and/or collections of families together is the opportunity for you to go to groups and do things, meet new people – so it makes life more interesting than just being with your family, doesn't it? Is that true?

Anna: Not always.

Michael: Depending on the activity: some of it involves the church, a lot of music and singing, which you love.

Anna: Yes, I have choir.

Michael: So getting involved in that as a group is good, and your interest in activities is good for building confidence, doing things you normally wouldn't do and that you don't do at school.

Anna: No, at school we don't do choir.

Michael: As you need small groups to do that.

Anna: Yes.

Michael: The other thing is to go out and have meals, and with the youth group and school there's a nice cafeteria and you can have a chat and sit down with people and find out what everybody's been doing and that's one of your favourite activities, I think.

Anna: Anything else?

Michael: No.

Anna: Thank you. **How can they improve the jobs they do?**

Michael: I think it would be seeing you, working with you more regularly, specially speech therapy, possibly physiotherapy with your foot. As you've got older the medical services have taken less interest because you're out of the early stages of development, and we think there should have been more input from all of them constantly, particularly from speech therapy.

In terms of schools and other people I think they do a fantastic job. The only thing is that some people might make it easy for you sometimes and that they give in too easily if the challenge gets a bit hard and you might give up. Or they say, 'Oh, OK Anna,' and you give up and I might say keep going.

Anna: Give me an example.

Michael: If there's a long walk and you say, 'I need to rest now', and you've stopped resting. If you were with me you'd keep going and I think sometimes people go easy on you. I think the other thing, Anna, is that some of the services might not know you as a person.

Anna: OK, keep on going. Anything more you want to say, anything more to increase my skills?

Michael: It would help in what they're trying to do with you if they knew you as a person. Not just what they're trying to do with your foot or your eyes or your speech – so they could help you more and link it to your life.

Diane Gray interviewed by Anna

Anna: **What did the services do for me when I was little?**

Diane: When you were little, when you were in the Special Care Baby Unit, they looked after you, so that you had enough food, and checked to see that you were putting on weight and that you didn't have any problems and the paediatrician used to come and see you every day to check everything was alright.

Anna: **What do you think adults and children think of these services?**

Diane: I think the services were quite good, apart from the speech therapy which was virtually

Diane's diagram of services for Anna when she was younger than 1-year-old.

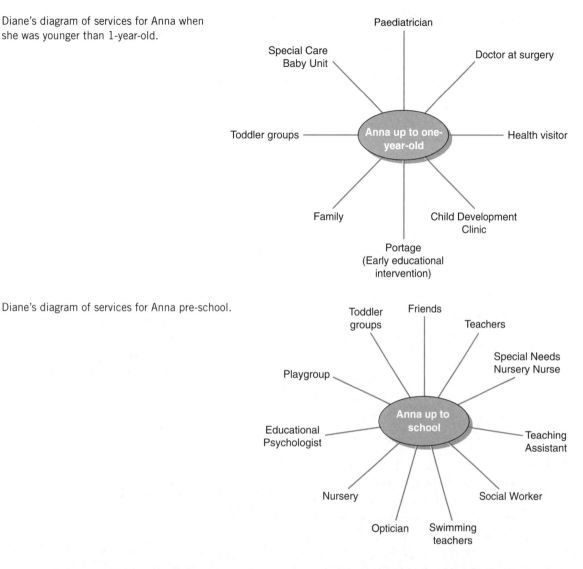

Diane's diagram of services for Anna pre-school.

non-existent, and everybody seemed to be there to help and give advice and to go and ask any questions we needed to ask and we don't have to wait too long for that, apart from when we went to get audiology appointments, and we always had to ring up to get your next appointment because they never sent one.

Instead of being seen every six months you were usually seen every nine months and that's only because I rang up, otherwise they probably wouldn't have seen you. The optician forgot to send an appointment for you which is why you had to wear a patch

at one stage – you'd stopped using your eye properly. But otherwise they were very good.

Anna: **How could they do better jobs?**

Diane: I think if they had more money they could do with having more speech therapists who could do speech therapy once a week rather than leaving it to once a term, or then speaking to the teaching assistant who was then told what they had to do and they did it with you regularly. You needed to be seen more. I don't think they could have really done more.

Diane's diagram of services for Anna as a teenager.

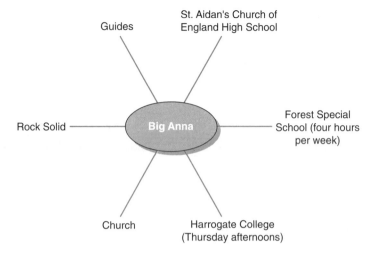

Anna: **What kind of services do teenagers like, or like to have?**

Diane: Teenagers like to have things to go to and you like to go to Guides, you like to go to church and the church youth group. I think you'd like to go to more things if there were more things available but there aren't.

Anna: Like for example going to Rangers?

Diane: Well you might go to Rangers after Guides because you're going to finish Guides aren't you? They do have groups for people with disabilities like yourself, but they usually are for people with severe disabilities and the social worker didn't think it would be appropriate, and there isn't anything that you can go to as a group.

Anna: **What effects do these services have on teenagers?**

Diane: It helps because it gives you something to go to and you can meet up with people who are the same age as you, so that's very important, so you're not just at home all the time. It gives you an interest, you can learn different things and carry on learning outside of school and you can go out and enjoy yourself.

Anna: **How can they improve the jobs they do?**

Diane: I think the Guides and the church youth group you go to are very well organised and very well set up for you to go to and integrate with everyone else because they make sure there are people watching you're safe so I don't think they can do any more. At school you have a teaching assistant who is there for you and that works very well. I don't think they could do much more there.

Anna Gray interviewed by Diane and Michael

Diane and Michael: **What did the services do for you when you were little?**

Anna: I'll start with Leeds, there was a playgroup I went to. There was a nursery and at school there was teachers and helpers and friends. I had speech therapy. There were different people to be with. At the nursery, for example, on the first day someone was there to help me find where to sit, tidying up, with my shoes. The helper was good because she helped me with what I needed to do. At the mothers and toddlers, well, they used to have books and toys there for little people to read and play with. It was children with and

Anna's diagram of services when she was little.

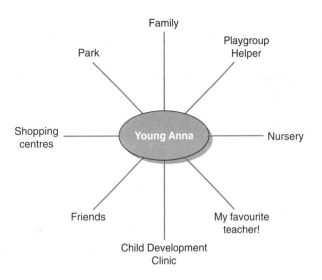

Family

Playgroup Helper

Park

Shopping centres — Young Anna — Nursery

Nursery

Friends

My favourite teacher!

Child Development Clinic

without disabilities. When parents bring their stuff like books and toys the littlies can go to different places in the room and they can sing and dance because there were different people there who helped. The child development centre was important to me. I remember that. At St Marks School there is a helper. The helpers helped me in different ways, showing me how to take control, I think, and making sure they know me and how to do things. I go to choir, the Star group and there are friends there and teachers. I also like the Guides. I like the Baptist church and I like reading books.

When I was little I loved the park and going to swings with my friends and going to the park and meeting people, 'Hello I'm Anna and I'm little.' Then sometimes we'd go to the shopping centre and then I'd go to the Centre for lunch. I know some friends from Stafford.

Diane and Michael: **What do you think adults and children think of these services?**

Anna: The Mothers and Toddlers worked well because I met new people and children with disabilities and play, sing, dance, drawing and writing. Mums would bring their children and also toys, books, stuff like that, and put their things on stalls, and then they buy

the things, books and toys, from the stalls. It's good so mum can meet other parents and discuss what I want to do.

Diane and Michael: **How could they do better jobs?**

Anna: It was a bit confused when the children wail and scream they want to go home at the end and the parents ignoring them and talking to each other. The parents could be a little bit chatterboxes.

Diane and Michael: **How could services be improved?**

Anna: Just improve their skills and help improve my opportunities. To help me, speech therapy, helping me to walk up steps, to count. How to do different things. To improve their skills to me, so I know their skills and tell other people to walk.

So, for parents 'do not talk' all the time because they are wasting time and people want to do different things.

I would also make more activities for Mothers and Toddlers, like more dancing, singing and being read to. If the leaders who will teach the dancing and singing will help them to learn more.

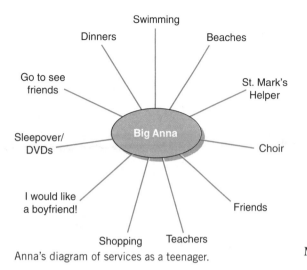

Swimming
Dinners
Beaches
Go to see friends
St. Mark's Helper
Big Anna
Sleepover/ DVDs
Choir
I would like a boyfriend!
Friends
Shopping
Teachers

Anna's diagram of services as a teenager.

Diane and Michael: What kind of services do teenagers like, or like to have?

Anna: There's school and Guides and after-school club and the church. As well now I like shopping, swimming, sending letters and sleepovers. I like DVDs and games. I would like a boyfriend. The clubs after school are also good.

They like to go to school, to church. I have a college I go to with activities and stuff. I like climbing, Guides. The best was when we went camping and it was fun, it was unstressful, it was a quiet life in the countryside. We did canoeing and games. I was up two nights, abseiling and dinner. Guides was fun. I like walking out of doors. I like swimming; I can do lots of swimming and dinners.

Diane and Michael: What effects do these services have on teenagers?

Anna: At school I have a helper and she helps me with my therapy, my walking. I have a planner and stickers. I also go to choir, we sing. It's my hobby. I feel really happy, it makes me really happy. I do PE.

I'm a big fan of the Star group. I like reading and getting books out.

It's my business, meeting and talking with other people. I really really like other people. I like being in capable hands and I like friends. There are students from the University of York and a study I'm in to do with language and people with Down's Syndrome. I like being in the study.

There's speech therapy and there's the library and the learning centre. I'm doing work experience. In hospitality. I like doing the tills, training and the experience.

Diane and Michael: How can they improve the jobs they do?

Anna: More after-school and help to think, concentrate to think and listen. I would like to baby-sit with my friends and I want a boyfriend and I want to go swimming.

School works well because I meet new people and old people that I know. So the teachers can teach us what to learn, and they teach others like me how to learn. Helpers are there as well to help people with disabilities such as me with Down's Syndrome.

School doesn't work well sometimes because there should be one rule saying 'do not mess around' and to stop people making noise (i.e. talking) because I can't learn and listen to my helper. That's general, but also specially hard because I have a disability. It could have been better on the first day you go back, it's confusing and hard to go and ask when to go, where to go on the first day back.

School could be made better if there were discos earlier after school. For Year 10. Also, if there were a ball for dancing for Year 10. I get tired, for example after PE and there should be places to rest with pillows if you are tired in the day. They should let me also change the way money is for education for children with disabilities. There should be a checklist and resource list for me to see and say what I want and what I think too. That's the best statement I have made in years. It's my favourite.

In after-school clubs they work well because they're easy to get to and go to. They're interesting and they help pupils. At times people do not learn and they talk and push and mess around and shoving and also swearing. They should be nicer to others, caring. When it works well it's clear, you can focus and work well. If teachers have other things, then helpers help people with disability problems like me, the helpers look after the disabled people and they would like more extra-curricular activities. More helpers to help out in after-school activities. Well they have school clubs like science club, choir club, worshipping club and start group, inside school time but like clubs. There should be more classes for children with a disability problem to work in different areas of the school to help them develop.

Annotated reading

Bignell, T. and Butt, J. (2000) *Between Ambition and Achievement: Young Black Disabled People's Views and Experiences of Independent Living*, London: Policy Press

Discusses research with young black disabled people on their experiences of accessing services for independent living including the barriers they face.

Davis, J., Watson, N. and Cunningham-Burley, S. (2000) 'Learning the lives of disabled children: developing a reflexive approach', in Christensen, P. and James, A. (eds) *Research with Children*, London: Routledge Falmer

Discusses the inadequacy of current models of disability to address the interests of disabled children and makes the case for including disabled children's own perspectives to get fuller insight into disability in childhood.

Davis, J. (2004) 'Disability and childhood: deconstructing the stereotypes', in Swain, J., French, S., Barnes, C. and Thomas, C. (eds) *Disabling Barriers: Enabling Environments*, 2nd edn, London: Sage

Draws attention to the 'screening' of disabled children, including segregation and restriction of choice, labelling, lack of home-based friendships, isolation at school playtime and breaks in mainstream schools, consultation with adult not child with regard to health issues, lack of recognition of a child's abilities and strengths, lack of information, poor quality and rationing in relation to services.

Detheridge, T. (2000) 'Research involving children with severe learning difficulties', in Lewis, A. and Lindsay, G. (eds) *Researching Children's Perspectives*, Buckingham: Open University Press

Discusses creative and visual methodology employed to develop research with children with severe learning difficulties.

Disability Rights Commission website <http://www.drc-gb.org/>

Clear, accessible and up-to-date coverage of the legal rights of disabled people, with examples of children who, with their families, have challenged discrimination.

French, S. and Swain, J. (2004) 'Young disabled people', in Roche, J., Tucker, S., Thompson, R. and Flynn, R. (eds) *Youth in Society: Contemporary Theory, Policy and Practice*, London: Sage/Open University

Argues that, when considering the inclusion of disabled children into mainstream school, an understanding of childhood culture is very important. Research with disabled children has raised important issues related to friendship, embarrassment, bullying, visibility, the desire to be one of the crowd and not feel under scrutiny.

Preston, G. (2005) *Helter Skelter: Families, Disabled Children and the Benefit System*, Case Paper 92: Disability Alliance and ESRC, p. 73

Explores key elements of social exclusion for families with disabled children in relation to benefits and services. Important issues such as powerlessness, discrimination, insecurity of income and social isolation are explored.

Chapter 17

Educating Refugee Children: A Class Teacher's Perspective

YINKA OLUSOGA

> Humble sentient beings, tormented
> by sufferings without cease,
> Completely suppressed by seemingly endless
> and terribly intense, negative deeds,
> May all their fears from unbearable war, famine,
> and disease be pacified,
> To freely breathe an ocean of happiness and well-being.
> (From *Words of Truth*: A prayer composed by the Dalai Lama, refugee)

Introduction

Refugees have rarely been out of the news during the past two decades. The approach of most of the media has been increasingly hostile, reactionary and derogatory. The public discourse has seen shifts in terminology as different governments have sought to frame the debate and be seen to address the 'problem'. Today, the discourse is still emotive and often ill-informed. Against this background, however, schools and teachers have sought to engage with children who are refugees. It must be borne in mind that children make up half of the world's population of refugees and displaced persons (Rutter and Jones, 2001). This chapter will examine the development of current policy in this area and will reflect on the real-life experiences of the author in meeting the needs of very young children from refugee families. Such families have proportionally more children under 5 than is the case in the general population (Rutter and Hyder, 1998).

Terminology and statistics

It is important, before beginning to discuss issues around refugees, to establish some facts and to consider the importance of words as labels. The terms 'refugee' and 'asylum seeker' are key to our discussion and both have legal definitions. The term 'refugee' denotes someone who, 'owing to a well-founded fear of being persecuted for reasons of race, religion, nationality, membership of a particular social group or political opinion', has fled their home country and is unable to return (UN Convention 1951, as amended by UN Protocol Relating to the Status of Refugees 1967, cited in Rutter, 2003, p. 4). The term 'asylum seeker' denotes someone who has fled from their own country and is seeking refugee status in a new country (Rutter, 2003, p. 4).

The concept of condensation symbols is very helpful at this point to this discussion of terminology. Developed in political science and media studies (Edelman, 1964; Graber, 1976), the concept identifies the power of words to come to symbolise and concentrate multiple meanings and to trigger strong, emotional responses. Words, therefore, can become a form of short-hand, and as such are particularly potent when used by politicians and the media to arouse or appease mass audiences. The terms 'refugee' and 'asylum seeker' have become powerful condensation symbols that encompass a number of public discourses. A sympathetic reading of the words identifies such people as victims who require support, shelter and sustenance, and prompts discourse around the rights of the victim and the responsibilities of humanity to respond to those in need. However, the terms are also open to unsympathetic interpretations and link to discourses around racial prejudice, the role and funding of the welfare state, globalisation and the existence (or not) of society.

> Further discussion of these interpretations can be found in Chapter 3, The Politics of Childhood, and Chapter 4, The Social Divisions of Childhood.

It is these discourses, and the negative concepts they contain, that have come to dominate and dictate the commonly held public 'image' of these groups of people. This image is a pernicious stereotype; in fact the Association of Chief Police Officers and research by the London Mayor have pointed to 'links between negative media reporting, increased community tensions, and hostility and violence aimed at asylum seekers' (Refugee Council, 2004, p. 3).

Refugee children in England

The Department for Education and Skills has no clear figures for the number of refugee children in English schools and relies instead on estimates from the Refugee Council. These estimates put the number of refugee children in 2005 at 82,000. Of this number, 62,000 live in Greater London (DfES, 2005e).

Refugee children in England are a diverse group. They have different religious, ethnic and class origins and they come to this country at different ages, from different countries, by different means, having had different experiences. They come from all over the world: from current war zones, from areas with political instability and with ethnic/religious/class conflict, from areas under economic and environmental stress. The majority of current refugees come from Africa and Asia, though in the 1990s considerable numbers also came from South America and from within Europe. They have had a range of experiences which include having witnessed violence, combat and murder. Some have had family members and friends killed, have themselves been injured or have undergone arrest, detention and torture (Rutter, 1994; Ofsted, 2003). Some have been separated from family; the Refugee Council estimates that there were over 6000 unaccompanied children seeking asylum in England in 2005 (DfES, 2005).

Refugee children may have spent time in refugee camps living under extremely difficult circumstances. Camps are often located in areas that are still at risk of attack and segregated from the local population on marginal land. Camps are characterised by overcrowding, a lack of healthy food and safe water, poor sanitation and a lack of play and recreational facilities. People in them have no control over basic aspects of their lives and have no idea how long their ordeal will last. They live under immense and chronic stress and in an atmosphere of conflict and fear. Violence and rape are commonplace.

Flight from persecution is again a stressful experience. It is not always planned and is physically and emotionally arduous. There is constant fear of discovery and asylum seekers often have little or no choice in their destination. Finally, on arrival in England asylum seekers are subject to detention by the immigration authorities. They are interviewed and fingerprinted (including children), issued with identity documentation and, in increasing number of cases, may be placed in a secure detention centre.

Legislation and the asylum process

Asylum seekers and refugees have been the subject of large amounts of legislation over the past 20 years. Since the early 1990s this legislation has been particularly focused on deterrent and containment policies. The result has been ever-tightening restrictions on the rights of asylum seekers with consequent implications for the quality of life of their children. Access to housing has been progressively curtailed, excluding asylum seekers from mainstream, local authority housing, moving them into the social housing and private sectors with families living in overcrowded bed and breakfast accommodation.

> Chapter 4, The Social Divisions of Childhood, and Chapter 13, Children's Experience of Community Regeneration, explain more about the effects of this kind of environment.

The intended culmination of this was the Nationality, Immigration and Asylum Act 2002. Outlined in the Act was the setting-up of three levels of centres for the processing, accommodation and removal of asylum seekers: Initial accommodation centres, detention centres and removal centres. Initial accommodation centres were to provide facilities for induction briefings, health screening and production of biometric identity cards for asylum seekers. Detention centres would house asylum seekers (including children) awaiting removal to their home country or a designated 'safe third country'. In the middle, accommodation centres would house asylum seekers awaiting the outcomes of their applications. The Act states that 'a child who is a resident of an Accommodation Centre may not be admitted to a maintained school or

a maintained nursery' (HMSO, 2002, s. 36(2)). Instead, children were to be educated in the accommodation centres rather than (to quote the then Home Secretary, David Blunkett) 'swamping' local schools (BBC, 2002). The Refugee Council argued that this set 'a dangerous precedent' and that withdrawing children from mainstream education provision was 'discriminatory' (Refugee Council, 2002, p. 18).

In June 2005, following protests at the proposed sites of a number of proposed accommodation centres (most notably at Bicester in Oxfordshire), the Home Office minister Tony McNulty quietly announced that the government would not proceed with plans to develop accommodation centres (Immigration and Nationality Directorate, 2005). However, initial accommodation centres and detention centres are still in use and more are proposed. Detention and removal centres routinely include children amongst their detainees, despite concerns voiced by numerous politicians, churches and non-governmental organisations. Indeed, this criticism extends even to other branches of government. For example, HM Inspectorate of Education has reported that facilities for children in one detention centre (Dungavel in Scotland) are 'unsatisfactory' and HM Inspector of Prisons has called for the cessation of the long-term detention of children (BBC, 2003).

Educating refugee children: a teacher's perspective

My first experience teaching refugees was in the early 1990s. I trained to teach English as a foreign language to adults and the practical element of the course involved providing free English lessons for adult refugees. A key turning point came when I was asked to teach the use of the future tense. How could I ask people for whom the future was so uncertain to discuss the future for 20 minutes and then move on to another area of the curriculum as though nothing of significance had happened? My eventual choice of activity was for pairs of students to write and then read out a horoscope for a chosen star sign for the coming week. This offered opportunities to practice the language required without asking anyone to look too far ahead or to reflect on their own genuine future. The activity turned out to be one that everybody understood and responded positively to, producing much laughter and silliness as well as productive use of the future tense. I considered the lesson to be a success, although my tutor did not. She could not understand why I did not ask the students to produce a horoscope for the coming year as this would have emphasised the concept of discussing 'future' events. My argument was, and remains, that, as a teacher, I had felt it more important to consider the personal circumstances of my students and the potential emotional impact of the activity. The curriculum had to respect and accommodate the needs of the individual. My tutor remained unconvinced. This episode made me understand the power and responsibility of being a teacher; it also made me, more than ever, want to become one.

Since training as a primary teacher, I have taught several refugee children in three local education authorities in England. The children ranged in age from 3 to 6. For some, my class was their very first experience of school; for others it was their first experience of a new school in a new country.

With all of these children my first task was to connect emotionally with them. To teach someone is to establish a relationship with them, a relationship involving trust, dialogue and sharing. Any lesson is a shared emotional experience, not just an educative episode. However, when a child and their family have been traumatised establishing trust can be difficult. Not knowing what each child has witnessed and experienced makes it easy to accidentally trigger disturbing memories or even flashbacks and the school day is full of noises, activities and smells that can evoke them. At the sound of a car backfiring, I have seen a child dive under a table, taking half an hour to be coaxed back. On another occasion, the same child seemed to be having difficulty getting changed for a PE lesson and looked very embarrassed. Not sure whether this was because he had never had a PE lesson before, I moved him to a quieter part of the classroom and began to help him undress only to find that his body was literally covered in shrapnel marks. This presented the dilemma of how to respond. Do I ignore them, tacitly verifying his shame and embarrassment? Do I comment (in a language he does not yet understand) violating his privacy?

Teaching children from refugee families often involves having to make decisions and take actions that a teacher does not normally have to consider. Maslow's hierarchy of need is of particular relevance in that, in order to reach a place where teachers can tend to the educative needs of the child, they first have to attend to their basic and emotional needs. Dilemmas can present themselves in the simplest of events. For example, as they most often arrive in this country with very little, families are often given clothing by charities. For some this will be their first experience of wearing Western-style clothing. On one occasion, a 6-year-old boy came to school wearing a pair of white ankle socks with a lace ruffle around the top. He was clearly embarrassed and was constantly attempting to tuck them into his track suit bottoms. It was his second week in school and he was desperate to be the same as everyone else and to make friends, particularly with other boys in the class. Wearing those socks had the potential to be the sort of defining event that would label him as different in the eyes of other children. I have to confess that, despite my dislike of gender stereotyping, I 'accidentally' spilled water on the socks, took them off to dry them and replaced them with boys' socks from the school supplies before the other children arrived in class.

If you want to know who a child is, and how they feel about themselves, watch them in the playground. This is a space where the need for adult intervention is minimal and physical play becomes a language in its own right. I found it fascinating to watch refugee children blossom in the playground. They tended to start either as uncertain observers or as hostile and even aggressive participants. Long before they had become confidently vocal inside the classroom, they seemed to have found a successful

> Chapter 12, Services to Children's Play, will give you a deeper understanding of the importance of this kind of play.

Maslow was a humanistic psychologist who argued that basic human needs (such as hunger) must be met before more sophisticated needs can be addressed. He developed a hierarchy of needs; at the base are physiological needs, then concerns such as safety; belongingness and love; self-esteem; cognitive needs (the need to know and understand), aesthetic needs and ultimately self-fulfilment (self-actualisation). (Hilgard, Atkinson and Atkinson, 1979).

way of negotiating life in the playground, losing their inhibitions and becoming verbally expressive and exuberant. The task for me therefore became how to harness this feeling and bring it into the classroom.

A key tool I discovered was music. When teaching a nursery class, I observed that two refugee children (from different parts of the world) were often drawn to the listening centre where they could select music tapes to listen to. I was unsure whether they were attracted to the opportunity to close themselves off from the world by putting on headphones or to the actual music itself. Either way, by sitting with headphones on, they were cut off from interaction with other children and at risk of becoming isolated. I decided to try playing the music out loud, as a background to the everyday experiences in the nursery. All of the children loved the music and would dance and sing as they played. The two refugee children joined in the dancing vigorously (indeed, it was the first time I saw a smile on the boy's face inside the classroom) and made the same connections (eye contact and laughing) that I had seen in the playground. They sang along with everyone else (their attempts at deciphering song lyrics were no worse than anyone else's) and discussed their favourite songs with their peers. These discussions continued into other areas of play. From then on, music was an integral part of my practice.

For the refugee child in a class, the trauma of being a refugee is ongoing. They may be affected by their own memories of the events that precipitated their flight. In addition, living with traumatised, stressed and often depressed adults will also impact on them. In such a situation, it is vital to establish communication and partnership with parents. Without wanting to pry, the more you know about the home and family circumstances, the more you understand the child and his or her behaviour and reactions.

This was the case for a 3-year-old girl I taught. Let's call her Mia. I conducted a home visit before Mia started nursery. I was shown into the tiny studio flat where she lived with her father and her heavily pregnant mother. Their entire flat was the size of my living room. The parents were just like all parents, very excited at the prospect of their first-born child starting school. I was sat down in the only chair in the flat, Mia was placed on my knee and the parents asked if they could take a photograph to record their little girl starting school. The juxtaposition of such normality in such strained circumstances was extremely poignant.

Mia quickly settled into nursery. Her Mum brought her to school every day and stayed with her until she had become happy and confident with adults and children alike. However, some months later Mia's behaviour suddenly changed. She became anxious and disengaged and stopped eating during snack time. At that point I spoke to Mia's mum. She confided that Mia's father was suffering from severe depression and that this was possibly affecting Mia. A week later, Mia's father came to pick her up from school. He had lost a great deal of weight since the initial home visit and was clearly very ill. Mia, it seemed had been echoing his behaviour and symptoms. I used the opportunity to invite Mia's father to spend some time in nursery with his daughter. He began to do this regularly and it did seem to help both him and Mia.

Normality and crisis

Teaching these children and connecting with their families taught me one thing above all others: refugees are ordinary people to whom extraordinary things have happened. Consequently, they have the same hopes, dreams and issues as everyone else, but with the added burden of trauma and dislocation from the familiar context in which they had expected to be living their lives.

It is important to note that within the population of children from refugee families, we should expect to find the same range of diversity that we would find in any other child population. There will be gifted and talented children, children with pre-existing learning difficulties, children with physical difficulties, children with speech and language difficulties and so on. Overlaying all of this, however, will be the results of the emotional trauma of being uprooted from their countries of origin, often in violent circumstances. Schools must attend to addressing these emotional needs, but must also ensure that, as with any other child, the full range of educational needs of each child is recognised and addressed.

In addition to the traumas undergone in their home countries, these children will also be living in an ongoing crisis situation in this country. Many have come from secure, even privileged socio-economic backgrounds, and are used to a high standard of living. They will now be living in poverty, often in extremely poor housing among populations that can be hostile towards them because of their refugee status and their ethnicity. The adults in the family will also be coping with their own personal trauma and loss, while trying to provide comfort for their children. Adult family members will also have to cope with the frustration of being denied the right to work or to undertake vocational training (Refugee Council, 2002, p. 4). They will be dealing with this complex and devastating situation without the extended support networks of family, community and language that existed in their homelands. Furthermore, asylum-seeker families will be living with the tension of uncertainty over the success or otherwise of their application for refuge.

The removal of the presumption that all destitute asylum seekers should receive support from the National Asylum Support Service (NASS) (Refugee Council, 2002, p. 16) means that some refugee families who have been granted leave to remain in the country take in other asylum-seeker families who would otherwise end up on the street.

> See Chapter 4, The Social Divisions of Childhood, for further discussion of racism.

The children of these joint households are therefore living under particularly cramped conditions.

In the rest of this chapter, the term refugees will be used to refer to people who have or are seeking refugee status. The political distinction between asylum seekers and refugees is not appropriate to this discussion and it could be argued that these distinctions are often unhelpful, particularly in relation to the education of children.

Refugees stand out. They are often visible minorities and they speak other languages (or speak English with an accent). They may wear non-Western clothing and may have a non-Christian religion. Furthermore, the public and media perception of refugees as scapegoats and 'scroungers' has made them targets. Refugee children and their families are often victims of overt racism both outside and inside school. They are usually housed within poor, disenfranchised communities at the margins of society where racist abuse and violence

are more likely to be aspects of everyday life. This has been further exacerbated by the recent policy of dispersal of refugees to towns and cities away from London. London has established ethnic communities from all over the world that can often support refugees and those working with them; this is not the case in some of the new areas that now are receiving refugees.

Educating children from refugee families: good practice

The Office for Standards in Education (Ofsted, 2003) reported on the education of refugee children in 2003. Their study (based on evidence from 37 schools in 11 local education authorities) identified a range of difficulties encountered by schools in meeting their needs and those of their families. These included:

- supporting children and families going through admission procedures (particularly in schools not used to significant pupil mobility);
- identifying and supporting children suffering severe psychological distress and trauma;
- developing expertise in supporting pupils new to English;
- coordinating with other agencies involved in supporting asylum-seeker families.

On the positive side, the report found that many refugee children made good progress due to their own determination and to the strong support they received from parents, though this also highlights the extra disadvantages experienced by unaccompanied child refugees (Wade, Mitchell and Bayliss, 2005). It also found that teaching of refugee children is most effective where teachers obtain advice, training and teaching support from staff funded by the Ethnic Minority Achievement Grant (EMAG).

The study's recommendations for schools included:

- ensuring that refugee children are admitted on days when EMAG staff are available in school to support the children, families and teaching staff;
- making flexible admissions arrangements – for example, phasing from part-time to full-time, placing children with siblings or placing them with other speakers of their home language;

- making links with local ethnic minority and refugee communities for language and cultural support for children and for parents (support that can continue outside of school premises and school hours);

- making links with agencies that can provide language assistance – for example, local colleges and universities and local hospitals;

- carrying out initial language-needs assessments to support effective planning and teaching of children new to English and those who are more advanced learners;

- selecting teaching strategies and resources that support children's language needs but provide appropriate cognitive challenge;

- celebrating diversity and incorporating home languages into classroom practice;

- using whole-school projects to promote inclusion and understanding;

- working with the local authority and other involved agencies to clarify roles, share information and streamline the response to the needs of the children and their families.

Good practice in educating refugee children is proactive rather than merely reactive. However, prior to the arrival of the first refugee family, many schools have never practically or philosophically considered how to respond. It is often only when a child actually arrives at the school that the school (or even just the teacher in isolation) begins to think about how to engage with, and meet the needs of, the child in question. Without previous experience of refugee families, schools can find themselves with little or no knowledge about possible sources of support for child or teacher.

In my experience of working with refugee children, this was almost invariably the case. Schools received very scant information to begin with and what was passed on to the class teacher may be more meagre still. In my experience, head teachers passed on the details only verbally and this often lacked basic information such as the home language and religion of the child. In addition, there was often little or no lead-in time; the child would be starting school within one or two days.

All of this made organising language support extremely difficult.

The Early Years curriculum, with its room for emergent learning outcomes rather than prescribed, pre-ordained learning objectives, is particularly well suited to the above. Time, space and respect for the child as an individual and as a constructor of knowledge offers opportunities for the members of the Early Years team to observe and work alongside the child, often on a one-to-one basis. The prevalence of practical, play-based experiences and the opportunity for children to choose their own activities are also well suited to the needs of refugee children.

By contrast, teachers in Key Stage 1 and above of the National Curriculum are constrained by a curriculum heavily loaded with content and increasingly abstract concepts and by teaching practices that emphasise whole-class teaching and minimise space for play. Availability of support from other adults, therefore, becomes crucial to promoting the active engagement of refugee children. However, this is a whole-school staffing issue, in a system that already has considerable demands placed on finite resources.

See Chapter 6, Education: Service or System?

On final reflection, the key to good practice in educating refugee children is the key to all good practice in educating any child.

- Get to know the child: personality, interests, circumstances.

- Develop a relationship with the family built on dialogue.

- Look for patterns of behaviour: progress, plateaus and dips.

- Find out what inspires each child.

The difference lies in how much more support and effort it may require to achieve. In an education system that is built on the duty to promote equality of opportunity and social responsibility, this should be regarded as simply another aspect of a commitment to inclusion. From personal experience, the opportunity to educate refugee children and to support their families is a deeply enriching one.

Reflective Activity 17.1

A refugee family's experience

Aisha is 25 years old. With her husband and two small children she escaped a violent regime in her home country after they witnessed the murders of other members of their family. The family are seeking asylum in the UK and are waiting to hear if they have been awarded refugee status. In the meantime they have been moved to a small town in northern England and are living in a small, damp flat. Aisha's husband Ahmed is suffering from post-traumatic stress causing depression and sleep-walking. Her baby Ari is only 3 months old. He is well but failing to put on weight at the expected rate.

Aisha's 5-year-old daughter, Mona, is in a reception class in the local school. The school has only recently begun receiving children from refugee families. The family speak no English and no one in the school speaks their home language. Mona had attended pre-school in her home country and had been a very bright, outgoing and confident child who was academically gifted. She had made friends very easily and had always been excited to talk about school to her parents. Mona has been in school in the UK for 6 weeks now, but does not want to talk about school to her family when she gets home. When Aisha leaves Mona in the mornings she notices that Mona sits alone with a book away from the other children.

1   What might Aisha need from the school?

2   What difficulties might Mona's class teacher face in meeting Aisha's needs as a parent and how could the school support this class teacher?

3   What impact might meeting Aisha's needs as a parent have on her child Mona's experience of school?

Reflective Activity 17.2

Educational difficulties for refugee children

This chapter describes some of the difficulties that refugee children (including those seeking asylum) and their families experience when trying to access the education service in the UK. Part I identifies how children's rights to services are affected by the images we have of children and young people and the groups they belong to.

1   What political and economic reasons might there have been for the government to have suggested the use of accommodation centres? Chapter 3 will help you to think about this.

2   What kind of images of asylum-seeking families might be behind the attitudes that have created such centres described in this chapter? Chapters 4 and 5 will help you to identify some of these images.

3   How does this differ from the picture of children that comes through this account of a teacher's relationship with the children she taught? Chapters 4 and 5 will help you to think about these images.

Annotated reading

Newcastle City Council (2004) *Refugee and Asylum Seekers Information Booklet and Directory for Schools*, Newcastle: Newcastle City Council, Available at: <http://www.qca.org.uk/downloads/cs_newcastle_refugee_sylum_seekers.pdf>

As refugees have been dispersed from London and the South-east to reception areas across the provincial towns and cities of England, Wales and Scotland, guides such as this have been created to inform and educate the professionals who will be providing key services for refugee children and their families. The Newcastle booklet and directory is a useful example of the kind of information that is needed and of the kinds of services that have been developed to respond to the dispersal programme.

Ofsted (2003) *The Education of Asylum-seeker Pupils*, London: Ofsted

After surveying 37 schools in 11 local authorities across England, Ofsted produced this report that examines the challenges and opportunities encountered by schools in educating and supporting refugee children. The report covers nursery to secondary education and features vignettes of practice observed by Ofsted inspectors, as well as testimonies from a refugee child and its mother, that help to illuminate the issues faced and the strategies developed to address them.

Rutter, J. (2006) *Refugee Children in the UK*, Buckingham: Open University Press

This up-to-date book explores asylum migration as a phenomenon and examines how migration and the highly emotive debates around it impact on policy and practice in a range of relevant areas. Within this framework, Rutter investigates, using a series of case studies, the impact that all of this has on the lives and education of young refugee children in the UK. It is a compelling and valuable read that puts the experiences of children at the heart of good practice for all professions involved in supporting refugee children and their families.

The Venture: Case Study of an Adventure Playground

FRASER BROWN, WITH CONTRIBUTIONS
FROM MALCOLM KING AND BEN TAWIL

An abridged version of the full case study published by PlayWales in May 2007.

We don't stop playing because we grow old; we grow old because we stop playing.

(attributed to George Bernard Shaw)

Introduction

The Venture is an adventure playground sited in the middle of one of the most deprived estates in Wales, Caia Park in Wrexham. While hundreds of open access play projects have come and gone during the last twenty-nine years, The Venture has moved from strength to strength, and is now one of the most respected projects of its type anywhere in the UK. It now employs around thirty staff, and has an annual turnover of approximately £450,000. The Venture has been used as the model for the programme of integrated children's centres in Wales, wherein one of the four key aspects is open access play (Welsh Assembly, 2002). A similar process has been adopted in Scotland. Recently the Secretary of State for Wales, Peter Hain,

described The Venture as 'one of the best in the country, if not in Europe' (St Co Deb, 2003).

How has this project managed to survive, and even expand, where so many others have failed? Perhaps the answer to that question will throw light on the minefield of government funding and help other projects in their quest for survival. The following case study looks at the history of The Venture, mainly through the eyes of one of its founders (Malcolm King), and later one of its recent playworkers (Ben Tawil). By exploring its history, the political battles and the creative manipulation of funding streams, it is possible to challenge the notion that open access play provision has inevitably been killed off by short-sighted fixed-term funding and/or our obsession with safety. It is also important to spell out the core philosophies that have informed

The Venture's practice for the last twenty-nine years. The Venture's success is not only the result of one individual's skill at overcoming political and financial obstacles, although that is clearly part of the story. It is also the result of the project's firm and ongoing commitment to the traditional values of playwork.

The Venture was started by Malcolm King and others on 31 July 1978. Malcolm remembers that first day with great affection. He was not entirely sure what to do, but his colleague Marten Kuiper, who had previous experience of adventure play from his time in Cardiff, suggested they light a fire. Children started to appear, drawn to the flames in primeval confirmation of what Hughes (2001) calls the need for recapitulative play.

> 'What's happening mate? What are you up to?'
>
> 'We're starting an adventure playground.'
>
> 'What's one of them?'
>
> 'Come and see!'

They were not sure what to expect, but understood the potential benefits of making connections with these disaffected youngsters. They understood in 1978 what Hughes (2001) and Brown (2003) have written about more recently: that in the adventure play setting strong relationships between adult and child are not just possible, but inevitable. If they could form such relationships with these youngsters, they might be able to help them.

Starting The Venture

In 1978 Malcolm King was in charge of the Intermediate Treatment (Juvenile Justice) programme for Wrexham. IT was the forerunner of today's Youth Offending Programme. The aim of IT programmes was to keep youngsters in their communities, rather than locking them up. IT was specifically targeted at young people who were thought to be at risk of offending or reoffending. Fifty per cent of the relevant target group came from the Caia Park estate, even though it

Chapter 9, Children Who Offend, discusses this in more detail.

only made up around 6 per cent of the total population of the area. A quick survey showed that these youngsters had nothing to do in their spare time. With strong support from Paul Eyre and Tony Chilton, the NPFA's play advisers, King suggested an adventure playground to the IT liaison committee. The following quote explains what adventure play is all about,

> A good adventure playground empowers its users by offering freedom of choice in a stimulating and empathetic setting, with the result that children constantly create and recreate their own play environment.   (Brown, 2003, p. 59)

Not only would that offer a suitable setting for working with youngsters who had been referred by Social Services, but an adventure playground might also help their younger brothers and sisters by 'heading them off at the pass' before they got into trouble. The committee was especially attracted to the preventative aspects of the adventure play approach. However, council officials wanted to delay starting the project for a year, because there were said to be 'difficulties in the planning process'.

That was deeply problematic because King was already committed to starting an adventure playground by the summer. What could be done? King formed a steering group, recruiting some very influential people, including the local councillor Agnes McConville, who also happened to be chair of the housing committee. He had already prepared the ground by exploring a series of basic lobbying questions: Who has influence over this decision? Who is for? Who is against? Who's in the middle ground, and how can we get them on our side? One very successful tactic was to report, 'We already have the support of . . .' People seemed to like the idea that they were joining a lobby that already had substantial support. Next, King put pressure on individual council officers. Eventually the Parks Officer gave a three-month licence which eventually led to full planning permission.

Two weeks before the official opening, the insurers suddenly said the adventure playground had to have a perimeter fence. However, there was no money for materials: there was no money full stop! King got hold of the personal telephone number of Jimmy McAlpine, the boss of one of the largest building firms in the UK, and a local resident. He told McAlpine about the project, and about the last-minute hitch, and finished with 'Only you can help.' McAlpine supplied two men and the fencing for free. Together with the young people, they erected the fence in time for the opening.

Agnes McConville became a committed lifetime supporter, and Jimmy McAlpine subsequently became The Venture's patron. It is very important to have such allies. It helps to build up friends and minimise enemies. It creates an impression of strength and solidity, and gives decision makers the impression that you're not going away. The Venture's committee has always included a mixture of local people, professionals, VIPs, and politicians.

During that first summer holiday most of the IT youngsters were involved, so King worked there for 90 per cent of his time. In theory there were about 25 IT ('wild bunch') youngsters (13- to 16-year-olds). Most were helping to run the adventure playground for the rest of the young people. That is still part of the philosophy of The Venture. Every Wednesday they all decided they needed some time off, ironically 'to get away from the kids', so they went back to the IT centre to wind down.

> You might like to compare this process with the case study in Chapter 14, The Swings and Roundabouts of Community Development.

Statutory funding streams and political battles

The Venture was initially funded by the Manpower Services Commission (MSC), one year at a time. That source of funding allowed the employment of four workers, and was renewed every year until the MSC was superseded by the Job Creation Programme. At the same time, the project was significantly supported by the Social Services IT Unit. IT support tailed off in 1982 after King left his job, although he stayed on as secretary to the management committee. From the earliest days he adopted a broad-based approach to funding, which meant the project's finances were always underpinned by more than one funding source. Thus, new funding sources were always in place before old sources dried up.

The success of these funding bids was based substantially on building contacts and thoroughness over the whole grant application process. It was important to make absolutely certain that the proposed outcomes of funding applications were tightly matched to the preferred criteria of the particular funding organisation. The borough council, who provided three staff and the building, were interested in play and leisure. Social Services, who provided two staff, were interested in addressing issues such as deprivation, social need and juvenile crime. The early Job Creation and STEP schemes, which provided four staff, were interested in improving the skills and employability of unemployed people.

At the end of each Urban Aid funding stream the council agreed a conversion to core funds. The second of these coincided with the first serious attempt to cut local authority budgets. The Venture was high on the list of proposed cuts. King had previously recruited key members of the council to The Venture's committee. He had developed lobbying notes on all the councillors, and proceeded to lobby each one in person. A children's letter-writing campaign was central to the process of fighting the cuts. The children were encouraged to write personal letters to individual councillors along The following lines: 'Dear Councillor . . . This is what The Venture means to me'. The children were not coached in any way, but nevertheless wrote amazingly powerful and emotional letters.

> 'My mum died when I was seven. The Venture staff look after me. If The Venture closed I'd never get over it.' Donna, age 11

> 'I love The Venture' cause it's not like school where I'm always in trouble. I am captain of The Venture's football team. All the staff are a good laugh and I help build structures. If The Venture closed none of us would have anything to do.' Wayne, age 14

> 'My dad's away in prison. Mum knows where I am. The staff make sure I'm all right. We'd have nowhere to go if The Venture closed.' Gary, age 9

Each councillor received about thirty-five letters. At the relevant council meeting, one councillor after another stood up and read their letters out. As a result the council abandoned any notion of cutting The Venture's budget, and agreed to make up the shortfall left at the end of the second Urban Aid grant. Some playworkers faced with this situation might have shied away from involving the children, but King argues that the children's letter-writing campaign is an example of good playwork in practice. The campaign actually empowered the children by providing a direct emotional connection between them and the decision makers. These tactics have worked twice with the county and once with the borough. There has never been another attempt by the council to cut The Venture's budget.

Non-statutory funding

During its life The Venture has received funding from hundreds of non-statutory organisations, big and small – everything from large grant-making trusts to young people's sponsorship schemes. A few examples will help to illustrate the wide diversity of support. In 1998 the National Lottery funded a three-year mentoring programme (worth around £50,000 pa). The multi-use games area has funding of £75,000 from the Sports Council for Wales. The Arts Council has made minor contributions (although they have not been approached very often). The Venture has had support from the European Social Fund, but found the whole process to be highly bureaucratic, so hardly worth the effort. Children in Need has helped each year from the early 1990s, mostly for camping, but in the last three years they have provided £25,000 to fund work with school-leavers. The Prince of Wales Committee (now Prince of Wales Trust) has given £30,000 over many years for environmental improvements. The Venture has also had numerous small grants from charitable trusts. For example the Charles Heywood Trust provided £10,000 to help kit out the building.

The Venture looks especially appealing to grant givers. It is safe and secure, but at the same time creative and innovative. That is a combination most grant givers are looking for.

Overall strategy

In the view of those involved with The Venture, the best strategy overall is to keep building around core funding from a local authority. Try to convince the local authority that you can do things they can't. They have to be persuaded that an adventure playground run by a voluntary organisation is a preferable option. There are lots of reasons why that is so. Scrounging is virtually impossible for a local authority project. Lots of grant-giving bodies only give to registered charities. Therefore voluntary organisations have access to a vast raft of money not normally available to local authorities. Also, in some people's minds, councils have a negative image. They make rules and punish you if you break them. Voluntary organisations do not. Therefore their ability to get through to the children is enhanced, and it becomes much easier to get the local community involved. Voluntary organisations have to live on their wits. This appeals to local people. They can get to places no one else can get to – especially on Sundays when everyone else tends to be closed. Finally, adventure playgrounds provide local people with a chance to get involved in something meaningful in their locality.

Reflections

It is often suggested that the complex benefits of play make it hard to secure financial commitment from potential funders as most statutory agencies are able to claim that an alternative agency is more suited to the task. For example, if an education authority is approached for funding they are likely to try to avoid their responsibility by suggesting another agency, such as leisure, community development, social services, housing, be approached. All those agencies are likely to adopt the same ploy. However, there is another way of looking at this, an altogether more optimistic view. Following this alternative line of argument it might be true to say that playwork is so complex that its outcomes cannot possibly be managed by a single local authority department, or funded from a single source. It necessarily has to be managed by an independent multi-faceted agency, and funded from a variety of sources. Taking this approach allows the grant applicant to focus the approach to each potential funding agency entirely on the aspect of their work that is most suited to that agency.

Chapter 12 explores the way in which the varied nature of children's play has led to confusion over responsibility for play provision. That in turn has produced an immense range of funding sources, mostly of a short-term nature. In most cases projects have struggled to survive much beyond the time limits of their funding. As a result some very good projects have fallen by the wayside. The Venture is a shining example of how that situation may be used to the benefit of a play project, rather than to its detriment. By following this approach The Venture has become probably the best-funded local children's project in the UK. Exactly how has that been possible? The following elements have proved to be important in the funding process:

- securing the involvement of people with influence gives the impression of strength and solidity;

- reliance on a single source of finance leaves a project vulnerable to changes in policy;

- the benefits of children's play are complex and varied – which means playwork is not easily pigeonholed – therefore playwork projects should expect to be funded from a number of different sources;

- having overlapping sources of finance presents an image of continuity to the outside world, and most importantly to the children;

- funding applications that are tightly matched to the preferred criteria of the particular funding organisation are more likely to be successful;

- targeting people who have influence in the decision-making process, and developing lobbying notes on those people support the application process;

- involving children so their points of view are highlighted not only empowers the children but is an effective way of influencing funding organisations, particularly if they meet them at the setting;

- decision makers need to be made aware of the benefits of the project and how the children would suffer if funds are not granted;

- using emotive arguments points out to grant givers the consequences of not giving financial support;

- adults had a childhood too, and may feel it ended too soon, so they may be naturally sympathetic to the need for children to play and open to emotional arguments;

- persistence in applications with adaptations in the light of feedback can eventually lead to success;

- organisations and individuals that give financial support need to be nurtured.

Philosophy and practice

Reliable funding is not the only factor underpinning The Venture's apparent stability. The project is sited in one of the most disadvantaged estates in Wales, and yet it has suffered little in the way of vandalism or theft. The core philosophy of the project, and the day-to-day practice of its staff are key factors in its continued survival. All those involved accept that play provides the best vehicle for a child's growth. Play is the child's fundamental tool for exploring the world, their environment, their interpersonal and physical relationships, and their sense of self. Give children a safe, staffed, open access play environment and they will not be able to resist the temptation to play. It is assumed at The Venture that children are biologically predisposed to playing and, once they start, their whole life is affected. The most fundamental lesson from practice is that play works.

For staff at The Venture, play is the base from which their relationship with the child and the community starts. Even today, when the project has become multi-faceted, play is still the core activity. Therefore all staff have to work on site for part of their working week. Everyone has to 'muck in', as well as run their own project. Justifying this to external funding agencies can sometimes create problems, and it is tempting to take refuge in simplistic justifications such as crime reduction, social inclusion, educational attainment. However, that would undervalue something that staff regard as the focus of their work. So what is it about the environment and culture of The Venture that has led to its continued success? What are the fundamental values and principles that underpin the work? They may be summarised as:

- adopting a child-centred approach;
- being non-judgemental, non-stigmatising;

- never giving up on anyone – always offering a second chance;

- being aware of, and trying to avoid, 'adulteration';

- employing home-grown staff;

- nurturing ownership by enabling children to create their own play space;

- targeting and responding to the most challenging children and young people;

- providing a broad range of engaging activities to counterbalance the ills in their lives;

- accepting that children's and young people's inclusion is of paramount importance;

- promoting positive reinforcement rather than criticism;

- reflective analytic practice.

Adopting a child-centred approach

A child-centred approach is essential, but a truly child-centred approach places incredible demands on the practitioner, and precipitates many a complex web of compromise and conflicts of interest – not only for the child-practitioner relationship, but also for the multi-professional staff team. A broad definition of play (and therefore of playwork) means the playworker has to get involved in the whole life of the child (Playboard, 1984). Stopping whatever you are doing, whenever you are doing it, and responding to a child's needs or wishes is a determining factor in that child's life and experience of the service. Often, many hours of considered consultation and planning will be thrown into disarray by new and/or revised demands from the children in attendance that day.

The Venture has always been open six days a week, including weekends. The playground closes at 7.45pm, but rarely do staff leave on time, often responding to a need that has only been revealed late in the day. Staff always respond to these needs. They are often some of the most serious and will simply not wait until tomorrow. Many of the staff's partners will testify to the adverse affect the application of the child-centred principle can have on their own personal relationships. The

child, their needs and wants, have to be at the centre of the service.

Being non-judgmental, non-stigmatising – always offering a second chance

One of the most challenging factors associated with adopting a child-centred approach is when a child continually engages in negative behaviour towards the staff or the other children. Although extremely infrequent compared with most projects of this type, The Venture and its staff have suffered acts of theft or vandalism from time to time. Staff have been threatened or assaulted both verbally and physically, and sometimes been the subject of unfounded accusations. Every child who has ever perpetrated any of these acts has eventually been allowed back to The Venture. Usually, they have also continued to receive the project's services during their time off the playground. The general attitude is that their need is greater than ours, pretty much no matter what. Often, careful inventive and creative reintegration strategies have been designed for the child (and sometimes for the worker), but no one has ever been permanently excluded. This is not the case in most children and young people's provisions.

Practice teaches that there must always be a second chance; there can be no bearing a grudge; a child's past must not be allowed to precede them; we must also be careful not to judge or stigmatise on the basis of evidence presented from external bodies. If there is to be any hope of working effectively with the most challenging children, then each child must be treated as an individual; each child must be taken at face value.

This is easier said than done – often barriers take years to break down. Practitioners and children alike have been heard to say 'Why do we carry on trying to work with them when they just keep destroying everything we do?' This is entirely understandable from people who are frustrated and upset, and often at their wits end, but many of these children have no one else. By sticking to the principles of being child-centred, non-judgemental and non-stigmatising, and always giving a second chance, The Venture encourages these children to keep coming back. Together in a gradually developing relationship, staff can begin to chip away at the damage they have endured. Through play and playful intervention, and sometimes by enabling access to specialist services, the project can facilitate growth, and sometimes enable recovery.

Being aware of, and trying to avoid, 'adulteration'

Adulteration comes in many forms: interfering in a child's play scenario; doing things for children rather than letting them do things for themselves; overly rigid programming; unnecessary planning; making decisions for them when they could easily make their own decisions; giving adult agendas primacy over those of the children; and many more (Else and Sturrock, 1998).

When a child is at play, or just at the play setting, they are in a special place where they feel in control of their environment and their relationship with it. They have personally chosen to be there, and what they do there depends on their wishes or needs at that particular time. What they are engaged in, more likely absorbed in, is real life: experiential learning. At any one time there is a strong likelihood that the child is experiencing complete absorption, as a matrix of varied but nonetheless connected information is processed by the brain at varying levels of understanding. The potential for growth and development in this scenario is immeasurable.

Hopefully, playworkers are sensitive to this, but even the best playworkers can get this wrong. Sometimes the playworker, recognising what is going on and feeling incredible joy that they have been able to provide such a stimulating environment, intervenes to impart the wisdom of their experience and some positive feedback to the child. In one fell swoop the possibility of untold personal growth and development is shattered. Of course, it would be impossible to get it right every time. The important thing is to be thinking at all times; to be considering your approach and reflecting both individually and as a team about the style and effect of any intervention.

The possibilities of adulteration in playwork practice are numerous, and difficult to spot. They pervade our body language, morals, social mores and personal value base. Our sensibilities can be affronted by some of the things children present to us, and our instinctive reactions can adulterate the child's play world. We have already alluded to the fact that playworkers cannot be expected to get it right all the time. However, this need not necessarily be a bad thing. The children who use The Venture know the staff are real people who have feelings, and strengths and weaknesses, and if these come to the fore on the odd occasion it may serve to make that member of staff slightly more human – and thus enhance the relationship with the child. Ironically, getting things wrong once in a while may be better than getting it right all the time. The important thing is, whenever possible, to give yourself the same status as the children. Their self-esteem is boosted immeasurably, and they begin to feel good about themselves (possibly for the first time).

Employing a mixture of outsiders and 'home-grown' staff

At any one time at least half of The Venture's staff are 'home-grown'. In most cases they are people who have grown up on the playground. They may have spent many thousands of hours as playground users prior to being employed. That gives them an invaluable insight into the way the children view the life of The Venture, and makes the bonding process that much easier. That is not to say there is no value in outsiders. Clearly the project has benefited greatly from employing staff with high-quality academic and professional qualifications, and/or particular specialist expertise. However, if the staff of The Venture were merely a group of 'do-gooders' parachuted in from outside of Caia Park, not only would they struggle to gain acceptance, they would also struggle to understand the rich nuances of the local culture.

Employing local people brings all manner of benefits. It helps cement the place of The Venture as a central pivot of the Caia Park community. Local people bring with them local knowledge, which sometimes helps the rest of the staff make sound decisions about what will be acceptable to the community. When children grow up to become staff, it helps to promote the concept of ownership. After all it would not make sense to tell the children 'we respect you', and 'this is your project' if it was obvious that there was no possibility of future involvement once they became adults. That would send out the message, 'We say we value you, but you're not good enough to work here,' which would obviously be totally unacceptable.

Nurturing ownership by enabling children to create their own play space

From an early age children can be observed creating their own space. Even babies arrange their favourite toys or objects in a way that pleases them. This phenomenon is often overlooked or misjudged as simply 'messing around', but in fact the child is creating an environment for themselves in which they feel comfortable. If the environment in which children operate does not provide a great enough range of experience, many will come nowhere near achieving their full potential. Some will become so disassociated from their immediate environment that they will cease to use it. Needless to say that sort of social alienation is not good for the individual child, nor is it good for society as a whole.

An adventure playground provides the most fulfilling and productive environment for children to grow in. In the words of Malcolm King, 'There is lots of space on The Venture for fifty different fantasies.' A self-built play space where children create and recreate their environment on a daily basis is the ideal vehicle both to nurture a sense of ownership, and to create a feeling of control (at the same time as facilitating and enabling their intrinsically motivated cognitive and affective development).

Visitors to the playground regularly exhibit signs of fear when considering self-build. However, The Venture is largely built by the children. It has taken over twenty-five years to reach its current state. For example, children and young people have dug holes, helped erect telegraph poles, cut floorboards and built all manner of structures. It is an organic process which develops at the children's own pace. If one day they don't want to work, then no work is carried out. For this reason building simple structures takes much longer than if adults had carried out the work – but, for the same

reason, when completed vandalism and/or abuse is virtually never a concern. By the same token neither is health and safety nor accident prevention. If children create their own play environment they know every trip or bump or fall hazard and calibrate themselves readily to the prevailing hazards, so that accidents are rare. Their awareness of health and safety matters is acute due to the level of inclusion they have encountered throughout the self-build process.

Visitors often ask how long it took to finish The Venture. To which the reply is 'It will never be finished.' It is the process that matters, not the finished product, and each new wave of children will change it again. It is this principle that creates a sense of belonging for the child and young person. The product is not the fixed structures, but the development of self that the child achieves from committing to a process of work from start to finish; from risking their ideas, vision, imagination and creativity; from participating in a social group; from the personal sense of achievement; and from practising and mastering the skills involved in a particular project.

Targeting and responding to the most challenging children and young people

The Venture had its foundations in a project that targeted and responded to the most challenging children and young people. Clearly, all children need play opportunities and play provision, but as with most interventionist treatments the neediest must be addressed first. If the most needy and deprived children are ignored by the play service provider, then those children will come to harbour the same resentful feelings about the provider, the service and other users as they do towards the rest of society (school, police, parents, social workers, etc.). There is also a strong likelihood that if the roughest, toughest young people are not included, they will vandalise and destroy the play provision. Treat them with respect and they are likely to defend the project from harm. The Venture stands by this principle to this day. There is a neat logic to the thinking: if we don't work with the most challenging youngsters we will not survive, and if we don't survive we can never help these youngsters again. The work is challenging, but through the development of strong and lasting relationships great headway can be made in a fairly short space of time.

Providing a broad range of engaging compensatory activities

Children at play need to connect with the elements: lighting fires; digging in the earth; rolling in the mud; feeling the wind on your face; engaging in water fights – the sort of activities Hughes (1996, 2003) calls recapitulative play. In the words of Malcolm King, 'Even though adventure playgrounds are scruffy places, they contain the essence of human existence.'

Children and young people have a diverse and broad range of interests and skills, fears and apprehensions. These cannot all be accommodated through play alone. Perhaps the child is so deprived of play experiences that they don't know how to play and therefore find the setting a bit intimidating. Perhaps The Venture's environment does not permit every type of activity the child is interested in, such as rock climbing, motorbike riding. In such cases The Venture will hire in experts or take the children to a specialist centre. It actually took three years to source a place where young people could be taken to ride motorbikes in relative safety, and with some educational gain.

Some of the children and young people who use The Venture are the most disadvantaged or at-risk children on the estate, the most socially excluded, the least loved – and the most feared! All too often these children are angry – angry at themselves, at society, at their parents – and this anger is evident in the way they play. Often they only engage in dangerous play, characterised by extreme risk-taking behaviour. These children are often the most challenging, and the staff are committed to finding a way into their lives. However, to engage these children fully, and to provide the extra services they require (education, training, advocacy, housing, therapeutic services), it is necessary to target services very specifically at them. This requires a more holistic approach to working with the child than is immediately obvious from a brief tour round the adventure playground.

Accepting that children's and young people's inclusion is of paramount importance

At The Venture the users are included in everything and in every way possible – from the planning of activities and play opportunities to applying for funding, and membership of the management committee; from the very basic acts of emptying litter bins and designing and building structures, to interviewing staff and giving guided tours to local and national dignitaries. The adventure playground cannot become a place that does things *to* children, or even be seen as a place that does things *for* them – it must be a place that they themselves feel they run, own and have similar rights to the staff. Although the staff have responsibility for the facility, it is important that they operate mostly as if they have the same status as the children. Obviously, there are limitations placed on that child–adult relationship by legislation, employment protection, etc. However, if a sense of inclusion is truly experienced by the child, then he or she will feel much more able to participate freely in any of the play opportunities that are open to them and will be able to immerse themselves in the play process free from the fear that there are other external forces which may at any time be used to stop them doing what they are doing. In the words of Malcolm King, 'This touches a part of the child that often no one has ever touched before.' He speaks of children 'immersing all their cells in pleasure'. They begin to feel differently about themselves, and so gain improved self-esteem.

When they don't have a sense of total inclusion, they will hold a bit of themselves back, which means they can't get the full benefit of the play process. A sense of inclusion also results in a heightened sense of responsibility. The children feel they are in charge of themselves. This means they consider and calculate their risk-taking behaviour more seriously. The Venture is substantially self-regulating as the players monitor and evaluate each others' behaviour raising the alarm if some behaviour seems inappropriate. Children are more likely to demonstrate their needs more openly because they feel trusted and that it is their space to do so.

Promoting positive reinforcement rather than criticism

Most playworkers know that positive reinforcement is the key to behaviour modification and a positive developmental process. However, more often than not the environments that youngsters find themselves in are riven with negativity. The child's play environment needs to be flexible with a range of different areas containing different possibilities (Brown, 2003). Access to equipment and tools should be free and easy; action should be self-motivated, without always having to seek consent. If the environment possesses these ingredients then the child can gain continued positive reinforcement without any practitioner intervention. This way a child can engage in an activity that they feel is theirs. They can take charge, and control the outcomes; their self-esteem will develop (Roberts, 1995). Even if they appear to be struggling it is *their* struggle. If things go wrong it is because the child chose to do it that way. Children are very resilient to failure, so long as it is a failure that they precipitated. For example, children learn to walk even though they fall over a lot at first. The damage comes when adults set tasks, and the child fails (Holt, 1967).

In addition to this, of course, is practitioner intervention. Every possible opportunity must be sought to provide the children and young people with positive reinforcement. Many of the children who attend The Venture will have been told regularly, elsewhere, how unsatisfactory they are in many different ways. They will overhear people talking about them in derogatory ways. They will feel all the negative subliminal messages that are fed to them by society as a whole. At The Venture it is the staff's job to observe constantly and find the tiniest thing for praise. Sometimes children spend all their non-Venture time being made to feel bad about themselves. So it is The Venture's job to provide as many hours as possible of unadulterated positive reinforcement, to try to find for that child some quality time to feel good about themselves.

Reflective Activity 18.1

Ensuring funding

Part of this project's success is down to the approach of targeting every funding stream that the government produces. This is possible because play has such wide-ranging benefits, not just for children, but for society as a whole. Clearly a lot of this depends on the social and political understanding of a single key character (Malcolm King). If Malcolm decided to leave The Venture would still remain.

1 How would you ensure a continued flow of money from south to the north?

2 What steps would you take to protect the children who use The Venture?

Reflective Activity 18.2

Linking this chapter with Part I

This chapter describes the success of an adventure playground and some of the factors that influenced this success. Chapters in Part I explain how services are influenced by the political and economic context from the top down and also by service users from the bottom up.

1 What kind of 'top down' economic and political factors influenced the success of The Venture? Chapter 3 will help you to identify these.

2 How did the views of children and young people influence the success of the project from the 'bottom up'? What sort of picture of children and young people does this involvement give? Chapters 2 and 4 will help you to identify the influences on the involvement of children and young people and help you to identify the pictures of children and young people that are conveyed in this chapter.

Annotated reading

Brown, F. (ed.) (2003) *Playwork: Theory and Practice*, Buckingham: Open University Press

Presents a range of theoretical and practical perspectives of playwork, with examples of playwork in practice, including adventure playgrounds, establishing play in a local authority, and a therapeutic playwork project with abandoned children in Romania.

Else, P. and Sturrock, G. (1998) 'The playground as therapeutic space: playwork as healing', in *Proceedings of the IPA/US Triennial National Conference: Play in a Changing Society: Research, Design, Application*, Colorado: IPA June, 1998

Hughes, B. (2001) *Evolutionary Playwork and Reflective Analytic Practice*, London: Routledge

Explores the complexities of children's play, and its meaning and purpose. Considers the fundamentals of evolutionary playwork, and looks at some key theoretical concepts underlying playwork.

Hughes, B. (2006) *Playtypes: Speculations and Possibilities*, London: London Centre for Playwork Education and Training

Analyses the playtypes as they appeared in the original 'Taxonomy of Playtypes', and suggests that there may be more playtypes than previously proposed.

Nicholson, S. (1971) 'The theory of loose parts', *Landscape Architecture Quarterly*, vol. 62, no. 1, October, pp. 30–34

A theory which suggests that 'loose', moveable parts in an environment will empower creativity, inventiveness and discovery.

Conclusion: Pulling the Threads Together and Furthering Understanding

What is the aim of Part IV?

Part IV focuses on the way that the book might be used as a learning resource and the way that knowledge and understanding of the shifting terrain of children's services and provision may be updated. Reflective activities are integrated in different chapters and Part IV focuses directly on other ways in which the book might be used and understanding of children's services and provision might be developed.

Guide to reading Part IV

Chapter 19 links back to themes and issues in the book, and looks to future directions in research and developing knowledge and understanding in the area of childhood service. It reviews the different types of

information and research that are available and how to go about finding them. The subjects within this book are continually on the political agenda and this leads to constant developments in policy and research. This chapter discusses the resources available to develop knowledge and understanding, and suggests how best to find and make use of them.

Chapter 20 links back to critical themes, areas of provision and case studies in the book. It introduces useful debates and dilemmas as a way of reading across the different contributing chapters. It provides some 'Focused Themes' and questions to help the reader review some of the ways in which the book can be used to see how themes connect. The chapter demonstrates the way that knowledge and understanding can be developed through drawing on different chapters to explore existing concepts, issues in this book and to pose new dilemmas.

Chapter 19 Searching and Researching Childhood: Making Full Use of Libraries

This chapter aims to demystify the academic library and the information searching and retrieval process. It is aimed at anybody who has read all or part of this book and wishes to find out more about the issues relating to children and childhood.

Chapter 20 Reading Between the Chapters

This chapter provides some 'Focused Themes' and questions to help you to review some of the ways in which the book can be used to see how themes connect, or how different chapters can offer material which can be looked at and studied to provide contrasting or complementary angles on an issue.

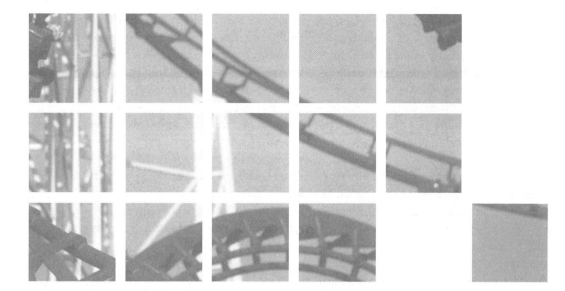

Chapter 19

Searching and Researching Childhood: Making Full Use of Libraries

GEORGINA SPENCER

'Sometimes you feel a bit stupid and you daren't say anything because you did feel that all the tutors here were really clever . . . For a lot of people they have said they've really been intimidated . . .'

(Diane)

The higher education culture, which positioned staff and students hierarchically in relation to knowledge production, reinforced the belief of some students that their knowledge and understanding had less validity.

(Moss, 2006, p. 165)

Introduction

This chapter aims to demystify the academic library and the information searching and retrieval process by using the following questions as key themes:

- How do we begin to access information, in particular academic research about childhood?

- How do we use book-based learning to explore theories related to childhood?

- How do we access journals to learn about recent research about childhood?

- How do we safely use the Internet to learn about debates and policies about children?

The chapter is aimed at anybody who has read all or part of this book and wishes to find out more about the issues relating to children and childhood. It will talk about the types of information that are available and how to go about finding them. Each section will deal with a different type of resource and give an example of when this resource might be used. Of course, it should be remembered that these are not mutually exclusive and one research question may need several different types of material in order to understand and answer it.

Learners as referred to in this chapter might be students, researchers, practitioners or anybody who wants to extend their knowledge in the field of childhood. The subject of children and their rights is consistently high on the political agenda (as can be seen in Chapter 3). This leads to constant changes in information and policy. Understanding the types of resources and how to find them is vital in this area due to these constant changes and developments.

As the quote at the beginning of the chapter illustrates, the first time a learner enters a higher education institution and then an academic library environment it can be a daunting experience. Learners often feel overwhelmed by the amount of resources and find it difficult to escape the feeling that everyone else knows exactly what they should be doing. These emotional uncertainties about their own ability and lack of confidence leave them feeling stupid and undeserving of help. Assuming they find the confidence to ask in the first place, learners will often start their enquiry with 'I know this is a stupid question but . . .', or 'You probably get asked this all the time . . .' Many learners do not recognise the increasing diversity of the student population and the readiness of library staff to deal with any question thrown at them. Feedback to surveys carried out in the library suggests that many students suffer a crisis leading them to ask how they got there and wonder how long it will be before their stupidity is recognised. These worries and anxieties are often amplified for learners studying more vocational courses such as those related to childhood and children.

Traditionally, libraries have been seen as physical buildings holding books that can be borrowed. Librarians were the custodians of the items held in libraries, and ensured order and quiet. Modern libraries are very different places. Although the physical building still exists, the introduction of electronic information means that many users need never visit the physical building but are still able to access the library resources from anywhere in the world using the Internet. Today, librarians are less custodians and more facilitators, ensuring easy access to the wealth of information that is available to their users.

Learners will use the library in different ways. Some will come to the library knowing exactly what information they want to find and how to find it. Some may know what they need but be unsure how to go about finding it. Others may have a question they need answering but have no idea what type of information they need or where to find it. The techniques in this chapter will allow the learner to start developing the skills they need to successfully use the academic library. Often the learner's time is precious and they need to go directly to what they need but practising these techniques will pay off. Learners will benefit from playing around with the process. When a child first visits a library their curiosity reaps rewards as they are not afraid to search and ask questions. Approaching the academic library with the same curiosity will lead to success and rewards.

How do we begin to access information, in particular academic research, about childhood?

One of the most important things a learner new to higher education can do is visit the library, either physically or virtually. Although many learners find this an initially daunting experience, an early visit to the library can allay many unfounded fears. Once they have taken the step of actually visiting then learners must not be afraid to ask questions. Despite the traditionally stern image of the librarian, library staff are there to help and point learners in the right direction. It is also well worth becoming familiar with the library's online resources. Libraries have an increasing number of resources available online which can be accessed from anywhere in the world. These range from electronic books, journals, statistics, market reports and government information to databases and information about the physical content of the library. Some of this is freely available to any member of the public while some is only accessible by members of the library. Electronic information only available through paid subscriptions is usually password protected and subject to strict licensing rules dictating who can access it. Knowing what is available can help the learner decide what information they need and how to find it for particular assignments or research.

When searching for resources there are several techniques that can be used to ensure learners find exactly what they need. Mastering these techniques will save countless frustrating hours and can be used with Internet search engines such as Google, as well as electronic library databases. These techniques can then be applied to the sections that follow when searching for journals, books and websites.

Keyword searching The error that many learners make when searching for resources is only using keywords in the question they are exploring. The belief, or hope, is often that a book or journal article has been written using the exact same words or, even better, the same question. It is important to think beyond these basic keywords in order to pull back all the relevant results. For example research into a topic relating to the so-called 'Third World' might also use 'underdeveloped countries', 'poor countries' or 'developing countries' as keywords.

The main concepts should be identified and then keywords listed for each one. For example the question might be 'Consider the impact of public opinion on UK government policy relating to children.' The main concepts in this question are 'public opinion' and 'UK government policy relating to children'.

The next step is to make a list of keywords for each concept which can be combined as a search. It may be necessary to use dictionaries or a thesaurus to find alternative synonyms. Try and think of broader as well as narrower terms, for example keywords for public opinion might include polls and voters.

Truncation Another technique that can be used to aid searching is truncation. This allows the user to cut down the number of searches they do while ensuring that all relevant information is retrieved. Different search tools may use different truncation symbols so it is always worth checking what is used before employing this technique. For example a search for 'child*' (in this case the truncation symbol is *) would retrieve search results including 'child', 'childhood', 'children', 'childlike', etc. Rather than having to do a search for each separate keyword, one search will retrieve all relevant results.

Wildcards As with truncation, wildcards allow us to cut down the number of searches that are needed.

Reflective Activity 19.1

Keyword searching I

1 Go to <www.google.co.uk> and search for: *our children are not our children.* What kind of results does this search retrieve? Are they what you might hope for?

2 Now repeat the search but enclose the words in quotation marks, 'our children are not our children'. Does this make a difference to the results? Which search retrieved the most relevant results?

Wildcards let the user solve the problem of variations of spelling. For example a search for 'organi*ation' would retrieve results containing both 'organisation' and 'organization'. Wildcards can be used for all words with alternative spellings such as 'globalisation', 'behaviour' and 'paediatric'.

Proximity searching This is a useful technique when searching for a phrase or name. Putting the keywords in quotation marks tells the database that these words must be found next to each other in the search results.

Stop words One of the reasons that the example above retrieves different results is that most of the words in the phrase are what are known as stop words. These are common words, often conjunctions, prepositions and articles that databases ignore as irrelevant when a search is entered. Examples of stop words are:

a, also, although, an, are, be, do, does, done, for, from, had, has, have, I, if, in, is, of, only, that, the, this, to, was, we, were, with, you

There are many more and unless the word is part of a phrase it is inadvisable to use them.

Boolean Logic Three little words that can make a huge difference to searches are AND, OR, NOT. They can be used to combine keywords and are known as Boolean Operators. These allow users to manipulate the search to be more precise and relevant.

AND logic This allows us to combine keywords and concepts, narrowing the search down to find the most specific results. As can be seen in the diagram below only documents containing the keywords child and poverty will be retrieved.

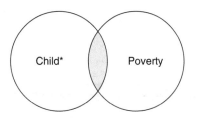

OR logic An OR search will broaden your search and allows inclusion of synonyms and other related terms.

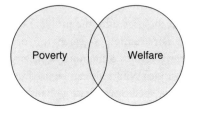

NOT logic Finally a NOT search will allow irrelevant terms to be eliminated from the search.

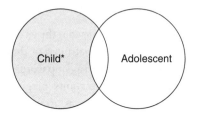

Date range Although it is not always possible using Internet search engines, many library databases will allow searches to be limited to a particular date range. It is useful to start searching the most recent information first, unless an historical perspective is sought. This means that when the learner finds they have found enough resources they also know they have the most recent.

Search tips

- Think about your search strategy before you begin.
- List all the search terms you might use.
- Don't dismiss the idea of using information from other disciplines as subject areas often overlap.

Reflective Activity 19.2

Keyword searching II: Applying the Techniques

Look at the following question:

Discuss the strengths and limitations of the different meanings and interpretations of children and childhood.

1   What are the main concepts in this question? Look back at the earlier concept example for help (p. 261).

2   Make a list of all the keywords that could be used to research this question. The word 'interpretation' could lead to a list of keywords including understanding, reading, explanation, analysis.

3   How might the techniques above be employed to ensure the most effective search possible? As mentioned earlier, the word 'child' is an excellent example of when truncation can be used.

- Work from the present to the past as this means when enough information has been found it will be the most recent.

- Note down all the references and where they were found.

We now move on to applying the learning from this section. All the chapters in this book deal with complex and overlapping meanings of the terms 'children' and 'childhood'. Chapter 5 in particular asks whose interpretation of childhood shapes services for children.

How do we use book-based learning to explore theories related to childhood?

As mentioned in the introduction, a first visit to a university library can be an intimidating experience for many learners. For this reason books are often a nice place to start as most visitors to a library expect it to be full of books. Books are the traditional resource of libraries. They are often the first point of call for the learner wishing to find more information out about a subject, in this case children's services. The Internet has in some ways replaced this traditional role, but many learners still find comfort in finding a book on their subject. In the modern library, books are still a main resource but not just those available on the shelf. Many university libraries now have access to web-based collections of books which can be accessed from anywhere with an Internet connection and a password.

The majority of libraries now have their full library catalogue available online. The catalogue is the best place to start investigating what books your library has to offer. Charles Ammi Cutter made the first explicit statement regarding the objectives of a bibliographic system (catalogue) in 1876 (Cutter, 1962). According to Cutter, those objectives were:

1 to enable a person to find a book of which either
   - the author,
   - the title, or
   - the subject
   is known

2 to show what the library has
   - by a given author
   - on a given subject
   - in a given kind of literature

3 to assist in the choice of a book
   - as to its edition
   - as to its character.

This gives some indication of how you might search the catalogue. Books can be found via author, title or general subject search.

Some learners find it difficult to know how to locate the book on the shelf from the information they find on the catalogue. The key to this is noting down the classmark (sometimes called shelfmark) from the catalogue. This will normally be a combination of letters and numbers indicating the location of the book in the library. Not all libraries use the same book classification system so it is best for learners to familiarise themselves with the library they are in. Some higher education libraries employ a colour coding system to indicate particular subject areas, which is useful for browsing the shelves to get a feel for what is available.

Why might a learner use a book? A good reason for using books is that it will be a complete work in one volume. This will usually include comprehensive information on the topic of the book. Learners should expect to gain a sense of scope, historical background and a thorough analysis of the issues. Alternatively a book may be a collection of essays with each chapter being written by different authors. All the chapters will be related somehow but will focus on a smaller aspect of the larger issue. Books are excellent places to gain an understanding of the wider theories and concepts behind a topic. Look at the references and bibliography in this book to see how books have supported the various chapters on children's services. The next section will look at journals which are useful for seeing the application of these theories.

Is the book academic enough? Sometimes learners can be concerned that they are not using the right type of information. It is always good to question resources and why they have been produced in the first place, but there are tricks for checking reliability. Books can be judged by the author and what his or her credentials are or what their reference list is like. Often the publisher can offer clues as to the type of book it is. For example, university presses generally publish scholarly works.

Academic textbooks may be very different from what learners have used previously: 'Academic texts could be intimidating . . . Suraya was shocked that the books in the library had no pictures. Her only previous experience of libraries was at school' (Moss, 2006, p. 162). This experience is quite normal for many learners. They feel there is an expectation that they will not only read a huge amount but also understand and digest it. It is important for learners to realise that academic reading is not easy and does take some practice but there are systems that can be used to make things easier. One such system is SQ3R which stands for survey, question, read, recall and review. There are other systems such as P2R and S-D4 (Wainwright, 2001), the learner should find the system that suits them best. SQ3R works as follows:

Survey Make sure that the book you have actually picked up is worth reading. When was it published? Some books may be too out of date or equally may provide an excellent historical perspective, make sure it is

Reflective Activity 19.3

Book searching

Consider the questions, 'Why are children poor?', 'How can this be overcome?'

Think about what type of books you might want to search the library catalogue for.

1 Would you need to look at books outside the field of children and childhood?

2 Would it be useful to look at books on social, economic and political theory?

Gabrielle Preston's *At Greatest Risk: The Children Most Likely to be Poor* might be a good starting point, as would Tony Novak's *Rich and Poor: The Growing Divide*. If you cannot find these books, don't worry!

3 Are there any other books in the library with the same classmark? The classmark of a book is subject specific so if the book you are looking for isn't available, check the other books nearby with the same number as they will cover the same subject area.

---

relevant for the purpose. Read the blurb on the back cover to gain an overview of what the book will cover, bearing in mind that this is the publisher's account (they want people to buy the book!). The contents page will also give a good indication of what can be expected. Be selective when choosing texts to read, time is precious so make judgements about what is important or not.

Question Start to formulate questions you would hope the book will answer based around the topic being researched. Think about how it fits in with what has already been read. Do you need to find out more about any particular aspects? Is the information useful?

Read Not everything needs to be read in depth. Some sections can be skimmed to get a feel for what is being said. Only read in more detail if you are sure the text is relevant. Constantly evaluate what is being read, does the argument make sense? What is the writer's perspective? Don't be afraid to question what you are reading, just because they have written a book doesn't make the argument right! It is also important to ensure understanding, if a word is difficult to understand visit the quick reference section of the library and borrow a dictionary. There are also many dictionaries available online.

Recall This part definitely takes practice. Making notes while reading can help but ensure it is the key points only and in your own words wherever possible. Remembering what you have read is important and

time spent making notes and recalling it will be well spent, unless you plan to read it all again.

Review This involves going back over what has already been done. Are there any more questions? Is there anything else worth reading in this book? Have the main points been recalled?

We now move on to applying the learning from this section. Chapters 3 and 4 both deal with quite complex theories.

How do we access journals to learn about recent research about children?

By the time learners arrive in higher education they will have had some experience of libraries. The level of the experience will vary tremendously as will the resulting satisfaction gained. It may have been visits to the public library or a school library. Whatever the experience, it is fair to say that most learners will have little or no experience at all of using journals. For many learners these mysterious volumes remain a puzzle throughout their time in HE and are seen as something they can probably get away without using. Unfortunately, this is not the case and learners will find it invaluable to gain an understanding early on of journals and how to search them.

So what are journals? Some libraries and literature will refer to them as periodicals (which includes newspapers) or serials but there is no difference. The dictionary definition of a journal is 'a serious magazine or newspaper which is published regularly, usually about a specialist subject: a medical/trade journal' (CUP, 2006). This means that journals can be published daily, weekly, quarterly, monthly and many other ways but as long as they are produced on a regular basis they are classified as a journal. There can be differences between titles but generally, as illustrated below, each journal issue is made up of several different articles. Each issue then builds to form a complete volume – usually each calendar year equals one volume.

Examples of journals in the area of children and childhood are:

- *Children & Society*
- *Childhood*
- *International Journal of Early Years Education*
- *Early Years: An International Journal of Research and Development*
- *Surestart: The Magazine for People Working with Children and Families*

The first four titles are what are known as peer-reviewed journals. This means that before an article is published the writer must send it to a group of experts in that field. They will review the article and decide whether it should be published in the journal. The aim is to ensure academic quality and ensures a reliable body of research and knowledge.

So why should you use a journal? It is in journal articles that the learner can read about the application of the theories learnt from books. Journals are excellent sources of up-to-date research as, compared to a book, journals can reach the shelves in a relatively short time. Books usually cover one particular theme or one perspective of a topic. Reading several journal articles on a topic related to children's services will expose the learner to a wider range of ideas and experiences. This gives an excellent overall grasp of the area being researched.

As each article may cover a different topic it would be time consuming to flick through every volume to find the most suitable articles. In order to shorten the time it takes to search for articles, abstracts and indexes are used. Originally these were print volumes but now most are available electronically as searchable databases. A university library will subscribe to these services according to the subjects taught and they will usually be password protected. The passwords ensure that only members of the university, and possibly particular exceptions, gain access to these very expensive resources. Some are very general:

- ASSIA (Applied Social Sciences Index and Abstracts)
- British Humanities Index
- Sociological Abstracts

while some are much more specialised:

- ERIC
- Physical Education Index
- PsychInfo

Abstracts and indexes list journal articles from journals in particular subject areas. This can be thousands of different journal titles. Printed abstracts and indexes are published as issues throughout the year and are usually bound into one volume at the end of the year. Electronic or web-based versions are updated on a regular basis. Using the services is a two-step process. First, the learner must search the database (using the techniques from section 1) to find articles of interest. Secondly, the learner must use the list of articles to find the full text either in print or electronically. It is useful for the learner to familiarise themselves with how journals are stored in their library. Are they kept alphabetically or by subject? Is there a separate section of the library where journals are stored? Does your library have access to a wide range of journals electronically?

If so, how do you access them? The most important thing is to ask: staff should always be around to help.

There are many different services available to search for journal articles and this chapter will mention only a few. This does not mean that others are not suitable; the choice of service used depends very much on the subject being researched. Many learners use the same service over and over again because they feel comfortable with the interface. This is fine, but remember that the perfect article may be out there and only retrievable via a different database. Don't be afraid to try something new. Good research takes time and practice.

It may not always be clear which service should be used to find information as there are a confusing number available. The library the learner is using should have information regarding the different services available. This should provide some guidance on which one to choose.

Reflective Activity 19.4

Journal searching

Consider the question:

Do the parents of a girl under 16 have the right to know if she is given advice on obtaining an abortion?

The first step would be to use the techniques discussed in the first part of this chapter. Think about the concepts being researched, make a list of keywords and consider if any of the other techniques can be applied. For example, can truncation or wildcards be applied to the keywords? How might the keywords be combined using Boolean Logic?

When the search strategy is clearly planned the search tool can be selected.

For this type of enquiry a database such as ChildData would be useful as it covers education, health and welfare of children and young people. It is provided by the National Children's Bureau and is a major source of information on children's issues with coverage going back to 1989. It would also be useful to research newspapers to find if any stories have been published recently on this topic. Databases such as Lexis Nexis Executive provide access to local, national and international newspapers.

We now move on to applying the learning from this section. The area explored in Chapter 2 is complex and changing. How might journal searching support our study of children's rights?

Here is an example of the type of articles that could be found. The following is a journal article found on ChildData.

HALL, A. (2006) Children's rights, parents' wishes and the State: the medical treatment of children. *Family Law,* vol. 36 (Apr) pp. 317–22. Abstract: Sue Axon, a mother of two teenage girls from Manchester, launched a High Court challenge against Department of Health guidance allowing young people under 16 to be given sexual health advice and treatment, including abortion and contraception, without their parents' knowledge. The High Court rejected Ms Axon's challenge. In his judgement, Mr Justice Silber said no parent had a right to know unless the child decided otherwise. He said that forcing a girl to tell her parents 'may lead her to make a decision that she later regrets or seek the assistance of an unofficial abortionist'. Hall reviews the Axon decision and reflects on what it says about the increasing social confusion over the modern role of the parent.

How do we stay safe searching the wider Web?

Bergman alludes to those oft-repeated estimates that scientific knowledge is doubling every three years, medical knowledge is doubling every eight years, biological knowledge is doubling every five years and the sum of all human knowledge today is just 1 percent of what it will be in the year 2050. (Ebisch, 2005)

The vast quantities of information on the Web often make it difficult to discern value. This is particularly true of websites relating to children's issues. These issues are so frequently high priority in the media that many websites publish opinions and information on the subject. Anyone can post information on the Web and this results in great variations in quality. No one controls, checks or filters most Web information, which means it is vitally important to understand how to evaluate it. It is often best to be suspicious of everything initially in order to be sure that it can be trusted. There are a series of questions that can be asked to evaluate a web page and decide if it contains suitable material.

The first thing to look at is the domain name of the URL or web address. This gives a clear indication of who has produced the site. Is it somebody's personal page? The URL may contain a personal name, for example jbarker or barker following a tilde (~), a per cent sign or the words 'users', 'members' or 'people'.

If the page is not a personal page then check to see who did create it. These will all give an indication of type of organisation produced the site:

- government sites: **.gov**
- educational sites: **.ac** (UK educational sites) or **.edu** (American/Australian educational sites)
- non-profit organisations: **.org**
- commercial sites: **.co** or **.com**

Every country has its own country code which is included in the URL:

- **.uk** = United Kingdom
- **.fr** = France
- **.au** = Australia
- **.ja** = Japan
- **.de** = Germany

The US has its own code (.us) but this is very rarely used. Often a URL that does not have a country code is usually from the US but this should not always be assumed to be the case.

The publisher of the page is also very important. The publisher is the person or agency operating the server computer from which the document is issued. The server is usually named in the first portion of the URL (between 'http://' and the first '/'), for example 'http://www.leedsmet.ac.uk/lis/lss'. The website should be constantly questioned, so have you ever heard of the publisher before? Does it correspond to the name of the site? Knowing the publisher of the page will then

also allow the reader to question their motives for creating the website. Is the publisher a private profit-making organisation? What might their motives be for publishing the page? What may at first appear to be independent research may have been published with profit in mind. The reader may well be viewed as a consumer and therefore a particular viewpoint will be communicated.

For many people the Internet is an opportunity to tell people about their favourite subject, or voice their opinions on a subject close to their heart. When reading a website, it is vital to think about why it was written in the first place. Always question why it was written and look beneath the rhetoric of the site. Remember the process that a peer-reviewed journal article goes through before publication (see pp. 264–6) and then think how easy it is for everyone to publish whatever they wish to on the Internet. Quality information certainly exists, but there are many pages that should not find their way into an academic reference list.

The most visible component of the Internet is the World Wide Web. Many learners do not realise that search engines do not search the entire web. The Online Computer Library Center stated that in 2002 there were over 8.5 million unique websites (OCLC, 2006). This is a huge amount for search engines to be able to search. Most search engines work by sending out Web crawlers (also known as spiders). The Web crawlers follow every link they see and the information on the page is analysed so it can be indexed according to particular words drawn from the page. This data is stored so that when a user enters a search term it can be matched against the website. Most search engines support Boolean searching and proximity searching. What makes a search engine successful is the relevance of the results it returns. Different search engines will use different techniques to rank the results and trial and error will help the learner find the one they like best. Metasearch engines are search engines which search several search engines at once, for example Dogpile.

Search engines also do not search what is known as the invisible or deep Web. This is composed of the contents of thousands of specialised searchable databases such as those mentioned earlier for searching for journal articles. Some search engines also exclude pages for policy reasons.

It is important to remember that often even pages that seem to be trustworthy actually are not. A good example of this is Wikipedia, which is a free online encyclopaedia <http://en.wikipedia.org/wiki/Wikipedia>. Although the clue is in the name (Wiki – meaning a website that any visitor can add to or edit), many people do not realise that anybody can contribute to Wikipedia. Many learners believe the information there is suitable for research. It is a very useful site and can give nice overviews of topics, perhaps as a starting point, but this does not mean the content is suitable to be used in a bibliography and should still be questioned.

Reflective Activity 19.5

Safer Web searching

As an example, a search for youth offending in the UK on a search engine like Google will bring up lots of results relating to anti-social behaviour. Below are two examples of results;

    <www.together.gov.uk>
    <http://www.thesleaze.co.uk/badneighbours.html>

1 Who has published these pages?

2 Would you trust the information?

3 When was the page published?

4 Repeat this search and have a look at two or three of the results. Would you use this information in an assignment or research paper?

Assess the quality of the information every time the Web is used. Remember, anyone can publish a website!

Conclusion

The most important thing to remember about libraries is that they are there to provide a service to their learners. Hopefully, this chapter has begun to demonstrate how to begin to make the best of that service when looking for information, ideas and research about children and childhood. All the resources mentioned in this chapter will be useful but none of them stand alone. Books are useful for an overview and background, while journal articles will offer the latest application of theory and research. Websites also offer a useful extra and large amounts of information is available online at any time of the day and night. Always remember to assess the quality of the information and question where it has come from. Learners will need to use a combination of these resources in order to complete assignments, research and fully understand the subject area.

Learners should make the most of their library service. Many academic libraries offer tours and workshops to familiarise their learners with the resources on offer. These may be tailored to the area of childhood. Academic libraries usually assign a professional librarian to each subject area. These subject librarians should have an excellent knowledge of their area so learners can make the most of their expertise. If the learner has any difficulties using the library or accessing resources it is useful to contact their subject librarian or help.

Chapter 20

Reading Between the Chapters

PHIL JONES

Introduction

The different sections of this book have considered children's services from a variety of perspectives. Part I provided ways of considering issues or debates which ranged across the various aspects of provision. Part II's chapters each identified an area or aspect of children's services and combined information with critical discussion about areas such as youth services or day care. Section III offered more in-depth case examples of aspects or specific experiences of services for children.

This chapter provides some 'Focused Themes' and questions to help you to review some of the ways in which the book can be used to see how themes connect, or how different chapters can offer material which can be looked at and studied to provide contrasting or complementary angles on an issue.

The Focused Themes are:

- How might the rights of disabled children and young people be recognised and progressed?

- How do poverty and inequality shape access to children's services?

- What underpins young people's social exclusion?

- How is access to children's services shaped by concepts of 'race' and 'racism'?

Each Focused Theme gives brief excerpts from chapters in this book. There are activities attached to each excerpt to help analyse the excerpt and to raise and develop issues which connect and contrast the material from the different chapters.

These can be used in themselves to consider the specific issues we identify, such as children's rights or inequality, but this chapter also demonstrates a way to work across the book. All the contributors to *Childhood: Services and Provision for Children* indicate useful cross-references between their chapters and other sections of this book. These can be used in the ways which this chapter demonstrates: to take material from different parts of the book and to combine it in order to compare and contrast ideas, issues and perspectives to deepen your familiarity with, or understanding of, related aspects of children's services.

The chosen themes reflect some of the central concerns running through this book. The first concerns children's rights. The book has considered debates and issues concerning children's rights in a number of arenas – education, protection and play, for example. The Focused Theme chooses a particular aspect of this area as a way of demonstrating how this crucial issue features in different chapters: the relationship between rights and disabled children. The second Focused Theme concerns poverty and inequality and highlights excerpts which show how different chapters look at the ways in which these areas must be considered as central to any discussion of children's services. The third looks at the different ways in which social exclusion can be understood and demonstrates how particular facets of the experiences of young people can be seen and compared to help understand the processes at work within exclusion. The fourth examines the concepts of race and racism, how these can be present in overt and covert ways within service provision for children. The excerpts show how the chapters in this book can be used to look at different understandings and explorations of such areas of children's experiences and to identify different responses to the same key issues of race and racism.

Focused Theme: How might the rights of disabled children and young people be recognised and progressed?

Chapter 2 excerpt: Childhood: Rights and Realities

If an individual has a right to something it places an obligation on others to ensure that that right is met. Sometimes this is a moral obligation: something that we feel we ought to do. Sometimes it is a legal obligation: something that we have to do by law. So, although we may say that someone has a right to food and shelter, unless there are legal imperatives that someone, usually the state, has to provide these, the safeguarding of that right will depend on the voluntary actions of others. (p. 8)

... when we talk about rights there is the expectation of entitlement to something; when we talk

about needs there is a sense of deficiency ... Within the context of rights and needs children are constrained by the social divisions across the societies in which they reside. Children may be construed as needy or entitled because of their social context, such as class, economic circumstances, gender or ethnic background. Within such a framework children can be differentiated and discriminated as being worthy of rights due to high familial status or unworthy due to perceived or actual deficiency. (pp. 8–9)

- Write a list of the rights that a child in the UK should have in your opinion.

- Discuss whether these are rights or needs.

- Do you think a child living in poverty might have less access to any of these rights than a child from a wealthy background living in a wealthy community? Which rights? Why or why not?

- Do you think a child or a young person with a learning disability might have less access to any of these rights than a child without a learning disability? Which rights? Why or why not?

This excerpt raises issues concerning the difference and relationship between rights and needs in relation to children. It's important, when considering most areas of a child's experience, to see how debates concerning rights feature. It can help to understand some of the power issues present, but not always immediately recognisable, in a child's experience of poverty or disability, for example. Power here can refer to the ways in which some groups or processes at work within society can exclude others. A key question running through many chapters in this book asks whether action or legislation defending the position of individuals or groups who are being excluded can reduce or address such exclusion. This might refer to the ways in which attitudes, policies and practices within schooling has served the 'majority' of pupils who are not disabled and has excluded children with disabilities from education. Such issues concerning, for example, the rights of all children to access to education can be connected to issues concerning social divisions as described in Chapter 3.

Chapter 4 excerpt: The Social Divisions of Childhood

Oliver (1990) has pointed out that the patronising or hostile treatment of disabled people in society comes from deeply embedded ideologies (ways of thinking) that disability is a personal tragedy and that individuals are 'afflicted' by disabilities. In this way society denies responsibility for the conditions in which disabled people live. Disabled children have been historically segregated and isolated in separate schools and institutions. Despite policies of inclusion espoused by government, practices of segregation and isolation still arise in mainstream settings which result in the less-favourable treatment of disabled children. Many mainstream schools lack the facilities needed to meet the inclusion of all pupils.

Laura Middleton discusses the way that, historically, disabled children have been 'screened out' of mainstream services. Screening is a process whereby able-bodied people removed disabled children from mainstream settings because it was considered better for society as a whole (Middleton, 1992). She considers this screening process in relation to birth, family acceptance, medical treatment; education; the market place; growing up and sexuality; acquiring skills; getting somewhere to live; and gaining employment. Although there has been progress in relation to the inclusion of disabled children in some mainstream services, children still face huge barriers as the case of Samuel demonstrates. (p. 47)

- What do you think 'policies of inclusion' might mean in relation to disabled people? What kinds of inclusion do you think it refers to?
- Identify how 'screening' might happen for a disabled person in relation to medical treatment, education, acquiring skills: you will find it useful to refer back to the case of Samuel in Reflective Activity 4.4 (p. 47)
- Look back at your list of rights you developed in response to the excerpt from Children's Rights and Realities. How might society exclude children and young people with disabilities from these rights? Think of two ways this can be changed.

In this excerpt ways of thinking and attitudes are linked to divisions in society and to the ways in which people become excluded through processes such as the one described as 'screening'. This is contrasted with the concept and practice of inclusion. The case of Samuel (Reflective Activity 4.4, p. 47) and the interviews created by Anna Gray in Chapter 16 can be compared and contrasted in relation to processes of exclusion and inclusion.

Chapter 16 excerpt: The Anna Rebecca Gray Interviews

Diane and Michael: **What kind of services do teenagers like, or like to have?**

Anna: . . . They like to go to school, to church. I have a college I go to with activities and stuff. I like climbing, Guides. The best was when we went camping and it was fun, it was unstressful, it was a quiet life in the countryside. We did canoeing and games. I was up two nights, abseiling and dinner. Guides was fun. I like walking out of doors. I like swimming; I can do lots of swimming and dinners.

Diane and Michael: **What effects do these services have on teenagers?**

Anna: At school I have a helper and she helps me with my therapy, my walking. I have a planner and stickers. I also go to choir, we sing. It's my hobby. I feel really happy, it makes me really happy. I do PE.

I'm a big fan of the Star group. I like reading and getting books out.

It's my business, meeting and talking with other people. I really really like other people. I like being in capable hands and I like friends. There are students from the University of York and a study I'm in to do with language and people with Down's syndrome. I like being in the study.

There's speech therapy and there's the library and the learning centre. I'm doing work experience. In hospitality. I like doing the tills, training and the experience.

Diane and Michael: **How can they improve the jobs they do?**

Anna: More after-school and help to think, concentrate to think and listen. I would like to baby-sit with my friends and I want a boyfriend and I want to go swimming.

School works well because I meet new people and old people that I know. So the teachers can teach us what to learn, and they teach others like me how to learn. Helpers are there as well to help people with disabilities such as me with Down's syndrome.

School doesn't work well sometimes because there should be one rule saying 'do not mess around' and to stop people making noise (i.e. talking) because I can't learn and listen to my helper. That's general, but also specially hard because I have a disability. It could have been better on the first day you go back, it's confusing and hard to go and ask when to go, where to go on the first day back.

School could be made better if there were discos earlier after school. For Year 10. Also, if there were a ball for dancing for Year 10. I get tired, for example, after PE and there should be places to rest with pillows if you are tired in the day. They should let me also change the way money is for education for children with disabilities. There should be a checklist and resource list for me to see and say what I want and what I think too. That's the best statement I have made in years. It's my favourite. (p. 234)

- Identify how the areas you identified as 'rights' in the excerpt from Children's Rights and Realities feature in Anna's interview. Do you think her rights are being met?

- Identify how the areas you identified in relation to 'screening' in the excerpt from The Social Divisions of Childhood feature in Anna's account of her life, for example medical treatment, education, acquiring skills.

- Compare Anna's account with the case example of Samuel. What are the differences and parallels? Why do you think these differences and parallels occur?

- Consider Anna's views about how her experience could be improved. Do you think her opinions will be taken into account by the services? Why or why not?

Focused Theme: How do poverty and inequality shape access to children's services?

Chapter 4 excerpt: The Social Divisions of Childhood

Although children from the lowest-income households are the focus of a wider range of state services and provision, in many areas of service provision children from wealthier households benefit more, in particular when private services are considered. In relation to education, better-off children tend to stay on at school longer, they go to the 'better' state schools (in terms of examination results), they enter higher education and many also have access to private education (which is sometimes subsidised by the state). In relation to health, better-off families tend to use health services on a more regular basis, they may experience better health due to living in less polluted environments and have better nutrition. Better-off children may also use libraries and leisure services more often than poorer children. They are also more likely to benefit from subsidised transport systems because of their greater mobility. This shows that poorer children may benefit more from particular specialist services targeted at them such as Sure Start, Connexions and community regeneration projects (which tend to be located in poorer neighbourhoods) and some state welfare benefits, but many areas of spending on children's services and provision do not reach the poorest children. (pp. 42–3)

- This portrait of government intervention states that, in many areas of service provision, children from wealthier households benefit more than those from lower-income households, and that in many areas government spending does not reach the poorest children. Take education or health services for children as a topic and consider why this might be.

- Why might better-off children benefit more than children from lower-income households from public transport systems? Try to identify two reasons.

- Why might poorer children benefit more from community regeneration projects which are located in poorer neighbourhoods? Try to identify two reasons.

This extract raises broad themes concerning the complex relationship between welfare and poverty. Analysis of the nature of the relationship between wealth, poverty and children's lives has featured in most of the chapters of the book. As such it can be seen as one of the most challenging issues within service provision for children: the effects of poverty and the inequality which is allied to it are far reaching and damaging to children. While the first extract gives attention to general perspectives and key debates, other chapters, such as the following excerpt from Chapter 8, concern how poverty and inequality shape specific service areas.

Chapter 8 excerpt: Provision for Child Health

The government is a key player and partner in provision of services for the health of children and young people. Government action to enhance children's and young people's health takes place across all sections of government at local, regional and national levels. As we have seen, health is affected by many complex factors and therefore

the sectors involved are varied – from education to housing to environment to the Home Office. This is illustrated through the work of the Department for Education and Employment which has been instrumental in leading the development of the National Healthy School Standard. In addition, the Department of Work and Welfare has been responsible for raising the levels of benefits and targeting them at some of those most in need, particularly families with young children as the Acheson Report recommended (Stretch, 2002) and we have already seen the importance of economics on health outcomes. It should be noted however, that this has had mixed results. Difficulties have been encountered with take-up of benefits and out-of-work benefits have been insufficiently addressed to date. (p. 116)

- The extract from the Social Divisions chapter stated that government benefits do not reach the poorest children. This extract from the Health chapter states that there have been difficulties in the take-up of health benefits. What difficulties might a family encounter in order to stop their take-up of benefits:
  - in relation to government information and their being aware of the benefit?
  - in relation to attitudes towards receiving benefit for children within the family?

- The 'Social Divisions' extract mentions the effect of a child's experience of poverty on their access to good education, health, leisure and transport. This extract from the Health chapter also mentions that education, housing and the environment have an important relationship to health. Try to identify how the quality of each of the following would relate to a child's health:
  - their education in relation to (i) healthy eating (ii) sexual health
  - their housing situation and (i) the standard of building lived in (ii) mental health
  - the environment and community they live in and (i) safety (ii) access to play facilities

The following excerpt considers the issue from another angle. It contains a brief analysis of legislation concerning children's service provision, but does so with a critique of the approaches of government to the issue of wealth, poverty and the choices made to try to address inequality. Its summary of arguments about the nature of the political issues beneath and within policy made to initiate service provision for children shows how reading between chapters can deepen any analysis of a service area or an issue.

Chapter 10 excerpt: Safeguarding Children

The final area to illustrate the contradictions between *Every Child Matters* and other legislation is child poverty. Figures for 2005 show that 3.6 million children – one in four – live in low-income households (Child Poverty Action Group, 2005). The official measure for poverty in 1999 was defined as households with incomes below 60 per cent of the median after housing costs (Flaherty et al., 2004). The government has pledged to halve child poverty by 2010, and to eradicate it by 2020, an ambitious target. By 2004, consensus seemed to be that the government were on target to reduce child poverty by a quarter (Lohde, 2004). However, there is equal consensus that the next stage, to halve child poverty by 2010, will be much more difficult (Piachaud, 1999; Lohde, 2004). The reasons for this are thus: direct benefits and other policies to help poor families are relatively simple ways of assisting families just below the level of official poverty, in order to lift them out of poverty. Much more difficult to access are those households in deeper poverty. This is not merely because these families need more resources and assistance; it is also a political consideration. Piachaud (1999) and Lister (2001) explain that there is a taboo by successive governments on overtly redistributing wealth to the poor, as this may be perceived as reducing the incentive to work and encouraging dependence upon the state. One of the fundamental principles of UK society is that where people do not contribute to the economy, they have to been seen to be treated more harshly than those that do so, in order not only to 'punish' them and make it uncomfortable, but to set an example to others. In other words, the government could end child poverty at a stroke by guaranteeing a minimum household income for every family; however, to do so may incur the wrath of those in work who may well demand more pay to maintain the income differential – a recipe for potential economic and political disaster. To put it bluntly, no government in the UK seems prepared to take the risk of self-destruction in order to end poverty for a quarter of children. (p. 150)

Summarise the reasons given relating to the problems of halving child poverty by 2010.

Focused Theme: What underpins young people's social exclusion?

Chapter 2 excerpt: Childhood: Rights and Realities

Franklin (2002) shows how media representations of children have changed over the last twenty years to increasingly emphasise a view of children as a group who are at least troublesome if not evil. Perhaps in response to the restrictions designed to protect children as victims, the behaviour of some children is now seen as much more challenging. Here the identified problem is not one of finding ways to protect children but of finding ways to make children conform to what adults perceive as appropriate standards of behaviour. Solutions to the problem tend to be in terms of increasing control over children and young people. While the UNCRC is pointing to the need for children to participate in decisions according to their developing capabilities government policies have been focusing on the control of children and young people. In earlier sections of this chapter we considered the status of children and the relationship between the rights of children and the rights of adults. This is particularly relevant here as Franklin (2002) suggests that one of the possible causes for this 'demonisation' of children might be the fear of losing control that adults have. He identifies the priority that is usually given to adult rights when there is a conflict between children's rights and adults' rights. This was reinforced in the previous discussion around citizenship of children being economically dependent on adults and having no right to vote so remaining comparatively powerless. (pp. 19–20)

- The extract says that the media increasingly depicts young people as 'troublesome if not evil'. Can you think of two examples of stereotypical ways in which the media depicts teenage young men as troublesome or evil, and two stereotypical ways in which they depict teenage young women as troublesome or evil?

- Why might the media do this? Discuss why this portrayal might help sell newspapers, for example.

- How might this kind of portrayal have an effect on the way some teenagers see themselves? Do you think it will make them feel more included in society or more excluded? Why or why not?

Chapter 5 excerpt: Pictures of Children

Another tension has been identified concerning whether children are seen as objects of concern and dependent on adults, or, agents in their own right capable of opinion, decisions and actions on their own behalf. Are they, for example, active participants in society rather than individuals for whom others 'know best' and make decisions?

Hill and Tisdall (1997) talk about the way needs are often seen as,

> mainly the responsibility of parents and families within the private sphere of the home, although wider society has a role in supporting families to do so. The collective needs of populations or communities are part of the realm of social policy which examines the nature and extent of societal responses through provision of services, financial benefits and legal regulation.   (Hill and Tisdall, 1997, p. 39)

Wyse has pointed out that the UK has been strongly criticised by the United Nations Committee on the Rights of the Child (UN, 2000) for its lack of progress on prioritising children's rights. He links this to an embedded, historical attitude towards children,

> The UK is criticized for doing little to adopt a rights-based approach because of a dependency

on the philosophies of service, welfare and interest. The word 'rights' hardly appears in UK legislation.   (Wyse, 2004, p. 100)

In our further discussion of case examples we will see how much the state is seen to be 'serving' children within specific and stringently defined contexts compared with promoting children's rights and views per se. We will also look at how much large and powerful organisations say they know what children need and will look after their welfare, compared with acknowledging children's rights.

Again, we can use these debates to create questions to help us see what pictures emerge of children in terms of needs, rights and risks. (pp. 60–1)

- Think of an example for each of the three following areas where what a child wants and what an adult such as a parent might want for them might be different:
  - health
  - education
  - safety

- Justify why the child's voice should be listened to in relation to your examples.

- Justify why the adult's voice should be listened to in relation to your examples.

- Discuss what the tensions are between the two in relation to areas such as risk, need, responsibility, age and gratification or pleasure.

- The extract from Chapter 2 talks about how important it is 'for children to participate in decisions according to their developing capabilities'. The extract from Chapter 5 emphasises the differences between services responding to *needs* as compared with *risks*. Identify a reason why the provision of services could be improved by listening to children's opinions about their needs, and allowing them to make decisions about the services provided for them in relation to:
  - health
  - education
  - safety

The first excerpt in this Focused Theme talked about the relationship between child rights and adult rights in terms of conflict. The following extract offers a contrasting experience where the rights of children to good facilities and opportunities for play are seen within the context of adults redressing aspects of their exclusion. The community's experience of exclusion is partly presented through the impact of poor service provision in a number of areas, including play facilities for children and young people. However, the excerpt can be seen to illustrate a parallel but different part of social exclusion.

Chapter 14 excerpt: The Swings and Round-abouts of Community Development

In the early 1990s a group of local residents (myself included) came together, without external professional help, with the vague purpose of wanting to bring about improvements to the area. Hirst Wood had something of a reputation in the 1980s as a tough place to live where 'problem families' were once housed. This reputation still persists today, despite the influx of new residents. This legacy can be attributed to the behaviour of a small minority of local young people and their families. This factor was the impetus for the community group coming together. The group was mostly comprised of parents and older people with grandchildren. One of the objectives was to look at creative ways of tackling the boredom and lack of facilities for children and young people in the area. From the outset, however, it was only adults that were involved in the meetings. A few tentative attempts were made to include young people but these were broadly unsuccessful. Young people, understandably, did not want to come along to 'boring' meetings dominated by adults. This factor was important since in later years, as the group became more established and active, the voices of children and young people were largely absent. (p. 205)

- What reasons might there be, do you think, for Hirst Wood not having good facilities?

- What impact would having good facilities have on children and young people?

- The excerpt says that 'the voices of children and young people were largely absent' in the process. Discuss how the following areas might play a role

in this absence: poverty, disenchantment, the relationship between young people and adults.

- Look at Chapter 14 and think about how this absence could be addressed.

Chapter 7 excerpt: Youth Services and Provision

The Bridging the Gap (SEU, 1999a) exposed the fact that a significant minority of young people had 'disappeared' and were not involved in education, employment or training. This is the group that is referred to by professionals as disengaged and hard to reach. It is also the group that recent evaluations suggest that services have continued to fail to engage. Their needs have been defined by the government and the lack of response has indicated a further social policy review, respect being a primary focus. (p. 97)

Many of the excerpts in this Focused Theme have referred to 'disengagement' in one form or another.

- What do you think this means?

- Identify some of the factors which contribute to this disengagement.

- Look at pages 97–8 in Chapter 7 and pages 208–10 in Chapter 14. What ideas are present to try to take positive action in relation to this disengagement?

Focused Theme: How is access to children's services shaped by concepts of 'race' and 'racism'?

A number of chapters in this book have shown how the services children receive or are involved in – such as health or education – are not simply designed as practical answers to simple questions such as 'How shall we educate children?' or 'What is the best way to help children remain healthy?' They have shown that there are a number of ways to ask and answer such questions, and that any service provision – from the location of a playground to decisions on which service identifies or supports a child who may be being sexually abused – involves debates and choices in selecting from the different ways something can be designed and provided. The policies which fuel changes in the way services are provided, the ways that children's lives are looked at in designing services and the way people work and use the services are connected to ideas and processes which concern and affect every individual child's experience. These occur within the ways organisations form and work as well as within the way people and children behave towards each other in daily encounters within the services. This book has explored a number of these. They include attitudes towards children: seeing them as victims or threats; as innocent or inherently dangerous; in need of training and control. They also include forces at work within society such as sexism, homophobia or prejudice against disabled children and adults. The following extracts explore some of these areas of ideas and processes: race, racism and equity. Though they focus on a particular aspect of these forces, they are included as an example of looking at such processes and ideas which are within all services and which need to be acknowledged in considering how services are designed, implemented and used.

Chapter 4 excerpt: The Social Divisions of Childhood

In what way is the concept 'minority' problematic in relation to services for children? Does it simply draw attention to children's group membership? Does it draw attention to 'minority needs' (for example, minority religious beliefs)? Does the concept 'minority' trigger different treatment by service providers? Should it? In recent years the concept 'minoritised' has been used to draw attention to the process whereby some groups are treated less well by service providers on the grounds of 'race' or 'culture' (Forbat, 2004; Burman et al., 2004). In the UK a black child of Afro-Caribbean heritage is clearly in the minority compared with a child of white European heritage. In the Caribbean, of course, black children are in the majority.

This section will use 'race' as an example of being in a minority group. In relation to the concept of race, there is in fact no pure race and the term is often used as a euphemism for other identifying factors such as colour, country of origin or religion. The concept has historically been used to conceal racism.

> Because racial prejudice is so deeply embedded in our society, it comes as no surprise to many people to learn that the concept of race is a social construct, and a recent one in human history. It did not emerge until the early days of capitalism . . . The myth of a Black race that is inferior was developed to rationalise the institution of enslavement of Black (people) from Africa.   (Jennes, 2001, p. 306)

The tailoring of children's services to meet the different needs of individual children is important, for example the recognition of an individual's language or dietary needs is imperative. Sometimes, however, difference in treatment is generalised to a 'minority' group on the basis of ill-informed stereotypes. Individual circumstances may be lost sight of when children are treated as part of a group. Stereotypes about 'race' and 'culture' may determine service provision with negative consequences. Sensitivity to cultural difference may override respect for children's rights. (p. 49)

Chapter 9 excerpt: Children Who Offend

Those who come into contact with the children crime and justice system are disproportionately boys from low-income households or looked-after situations, and disproportionately from some black and minority ethnic communities (Muncie, 2004). Although the numbers of girls going through the courts has increased there is little evidence to suggest the numbers actually offending have increased, just that more are being taken to court (Nacro, 2005). There has been long-standing debate on how accurate statistics are in reflecting the relationship between class and crime. As early as 1958, Short and Nye argued that middle-class boys were engaged in as many criminal acts as working-class boys but they were less likely to end up in the criminal statistics (cited in Maguire, 1994). Although this argument has been challenged there is a general consensus that the offences of middle-class young people are underestimated.

In relation to 'race' there is evidence that black young people are over-represented within the youth justice system and generally treated more harshly:

> According to Youth Justice Board data, for instance, children classified as black or black British made up 6.2% of the youth offending population during 2003/4. At the remand stage, such children were less likely to be granted unconditional bail than their white counterparts, and more likely to be remanded to secure facilities . . . black or black British young people constituted 12.2% of those receiving a custodial sentence. (Nacro, 2005, p. 6) (p. 130)

- This excerpt from Chapter 9 states that 'the offences of middle-class young people are underestimated'. Identify reasons why that might be, why these offences might not be seen or acknowledged.

- The quotation from Nacro states that black or black British children are 'less likely to be granted unconditional bail than their white counterparts'. Why might this be? Why might the justice system see black and black British young people differently and treat them differently? Look back into the chapter (pp. 130–2) to help you consider this.

Chapter 17 excerpt: Educating Refugee Children: A Class Teacher's Perspective

The Nationality, Immigration and Asylum Act 2002 . . . outlined . . . the setting-up of three levels of centres for the processing, accommodation and removal of asylum seekers . . . Initial accommodation centres were to provide facilities for induction briefings, health screening and production of biometric identity cards for asylum seekers. Detention centres would house asylum seekers (including children) awaiting removal to their home country or a designated 'safe third country'. In the middle, accommodation centres would house asylum seekers awaiting the outcomes of their applications. The Act states that 'a child who is a resident of an Accommodation Centre may not be admitted to a maintained school or a

maintained nursery' (HMSO, 2002: s. 36(2)). Instead, children were to be educated in the accommodation centres rather than (to quote the then Home Secretary, David Blunkett) 'swamping' local schools (BBC, 2002). The Refugee Council argued that this set 'a dangerous precedent' and that withdrawing children from mainstream education provision was 'discriminatory' (Refugee Council, 2002, p. 18).

In June 2005, following protests at the proposed sites of a number of proposed accommodation centres (most notably at Bicester in Oxfordshire), the Home Office minister Tony McNulty quietly announced that the government would not proceed with plans to developed accommodation centres (Immigration and Nationality Directorate, 2005). However, initial accommodation centres and detention centres are still in use and more are proposed. Detention and removal centres routinely include children amongst their detainees, despite concerns voiced by numerous politicians, churches and non-governmental organisations. Indeed, this criticism extends even to other branches of government. For example, HM Inspectorate of Education has reported that facilities for children in one detention centre (Dungavel in Scotland) are 'unsatisfactory' and HM Inspector of Prisons has called for the cessation of the long-term detention of children (BBC, 2003). (p. 238)

- How might refugee children be affected by not attending school?

- The Refugee Council stated that the Nationality, Immigration and Asylum Act 2002 was 'discriminatory'. Identify what you think the Council means by the Act being discriminatory in its treatment of refugee children and their education compared with children who are not refugees.

- The Chapter 9 extract talked about the ways in which young people who are black or black British are seen and treated differently than other children. The description of the treatment of refugee children in the extract here suggests that refugee children are seen and treated differently under the Act than children who are not refugees. Look at

Chapter 17, pp. 240–1, to see how the teacher welcomed and worked with Mia, as well as her mother and father, then answer the following questions:

- Why might it be important for the welfare and interests of a child such as Mia to have full access to education services?
- Identify three things that you think are positive or helpful in the way the teacher and school see Mia and her family's situation and work with it?
- Think of two ways in which this treatment and experience differs from notions of refugees 'swamping' existing classes.

Focused Theme: How do ways of thinking about childhood affect services for children?

The following extract from the Politics of Childhood identifies one of the ways of thinking about 'the child' – as an investment for the future

Chapter 3 extract: The Politics of Childhood

Child as investment

- Children may be viewed as investments to satisfy future society needs.
- Population policies may be introduced to influence both quality and quantity.
- Children may be viewed in terms of their potential to produce economic wealth for themselves and society.
- 'Success' in the future may be the focus.
- The child as 'investment' influences approaches to various aspects of social policy, such as education and health. (p. 28)

This way of thinking about the child influences the type of services that are provided for children and this is discussed in Chapter 2.

- What do you understand the idea of the child as an 'investment' to mean?
- What would a contrasting idea of childhood be? Consider the ideas discussed in Chapter 2, pp. 8–9.
- How might the practice of preparing children to be good contributors to the economic wealth of the

country through educational attainment create tension with a child-centred approach to their experience of childhood?

Chapter 2 extract: Childhood: Rights and Realities

Bellamy suggests that a reason for providing services for children (and their mothers) is because the investment will pay off in the future by ensuring that the adults of tomorrow are productive and happy. She may be using this as an argument because the view that children should be provided with services because they are children doesn't have such a strong political appeal. The earlier discussion concerning the status of children suggests that in the UK the higher status of adults through being voters and tax payers leads to the likelihood of services reflecting the interests of adults rather than children. (p. 16)

- Consider the two different frameworks referred to in this extract. Make two points in favour of the development and design of services being the rationale that good services for children make for 'productive and happy' adults. Make two points in favour of the rationale that the development and design of services for children should be based on the rights, needs and demands of children in their own right, not on trying to ensure they grow into a particular kind of adult.
- What do you think you would have wanted as a child?
- The excerpt says that 'the view that children should be provided with services because they are children' doesn't have a 'strong political appeal' with adult voters. Why do you think that might be?

An example of this tension can be seen in the following discussion of the education system from Chapter 6.

Chapter 6 extract: Education: Service or System?

Underlying both the GNP and cultural-transmission models, which are very prominent within the National Curriculum and the structures around it, is the notion of the passive child and the view of childhood as preparation for adulthood.

As long as children do as they are told they will go through the system smoothly and come out as an acceptable adult.

Linked with this is the assumption that children don't or won't learn unless their learning is clearly directed by adults and they are made to attend school: a view of children as vulnerable but also potential villains.

Other aspects of policy also indicate a perception of childhood as being of low status and a time of preparation for adulthood. Instances of this relate to the relationship that schools have with parents. In the market-led education system devised under the Education Reform Act (1988) focus is on the parent as the consumer of education and schools as the providers of education. Children, who actually experience being in school, are not seen as the consumers! The accountability of teachers and schools, which is such an important feature of the current system, is directed towards parents rather than children, but even then the accountability is on the government's terms as it centres round the testing of the core curriculum (p. 89).

- What do you think a 'market-led education system' means? Consult Chapter 6, pp. 84–9.

- The extract links this approach with the National Curriculum and 'the notion of the passive child' and rewarding children who 'go through the system smoothly and come out as an acceptable adult'. What might an alternative view on the value of the National Curriculum be? Consult Chapter 6 pp. 92–3.

- If you consider this interpretation of the relationship between education and the child, what kind of adult might this produce? What kinds of attitude will this passivity and reward system encourage?

- How might the promotion of child rights and child-centred perspectives feature in education? Consider the points made in Chapters 2 and 6.

Conclusion

This chapter has shown how it is valuable to refer across chapters in order to deepen your understanding of service provision. It has provided specific, detailed, structured questions and activities to show how thorough attention to connections can add significantly to the range and depth of understanding and value of the different chapters. Such cross-referencing can provide different perspectives from different authors on a theme or issue such as equality, or of children's voices being heard and responded to in developing, implementing and evaluating service provision. In part this is good practice in studying children's services, ensuring that an area is thoroughly and broadly researched and considered. The book assists this way of working by providing references throughout to encourage connections between chapters. However, this is not just about a way of reading.

This approach is one that reflects a central principle in the ways in which all the authors of this book see the relationship between children and services. The core concept is that it is impossible to section off one aspect of a child's life and circumstance from another: context and the inter-relationship between different factors must be paid attention to at all times in considering children and the services which relate to them. Hence while this chapter presents a useful series of activities to help maximise its use in studying services, it also represents a political position about the crucial nature of considering and working with the complex interactions between children, the world they live in and the services which relate to them.

As the introduction to this book made clear, there is not one 'childhood'; rather there are many childhoods. The many chapters and interconnections within the book have represented and analysed the inter-relationship of the many things that impact on how different children experience different childhoods: the dynamic tensions between prevailing policies and provision, the critical context within which these exist, the range of services and the adults and children involved as decision makers, providers and users. By paying attention and trying to understand these relationships and interactions, the book has attempted to help the reader to critically encounter existing and developing services and how they feature within children's lives.

References

Abernethy, D. (1968) *Playleadership,* London: National Playing Fields Association

Abernethy, D. (1973) *Playgrounds,* London: National Playing Fields Association

Adamson (ed.) (1989) *The State of the World's Children,* Oxford: Oxford University Press for UNICEF

Aggleton, P. (1990) *Health,* London: Routledge

Albemarle Report (1959) *The Youth Service in England and Wales,* London: The Stationery Office

Albert Kennedy Trust (2005) <http://www.akt.org.uk/> accessed 24 November 2005

Alcock, P., Erskine, A. and May M. (eds) (2003) *The Students Companion to Social Policy,* 2nd edn, Oxford: Blackwell Publishing

Alcoff, L. (1997) 'Cultural feminism versus post structuralism: the identity crisis in feminist theory', in Nicholson, L. (ed.) *The Second Wave: A Reader in Feminist Theory,* London: Routledge

Alderson, A. (2003), cited in Katz, A. (2003) 'A step backwards', *The Guardian,* Thursday 6th February 2003.

Alexander, C. (1977) *A Pattern Language,* Oxford: Oxford University Press

Alinsky, S. (1971) *Rules for Radicals,* New York: Random House

Allen, C. (2003) *Fair Justice: The Bradford Disturbances, the Sentencing and the Impact,* London: FAIR

Archard, D. (1993) *Children: Rights and Childhood,* London: Routledge

Atkinson, R. L. and Atkinson, R. C. (1979) *Introduction to Psychology.* New York: Harcourt Brace Jovanovich

Attree, P. (2004) '"It was like my little acorn and its going to grow into a big tree": a qualitative study of a community support project', *Health and Social Care in the Community,* 12(2), 155–61

Audit Commission (1996) *Misspent Youth: Young People and Crime,* London: Audit Commission Publications

Avery, J. G. and Jackson, R. H. (1993) *Children and their Accidents,* London: Edward Arnold

Axline, V. (1969) *Play therapy* (rev. edn), New York: Ballantine Books

Bachpan Bachao Andolan (2007) South Asian Coalition on Child Servitude, http://www.bba.org.in

Baldock, P. (2001) *Regulating Early Years Services,* London: David Fulton

Ball, D. M. B. (1996) *Health for All Children,* 3rd edn, Oxford: Oxford University Press

Banksy (2002) 'Creative vandalism: Out and about with Banksy in London', in Squall May 2002 <http://www.squall.co.uk/squall.cfm/ses/sq=2002053001/ct=2> accessed 4 November 2004

Barr, A. and Hashagan, S. (2000) *ABCD Handbook: A Framework for Evaluating Community Development,* London: Community Development Foundation

Barrett, S. (2005) 'Draft Green Paper begs many questions', *Young People Now,* 16–22 March

Barry, M. (2005) *Youth Policy and Social Exclusion: Critical Debates with Young People,* London: Routledge

Bassam, Lord (2003) 'Voting Age (Reduction to 16) Bill debate', *Lords Hansard,* 9 January, Column 1120

Bateson, G. (1955) 'A theory of play and fantasy', *Psychiatric Research Reports,* 2, 39–51

Batsleer, J. and Humphries, B. (eds) (2000) *Welfare, Exclusion and Political Agency,* London: Routledge

Bauman, Z. (1998) *Work, Consumerism and the New Poor,* Buckingham: Open University Press

Bauman, Z. (2004) *Wasted Lives: Modernity and its Outcasts,* Oxford: Polity

BBC (2000) 'Young killers shown compassion', BBC News, Friday 30 June, available at <http://news.bbc.co.uk/1/hi/programmes/correspondent/803151.stm> accessed 10 September 2005

BBC (2002) 'Blunkett stands by "swamping' remark"', BBC News, Thursday 25 April, available at <http://news.bbc.co.uk/1/hi/uk_politics/1949863.stm> accessed 23 April 2007

BBC (2003) 'Asylum centres "not for children"', BBC News, Friday 15 August, available at <http://news.bbc.co.uk/1/hi/scotland/3151535.stm> accessed 23 April 2007

BBC (2005) 'Boy, 15, wins legal battle', BBC News, Wednesday 20 July, available at <http://news.bbc.co.uk/1/hi/england/london/4699095.stm> accessed 28 March 2006

Beck, U. (1992) *Risk Society: Towards a New Modernity,* trans, Mark Ritter, Introduction by Scott Lash and Brian Wynne, London: Sage Publications

Bee, H. and Boyd, D. (2002) *Lifespan development,* Boston MA: Allyn and Bacon

Berlyne, D. E. (1960) *Conflict, arousal and curiosity,* New York: McGraw-Hill

Berridge, D. (2000) *Placement Stability,* London: Department of Health

Best, S. (2005) Understanding Social Divisions, London: Sage

BIG (2006) *Children's Play: £155 million England wide children's play initiative,* The Big Lottery Fund. <http://www.biglotteryfund.org.uk/programmes/childrensplay> accessed 16 April 2006

Bignell, T. and Butt, J. (2000) *Between Ambition and Achievement: Young Black Disabled People's Views and Experiences of Independent Living,* London: Policy Press

Blanden, J. and Gibbons, S. (2006) *The persistence of poverty across generations: A view from two British cohorts,* London: The Policy Press

Blanden, J., Gregg, P. and Machin, S. (2005) *Intergenerational Mobility in Europe and North America,* A Report by the Sutton Trust Centre for Economic Performance LSE <http://cep.lse.ac.uk/about/news/IntergenerationalMobility.pdf> accessed 12 May 2005

Blaxter, M. (1990) *Health and Lifestyles,* London: Routledge

Borland, M. (1998) 'Education for Children in Residential and Foster Care', available at <http://www.scre.ac.uk/rie/nl63/nl3borland.html>

Bottery, M. (1990) *The Morality of the School,* London: Cassell

Bradbury, B. and Jäntti, M. (1999) *Child Poverty across Industrialized Countries,* Innocenti Occasional Paper 71, Florence: UNICEF

Bradbury, B. and Jäntti, M. (2001) 'Child poverty across twenty-five countries', in Bradbury, S. Jenkins, P. and Micklewright, J. (eds) *The Dynamics Journal of Population and Social Security (Population),* Supplement to Volume 1 of Child Poverty in Industrialised Countries', Cambridge: Cambridge University Press, Chapter 3, pp. 62–91

Bradbury, B., Jenkins, S. and Micklewright, J. (2001) *The Dynamics of Child Poverty in Industrialised Countries,* Cambridge: Cambridge University Press

Bradshaw, J. (1990) *Child Poverty and Deprivation in the UK,* Innocenti Occasional Paper 8, Florence: UNICEF

Brannen, J. and Moss, P. (eds) (2003) *Rethinking children's care,* Buckingham: Open University Press

Brannen, J. and Storey, P. (1996) *Child Health in Social Context: Parental Employment and the Start of Secondary School,* London: Health Education Authority

Brewer, M., Goodman, A., Shaw, J. and Shephard, A. (2005) *Poverty and Inequality in Britain: 2005,* London: Institute for Fiscal Studies

Bright, M. (2005) 'Crime czar: stop calling children yobs', The *Observer,* Sunday 22 May

Brogan, D. (2005) 'Anti-Social Behaviour Orders: An Assessment of Current Management Information Systems and the Scale of Anti-Social Behaviour Order Breaches Resulting in Custody', available at <http://youth-justice-board.gov.uk/NR/rdonlyres/74AEB491-2440-4C4C-A975-83F65C82DBC7/0/AntiSocialBehaviourOrdersfullreport.pdf> accessed 27 May 2005

Brown, B. (1998) Unlearning discrimination in the early years, Stoke-on-Trent: Trentham Books

Brown, F. (ed.) (2003a) *Playwork: Theory and Practice,* Buckingham: Open University Press

Brown, F. (2003b) 'An evaluation of the concept of play value and its application to children's fixed equipment playgrounds', unpublished PhD thesis, Leeds Metropolitan University

Brown, F. (2003c) 'Compound flexibility: SPICE revisited', in Brown, F. (ed.) (2003) *Playwork: Theory and Practice,* Buckingham: Open University Press

Brown, F. (2006) *Play Theories: What Do They Tell Us About the Value of Play?*, London: National Children's Bureau

Brown, F. (2007) 'Playwork theory', in Brown, F. and Taylor, C. (2007) *Foundations of Playwork*, Buckingham: Open University Press

Brown, F. and Cheesman, B. (2003) 'Introduction: childhood and play', in Brown, F. (ed.) (2003) *Playwork: Theory and Practice*, Buckingham: Open University Press

Brown, F. and Webb, S. (2002) 'Playwork: an attempt at definition', *Play Action*, Spring, Bognor Regis: Fair Play for Children

Brown, F. and Webb, S. (2005) 'Children without play', *Journal of Education*, 35, March, special issue 'Early childhood research in developing contexts'

Brown, S. (1998) *Understanding Youth and Crime: Listening to Youth*, Buckingham: Open University Press

Bruner, J. S. (1972) 'Nature and uses of immaturity', in Bruner, J. S., Jolly, A. and Sylva, K. (eds) (1976) *Play: Its Role in Development and Evolution*, New York: Basic Books

Bruner, J. S. (1996) *The Culture of Education*, London: Harvard University Press

Brynin, M. and Scott, J. (1996) *Young People, Health and the Family*, London: Health Education Authority

Burden, T. (1998) *Social Policy and Welfare*, London: Pluto Press

Burke, C. and Grosvenor, I. (2003) *The School I'd Like*, London: Routledge

Burman, E., Smailes, S. L. and Chantler, K. (2004) 'Culture as a barrier to service provision and delivery', in *Critical Social Policy*, 24(3), August, 332–57

Burton, P. (1993) *Local authorities and children's play*, Bristol: SAUS Publications

Bynner, J. and Joshi, H. (2002) 'Equality and Opportunity in Education: Evidence from the 1958 and 1970 Birth Cohort Studies', *Oxford Review of Education*, 28(4), 405–25

Callaghan, J. (1976) Ruskin speech, available at <http://education.guardian.co.uk/thegreatdebate/

Calnan, M. (1987) *Health and Illness: The Lay Perspective*, London: Tavistock Publications

Cameron, C. (2003) 'An historical perspective on changing child care policy', in Brannen, J. and Moss, P. (eds) *Rethinking Children's Care*, Buckingham: Open University Press

Cannan, C. and Warren, C. (1997) *Social Action with Children and Families: A Community Development Approach to Child and Family Welfare*, London: Routledge

Cantle, T. (2001) *See* CCRT (2001)

Carrabine, E., Cox, P., Lee, M. and South, N. (2002) *Crime in Modern Britain*, Oxford: Oxford University Press

Carvel, J. and Elliot, L. (2005) 'Child poverty defies government targets', *Guardian Unlimited*, Thursday 31 March, available at <http://www.guardian.co.uk/uk_news/story/0,,1448634,00.html> accessed 12 May 2005

CCRT (2001) *Community Cohesion: A Report of the Independent Review Team*, chaired by Ted Cantle, London: Home Office

Chanan, G. (2000) 'Community responses to social exclusion', in Percy-Smith, J. (ed.) *Policy Responses to Social Exclusion*, Buckingham: Open University Press

Chapman, N., Emerson, S., Gough, J., Mepani, B. and Road, N. (2000) *Views of Health 2000*, London: Save the Children

Chawla, L. and Malone, K. (2003) 'Neighbourhood quality in children's eyes', in Christensen, P. and O'Brien, M. (2003) *Children in the City: Home, Neighbourhood and Community*, London: Routledge Falmer

Childcare Act 2006, London: The Stationery Office, available at <http://www.opsi.gov.uk/acts/acts2006/ukpga_20060021_en.pdf> accessed 24 July 2007

Childcare Bill Summary (2006) available at <http://www.publications.parliament.uk/pa/cm200506/cmbills/080/2006080.htm> accessed 24 July 2007

Children Act 2004, London: The Stationery Office, available at <http://www.opsi.gov.uk/acts/acts2004/20040031.htm> accessed 24 July 2007

Children's Rights Alliance for England (2005) 'State of Children's Rights in England, Annual Review of UK Government Action of the Concluding Observations of the United Nations Committee on the Rights of the Child', available at <www.crae.org.uk/cms/dmdocuments/State> accessed 28 April 2007

Children's Society (2003) 'Children warn anti-social plans could create tension with police', 23 October, available at <http://www.the-childrens-society.org.uk/whoareyou/media/SG_Feature/6882/1/> accessed 4 November 2004

Children's Society, The (2005) Parliamentary Briefing, The Queens Speech, 17 May, available at <http://www.the-childrens-society.org.uk> accessed 24 July 2007

Children's Workforce Development Council (2006) available at <http://www.cwdcouncil.org.uk/projects/earlyyears.htm> accessed 24 July 2007

Chitty, C. (1997) 'Interview with Sir Keith Joseph', in Ribbins, P. and Sherratt, B. (eds) *Radical Educational Policies and Conservative Secretaries of State*, London: Cassell

Chitty, C. (2002) *Understanding Schools and Schooling*, London: Routledge Falmer

Chitty, C. (2004) *Education Policy in Britain*, Basingstoke: Palgrave Macmillan

Christensen, P. and O'Brien, M. (2003) *Children in the City: Home, Neighbourhood and Community*, London: Routledge Falmer

Cohen, D. and Prusak, L. (2001) *In Good Company: How Social Capital Makes Organizations Work*, Boston, MA: Harvard Business School Press

Cohen, R. and Long, G. (1998) 'Children and anti-poverty strategies', *Children & Society*, 12, 73–85

Cole-Hamilton, I. and Gill, T. (2002) *Making the Case for Play: Building Policies and Strategies for School-aged Children*, London: National Children's Bureau (detailed research evidence is available in the companion report, Cole-Hamilton et al., 2002)

Coleman, S. and Rowe, C. (2005) *Remixing Citizenship: Democracy and Young People's Use of the Internet*, London: CarnegieYPI, available at <http://cypi. carnegieuktrust.org.uk/files/Carnegie_v3LRES_0.pdf> accessed 23 April 2007

Coles, B. (1998) *See* Alcock, P. et al. (1998)

Coles, B. (2004) 'Slouching towards Bethlehem: youth policy and the work of the Social Exclusion Unit', in *Social Policy Review* 12

Coles, B. (2005) Youth policy 1995–2005: from the 'best start' to 'youth matters' in *Youth and Policy* 89

Communities and Local Government (2004) 'Learning to Listen: Action Plan For Children and Young People 2003/4'. 4.3 The Urban Summit Youth Fringe Event 2002, available at <www.communities.gov.uk> accessed 27 April 2007

Communities Today (2005) 'Forward Thinker, David Orr', 31 August, available at <http://www. communitiestoday.co.uk/default.aspx?contentid= e529fea1-eeb3-49ae-8adc-eebe9d9bb0e1&newsid=41> accessed 24 July 2007

Community Care (2004) *See* Wise, K. (2004)

Cornia, G. A. and Danziger, S. (eds) (1997) *Child Poverty and Deprivation in the Industrialized Countries 1945–1995*, Oxford: Oxford University Press

Corson, D. (1998) *Changing Education for Diversity*, Buckingham: Open University Press

Coxall, B. and Robins, L. (1998) *Contemporary British Politics*, 3rd edn, Basingstoke: Macmillan Press Ltd

CPAG (2001) 'Campaigns Newsletter No 16', June, Child Poverty Action Group, available at <http://www.cpag. org.uk> accessed 24 November 2005

CPAG (2005a) 'Poverty: the facts', Child Poverty Action Group, available at <http://www.cpag.org.uk> accessed 24 November 2005

CPAG (2005b) *Ten Steps to a Society Free of Poverty*, London: Child Poverty Action Group

CPAG (2006) *The Welfare Benefits and Tax Credits Handbook 2006/7*, 8th edn, London: Child Poverty Action Group

CPC (2001) 'Chris Smith announces £200 million lottery funding for play', Children's Play Council, *Playtoday*, 25, July/August

CPC (2002) *More than Swings and Roundabouts: Planning for Outdoor Play*, London: National Children's Bureau

CPIS (2003) *How to raise funds for children's play*, rev. edn, Children's Play Information Service factsheet, London: National Children's Bureau

Craig, G. (1999) *Unfinished Business: Local Government Reorganisation and Social Services*, Bristol: Policy Press

CRE (2002) Impact assessment criminal justice statistics, Commission for Racial Equality, available at <http://www.cre.gov.uk/duty/reia/statistics_justice. html> accessed 4 November 2004

Crime and Disorder Act 1998, London: The Stationery Office, available at <http://www.opsi.gov.uk/acts/ acts1998/98037—a.htm>

Crimmens, D., Factor, F., Jeffs, T., Pitts, J. and Pugh, C. (2004) *Reaching Socially Excluded Young People: A National Study of Street-based Youth Work*, Leicester: National Youth Agency

Crompton, R., Brockmann, M. and Lyonette, C. (2005) 'Attitudes, women's employment and the domestic division of labour: a cross-national analysis in two waves', *Work, Employment and Society*, 19(2), 213–33

Cunningham, S. and Tomlinson, J. (2005) '"Starve them out": does every child really matter?: A commentary on section 9 of the Asylum and Immigration (Treatment of Claimants, etc.) Act 2004', in *Critical Social Policy*, 25(2), May, 253–75

CUP (2006) *Cambridge Advanced Learner's Dictionary*, Cambridge: Cambridge University Press, available at <http://dictionary.cambridge.org/> accessed 12 June 2006

Curtis, S. (2004) *Health and Inequality: Geographical Perspectives*, London: Sage

Cutter, C. A. (1962) *Rules for a Dictionary Catalog*, London: Library Association

CWS (2007) Child Welfare Scheme, Nepal, available at <http://www.childwelfarescheme.org/homef.php> accessed 24 July 2007

CYPU (2001a) *Building a Strategy for Children and Young People*, London: Children and Young People's Unit

CYPU (2001b) *Learning to Listen: Core Principles for the Involvement of Children and Young People*, London: Children and Young People's Unit

Dahlberg, G. and Moss, P. (2004) *Ethics and Politics in Early Childhood Education,* London: Routledge Falmer

Dahlberg, G., Moss, P. and Pence, A. (1999) *Beyond Quality in Early Childhood Education and Care,* London: Routledge Falmer

Daniel, P. and Ivatts, J. (1998) *Children and Social Policy,* Basingstoke: Macmillan

Daniels, K. and Macdonald, L. (2005) *Equality, Diversity and Discrimination,* London: Chartered Institute of Personnel and Development

David, T. (1994) 'Supporting children and families: an optimistic future?', in David, T. (ed.) *Working Together for Young Children: Multi-Professionalism in Action,* London: Routledge

Davies, B. (2005a) 'If youth matters, where is the youth work?', *Youth Policy* 89, Leicester: National Youth Agency

Davies, B. (2005b) 'Youth work: a manifesto for our times', *Youth Policy,* summer, Leicester: National Youth Agency

Davies, B. (2005c) 'Threatening youth revisited: youth policies under New Labour', available at <http://www.infed.org/archives/bernard_davies/revisiting_threatening_youth.htm> accessed 23 April 2007

Davies, B. and Docking, J. (2004) *Transforming lives: Re-engaging Young People Through Community-based Projects,* Sheffield: DfEE

Davis, J. (2004) 'Disability and childhood: deconstructing the stereotypes', in Swain, J., French, S., Barnes, C. and Thomas, C. (eds) *Disabling Barriers: Enabling Environments,* London: Sage

Davis, J., Watson, N. and Cunningham-Burley, S. (2000) 'Learning the lives of disabled children: developing a reflexive approach', in Christensen, P. and James, A. (eds) *Research with Children,* London: Routledge Falmer

DCMS (2004a) *Getting Serious About Play: A Review Of Children's Play,* The Report of the Review of Children's Play chaired by the Rt. Hon Frank Dobson MP, London: Department for Culture, Media and Sport

DCMS (2004b) *Getting Serious About Play: A Review of Children's Play: Children's Play Review: Feedback To Children And Young People,* London: Department for Culture, Media and Sport, available at <http://www.culture.gov.uk/global/publications> accessed 24 July 2007

Deacon, B. (1998) 'Social policy in a shrinking world', in Alcock, P., Erskine, A. and May, M. (eds) (2003) *The Students Companion to Social Policy,* Oxford: Blackwell Publishing

Dehghan, M., Akhtar-Danesh, N. and Merchant, A. T. (2005) 'Childhood obesity, prevalence and prevention', *Nutrition Journal,* 4(24)

Department for Work and Pensions (2003) 'United Kingdom National Action Plan on Social Inclusion 2003–2005', available at www.dwp.gov.uk/publications/dwp/2003/nap/ accessed 28 April 2007

Detheridge, T. (2000) 'Research involving children with severe learning difficulties', in Lewis, A. and Lindsay, G. (eds) *Researching Children's Perspectives,* Buckingham: Open University Press

Dewey, J. (1916) *Democracy and Education,* New York: Macmillan

DfEE (1998a) *Meeting the Childcare Challenge: A Framework and Consultation Document,* London: Department of Education and Employment

DfEE (1998b) *The National Literacy Strategy: Framework for Teaching,* London: Department for Education and Employment

DfEE (1998c) *The National Numeracy Strategy: Framework for Teaching,* London: Department for Education and Employment

DfEE (1999) *Learning to Succeed: A New Framework for Post-16 Learning,* London: The Stationery Office

DfEE (2000) *The Childcare Start-up Guide* (Good Practice in Childcare 12), Nottingham: Department for Education and Employment (EYDCP Rep 26)

DfEE (2001) *Transforming Youth Work,* London: The Stationery Office

DfEE and DoH (2000) *Education of Young People in Public Care: Guidance,* London: Department for Education and Employment & Department of Health

DfES (2001) *Schools Achieving Success,* available at <http://www.dfes.gov.uk/achievingsuccess/foreword.shtml> accessed 24 July 2007

DfES (2002) *Resourcing Excellent Youth Services,* London: The Stationery Office

DfES (2003a) *Building a Culture of Participation Handbook,* London: Department for Education and Skills

DfES (2003b) *Every Child Matters* (Green Paper on Children's Services), London: Department for Education and Skills, available at <http://www.dfes.gov.uk/everychildmatters> accessed 24 July 2007

DfES (2003c) *Every Child Matters: Change for Children,* London: Department for Education and Skills, available at <http://www.everychildmatters.gov.uk> accessed 24 July 2007

DfES (2003d) *Excellence and Enjoyment: A strategy for Primary schools,* London: Department for Education and Skills

DfES (2004a) *Every Child Matters: Change for Children in Health Services,* London: Department for Education and Skills, available at <http://www.everychildmatters.gov.uk> accessed 24 July 2007

DfES (2004b) *Every Child Matters: Change for Children in the Criminal Justice System*, London: Department for Education and Skills, available at <http://www.everychildmatters.gov.uk> accessed 24 July 2007

DfES (2004c) *Every Child Matters: Next Steps*, London: Department for Education and Skills, available at <http://www.everychildmatters.gov.uk> accessed 24 July 2007

DfES (2004d) The Children Act 2004, London: The Stationery Office, available at <http://www.dfes.gov.uk/publications/childrenactreport/#2004> accessed 24 July 2007

DfES (2004e) *Primary National Strategy, Excellence and Enjoyment: Learning and Teaching in the Primary Years*, London: Department for Education and Skills

DfES (2005a) 'Welcome to Gifted and Talented', London: Department for Education and Skills, available at <http://www.standards.dfes.gov.uk/giftedandtalented/> accessed 13 May 2005

DfES (2005b) *Common Assessment Framework for Young People*, London: Department for Education and Skills

DfES (2005c) *Every Child Matters: Change for Children*, London: Department for Education and Skills, available at <http://www.everychildmatters.gov.uk/culturesportplay/> accessed 17 January 2006

DfES (2005d) *Every Child Matters: Change For Children – An Overview of Cross Government Guidance*, London: Department for Education and Skills, available at <http://www.dfes.gov.uk/everychildmatters> accessed 24 July 2007

DfES (2005e) *Supporting the Education of Asylum Seeking and Refugee Children*, London: Department for Education and Skills

DfES (2005f) *The National Evaluation of Children's Trusts: Interim Report*, London: Department for Education and Skills, available at <http://www.dfes.gov.uk/everychildmatters> accessed 24 July 2007

DfES (2005g) *Youth Matters* (Green Paper), available at <http://www.dfes.gov.uk/publications/youth

DfES (2005h) *Children and Young People's Plan (England) Regulations 2005*, London: The Stationery Office

DfES (2005i) *Guidance on the Children and Young People's Plan*, Nottingham: Department for Education and Skills

DfES (2005j) *Children's Workforce Strategy*, London: Department for Education and Skills

DfES (2006a) *Children's Workforce Strategy: Building a World-class Workforce for Children, Young People and Families*, London: Department for Education and Skills, available at <http://www.everychildmatters.gov.uk/_files/7D2DD37746721CC8E5F81323AD449DD7.pdf> accessed 24 July 2007

DfES (2006b) *Outcome Indicators for Looked After Children: Twelve Months to 30 September 2005, England*, available at <http://www.dfes.gov.uk/rsgateway/DB/SFR/s000651/SFR16-2006textv1.pdf> accessed 15 June 2006

DfES (2006c) *Working Together to Safeguard Children: A Guide to Inter-Agency Working to Safeguard and Promote the Welfare of Children*, London: The Stationery Office

DfES (2006d) *Youth Matters: Next Steps* <http://www.dfes.gov.uk/publications/youth accessed 24 July 2007

DfH (2000) 'The NHS Plan: a plan for investment, a plan for reform'

DfID (1997) *Eliminating World Poverty: A Challenge for the 21st Century*, White Paper on International Development, London: The Stationery Office, available at <http://www.dfid.gov.uk/pubs/files/whitepaper1997.pdf> accessed 24 July 2007

Dimond, B. (1996) *The Legal Aspects of Child Health Care*, London: Mosby

Disability Rights Commission (2004) 'DRC/03/9599', available at <http://www.drc-gb.org/thelaw/casedetails.asp?id=515&category=disability&subcat=learning> accessed 24 November 2005

Disability Rights Commission (2005a) 'Discrimination education', available at <http://www.drc-gb.org/knowyourrights/discrimination.asp> accessed 24 November 2005>

Disability Rights Commission (2005b) 'Sendist ref: 03-50019 (DIS)', available at <http://www.drc-gb.org/thelaw/casedetails.asp?=453&category=disability&subcat=learning> accessed 24 July 2007

Dispatches (2004) *Spiked*, Channel 4, First Frame, Guardian Films, 13 September 2004

DoH (1989) *An Introduction to the Children Act 1989*, London: The Stationery Office

DoH (1990) *The Children Act 1989: Guidance and Regulations II*, London: The Stationery Office

DoH (1991) *Working Together under The Children Act 1989: A Guide to Arrangements for Inter-Agency Co-operation for the Protection of Children from Abuse*, London: The Stationery Office

DoH (1999a) *Saving Lives: Our Healthier Nation*, London: The Stationery Office

DoH (1999b) *Working Together to Safeguard Children: A Guide to Inter-Agency Working to Safeguard and Promote the Welfare of Children*, London: The Stationery Office

DoH (2002) *Safeguarding Children: A Joint Chief Inspectors' Report on Arrangements to Safeguard Children*, London: Department of Health

DoH (2003) 'Statistical work areas – public health', available at <www.publications.doh.gov.uk/public/work_public_health.htm> accessed 30 April 2007

DoH (2004a) *Choosing Health: Making Healthier Choices Easier,* London: The Stationery Office

DoH (2004b) *National Service Framework for Children, Young People and Maternity Services,* London: Department of Health

DoH (2005) *National Service Framework for Children, Young People and Maternity Services: Executive Summary,* London: Department of Health, available at <http://www.dh.gov.uk> accessed 24 July 2007

Donaldson, M. (1978) *Children's Minds,* London: Fontana

Driskell, D. (2002) *Creating Better Cities with Children and Youth: A Manual for Participation,* London: Earthscan/UNESCO

DTLR (2002) *Improving Urban Parks, Play Areas and Green Spaces: Interim Literature Review,* London: Department of Transport, Local Government and the Regions

DWP (2002) *Children and Young People's Participation in Planning, Delivery and Evaluation of Policies and Services: The Action Plan of Department of Work and Pensions,* London: Department for Work and Pensions

DWP (2003) *UK Action Plan on Social Inclusion 2003–2005,* London: Department for Work and Pensions

DWP (2004) *Building on New Deal: Local Solutions Meeting Individual Needs,* London: Department for Work and Pensions

Ebbeling, C. B., Pawlak, D. B. and Ludwig, D. S. (2002) 'Childhood obesity: public health crisis, common sense cure', *Lancet,* 360: 473–82

Ebisch, R. (2005) 'Grand slam home run', available at <http://www.delta-sky.com/2005_12/Doctor/index.html> accessed 24 May 2006

Edelman, M. (1964) *The Symbolic Uses of Politics,* Illinois: University of Chicago Press

Education Reform Act 1988, available at <http://www.opsi.gov.uk/acts/acts1988> accessed 24 July 2007

Edwards, L. and Hatch, B. (2003) *Passing Time,* London: Institute of Public Policy Research

Edwards, R. and Duncan, S. (1996) 'Rational Economic Man or Lone Mothers in Context?', in Silva, E. B. *Good Enough Mothering?: Feminist Perspectives on Lone Motherhood,* London: Routledge

Electoral Commission (2004) <www.electoralcommission.org.uk> accessed 30 April 2007

Else, P. and Sturrock, G. (1998) 'The playground as therapeutic space: playwork as healing', in *Proceedings of the IPA/USA Triennial National Conference: Play in a Changing Society: Research, Design, Application,* Colorado, June, available at <http://www.ludemos.co.uk/COLFULLa4%20final%2007.pdf> accessed 24 July 2007

Equal Opportunities Commission (2006) available at <http://www.eoc.org.uk/> accessed 24 July 2007

ESRC Society Today (2006) *Welfare and Single Parenthood in the UK,* available at <http://www.esrc.ac.uk/ESRCInfoCentre/facts/UK/index40.aspx?ComponentId=12614&SourcePageId=14975> accessed 15 October 2006

European Commission (2001) *A New Impetus for European Youth,* White Paper, Brussels: European Commission

Ewles, L. and Simnett, I. (1999) *Promoting Health,* 4th edn, London: John Wiley and Sons

Fanon, F. (1986) *Black Skin, White Masks,* London: Pluto Press

Farrington, D. (2002) 'Understanding and preventing youth crime', in Muncie, J., Hughes, G. and McLaughlin, E. (eds) *Youth Justice Critical Readings,* London: Sage

Fatchett, A. (1995) *Childhood to Adolescence: Caring for Health,* London: Bailliere Tindall

Faux, K. (2004) 'Warning signs: special report child protection', *Nursery World,* 7 October

Fisher, E. P. (1992) 'The impact of play on development: a meta-analysis', *Play and Culture,* 5, 159–81

Fitzpatrick, S., Hastings, A. and Kintrea, K. (2000) 'Youth involvement in urban regeneration: hard lessons, future directions', *Policy and Politics,* 28(4), 493–509

Flaherty, J., Veit-Wilson, J. and Dornan, P. (2004) *Poverty: The Facts,* 5th edn, London: Child Poverty Action Group

Fletcher-Campbell, T., Archer, T. and Tomlinson, K. (2003) *The Role of the School in Supporting the Education of Children in Public Care,* Slough: National Foundation for Educational Research

Foley, P., Roche, J. and Tucker, S. (eds) (2001) *Children in Society,* London: Palgrave

Foot, M. (2004) 'ASBO absurdities', *The Guardian,* 1 December 2004, available at <http://society.guardian.co.uk/societyguardian/story/0,,1362899,00.html> accessed 27 May 2005

Forbat, L. (2004) 'The care and abuse of minoritized ethnic groups', *Critical Social Policy,* 24(3), August 312–31

Fortin, J. (1998) *Children's Rights and the Developing Law,* London: Butterworths

Fortin, J. (2002) 'The Human Rights Act 1998: Human rights for children', in Franklin, B. (2002) *The New Handbook of Children's Rights,* London: Routledge

Foucault, M. (1977) *Discipline and Punish: The Birth of the Prison,* trans. Alan Sheridan, Harmondsworth: Penguin

Franklin, B. (2002) *The New Handbook of Children's Rights: Comparative Policy and Practice,* 2nd edn, London: Routledge

Fransman, L. (1994) 'Future citizenship policy', in Spencer, S. (ed.) *Strangers and Citizens: A Positive Approach to Migrants and Refugees,* London: Rivers Oram Press

Freeman, C., Henderson, P. and Kettle, J. (1999) *Planning with Children for Better Communities,* Bristol: The Policy Press

Freeman, M. (2002) 'Children's rights ten years after ratification', in Franklin, B. (ed.) *The New Handbook of Children's Rights,* London: Routledge

French, S. and Swain, J. (2004) 'Young disabled people', in Roche, J., Tucker, S., Thompson, R. and Flynn, R. (eds) *Youth in Society,* London: Sage, Open University

Freud, S. (1974) The standard edition of the complete psychological works of Sigmund Freud, 24 volumes, trans. under the general editorship of James Strachey, with Anna Freud, Alix Strachey and Alan Tyson, London: Hogarth Press, Institute of Psychoanalysis

Friere, P. (1972) *Pedagogy of the Oppressed,* Harmondsworth: Penguin

Furling, A. and Carmel, F. (1997) *Young People and Social Change,* Buckingham: Open University Press

Gallagher, C. (1997) '*Our Town': An Architectural Perspective – Architecture and Inner-City, At Risk Children,* VisionQuest: Journeys towards visual literacy, Blacksburg VA: International Visual Literacy Association

Gallagher, C. (2004) ' "Our Town": children as advocates for change in the city', *Childhood,* 11(2), 252–62

Garvey, C. (1991) *Play,* 2nd edn, London: Fontana

Getaway Girls (2005) available at <http://www. getawaygirls.co.uk/about.asp> accessed 24 November 2005

Gilchrist, A. (2004) *The Well-Connected Community: A Networking Approach to Community Development,* Bristol: The Policy Press/CDF

GLA (2005) *Guide To Preparing Play Strategies: Planning Inclusive Play Spaces and Opportunities for All London's Children and Young People,* London: Greater London Authority

Goldson, B. (2002a) 'Children, Crime and the State', in Goldson, B., Lavalette, M. and McKechnie, J. (eds) *Children, Welfare and the State,* London: Sage

Goldson, B. (2002b) *Vulnerable Inside: Children in Secure and Penal Settings,* London: Children's Society

Goldson, B. and Muncie, J. (eds) (2006) *Youth Crime and Justice,* London: Sage

Goldson, B., Lavalette, M. and McKechnie, J. (eds) (2002) *Children, Welfare and the State,* London: Sage

Graber, D. (1976) *Verbal Behavior and Politics,* Illinois: University of Illinois Press

Graham, J. and Bowling, B. (1995) *Youth and Crime,* London: Home Office

Griffin, C. (1993) *Representations of Youth: The Study of Youth and Adolescence in Britain and America,* Cambridge: Polity Press

Griffith, R. (2000) *National Curriculum: National Disaster?: Education and Citizenship,* London: Routledge Falmer

Guardian, The (2003) 'We were in prison: I did not understand' 9 October 2003, available at <http://www. guardian.co.uk/child/story/0,7369,1058877,00.html> accessed 12 May 2005

Guardian, The (2005) 'Piggy in the Middle', by Alison Benjamin, 12 January

Hall, D. M. B. (1993) *Promoting Child Health,* Oxford: Radcliffe Medical Press

Hall, D. M. B. and Elliman, D. (eds) (2003) *Health For All Children,* 4th edn, Oxford: Oxford University Press, available at <http://www.health-for-all-children.co.uk> accessed 24 July 2007

Hall, G. S. (1904) *Adolescence: Its Psychology and its Relations to Physiology, Anthropology, Sociology, Sex, Crime, Religion and Education,* Vol. 1, New York: Appleton

Hall, S. (2003) 'The "Third Way" revisited: "New" Labour, Spatial Policy and the National strategy for neighbourhood Renewal', London: Routledge Taylor and Francis

Hallden, G. (1991) 'The child as project and the child as being: Parents' ideas as frames of reference', *Children and Society,* 5(4), 334–46

Hamilton, P. (2003) *Specialist Health Services for Children and Young People,* January 2003, London: Royal College of Paediatrics and Child Health

Hammer, T. (2000) 'Youth unemployment and social exclusion in Europe', available at <www.nuff.ox.ac.uk/ projects/uwwclus/papers> accessed 30 April 2007

Handbook (1904) *Handbook for Workers Involved in Homes for Waifs and Strays,* Church of England

Handelman, D. (1992) 'Passages to play: paradox and process', *Play and Culture,* 5, 1–19

Harding, L. (1996) *Family State and Social Policy,* Basingstoke: Macmillan

Harker, L. (2005) 'Lessons from Reggio Emilia', *The Guardian,* 11 November, pp. 11–12

Harper, S. (ed.) (2003) *The Family in Ageing Societies,* Oxford: Oxford University Press

Harper, S. (2003) *Changing Families as Societies Age,* Research Report Number RR103 Oxford: Oxford Institute of Ageing, University of Oxford

Harrison, A. (2003) 'Higher Degrees for State School Pupils' BBC News 24 July citing Higher Education Funding Council Report available at <http://news. bbc.co.uk/1/hi/education/3094023.stm> accessed 24 November 2005

Hart, R. (1995) 'The right to play and children's participation', in Shier, H. (ed.) *Article 31 Action Pack: Children's Rights and Children's Play*, Birmingham: Play Train

Hart, R. (1997) *Children's Participation: The Theory and Practice of Involving Young Citizens in Community Development and Environmental Care*, London: Earthscan

Haw, K. (1998) *Educating Muslim Girls*, Buckingham: Open University Press

Hayes, A. (2002) 'Making the best of Best Value', *Playtoday*, 33(Nov/Dec), 4–5

Hayes, N. (1994) *Foundations of Psychology*, London: Routledge

Health for All Children, see Hall and Elliman (2003)

Henderson, P. (ed.) (1995) *Children and Communities*, London: Pluto Press

Henderson, P. (1997) 'Community development and children: a contemporary agenda', in Cannan, C. and Warren, C. (eds) *Social Action with Children and Families*, London: Routledge

Henderson, P. and Thomas, D. (2002) *Skills in Neighbourhood Work*, 3rd edn, London: Routledge

Highland Council/NHS Highland (undated) 'All to Play for, Highland Play Strategy 2006–10, Highland Council', p. 12, available at <www.highland.gov.uk> accessed 22 October 2006

Hilgard, E. and Atkinson, R. L. (1979) *Introduction to Psychology*, New York: Harcourt Brace Jovanovich

Hill, M. and Tisdall, K. (1997) *Children and Society*, London: Longman

HLF (2006) *Parks for people*, Heritage Lottery Fund and the Big Lottery Fund, available at <http://www.hlf.org.uk/English/HowToApply/OurGrantGivingProgrammes/Parks+for+People/> accessed 24 July 2007

HM Treasury (2004) *Choice for Parents, The Best Start for Children: A Ten Year Strategy for Childcare*, London: The Stationery Office

HMSO (2002) Nationality, Immigration and Asylum Act 2002, Section 36(2) <http://www.opsi.gov.uk/ACTS/acts 2002>

Holman, B. (1981) *Kids at the Door*, Oxford: Blackwell

Holman, B. (2000) *Kids at the Door Revisited*, Lyme Regis: Russell House Publishing

Holt, J. (1967) *How Children Fail*, New York: Pitman

Home Office (1997) *Preventing Children Offending: A consultation document*, available at <http://www.homeoffice.gov.uk/docs/tyc1.html> accessed 7 June 2005

Home Office (2005) Extracts from Table A2: Persons of all ages and unknown, Number of anti-social behaviour orders issued at all courts by area and year, April 1999 to September 2004, available at <http://www.crimereduction.gov.uk/asbos2.htm> accessed 22 April 2005

Hope, A. and Timmel, S. (1995) *Training for Transformation: A Handbook for Community Workers*, Gweru: Mambo Press

Horton, C. (ed.) *Working with Children* 2004–5, London: Guardian Books

House of Commons (2004) *Select Committee on Work and Pensions*, 2nd report, Session 2003–4, 31 March, available at <http://www.publications.parliament.uk/pa/cm200304/cmselect/cmworpen/85/8506.htm> accessed 4 November 2005

Howard League for Penal Reform (2004) Press Release, September, available at <http://www.howardleague.org/press/2004/220904.htm> accessed 25 November 2004

Howard League for Penal Reform (2005) campaigns, available at <http://www.howardleague.org/campaigns/campaignsindex.htm> accessed 22 April 2005

Howard, M. (2004) *Tax Credits One Year On*, London: Child Poverty Action Group

Hudson, A. (2002) ' "Troublesome girls": towards alternative definitions and policies', in Muncie, J., Hughes, G. and McLaughlin, E. (eds) *Youth Justice Critical Readings*, London: Sage

Hughes, B. (2001) *Evolutionary Playwork and Reflective Analytic Practice*, London: Routledge

Hughes, B. (2006) *Play Types: Speculations and Possibilities*, London: London Centre for Playwork Education and Training

Hughes, B. and Williams, H. (1982) 'Looking at Play', *Play Times*, 35 (also in 31–34), London: National Playing Fields Association

Hughes, B. (1996) *A playworker's taxonomy of play types*, London: Playlink

Hughes, F. P. (1999) *Children, Play and Development*, 3rd edn, Needham Heights MA: Simon and Schuster Company

Hughes, B. (2003) 'Play deprivation and bias', in Brown, F. (ed.) *Playwork Theory and Practice*, Buckingham: Open University Press

Huizinga, J. (1949) *Homo Ludens: A Study of the Play Element in Culture*, London: Routledge & Kegan Paul

Hultqvist, K. and Dahlberg, G. (2001) *Governing the child in the new millennium*, London: Routledge Falmer

Hulyer, B. (1997) 'Long-term development: neighbourhood community development work on estates', in Cannan, C. and Warren, C. (1997) *Social Action with Children and Families: A Community Development Approach to Child and Family Welfare*, London: Routledge

Hunt, R. (2000) *The Educational Performance of Children in Need and Children Looked After*, London: Department of Health

ILO (2002) 'A future without child labour', London: International Labour Office

Immigration and Nationality Directorate (2005) 'Frequently Asked Questions', London: Home Office

Jackson, S. (1987a) *The Education of Children in Care*, Bristol: University of Bristol

Jackson, S. (1987b) 'Residential care and education', *Children & Society*, 2(4), 335–50

Jackson, S. and Sachdev, D. (2001) *Better Education, Better Futures: Research, Practice and the Views of Young People in Public Care*, Ilford: Barnardo's

Jaggi, M. (1999) 'Swaddled in red tape', *The Guardian*, 7 July, available at <http://arts.guardian.co.uk/features/story/0,,701469,00.html> accessed 7 July 1999

James, A. and James, A. (2004) *Constructing Childhood: Theory, Policy and Social Practice*, Basingstoke: Palgrave Macmillan

James, A. and James, A. L. (2004) *Constructing Childhood*, Basingstoke: Palgrave Macmillan

James, A. and Prout, A. (eds) (1997) *Constructing and Reconstructing Childhood: Contemporary Issues in the Sociological Study of Childhood*, London: Falmer

Jeffs, T. (1997) 'Changing their ways: youth work and underclass theory', in MacDonald, R. (ed.) *Youth, the Underclass and Social Exclusion*, London: Routledge

Jeffs, T. and Smith, M. K. (1999) 'The problem of "youth" for youth work', *Youth and Policy*, 62, 45–66

Jeffs, T. and Smith, M. (2005) *Informal Education: Conversation, Democracy and Learning*, Nottingham: Educational Heretics Press

Jennes, D. (2001) 'Origins of the myth of race', in Cashmore, E. and Jennings, J. (eds) *Racism: Essential Readings*, London: Sage

Jensen, A. and McKee, L. (2001) *Children and the Changing Family*, London: Routledge Falmer

Johnson, J. E., Christie, J. F. and Yawkey, T. D. (1987) *Play and Early Childhood Development*, London: Scott, Foresman and Company

Johnson, M. (2004) *Beyond the Boundaries, Children Now: Guide to Careers*, London: Haymarket

Johnson, V., Ivan-Smith, E., Gordon, G., Pridmore, P. and Scott, P. (1998) *Stepping Forward: Children and Young People's Participation in the Development Process*, London: Intermediate Technology Publications

Jones, G. (2002) *The Youth Divide: Diverging Paths to Adulthood*, York: Joseph Rowntree Foundation

Jones, S. (2004) 'Language barriers', *The Guardian*, Wednesday 11 August 2004

Jones, C. and Novak, T. (1999) *Poverty and the Disciplinary State*, London: Routledge

Joseph Rowntree Trust (2002) Comprehensive research 1997–2002, available at <http://www.jrf.org.uk> accessed 24 July 2007

Kane, E. (2005) *The Big Lottery*, UKplayworkers Website entry, available at <http://groups.yahoo.com/group/UKplayworks> accessed 2 December 2005

Katz, A. (2003) 'A step backwards', *The Guardian*, Thursday 6 February 2003, available at <http://politics.guardian.co.uk/apathy/comment/0,,890564,00.html> accessed 6 February 2003

Kay, J. (2000) *Good Practice in Childcare*, London: Continuum

Kettle, J., Littlewood, S. and Maye-Banbury, A. (2004) *Impact Evaluation of the Selected Demolition of Housing*, London: Office of the Deputy Prime Minister

Kids' Clubs Network (2002) *Ready Steady Go!: Starting Up and Running Your Out of School Kids' Club*, rev. edn, London: Kids' Clubs Network

Kidsource (2002) available at <www.kidsource.com/kidsource/content> accessed 27 April 2007

Kincaid, J. (1976) *Poverty and Equality*, London: Penguin

Kirby, P. (2001) *Involving Children and Young People in Regeneration: Learning from 'Young Voices'*, Birmingham: Groundwork UK and Save the Children

Kirby, P. and Bryson, S. (2002) *Measuring the Magic?: Evaluating and Researching Young People's Participation in Public Decision Making*, London: Carnegie Young People Initiative

Klein, M. (1955) 'The psychoanalytical play technique: its history and significance', in Mitchell, J. (ed.) (1986) *The Selected Melanie Klein*, Harmondsworth, Penguin, pp. 35–54

Laming, Lord (2003) *The Victoria Climbié Inquiry*, London: The Stationery Office, available at <http://www.victoria-climbie-inquiry.org.uk> accessed 24 July 2007

Lazarus, M. (1883) *Uber die Reize des Spiels*, Berlin: Dummler

Lea, J. and Young, J. (1993) *What Is to be Done About Law and Order?*, London: Pluto

Leach, P. (1994) *Children First*, London: Michael Joseph

Learning and Skills Council (2005) 'Response to the Green Paper Youth Matters', available at <www.readingroom.lsc.gov.uk/LSC/2005/research> accessed 27 April 2007

Lees, S. (1993) *Sugar and Spice: Sexuality and Adolescent Girls*, Harmondsworth: Penguin

Lees, S. (1997a) *Carnal Knowledge: Rape on Trial*, Harmondsworth: Penguin

Lees, S. (1997b) *Ruling Passions: Sexual Violence, Reputation and the Law,* Buckingham: Open University Press

Lenton, S. (2004) 'Child Healthcare goals unveiled', available at <http://news.bbc.co.uk/1/hi/health> accessed 15 September 2004

Lester, S. (2004) *Nine Processes of Playwork,* London: SkillsActive available at <http://www.playwork.org.uk/downloads/9processes.doc> accessed 4 April 2006

Link, R. J. and Bibus, A. A. with Lyons, K. (2000) *When Children Pay: US Welfare Reform and Its Implications for UK Policy,* London: Child Poverty Action Group

Lister, R. (2001) 'Foreword', in Fimister, G. (ed.) *An End in Sight?: Tackling Child Poverty in the UK,* London: Child Poverty Action Group

Littlewood, M. (2003) *Response to 'Every Child Matters' and 'Keeping Children Safe',* London: Liberty, available at <http://www.liberty-human-rights.org.uk/press.press-releases-2003/response-to-every-matters.shtml> accessed 6 May 2005

Lloyd, T. (2005) 'Respect agenda calls for more responsibility in communities', *Young People Now,* available at <http://www.ypnmagazine.com/> accessed 24 July 2007

Local Authority Social Services Act 1970, London: The Stationery Office, available at <http://www.parliament.the-stationery-office.co.uk> accessed 24 July 2007

Local Government Finance Report (2005/06) 'Communities and Local Government', available at www.local.odpm.gov.uk/finance/0506/grant.htm accessed 27 April 2007

Lohde, L. (2004) 'Will the poor measure up?', *The Guardian,* 18 March 2004, available at <http://society.guardian.co.uk/socialexclusion/comment/0,,1171392,00.html> accessed 27 May 2005

London Development Agency (2004) *The Educational Experiences of Black Boys in London Schools 2000–2003,* available at <http://www.lda.gov.uk/server.php?show=ConWebDoc.568>

Macauley, N. (2003) *Comment,* London: British Association of Social Workers, available at <http://www.basw.co.uk/articles.php?article=109> accessed 27 May 2005

MacFarlane, A. and Mitchell, R. (1988) 'Health services for children and their relationship to the educational and social services', in Forfar, J. O. (ed.) *Child Health in a Changing Society,* Oxford: British Paediatric Association

MacFaul, R. et al. (2004) *See* ONS (2004)

McGillycuddy, K. (1991) *Response to Karen Pitman: Future Choices,* Washington DC: Youth Policy Institute

McInroy, N. and MacDonald, S. (2005) *From Community Garden to Westminster: Active Citizenship and the Role of Public Space,* London: Centre for Local Economic Strategies

McKendrick, J. H., Bradford, M. G. and Fielder, A. V. (2000) 'Kid customer?: Commercialization of playspace and the commodification of childhood', *Childhood: A global journal of child research, Special Issue: Spaces of childhood,* Vol. 7, Issue 3, August

MacPherson, W. (1999) *The Stephen Lawrence Enquiry,* London: The Stationery Office

Maguire, M. (1994) 'Crime statistics, patterns and trends: changing perceptions and their implications', in Maguire, M., Morgan, R. and Reiner, R. (1994) *The Oxford Handbook of Criminology,* Oxford: Oxford University Press

Marketlooks (2001) *The US Tween Market: Overall,* Marketlooks Packaged Facts available at <http://www.packagedfacts.com/Tween-Overall-423696/> accessed 24 July 2007

Matthews, H. (2001) *Children and Community Regeneration,* London: Save the Children

Matthews, H. (2002) 'Children and regeneration: setting and agenda for community participation and integration', *Children and Society,* 17, 264–76

Mayall, B. (ed.) (1994) *Children's Childhoods,* London: Falmer

Mayall, B. and Foster, M. (1989) *Child Health Care,* Heinemann Nursing, London

Means, R. and Smith, R. (1996) *Community Care, Housing and Homelessness: Issues, Obstacles and Innovative Practice,* London: Policy Press

Melville, S. (1999) 'Creating spaces for adventure', *Built Environment,* 25, 1

Mental Health Foundation (1999) *Bright Futures,* London: Mental Health Foundation

Merton, B., Payne, M. and Smith, D. (2004) *An Evaluation of the Impact of Youth Work in England,* Nottingham: DfES Publications

Micklewright, J. (2000) *Macroeconomics and Data on Children,* Innocenti Working Papers, ESP No. 73. Florence: UNICEF

Middleton, L. (1992) *Children First: Working with Children and Disability,* Birmingham: Venture Press

Millie, A., Jacobson, J., McDonald, E. and Hough, M. (2005) *Anti-Social Behaviour Strategies: Finding a Balance,* Bristol: The Policy Press

Mills, J. and Mills, R. (1999) *Childhood Studies,* London: Routledge Falmer

Ministry of Education (1944) *Education Act* (Sections 41 and 53), London: The Stationery Office

Ministry of Education (1960) *The Youth Service in England and Wales* (The Albemarle Report), London: The Stationery Office

Mitzen, P. (2003) 'The best days of your life?: Youth policy and Blair's New Labour', *Critical Social Policy*, Vol. 23

Monk, D. (2004) 'Childhood and the law: in whose "best interests"?', in Franklin, B. (ed.) *The New Handbook of Children's Rights*, London: Routledge

Montalembert, C. F. R. (1856) *The Political Future of England*, (Chapter 10), London: J. Murray (this is the earliest reference to a remark that is usually attributed to the Duke of Wellington)

Montgomery, H., Burr, R. and Woodhead, M. (eds) (2003) *Changing Childhoods: Local and Global*, Chichester: Wiley and The Open University

Moore, S. (2005) 'The State of the Youth Service: recruitment and retention rates of youth workers in England's National Youth Agency (1998) *England's Youth Service*, The 1998 Audit, Leicester: National Youth Agency

Moorhead, J. (2000) 'Kids rule', *The Guardian*, 24 October 2000

Morrow, V. (2002) 'Children's Rights to Public Space: Environment and Curfews', in Franklin, B. *The New Handbook of Children's Rights*, London: Routledge

Moss, D. (2006) *Gender, Space and Time: Women and Higher Education*, Lanham MD: Rowman & Littlefield

Moss, P. (2001) 'The otherness of Reggio', in Abbott, L. and Nutbrown, C. (2001) *Experiencing Reggio Emilia: Implications for Preschool Provision*, Buckingham: Open University Press

Moss, P. (2002) Time to say farewell to 'early childhood'? *Contemporary Issues in Early Childhood*, 3(3), 435–8

Moss, P. and Penn, H. (1996) *Transforming Nursery Education*, London: Paul Chapman Publishing

Moss, P. and Petrie, P. (2002) *From Children's Services to Children's Spaces: Public Provision, Children and Childhood*, London: Routledge Falmer

Muncie, J. (2004) *Youth and Crime*, 2nd edn, London: Sage

Muncie, J. and Hughes, G. (2002) 'Modes of youth governance: political rationalities, criminalization and resistance', in Muncie, J., Hughes, G. and McLaughlin, E. (eds) *Youth Justice Critical Readings*, London: Sage

Murray, C. (1990) *The Emerging British Underclass*, London: Institute of Economic Affairs

Nacro (2005) 'Youth Crime briefing: Some Facts About Young People who Offend – 2003', London: Nacro Youth Crime (March)

Naidoo, J. and Wills, J. (2000) *Health Promotion: Foundations for Practice*, 2nd edn, London: Bailliere Tindall

National Strategy for Neighbourhood Renewal (2000) *Report for Policy Action Team 12: Children and Young People*, available at <http://www.socialexclusionunit. gov.uk/downloaddoc.asp?id=125> accessed 24 July 2007

NCO (2004) *Ready, Steady, Play!: A National Play Policy*, Dublin: National Children's Office

Neighbourhood Renewal Unit (2005) *Making It Happen in Neighbourhoods*, available at <http://www. neighbourhood.gov.uk/publications.asp?did=1193> accessed 24 July 2007

Neill, A. S. (1968) *Summerhill*, Harmondsworth: Penguin Books

New Deal for Communities (2004) *Young People in NDC Areas: Findings from Six Case Studies*, Research Report 20, available at *www,ndcevaluation,adc,shu, ac,uk/ndcevaluation/home,asp* accessed 24 July 2007

Newcastle City Council (2004) Refugee and Asylum Seeker Information Booklet and Directory for Schools <http://www.qca.org.uk/downloads/ cs-newcastle-refugee-asylum-seekers.pdf>

Novak, T. (2002) 'Rich children, poor children', in Goldson, B., Lavalette, M. and McKechnie, J. *Children, Welfare and the State*, London: Sage

NPFA (1926) *Proceedings of the Inaugural Meeting of the National Playing Fields Association*, London: National Playing Fields Association

NPFA (1933) *Royal Charter of Incorporation (18th January 1933)* Section 5 (B), London: National Playing Fields Association

NPFA (1952) *Conference for local authorities*, London: National Playing Fields Association

NPFA (1954) *Conference for local authorities*, London: National Playing Fields Association

NPFA (2000) *Best Play: What Play Provision Should Do for Children*, London: NPFA/Children's Play Council/ Playlink and Department of Culture, Media and Sport

NYA (2004) *The Youth Manifesto: A Pocket Guide for Local National Politicians from the National Youth Agency*, Leicester: National Youth Agency

Oakley, A. (1994) 'Women and children first and last: parallels and differences between women's and children's studies', in Mayall, B. (ed.) *Children's Childhoods*, London: Routledge Falmer

OCLC (2007) *Size and Growth Statistics*, Dublin OH: Online Computer Library Center <http://www.oclc. org/research/projects/archive/wcp/stats/size.htm> accessed 23 April 2007

ODPM (2000a) *Our Towns and Cities: The Future: Delivering an Urban Renaissance*, White Paper, London: Office of the Deputy Prime Minister, available at <http://communities.gov.uk/index. asp?id=1127168> accessed 24 July 2007

ODPM (2000b) Report of Policy Action Team 12: Young people, available at <www.crimereduction.gov.uk> accessed 30 April 2007

ODPM (2002) *A Learning Curve: Developing Skills and Language for Neighbourhood Renewal,* London: ODPM

ODPM (2003) *Learning to Listen: Action Plan for Children and Young People,* available at <www.communities.gov.uk/embeddedobject> accessed 30 April 2007

ODPM (2004) *Making it happen: The Northern Way,* available at <www.odpm.gov.uk/index> accessed 30 April 2007

ODPM (2006) 'Research Report 17, New Deal for Community 2001–2005, an interim evaluation', CRESER, Sheffield Hallam University: Sheffield

Ofsted (2001) *Raising Achievement of Children in Public Care,* London: Ofsted

Ofsted (2003) The Education of Asylum-Seeker Pupils, London: Ofsted

Ofsted (2005) *Every Child Matters: Inspection of Children's Services; Key Judgements and Illustrative Evidence,* Section 3.6 available at <http://www.ofsted.gov.uk/publications> accessed 17 April 2006

Ofsted (2006) *Framework for the Regulation of Childminding and Day Care,* available at <http://www.ofsted.gov.uk/publications> accessed 24 July 2007

Oliver, M. (1990) *The Politics of Disablement,* London: Macmillan

Oliver, M. and Barnes, C. (1998) *Disabled People and Social Policy: From Exclusion to Inclusion,* London: Longman

ONS (1998) www.statistics.gov.uk/downloads/theme_compendia accessed 30 April 2007

ONS (2004) 'The health of children and young people', available at <http://www.statistics.gov.uk/children/downloads/prov_use_services.pdf> accessed 24 July 2007

Oxley, H., Dang, T.-T., Forster, M. F. and Pellizzari, M. (2001) 'Income inequalities and poverty among children and households in selected OECD countries', in Vleminekx, K. and Smeeding, T. M. (eds) *Child Well-being, Child Poverty and Child Policy in Modern Nations,* Bristol: Policy Press

Payne, G. (2000) 'An introduction to social divisions', in Payne, G. (ed.) *Social Divisions,* Basingstoke: Palgrave Macmillan

Pearson, G. (1983) *Hooligan, History of Respectable Fears,* London: Macmillan

Penn, H. (2005) *Understanding Early Childhood: Issues and Controversies,* Maidenhead: Open University Press

Perri, G. (1997*) Holistic Government,* London: Demos

Piachaud, D. (1999) 'Means to an end', *The Guardian,* 31 March, available at <http://society.guardian.co.uk/guardiansociety/story/0,,308014,00.html> accessed 27 May 2005

Piachaud, D. (2005) 'Child poverty: an overview', in Preston, G. (ed.) *At Greatest Risk: The Children Most Likely to Be Poor,* London: Child Poverty Action Group

Piaget, J. (1951) *Play, Dreams and Imitation in Childhood,* London: Routledge & Kegan Paul

Pierson, J. (2002) *Tackling Social Exclusion,* London: Routledge

Pitts, J. (ed.) (2003) *Crime, Disorder and Community Safety,* London: Routledge

Play Wales (2005) *Playwork Principles,* Cardiff: Play Wales

Powell, R. (ed.) (2004) *People Making Places: Imagination in the Public Realm,* Wakefield: PublicArts

Preston, G. (2005) *Helter Skelter: Families, Disabled Children and the Benefit System,* Case Paper 92: Disability Alliance and ESRC, London: Centre for Analysis of Social Exclusion

Pridmore, P. (1996) 'Visualizing health: exploring perceptions of children using draw-and-write method', *Health Promotion and Education,* December, 3(4): 11–15

Pridmore, P. and Stephens, D. (2000) *Children as Partners for Health: A Critical Review of The Child-to-Child Approach,* London: Zed Books

Pringle, K. (1998) *Children and social welfare in Europe,* Buckingham: OUP

Pringle, M. L. K. (1974) *The Needs of Children,* London: Hutchinson

Prout, A. (2000) 'Children's participation: control and self-realisation in British late modernity', *Children & Society* 14, 304–15

Prout, A. (2003) 'Children, representation and social change', keynote address European Early Childhood Education Research Association (EECERA)

QCA (2000) *The National Curriculum,* London: Qualifications and Curriculum Authority

QCA (2005) *Futures: Meeting the Challenges,* available at <http://www.qca.org.uk/>

Qvortrup, J. (1994) 'A new solidarity contract?: The significance of a demographic balance for the welfare of children and the elderly', in Qvortrup, J., Bardy, M., Sgritta, G. B. and Winterberger, H. (eds) *Childhood Matters: Social Theory, Practice and Politics,* Aldershot: Avebury, pp. 319–34

Qvortrup, J., Bardy, M., Sgritta, G. and Wintersberger, H. (eds) (1994) *Childhood Matters: Social Theory, Practice and Politics,* Aldershot: Avebury

Reaney, M. J. (1916) *The Psychology of the Organized Game,* Cambridge: Cambridge University Press, cited in Schwartzman, H. B. (1978) *Transformations: The Anthropology of Children's Play,* London: Plenum Press

Redhead, Z. (2003) 'Summerhill by Zoe', available at <http://www.summerhillschool.co.uk/pages/summerhill_by_zoe.html> accessed 24 July 2007

Refugee Council Information (2004) 'Nailing Press Myths about Refugees', London: Refugee Council

Refugee Council (2006) *The Nationality, Immigration and Asylum Act 2002: Changes to the Asylum System in the UK,* London: Refugee Council

Riddell, S. and Tett, L. (eds) (2001) *Education, Social Justice and Inter-Agency Working: Joined-up or Fractured Policy?,* London: Routledge

Roaf, C. (2002) *Coordinating Services for Included Children: Joined Up Action,* Buckingham: Open University Press

Roberts, P. (2005) 'Launch of the Academy for Sustainable Communities', available at <www.ascskills.org.uk> accessed 14 November 2005

Roberts, H. (2000) *What Works in Reducing Inequalities in Child Health: Summary,* available at <http://www.barnardos.org.uk/resources> accessed 24 July 2007

Roberts, R. (1996) 'In the schema of things', *The Times Educational Supplement,* November

Rogers, W. S. *See* Foley, P. et al. (2001)

ROSPA (2006) *Accidents to Children,* Birmingham: Royal Society for the Prevention of Accidents, available at <http://www.rospa.com/homesafety/advice/child/accidents.htm> accessed 24 July 2007

Rutter, J. (1994) *Refugee Children in the Classroom,* Stoke-on-Trent: Trentham Books

Rutter, J. (2003) *Supporting Refugee Children in 21st Century Britain,* Stoke-on-Trent: Trentham Books

Rutter, J. and Jones, C. (eds) (2001) *Refugee Education: Mapping the Field,* Stoke-on-Trent: Trentham Books

Rutter, J. and Hyder, T. (1998) *Refugee Children in the Early Years: Issues for Policy-makers and Providers,* London: Save the Children

Rutter, J. (2006) *Refugee Children in the UK,* Buckingham: Open University Press

Sahota, P., Rudolf, M., Dixey, R., Hill, A., Barth, J. and Cade, J. (2001) 'Evaluation of implementation and effect of school-based intervention to reduce risk factors for obesity', *British Medical Journal,* 323: 1027–9

Save the Children Sweden (2002) *Children's Environmental Rights,* Stockholm: Save the Children Sweden

SCCD (2001) *A Strategic Framework for Community Development,* Sheffield: Standing Conference for Community Development (now CDX, available at <http://www.cdx.org.uk/>)

Schwartzman, H. B. (1978) *Transformations: The Anthropology of Children's Play,* London: Plenum Press

Scott, C. (2002) 'Citizenship education: who pays the piper?', in Franklin, B. (2002) *The New Handbook of Children's Rights: Comparative Policy and Practice,* London: Routledge

Scraton, P. (ed.) (1987) *Law, Order and the Authoritarian State,* Milton Keynes: Open University Press

Scraton, P. and Haydon, D. (2002) 'Challenging the criminalisation of children and young people: securing a rights based agenda', in Muncie, J., Hughes, G. and McLaughlin, E. (eds) *Youth Justice Critical Readings,* London: Sage

Seebohm, F. (1968) *Report of the Committee on Local Authority and Allied Personal Social Services,* (Seebohm Report) London: The Stationery Office

SEU (1998a) *Bringing Britain Together: A National Strategy for Neighbourhood Renewal,* London: The Stationery Office, Cm4045

SEU (1998b) *Rough Sleeping,* London: The Stationery Office, Cm 4342

SEU (1998c) *Truancy and Exclusion,* London: The Stationery Office, Cm 3957

SEU (1999a) *Bridging the Gap,* London: The Stationery Office, Cm 4404

SEU (1999b) *Teenage Pregnancy,* London: The Stationery Office, Cm 4342

SEU (2000) *Children and Young People,* Policy Action Team 12 report available at <http://www.socialexclusion.gov.uk>

SEU (2001) *A New Commitment to Neighbourhood Renewal: National Strategy Action Plan,* London: Office of the Deputy Prime Minister

SEU (2003) *A Better Education for Children in Care,* London: Social Exclusion Unit

Shah, R. and Hatton, C. (1999) *Caring Alone: Young Carers in South Asian Communities,* Ilford: Barnardo's

Shipman, A. (1999) *The Market Revolution and Its Limits: A Price for Everything,* London: Routledge

Singer, J. L. (1995) 'Imaginative play and adaptive development', in Goldstein, J. (ed.) *Toys, Play and Child Development,* Cambridge: Cambridge University Press

SkillsActive (2005) *Skills Needs Assessment for Playwork,* London: SkillsActive

Sluckin, A. (1981) *Growing Up in the Playground: The Social Development of Children,* London: Routledge & Kegan Paul

Smith, P., Cowie, H. and Blades, M. (2003) *Understanding Children's Development,* 4th edn, Oxford: Blackwell Publishing

Smith, R. (2006) 'Actuarialism and early intervention in contemporary youth justice', in Goldson, B. and Muncie, J. (eds) *Youth Crime and Justice,* London: Sage

Social Services Inspectorate (1995) *The Education of Children Who Are Looked After by Local Authorities,* London: Social Services Inspectorate

Sorensen, C. Th. (1931) *Open Spaces for Town And Country,* quoted in Allen of Hurtwood, Lady M. (1968) *Planning for Play,* London: Thames and Hudson

Spariosu, M. (1989) *Dionysus Reborn: Play and the Aesthetic Dimension in Modern Philosophical and Scientific Discourse,* Ithaca NY: Cornell University Press

Spencer, H. (1873) *Principles of Psychology,* New York: Appleton, cited in Hayes, N. (1994) *Foundations of Psychology,* London: Routledge

Spencer, N. J. (1996) *Poverty and Child Health,* Abingdon: Radcliffe

St Co Deb (2003) Welsh Grand Committee *The Economy in Wales* col. 3 http://www.publications.parliament.uk/pa/cm200304/cmstand/welshg/st031216/am/31216s01.htm

Stainton Rogers, W. (1989) 'Effective co-operation in child protection work', in Morgan, S. and Righton, P. (eds) *Child Care: Concerns and Conflicts,* London: Hodder & Stoughton

Stanley, K. (2005) 'Young asylum seekers and refugees in the UK', in Barry, M. (ed.) *Youth Policy and Social Inclusion: Critical Debates with Young People,* London: Routledge

Stanley, K., Bellamy, K. and Cooke, G. (2006) *Equal Access?: Appropriate and Affordable Childcare for Every Child,* London: IPPR

Stonewall (1996) *Queer Bashing: A National Survey of Hate Crimes Against Lesbians and Gay Men,* available at <http://wwwstonewall.org.uk/stonewall/information_bank/violent_hate_crime/resources/queer_bashing.html> accessed 25 November 2004

Stonewall (2004) *Age of Consent,* available at <http://www.stonewall.org.uk/docs/Scan3.pdf> accessed 24 September 2004

Stonewall (2005) *Help Us Stamp Out Homophobic Bullying in Schools Campaign,* available at <http://www.stonewall.org.uk/education_for_all/default.asp> accessed 24 November 2005

Stretch, B. (ed.) (2002) *BTEC National Health Studies,* Oxford: Heinemann

Sturrock, G., Russell, W. and Else, P. (2004) *Towards Ludogogy, Parts I, II and III: The Art of Being and Becoming Through Play* (The Birmingham Paper), Leigh-on-Sea: Ludemos Press

Sure Start (2002) *Birth to Three Matters,* London: DfES/Sure Start, available at <http://www.surestart.gov.uk/> accessed 24 July 2007

Sure Start (2004) *Spending Review 2004 DfES Public Service Agreement,* London: DfES/Sure Start, available at <http://www.surestart.gov.uk/improvingquality/targets/psatargets200508/fulldetails/> accessed 23 April 2007

Sutton, P. (1997) 'All in the same boat: rowing in the same direction?: Influences on collaboration over children's services', in Cohen, B. and Hagen, U. (eds) *Children's Services: Shaping up for the Millennium,* Edinburgh: Stationery Office

Sutton-Smith, B. (1997) *The Ambiguity of Play,* London: Harvard University Press

Sylva, K. (2004) *The Effective Provision of Pre-school Education (EPPE) Project: Effective Pre-school Education: A Longitudinal Study Funded by the DfES 1997–2004,* Annesley: Department for Education and Skills

Thomas, G. (2003) 'A vote at birth', *The Guardian,* Thursday 6 February 2003

Thomas, K. (1990) *Gender and Subject in Higher Education,* Milton Keynes: Society for Research into Higher Education and Open University Press

Thomas, P. (2003) 'Community cohesion and the role of youth work in building social capital, young people', *Youth and Policy* 81

Thompson, N. (1997) *Anti-Discriminatory Practice,* 2nd edn, BASW Practical Social Work, Basingstoke: Macmillan

Thomson, H., Aslangul, S., Holden, C. and Meggitt, C. (2000) *Health and Social Care,* 3rd edn, London: Hodder & Stoughton

Towner, E., Dowswell, T. and Jarvis, S. (1993) *Reducing Childhood Accidents: The Effectiveness of Health Promotion Interventions: A Literature Review,* London: Health Education Authority

Toynbee, P. and Walker, D. (2005) *Better or Worse?: Has Labour Delivered?,* London: Bloomsbury

Toys and Games Market Report (2005) 'Toys and games market report', May, Hampton: Key Note Publications Ltd, available at <http://www.keynote.co.uk/> accessed 24 July 2007

Turner, D. and Martin, S. (2002) 'Managerialism meets community development: contracting for social inclusion?', *Policy and Politics,* 32, 21–32

UN (1989) *Convention on the Rights of the Child,* available at <http://www.unicef.org/crc/fulltext> accessed 23 April 2007

UN (2000) *Committee on the Rights of the Child*, available at <http://193.194.138.190> accessed 23 April 2007

UN (2007) UN Resolution A/RES/50/81 'The World Programme of Action for Youth to the Year 2000 and Beyond', available at <http://www.un.org/esa/socdev/unyin/global.htm> accessed 23 April 2007

UNHCR (2005) <www.unhcr.org.uk/info/briefings/statistics/index> accessed 30 April 2007

UNICEF (1991) *United Nations Convention on the Rights of the Child, Article 31*, Svenska UNICEF Kommitten

UNICEF (2000) *League Table of Child Poverty in Rich Nations*, Innocenti Report Cards 1, Florence: UNICEF available at <http://www.unicef-icdc.org/research> accessed 24 July 2007

UNICEF (2004) *The State of the World's Children 2004*, New York: UNICEF

UNICEF (2005a) *The State of the World's Children 2005: Childhood Under Threat*, New York: UNICEF

UNICEF (2005b) *Human Rights Issues*, available at <http://www.unicef.org.uk/crc/humanr.htm> accessed 24 July 2007

UNICEF (UK) / United Nations Children's Fund (2007) 'Child labour: international and UK perspectives', available at www.eldis.org/static/DOC17940 (under Child Labour today) accessed 28 April 2007

Utting, W. (1997) *People like Us: A Review of the Safeguards of Children Living Away From Home*, London: The Stationery Office

Vernon, J. (1998) *Maintaining Children in School: The Contribution of Social Services Departments*, London: National Children's Bureau

de Vylder, S. (2001) 'A macroeconomic policy for children in the era of globalization', in Cornia, G. A. (ed.) *Harnessing Globalisation for Children: A Report to UNICEF*, Florence: UNICEF

Wade, J., Mitchell, F. and Bayliss, G. (2005) 'Unaccompanied asylum seeking children. The response of social work services', London: British Association of Adoption and Fostering

Wainright, M. (2002) 'The Gated Community', *The Guardian*, 28 November

Wainwright, G. (2001) *Read Faster, Recall More: Use Proven Techniques for Speed Reading and Maximum Recall*, Oxford: How To Books

Warburton, D. (1998) *Community and Sustainable Development: Participation in the Future*, London: Earthscan Publications

Webster, C. (1994) *Youth Crime, Victimisation and Racial Harassment: Keighley Crime Survey*, Bradford: Bradford and Ilkley College, Centre for Research in Applied Community Studies

Webster, C. (2006) '"Race", youth crime and justice', in Goldson, B. and Muncie, J. (eds) *Youth Crime and Justice*, London: Sage

Wells, K. (2005) 'Strange practices: children's discourses on transgressives unknown in urban public space', *Childhood*, 12(4), 495–506

Welsh Assembly (2002) *Play Policy*, Cardiff: Welsh Assembly Government

Welsh Assembly (2006) *Play Policy Implementation Group Recommendations*, available at <http://www.wales.gov.uk/subichildren/content/play/playpolicy-impgroup-e.pdf> accessed 19 April 2006

White, R., Carr, P. and Lowe, N. (1991) *A Guide to The Children Act 1989*, London: Butterworths

WHO (1946) *Constitution*, Geneva: World Health Organization

Who Cares? Trust, The (1999) *Equal Chances: Improving the Education of Looked After Children and Young People*, London: The Who Cares? Trust and Calouste Gulbenkian Foundation

Who Cares? Trust, The (2003) *Education Matters*, London: The Who Cares? Trust

Wilcox, D. (1994) *The Guide to Effective Participation*, available at <http://www.partnerships.org.uk/guide> accessed 24 July 2007

Williams, J. (2002) 'The neglect we tolerate', *The Guardian*, Saturday 22 June 2002

Williamson, H. (1995) *Social Action for Young People*, Lyme Regis: Russell House Publishing

Williamson, H. (1997) 'Status zero, youth and the underclass', in MacDonald, R. (ed.) *Youth, the Underclass and Social Exclusion*, London: Routledge

Willow, C. (2001) *Participation in Practice: Children and Young People as Partners in Change*, London: The Children's Society

Wilson, D. (2003) 'No holds barred: racism in the Prison Service', *The Guardian*, 10 December

Wilson, M. and Wilde, P. (2000) *Active Partners: Benchmarks for Community Participation in Regeneration*, Yorkshire Forward, Yorkshire and Humber Regional Development Agency, Leeds

Wise, K. (2004) 'Wand waver lacks magic in community care', available at <www.communitycare.co.uk/Articles/2004/06/03/44989/wand-waver-lacks-magic.html?key=CHILDREN%COMMISSIONER> accessed 3 June 2004

Woman's Own (1987) *Interview with Margaret Thatcher,* 31 October 1987

Woodhead, C. (2003) *Class War: The State of British Education,* London: Time Warner Books

Woodhead, M. (1997) 'Psychology and the cultural construction of children's needs', in James, A. and Prout, A. (eds) (1997) *Constructing and Reconstructing Childhood,* London: Falmer

Woodroffe, C., Glickman, M., Barker, M. and Power, C. (1993) *Children, Teenagers and Health: Key Data,* Buckingham: Open University Press

Working with Children (2004) *See* Horton, C. (ed.)

Writing Renewal 2 (2005) Government Office for Yorkshire and the Humber, Leeds: Government Office for Yorkshire and the Humber, with Interculture

Wyse, D. (2004) *Childhood Studies: An Introduction,* Oxford: Blackwell

Yeatman and Reifel (1992) 'Sibling play and learning', *Play and Culture 5,* 141–58. Champaign, IL: Human Kinetics

Index